Introduction to
Structured Finance

FRANK J. FABOZZI

HENRY A. DAVIS

MOORAD CHOUDHRY

WILEY

John Wiley & Sons, Inc.

FJF
To my wife Donna
and my children, Karly, Patricia, and Francesco

HAD
To my ever-supportive family and friends.

MC
To my Mum and Dad, to whom I owe everything

ISBN-13 978-0-470-04535-0
ISBN-10 0-470-04535-3

Printed in the United States of America.

10 9 8 7 6 5 4 3 2 1

Contents

This purpose of this book is to provide a broad, comprehensive introduction to structured finance. It is intended for people generally knowledgeable in financial markets who want to learn the fundamentals of structured finance and also for experts in certain areas of structured finance who would like to broaden their knowledge in other areas. This preface briefly walks through an outline of the book and introduces the reader to some of its more important concepts and terms

Our introduction in Chapter 1 recognizes that structured finance is a broad field and that not everyone even agrees on how structured finance is defined and where the boundaries are. We summarize a survey of experts on the definition of structured finance and conclude that our definition should include not only securitization and most applications of credit derivatives, but also leasing, project finance, the use of complex derivatives, and most other unusual, complex financing transactions. We also summarize another survey of experts on how the Enron debacle tested the boundaries of structured finance.

Our definitional survey confirms that derivatives and securitization are the most fundamental building blocks of structured finance. We show numerous combinations of those building blocks as we explain the most important instruments of structured finance in Chapters 2 through 10, followed by a discussion of leasing and project finance in Chapters 11 through 13.

While an interest rate derivative contract does not in itself constitute structured finance, the use of derivatives is one of the features that distinguish large structured financings. Chapter 2 includes coverage of interest rate swaps, interest rate options, and their specialized variations, including caps, floors, and collars.

While interest rate and currency derivatives were the most important financial innovations of the 1980s, credit derivatives were among the most important in the 1990s. In Chapter 3, we explain the structure and the uses of the major types of credit derivatives, including documentation, key terms and a discussion of credit default swaps (single name, basket, and index credit default swaps), asset swaps, and total return swaps. The credit derivatives explained in this chapter are essential components of structured finance products described in later chapters of this book such as synthetic collateralized debt obligations, synthetic securitizations, and credit-linked notes.

Then we have two chapters on securitization, starting with the basic principles of securitization in Chapter 4. We cover the motivations for securitization from the issuer's perspective, the benefits of securitized debt instruments for investors, the basic mechanics of a securitization, the role of the special purpose vehicle, and how investors and rating agencies analyze asset-backed securities, including the way they measure and monitor the cash flows of the pool of assets that serves as collateral backing a securitization.

In Chapter 5, we show how interest rate derivatives are used in a securitization and we explain credit enhancement mechanisms. We discuss external credit enhancement mechanisms, such as letters of credit and bond insurance, and internal credit enhancement mechanisms, such as senior-subordinate structures, overcollateralization, and reserve funds.

The next two chapters are concerned with collateralized debt obligations (CDOs). We explain the basis structure of cash flow CDOs in Chapter 6, discussing how CDOs are categorized according to the motivations of their sponsors and how the quality of the collateral pool is monitored through compliance tests, including quality tests and coverage tests.

With a synthetic CDO, discussed in Chapter 7, the credit risk of a pool of assets is transferred from the sponsor or originator to investors by means of credit derivative instruments. We discuss the motivations for synthetic CDOs as well as the mechanics, investor risks, and variations such as arbitrage and balance sheet CDOs.

Then, in Chapter 8, we explain the various securitized and synthetic money market funding structures, including commercial paper and medium-term notes structured as synthetic securitizations. We show how total return swaps can be combined with commercial paper and medium-term note issuance vehicles in structures that are similar in purpose to repurchase agreements (repos).

Credit derivatives may be either funded or unfunded. With unfunded credit derivatives such as credit default swaps, the protection seller does not make an upfront payment to the protection buyer. Credit-linked notes (CLNs), described in Chapter 9, are funded credit derivatives. The investor is the credit protection seller, which makes an upfront payment to the protection buyer, the issuer of the note. There are numerous forms of CLNs, but in all of them there is a link between the return they pay and the credit performance of the underlying pool of assets.

In Chapter 10, we explain and show numerous examples of structured notes. Compared to traditional bonds with fixed principal amounts and due dates, and coupon interest rates that are either fixed or floating at a fixed spread to a reference rates, structured notes have one or more embedded options with much more complicated provisions for the interest rate payable, the redemption amount, or the timing of the principal repayment. For investors, structured notes may offer the opportunity to enhance yield or gain exposure to alternative asset classes. For the issuer, creating a customized product for the investor may be an opportunity to reduce funding cost.

Next we devote two chapters to leasing, starting with the fundamentals of large-ticket leasing in Chapter 11. We compare leasing with other methods of financing; show various types of tax-oriented and non-tax-oriented leases; describe different types of lessors, lease programs, lease brokers, and financial advisors; explain synthetic leases; discuss accounting, tax, and financial reporting issues; and explain how leases are valued from the perspective of the lessee.

Leveraged leases, which allow lessees to harness lessors' capital and allow lessees to reduce their financing costs by passing depreciation tax benefits to lessors, are explained in Chapter 12. We show the parties to a leveraged lease, how the debt financing is arranged, various applications ranging from equipment to large industrial facilities, and the steps in structuring, negotiating, and closing a transaction.

In Chapter 13, we provide an introduction to project finance, in which lenders look to the cash flows of the project being financed rather than the credit of the project sponsors. As with securitization, project finance uses a special-purpose vehicle, but project finance involves cash flows from operating assets whereas securitization involves cash flows from financial assets such as loans or receivables. We explain the reasons for jointly owned or sponsored projects, the credit exposures for lenders during the course of project construction and operation, the key elements of a successful project financing, risks and causes for project failures with recent case examples, accounting and tax considerations, and recent trends.

And that's not all! We have lots more useful information in the appendices.

In recent years, the motivations for large banks to securitize have been driven partly by complex capital adequacy regulations. In Appendix A, we explain the Basel capital rules for banks, starting with the Basel I rules for core (Tier 1) and supplementary (Tier 2) capital and the requirement for banks to hold capital equal to 8% of risk-weighted assets. We proceed to explain the three pillars of Basel II: new capital requirements for credit risk and operational risk, a requirement for supervisors to take action when they see a bank's risk profile rise, and a requirement for banks to disclose more about their underlying risks. Basel II applies to all European financial institutions but only the largest banks in the United States. It is expected to give those large banks a competitive advantage by allowing them to categorize assets according to their own internal risk assessment systems and justify thinner capital charges than would be allowed under more standardized risk measurement systems. We explain the impact of the Basel rules on securitization and credit derivatives.

In Appendix B, we discuss synthetic mortgage-backed securitization, a way of removing the credit risk associated with a pool of mortgages by means of credit derivatives. The originator, typically a mortgage bank, is the credit protection buyer, which retains the ownership as well as the economic benefit of the assets. Synthetic mortgage-backed securitization follows similar principles, has similar funded and unfunded structures, and is done for similar reasons as synthetic CDOs, discussed in Chapter 7.

We follow with two articles from the *Journal of Structured Finance* (reprinted with the permission of Institution Investor) on unusually interesting applications of structured finance.

The article in Appendix C is the story of a structured financing for the recently opened Busch Stadium, home of the St. Louis Cardinals. The article describes how a special-purpose vehicle was formed to originate contracts giving rise to contractually obligated income (COI) pledged to support the ballpark financing in a way that isolated the COI receivables from the credit risk of the team. The authors also describe why this structure was chosen instead of a hybrid securitization/leveraged lease structure and complications that arise when different financing disciplines such as leasing, project finance, and securitization must be reconciled in one hybrid transaction.

The article in Appendix D reviews how future-flow securitizations have allowed public and private companies in below-investment-grade countries access to affordable international financing, how a municipal future-flow mechanism was developed in Mexico based on the principles of future-flow securitization, and the opportunities and problems in applying this mechanism in other developing countries. The Mexican municipal future-flow mechanism is based on the use of administrative trusts into which tax-sharing revenues are deposited directly by Federal authorities, and out of which debt service payments are made directly to bondholders.

The last six appendices to this book contain rating agency presales reports from Moody's Investors Service (Appendices E and F), Standard & Poor's Ratings Services (Appendices G and H), and FitchRatings (Appendices I and J) representing six different types of securitized debt issues. The analyses cover factors such as legal, transaction, and payment structure; collateral analysis; historical portfolio performance; cash flow modeling; and the agencies' overall evaluation of the transactions' credit strengths and weaknesses.

The cash flow stream for the Crown Castle Towers securitization in Appendix E comes from leases of site space on Crown Castle International Corporation's wireless communication towers to wireless service providers. Credit strengths cited by Moody's include the quality of the collateral, cross-collateralization of a large pool with diverse sites, and revenues from telephony tenants. The agency's concerns include lack of principal amortization during the term of the loan, the borrower's right to release collateral, and special arrangements with Verizon an AT&T-Cingular.

The MVL Film Finance revolving credit securitization facility, described in Appendix F, provides partial financing for Marvel Studios' production of 10 live-action and animated films. The special purpose vehicle issuing the securities owns film rights to the characters and the film library featuring the characters. Cash flow for debt service is provided by film revenues net of participations, residuals, and print, advertising and distribution expenses.

In the case of the Honda Auto Receivables retail auto loan securitization described in Appendix G, credit enhancement takes the form of subordinated certificates, a reserve fund, excess spread, and a yield-supplement account. The analysis describes the payment distribution schedule in order of priority, Honda's performance as originator and servicer of the receivables, the portfolio's loss performance, its delinquencies and repossessions, and characteristics of the collateral pool such as the auto loans' weighted term to maturity, their weighted-average annual payment rate (APR), and the average FICO score of the borrowers.

ACG Trust III, covered in Appendix H, is a securitized portfolio of aircraft operating leases and residual cash flows. A financial guarantee policy provides for an AAA rating on the most senior tranche. Standard & Poor's rating is based the credit quality of the aircraft lessees, collateral pool characteristics such as ages and models of the aircraft, the legal and cash flow structure of the transaction, the cash flow modeling of stress tests, the experience of the servicer, and the role of the aircraft remarketing agent.

In the CNH Equipment Trust, notes are backed by retail installment contracts on new and used agricultural and construction equipment. Fitch's rating, as described in Appendix I, is based on the geographic diversity of obligors; loan attributes such as seasoning, contract balance, and APR; historic portfolio performance; the possibility that a weak economic environment could accelerate near-term repossessions and losses; the role of the master servicer and a named back-up servicer; integrity of the transaction's legal structure; cash flow stress tests; other structural considerations such as a prefunding account, interest and principal allocation, the payment waterfall, and events of default; and an operations review covering origination, underwriting, collections, and servicing.

Finally, in the CIT equipment collateral securitization described in Appendix J, notes are backed by equipment lease contracts on new and used technology and other small-ticket equipment. Credit strengths cited by Fitch include the financial strength of the seller/servicer, the quality of the collateral, and the geographic diversity of the lessees. The agency's concerns include vendor and equipment concentration.

Frank J. Fabozzi
Henry A. Davis
Moorad Choudhry

About the Authors

Frank J. Fabozzi is an Adjunct Professor of Finance and Becton Fellow in the School of Management at Yale University. He was a visiting professor of finance at MIT's Sloan School of Management from 1986 to 1992. Dr. Fabozzi is a Chartered Financial Analyst and Certified Public Accountant and earned a doctorate in economics from the Graduate Center of the City University of New York in 1972. Some of the books he has coauthored in the area of structured finance published by John Wiley include *Collateralized Debt Obligations: Structures and Analysis, Second Edition; Collateralized Mortgage Obligations: Structures and Analysis, Third Edition; Credit Derivatives: Instruments, Pricing, and Applications; Real Estate Backed Securities; Managing MBS Portfolios; Valuation of Interest Rate Swaps and Swaptions;* and, *Equipment Leasing, Fourth Edition.* He is the coauthor of *Project Finance, Seventh Edition* published by Euromoney. Dr. Fabozzi was inducted into the Fixed Income Analysts Society Hall of Fame in November 2002.

Henry A. (Hal) Davis is an editor, writer, and consultant working in the fields of banking and corporate finance. He currently serves as editor of two quarterly professional journals, *The Journal of Structured Finance* and the *Journal of Investment Compliance.* Mr. Davis has written four books of project finance case studies for Euromoney Books, most recently: *Project Finance: Practical Case Studies—Second Edition, Volumes I & II.* Books he has written and coauthored for the Financial Executives Research Foundation include: *Financial Turarounds: Preserving Value; Building Value with Capital Structure Strategies; Cash Flow and Performance Measurement: Managing for Value; Foreign Exchange Risk Management: A Survey of Corporate Practices;* and *The Empowered Organization: Redefining the Roles and Practices of Finance.* He earned his bachelor's degree at Princeton University and his MBA at the Darden Graduate Business School at the University of Virginia.

Moorad Choudhry is Head of Treasury at KBC Financial Products in London. He is a Visiting Professor at the Department of Economics, London Metropolitan University, a Visiting Research Fellow at the ICMA Centre, University of Reading, a Senior Fellow at the Centre for Mathematical Trading and Finance, Cass Business School, and a Fellow of the Securities and Institute. Dr. Moorad is the author of several books published by John Wiley: *Structured Credit Products: Credit Derivatives and Synthetic Securitisation*, *Measuring and Controlling Interest Rate and Credit Risk*, *Credit Derivatives*, and *The Money Markets Handbook*. He obtained his PhD from Birkbeck, University of London.

CHAPTER 1

Introduction

The definition of structured finance is broad, and not everyone agrees on exactly what it is. This introductory chapter begins with our working definition of structured finance and then follows with views and opinions from a variety of experts. It concludes with a case study of how the boundaries of structured finance were tested by the Enron debacle.

DEFINITION OF STRUCTURED FINANCE

There is no universal definition of structure finance. It is apparent from the way that structured finance teams are organized in banks that the term covers a wide range of financial market activity. We believe a good working definition for structured finance is the following:

> . . . techniques employed whenever the requirements of the originator or owner of an asset, be they concerned with funding, liquidity, risk transfer, or other need, cannot be met by an existing, off-the-shelf product or instrument. Hence, to meet this requirement, existing products and techniques must be engineered into a tailor-made product or process. Thus, structured finance is a flexible financial engineering tool.

We believe one or more of following elements generally characterize a structured finance transaction:

■ a complex financial transaction that may involve actual or synthetic transfer of assets or risk exposure, aimed at achieving certain accounting, regulatory, and/or tax objectives;

■ a transaction ring-fenced in its own special purpose vehicle;

■ a bond issue that is asset-backed and/or external reference index-linked;

■ a combination of interest-rate and credit derivatives;

■ a transaction employed by banks, other financial institutions, and corporations as a source of funding and/or favorable capital, tax, and accounting treatment; and

■ disintermediation between banks and other corporate entities.

As we just noted, there are alternative definitions of structured finance and we will identify in the next section some definitions proposed by practitioners and regulators. As will be seen, the working definition above, as well as the elements of structured finance given above, tie together many of the alternative definitions identified in the next section.

OTHER DEFINITIONS OF STRUCTURED FINANCE

One obvious way to define structured finance is to rely on already-published definitions. Here are three examples.

In a recent report, the Bank for International Settlements (BIS) defines structured finance in this way:

> Structured finance instruments can be defined through three key characteristics: (1) pooling of assets (either cash-based or synthetically created); (2) tranching of liabilities that are backed by the asset pool (this property differentiates structured finance from traditional "pass-through" securitizations); (3) de-linking of the credit risk of the collateral asset pool from the credit risk of the originator, usually through use of a finite-lived, standalone special purpose vehicle (SPV).[1]

A 1995 report written by the Committee on Bankruptcy and Corporate Reorganizations of the Association of the Bar of the City of New York, entitled "New Developments in Structured Finance," defines structured financing and the parties involved as follows:

---

[1] "The Role of Ratings in Structured Finance: Issues and Implications," Committee on the Global Financial System, Bank for International Settlements, 2005.

Structured financings are based on one central, core principle: a defined group of assets can be structurally isolated and thus serve as the basis of a financing that is independent from the bankruptcy risks of the originator of the assets. By isolating the assets, an originator obtains easier access to the capital markets by generating note proceeds at a lower cost of funds than it otherwise might if it issued notes directly to investors. One of the principal benefits from structured financings is a reduction in the cost of financing (e.g., through lower yield on issued debt).

The parties involved in a structured financing typically include many, if not all, of the following entities (of which there may be more than one): the originator of the assets; a "special purpose vehicle;" credit enhancers (i.e., financial guarantors); the servicer (who makes collections on the receivables, directs cash-flow allocation, and otherwise acts as agent for the bondholders); a liquidity provider (letter of credit bank); a trustee or collateral agent; a securities underwriter or placement agent; and a rating agency.[2]

Andrew Silver of Moody's Investors Service defines structured finance as:

Structured finance is a term that evolved in the 1980s to refer to a wide variety of debt and related securities whose promise to repay investors is backed by (1) the value of some form of financial asset or (2) the credit support from a third party to the transaction. Very often, both types of backing are used to achieve a desired credit rating.

Structured financings are offshoots of traditional secured debt instruments, whose credit standing is supported by a lien on specific assets, by a defeasance provision, or by other forms of enhancement. With conventional secured issues, however, it is generally the issuer's earning power that remains the primary source of repayment. With structured financings, by contrast, the burden of repayment on a specific security is shifted away from the issuer to a pool of assets or to a third party.

---

[2] Committee on Bankruptcy and Corporate Reorganizations of the Association of the Bar of the City of New York, "New Developments in Structured Finance," Report 56, *Business Lawyer* 95, 2000–2001.

Securities supported wholly or mainly by pools of assets are generally referred to as either mortgage-backed securities (mortgages were the first types of assets to be widely securitized) or asset-backed securities, whose collateral backing may include virtually any other asset with a relatively predictable payment stream, ranging from credit card receivables or insurance policies to speculative-grade bonds or even stock. Outside the United States, both types of structured financing are often referred to simply as "asset-backed securities," which is the convention that we will employ here.[3]

The problem with the three definitions above is that they focus only on one area of what many market participants might view as structured finance: securitization. Our view is that securitization is a subset of structured finance.

In 2005 the Editor and the Editorial Board of the *Journal of Structured Finance* recognized the elusive definition of structured finance as a challenge. They considered it important to get their arms around the full range of views concerning how structured finance should be defined in today's financial markets. They thought that the best source of those views would be expert contributors to the journal. They sent questionnaires to 53 people and received responses from 25.[4] Some replied individually while others participated in group responses from their firms.[5]

The survey asked the experts two basic questions:

---

[3] Andrew A. Silver, "Rating Structured Securities," Chapter 1 in Frank J. Fabozzi (ed.), *Issuer Perspectives on Securitization* (Hoboken, NJ: John Wiley & Sons, 1998).

[4] Survey respondents were: Phil Adams, Barclays Capital; Mark H. Adelson, Nomura Securities International; Beth Bartlett, Nomura Securities International; Terry Benzschawel, Citigroup; Ronald Borod, Brown Rudnick; Moorad Choudhry, KBC Financial Products; Edward DeSear, McKee Nelson LLP; Frank J. Fabozzi, Yale University School of Management; J. Paul Forrester, Mayer, Brown, Rowe & Maw LLP; Edward Gainor, McKee Nelson LLP; Brian P. Gallogy, Brown Rudnick; Stav Gaon, Citigroup; Paul Geertsema, Barclays Capital; Barry P. Gold, Citigroup; Jeffrey J. Griffiths, Columbia University/Bear Stearns; Andreas Jobst, International Monetary Fund; Jason Kravitt, Mayer, Brown, Rowe & Maw LLP; Douglas Lucas, UBS; Jeffrey Prince, Citigroup; Madeleine M. L. Tan, Brown Rudnick; Janet Tavakoli, Tavakoli Structured Finance, Inc.; Jon Van Gorp, Mayer, Brown, Rowe & Maw LLP; Lawrence E. Uchill, Brown Rudnick; Hans Vrensen, Barclays Capital; Jacob J. Worenklein, U.S. Power Generating Company; and Boris Ziser, Brown Rudnick.

[5] One survey respondent offered a humorous definition of structured finance: "A complicated transaction that results in large legal fees."

- What is your definition of structured finance?
- Where do you think the boundaries are?

Survey recipients were also asked to cite some borderline cases they thought were just inside or outside the boundaries.

As expected, the definitions received ranged from narrow to broad. In this section, we discuss those definitions based on:

- basic conceptual definitions;
- instruments and techniques;
- when or where structured finance is used;
- benefits provided by structured finance; and
- emphasis on securitization.

Even the above definitions do not fully cover the diverse range of structured finance activity in the market. Exhibit 1.1 describes more esoteric transactions that also fall into the universe of structured finance as suggested by respondents.

Basic Conceptual Definitions

It is apparent from the survey responses that "structured finance" covers a wide range of activities and products. We present here a number of conceptual definitions from respondents that help us to see the different nuances by the variety of terminology used. Structured finance has been defined as:

- A synthetic transaction that transfers risk; such a transaction may or may not involve raising capital.
- A complex financial transaction involving the transfer of assets to raise cash, frequently with the additional goal of achieving certain accounting, regulatory, and/or tax treatment. Such a transaction may or may not involve a securities offering.
- The monetization of any rights to payments by a party having the legal right to transfer those payments to others.
- A financing transaction where legal structures are used to isolate asset or entity risk, resulting in decreased risk for the originator.
- The identification and isolation of inherent risk in a particular asset (or liability) or portfolio of assets (or liabilities) and the financing of such asset or assets (or liability or liabilities) in an economically efficient manner using specific risk transfer mechanisms when justified.
- The process whereby cash flows from cash-generating assets are molded into legal and financial structures designed to insulate those cash flows from insolvency risk and to invest those cash flows with greater predictability than they would be in their natural state.

EXHIBIT 1.1   Borderline Cases and Boundaries

This exhibit identifies some survey responses on structured finance that encompasses a wider range of transactions. Respondents had numerous ideas about the borderline between what should and should not be considered structured finance and also about how the boundaries of structured finance are expanding in the course of continued product innovation.

- There is general agreement that ABS, CMBS, RMBS, and CDOs fall squarely within the realm of structured finance. Borderline cases cited by respondents include credit opportunity funds, project finance loans, other tranched loans, credit default swaps (CDS), and hedge funds. For example, most respondents as well as the authors of this book consider project finance loans and CDS to be part of structured finance but some do not.

- In one respondent's opinion, pure credit derivatives are examples of structured products for credit risk transfer that allow very specific, capital-market-priced credit risk transfer. That is why they should be considered part of structured finance. Credit insurance and syndicated loans share the same financial objective; however, they do not constitute arrangements to create new risk-return profiles from existing reference assets.

- Another respondent considers structured finance to include any financial transaction that is not standard, or in market jargon, "plain vanilla" in terms and conditions. In this respondent's view, structured transactions add nonstandard terms, conditions, and other characteristics to create additional economic value for the principal, the agent, or both. So plain vanilla transactions such as syndicated loans, straight equity offerings (including preferred), and straight debt offerings would be outside the boundaries of structured finance. All of these types of financings are relatively commoditized in nature, meaning that there are very standard terms and conditions that govern the vast majority of simple capital-raising activities. In this respondent's view, we enter the realm of structured finance when we add bells and whistles to these straight, standard capital-raising activities. Structured finance can include straight equity and debt offerings that incorporate complex structures to provide some additional economic value to all transaction parties. Examples of features that can be added to plain vanilla capital offerings to make them "structured" include the creation of offshore, special-purpose vehicles; interest rate and currency swaps; embedded options; forward sales; and any other exotic derivatives. Also included under this respondent's definition of structured finance would be "hybrid" debt or equity securities such as trust preferred securities, warrants, and convertible bonds.

- There are differing opinions as to whether we should categorize the derivatives market and derivative securities as "structured finance." We might consider derivative securities to be the elements that can cause certain plain vanilla transactions to become "structured." Although derivative securities are highly structured products within themselves, some believe structured finance pertains mostly to capital-raising transactions that have nonstandard elements attached to them. But others point to numerous derivatives-based synthetic transactions that are designed not to raise capital but merely to transfer risk. Those transactions are becoming an increasingly important part of structured finance.

EXHIBIT 1.1 (Continued)

- The boundaries of structured finance, in terms of the assets that can be securitized on a repeated basis, are continuing to expand with the inclusion of intellectual property, time-share loans, tobacco legal fees, and life settlements. Other assets that may soon be added to this category are renewable energy project cash flows and greenhouse gas emission credits. The boundary between structured finance and project finance is steadily blurring, as ABS technology is applied to cash flows (e.g., wind power) that previously were financed exclusively through the traditional project finance paradigm.

- Another respondent addresses the expanding boundaries of structured finance with two questions: (1) How specific and identifiable are the assets? In a lot of transactions the borrower has flexibility within certain covenants and can bring in new assets as well as take out existing assets. But as assets become less specific and identifiable, it may become more difficult to design structured finance transactions around them. (2) How exactly does the security work? In a lot of transactions there are no registered mortgages on day one, but registration is triggered by certain events. In other words, structured finance is being applied to "assets to come" as well as assets already securely in place.

- One who sees no limit to the boundaries cites future-flow credit card securitizations originated by banks that have higher credit ratings than their native countries, for example Argentina and Turkey. Whereas assets are isolated from the credit risk of the originator in most securitizations, in this case the transaction is actually enhanced by the originating bank's credit rating. The continuing flow of credit card payments underlying the securitization depends on the creditworthiness of the bank.

- Weather-related securities are another definition-stressing example of securitization. Investors pay money into an account where it is invested in money-market-type instruments. The negative arbitrage (the difference between the low reinvestment rate on the escrowed proceeds and the significantly higher interest payable to the investors in the weather-related securities) is made up by a reinsurance premium paid by the U.S. property and casualty insurance company buying this capital-markets-provided reinsurance. The assets being securitized are the escrow investments and the future reinsurance payments from the single obligor.

- A bank may offer a savings product that pays a return linked to an index, but with a minimum guaranteed return as well. To hedge this product, the bank may buy a combined exotic option (an Asian option linked to the index) from an options market maker as well as a zero-coupon bond. The options product will pay what the bank is obliged to pay on its savings product. This combination of a vanilla product, a zero-coupon bond, and an exotic option linked to an index is another example of structured finance.

EXHIBIT 1.1   (Continued)

- Some aspects of Islamic finance also may fall within the realm of structured finance. For example, an Islamic loan becomes a structured finance instrument whenever its formation through replication of conventional asset classes involves a contingent claim. In Islamic finance, traditional fixed income instruments are replicated via more complex arrangements in order to establish (1) compliance with the religious prohibition on both interest earnings (*riba*); (2) the exchange of money for debt without an underlying asset transfer; and (3) nonentrepreneurial investment. Structured finance redresses these moral impediments to conventional forms of external finance. For instance, Islamic banks create synthetic loans for debt-based bond finance, where the borrower repurchases, or acquires the option to repurchase, its own assets at a markup in a sell-and-buyback transaction. That might entail a cost-plus sale of existing assets (*murabahah*) or project financing for future assets (*istina*). The lender can refinance the selling price and/or the indebtedness of the borrower via the issuance of commercial paper. Alternatively, the *ijarah* principle prescribes an asset-based version of refinancing a synthetic loan, where the lender securitizes the receivables from a temporary lease-back agreement as quasi-interest income. The debt transaction underlying each of these forms of refinancing reflects a put-call, parity-based replication of interest income, where the lender holds stock ownership of the notional loan amount and writes a call option to the borrower, who thereby has a put option to acquire these funds at an agreed premium payment subject to the promise of full payment of principal and markup after time. Both options have a strike price equal to the markup and the notional loan amount. So the lender's position at the time the synthetic loan is made is the value of the stock ownership minus the value of the call option plus the value of the put option, which equals the present value of principal and interest repayment of a conventional loan.
- A respondent believes the boundaries of structured finance will be set by investors, who will weigh the benefits of a particular transaction against the risk that the investment entails, and by public opinion and the legal system, as with Enron and Orange County, California.
- The Enron deals that used structured finance techniques are a difficult gray area. The securitization industry tried hard to distinguish its deals from the ones that Enron did. In the end, however, the main difference was simply that Enron was crooked and deceitful, in this respondent's opinion.

- A method of raising capital that involves the monetization of a cash flow stream, either due currently or to become due in the future, utilizing nonrecourse financing techniques to achieve a lower cost of funds, while enabling the borrower to meet its other operational objectives.
- A way of reorganizing an illiquid asset or group of assets for them to become liquid; a way to pool assets together for securities/certificates/

notes to be sold to investors, who otherwise would not want to purchase the underlying assets; a way to allocate risk by isolating some assets from other assets owned by the originator of the assets or the issuer of the securities; a way to create an efficient market in an asset initially unsuitable for investment and then trade the resulting investment instrument based on current market conditions.

■ The art or business of partitioning the risk of an investment (security) or investments (securities) into three or more unique securities—none being identical—that derive their value from the initial investment(s).

■ Encompasses all advanced private and public financial arrangements that serve to efficiently refinance and hedge any profitable economic activity beyond the scope of conventional forms of on-balance-sheet securities (debt, bonds, equity) in the effort to lower cost of capital and to mitigate agency costs of asymmetric information and/or market impediments to liquidity. In particular, most structured financings (1) combine traditional asset classes with contingent claims, such as risk transfer derivatives and/or derivative claims on commodities, currencies, or receivables from other reference assets; or (2) replicate traditional asset classes through synthetication.

In essence, the last definition here is probably the closest to what we believe the concept to be. Clearly structured finance encompasses more than simply securitization, although that is a popular definition for it.

Instruments and Techniques

Some survey respondents' definitions emphasize the instruments and techniques used in structured finance:

■ A term used in two different ways: (1) asset-backed securities (ABS), residential mortgage-backed securities (RMBS), commercial mortgage-backed securities (CMBS), and collateralized debt obligations (CDOs); and (2) credit derivatives on corporate names. This respondent puts asset-backed securities credit default swaps (ABS CDS) in both categories.[6]

■ Involves some or all of the following components: derivatives, securitizations, and/or special purpose entities. A structured financing can be as simple as a callable bond with an embedded option or as complicated as a cross-border, tax-advantaged securitization.

■ Any transaction that is specifically structured using a special-purpose vehicle (removed from the corporation and bankruptcy remote), issues

---

[6] The instruments cited here are described in later chapters.

bonds listed with an exchange, and is secured by ring-fenced assets producing cash flows solely for supporting the transaction. These elements allow the issuer to obtain better credit ratings and/or more leverage than it would by issuing senior unsecured debt.

- Incorporates the use of securitization techniques, leasing structures, tax credits, derivatives, and financial and regulatory arbitrage with respect to taxes, securities and related laws, regulatory requirements, and accounting issues.

- A method of providing financing that attempts to maximize proceeds that can be funded to an issuer through the use of various techniques that attract investors to provide such financing, including: (1) the use of special-purpose, bankruptcy-remote entities that function in the roles of borrowers or holders relative to such loans; (2) the use of pass-through entities to avoid "double" taxation entities that function in the roles of borrowers or holders relative to such loans; (3) the use of techniques to mitigate risks that, if they occurred, would divert or eliminate cash flow necessary to pay debt service; and (4) the use of techniques to maximize tax advantages for the issuer.

- Includes financial instruments such as credit derivatives that isolate and transfer credit risk.[7] As a common working principle, credit derivatives involve the sale of contingent credit protection for predefined credit events of lending transactions. In their basic concept, credit derivatives sever the link between the loan origination and associated credit risk, but leave the original borrower-creditor relationship intact. The protection buyer of a credit derivative hedges specific credit risk in return for periodic premium payments to the protection seller, who assumes the credit exposure of a financial contract isolated from the underlying transaction. The significance of credit derivatives lies in their ability to supplement traditional ways of hedging credit risk through the transfer of credit-related exposures to a third party. Pure credit derivatives are clear examples of structured products for credit risk transfer that allow very specific, capital-market-priced risk transfer. Other noncredit-

---

[7] If one agrees with this definition, then one must, logically, include interest-rate derivatives such as swaps and describe them as structured finance products as well. A plain vanilla credit derivative such as a credit default swap consists of fixed and floating cash flows (the "floating" cash flow is the payment on occurrence of a terminating credit event), the value of both of which are linked to the credit quality of the underlying reference. Replace "credit quality" with "interest rate level" and we have described an interest-rate swap. The authors do not extend the definition of structured finance to include plain vanilla credit or interest-rate derivatives themselves, but indeed the use of those instruments may put an otherwise conventional financing into the structured category.

derivative based forms of credit risk transfer include credit insurance, syndicated loans, loan sales, bond trading, and asset swaps. Those instruments share the same financial objectives as credit derivatives, but they do not constitute arrangements to create new risk-return profiles from reference assets.

This respondent distinguishes between credit derivatives in the narrower and in a wider sense. The latter classification includes pure credit derivatives, such as credit default swaps (CDSs), total return swaps, and credit spread options, as well as securitization products with significant contributions by credit-derivative elements, such as collateralized debt obligations (CDOs). Some unfunded/partially funded structured finance transactions, such as credit-linked notes (CLNs) and synthetic CDOs contain both securitization and credit derivative elements by providing refinancing through cash flow restructuring and tranche-specific credit risk transfer (which does not apply to fully funded asset-backed securities (ABS) and mortgage-backed securities (MBS)). These hybrid products, which are considered credit derivatives in a wider sense, usually condition the repayment of securitized debt on the nonoccurrence of a defined credit event (in the case of CLNs), the premium income generated from credit protection sold on reference assets (in the case of synthetic CDOs), or the returns from investment in securitization transactions as reference assets ("pools of pools").

CDOs have been the fastest growing area of structured finance. Generally, a CDO represents a form of asset-backed securitization (ABS), which converts a large, diversified pool of exposures into tradable capital market debt instruments (tranches). In a CDO structure, asset managers can increase assets under management while locking in committed funds and achieving some protection from market-value volatility. While cash CDOs are backed by the collateral of actual bonds and loans as reference assets, whose legal title is transferred to the purchaser, issuers of synthetic CDOs enlist large amounts of credit derivatives and various third-party guarantees to create partially funded and highly leveraged investments from synthetic claims on the performance of designated credit exposures. CDOs involve either cash flow or arbitrage mechanisms to fund either expected principal and interest payments or expected trading and sales activity. CDOs enable issuers to achieve a broad range of financial goals that include the off-balance-sheet treatment of securitized exposures, reduced regulatory capital requirements, and access to alternative sources for asset funding and liquidity support. The conventional security design of CDOs assumes a typical three-tier securitization structure of junior, mezzanine, and senior tranches. Expected losses are concentrated in a small first-loss position as equity claim, which bears the majority of the credit exposure and is frequently covered by a junior CDS, shifting most unexpected risk to larger, more senior tranches, which display distinctly different risk profiles. This risk-sharing arrangement induces a leverage effect on constituent tranches, whose distinct risk-return profiles can be tailored to specific investment preferences.

When or Where Structured Finance is Used

Some of the survey respondents emphasized when or where structured finance is used:

- Employed by financial and nonfinancial institutions in both banking and capital markets if (1) established forms of external finance are either unavailable or depleted for a particular financing need, or (2) traditional sources of funds are too expensive.
- Used wherever there is a reliable cash flow stream that should continue to exist over the maturity of the loan, which the owner wants to utilize to obtain a sizable cash payment from the financing proceeds, in a situation where the owner would like to retain ownership of, and manage, that cash stream. Could be utilized in connection with a variety of cash streams such as proceeds from power purchase agreements, rents from real estate assets, credit card revenues, toll revenues, payments in lieu of taxes, patent revenues, and the like.
- Seeks to substitute capital-market-based finance for credit finance through disintermediation, that is, sponsoring financial relationships outside the lending and deposit-taking capabilities of banks. The issuer raises funds by issuing certificates of ownership as pledges against existing or future cash flows from an investment pool of financial assets in a bid to increase the issuer's liquidity position without increasing the capital base or by selling these reference assets to a special-purpose vehicle, which subsequently issues debt to investors to fund the purchase.

Benefits of Structured Finance

Other definitions emphasize the benefits provided by structured finance:

- Enables the financing of a unique asset class that (1) previously may have been financed only by traditional borrowing methods or (2) could not be financed at all without structured finance.
- Offers issuers flexibility in terms of maturity structure, security design, and asset types, which in turn allows issuers to provide enhanced

return and a customized degree of diversification commensurate with investors' appetite for risk.

■ Contributes to a more complete capital market by offering a trade off along the efficient frontier of optimal diversification at minimum transaction cost.

■ Allows the issuer to obtain better credit ratings and/or more leverage compared to senior unsecured debt issuance.

■ May reduce borrowing costs; often captive finance companies and independent companies can obtain capital at rates better than those obtainable for the originator of the securitized assets.

■ May provide funding and liquidity by converting illiquid assets into cash.

■ May transfer the risk of assets or liabilities to allow a bank originator to do additional business without ballooning its balance sheet.

■ May enable a financial institution to exploit regulatory capital arbitrage, for example through securitization of assets that offer a low return on regulatory capital.

■ Can be used to shelter corporations from potential operating liabilities.

Securitization

A large part of what is considered to be structured finance in today's markets involves securitization, as can be seen from the three published definitions provided earlier. Some respondents provided us with their definitions of securitization as well. Those definitions included the following:

■ The use of superior information on how given assets will perform, or given risks will occur, in a way that such assets will be financed, or such risks allocated, more efficiently, usually by some means of structuring to isolate such assets or risks, and most commonly through offerings into the capital markets.

■ An alternative means of raising money through the transfer of financial assets to a special-purpose entity that issues securities, payments on which are based on collections on the financial assets to investors in a transaction in which the financial assets are isolated from the credit risks of the originator/sponsor.

■ Some people think that single assets can be "securitized." In this respect, bonds are securities that could be considered the securitization of a promise to pay, a stream of cash, or the value of assets.

■ One respondent describes securitization as a close cousin to traditional secured debt. Securitizations are intended to provide a lender or investor with greater protection against the corporate credit risk of the originator of the assets than with traditional secured debt. In principle, a securitization lender/investor is a kind of "super-secured creditor," with rights that surpass those of a traditional secured lender. Securitization employs the notion that the subject assets have been "sold" by the originator and, therefore, will not become entangled in bankruptcy proceedings if the originator files for protection under the bankruptcy code.

This respondent goes on to provide a working, functional definition of securitization. In a securitization, a company raises money by issuing securities that are backed by specific assets. In most cases, the underlying assets are loans, such as mortgage loans or auto loans. The cash flow from the underlying assets usually is the source of funds for the borrower/issuer to make payments on the securities. Securitization products generally are viewed as including the following: ABS, RMBS, CMBS, CDOs, and asset-backed commercial paper.

Accomplishing a "sale" of the securitized assets often requires the use of a special-purpose entity (SPE). A typical securitization is structured as a two-step transaction. In the first step, the originator transfers the subject assets to an SPE in a transfer designed to constitute a "true sale." In the second step, the SPE issues securities backed by the assets. The SPE uses the proceeds from selling the securities to pay the originator for the assets. In addition, part of the "consideration" that the originator receives for transferring the assets to the SPE is its ownership of the SPE. In some securitizations, the originator does not receive the equity in the SPE. Instead, the originator may retain the subordinate or equity position in the securitized assets through other means, such as a variable fee structure.

■ Aside from being a flexible and efficient source of funding, the off-balance-sheet treatment of securitization serves (1) to reduce both the economic cost of capital and regulatory minimum capital requirements as a balance sheet restructuring tool and (2) to diversify asset exposures (especially interest rate risk and currency risk), says another respondent.

■ The generation of securitized cash flows from a diversified asset portfolio represents an effective method of redistributing asset risks to investors and broader capital markets; it amounts to a transformation and fragmentation of asset exposures. As opposed to ordinary debt, a securitized contingent claim on a promised portfolio performance allows investors at low transaction costs to quickly adjust their investment holdings in response to changes in personal risk sensitivity, market sentiment, and/or consumption preferences.

Arguments for Broader Definitions

One respondent favors a broad definition that would include project finance, leveraged leasing, securitization, structured risk transfer (catastrophe and other insurance-linked securities and embedded-value securitization), and various other applications of derivatives. Indeed, most of the conceptual definitions appearing earlier in this article would apply to all aspects of structured finance under such a broad definition. In this respondent's view, one of the most interesting attributes of structured finance is that it may defy definition. That very hard-to-define attribute may help preserve its creativity, vibrancy, and flexibility and generally contribute to the success of structured finance in the face of repeated challenges by accountants, regulators, and others.

Another respondent recommends that we err on the side of inclusiveness, even for gray areas such as project finance and equipment trust certificates. In a similar vein, another respondent believes that in today's market, structured finance simply refers to more sophisticated, complex transactions. It is no surprise that the market has not standardized these distinctions because, as we know, the field of finance is extremely dynamic and constantly changing. What was complex and structured today may become plain vanilla and standard tomorrow. This leads the respondent to conclude that the market really does not need a clear definition for structured finance. And a consultant in the field agrees, saying, "It is to my advantage to leave the definition ambiguous."

The overall tone of the responses and the opinions strongly support the our notion that we should take a broad, inclusive view of structured finance. Thus in this book, we cover not only securitization, but other transactions that we believe should be viewed as structured financing.

CASE STUDY: HOW ENRON HAS AFFECTED THE BOUNDARIES OF STRUCTURED FINANCE

One of the respondents to our survey cautions that the increasing complexity of the structured finance market and the ever growing range of products being made available to investors are invariably creating challenges in terms of efficient information assembly, management, and dissemination. Another warns that structured finance and securitization create flexibility, but also can be vehicles for manipulating accounting statements and committing fraud, but these applications ultimately tend to work to the detriment of the deal sponsor. And in the course of providing us their definitions, several respondents mentioned Enron as pushing beyond the legal and ethical boundaries of structured finance.

In the spring of 2002, the *Journal of Structured and Project Finance* surveyed nine frequent contributors and leading experts to hear their views of how the Enron debacle affected project finance and the broader realm of structured finance.[8] Their general view is that the Enron bankruptcy and related events have changed neither the nature nor the usefulness of traditional project finance but they have led to a slowing down of some of the more innovative forms of structured and project finance. Among the other direct and indirect effects of Enron have been increased caution among lenders and investors toward the energy and power sectors; increased scrutiny of off-balance-sheet transactions; increased emphasis on counterparty credit risk, particularly with regard to companies involved in merchant power and trading; and deeper analysis of how companies generate recurring free cash flow. There is increased emphasis on transparency and disclosure, even though disclosure in traditional project finance has been more robust than in most types of corporate finance. In the recent market environment, for reasons that extend beyond Enron, some power companies have been canceling projects and selling assets to reduce leverage and resorting to on-balance-sheet financing to fortify liquidity.

Background

The immediate cause of the Enron bankruptcy was a loss of confidence among investors caused by that company's restatement of earnings and inadequate, misleading disclosure of off-balance-sheet entities and related debt. There were also secondary causes related more to conditions in the energy and power business than to structured finance, including (1) the California power crisis in 2001; (2) the related Pacific Gas & Electric bankruptcy; (3) falling spot power prices, caused largely by recent overbuilding of power plants; (4) increasing perception by investors, lenders, and rating agencies of the risk related to independent power producers; and (5) increasing skepticism of the energy trading business, including suspicion that some parties were manipulating their earnings through the marking to market of power contracts and off-balance-sheet vehicles.

Effect on Traditional Project Finance

Jonathan Lindenberg, Managing Director of Citigroup, reminds us that traditional project finance is cash-flow-based, asset-based finance that has little in common with Enron's heavily criticized off-balance-sheet partnerships. According to Roger Feldman, Partner of Bingham McCutchen, the historic elements of project finance are firmness of cash flow, counterparty

---

[8] Henry A. Davis, "How Enron Has Affected Project Finance," *Journal of Structured and Project Finance* 8 (Spring 2002), pp. 19–26.

creditworthiness, ability to deal over a long timeframe, and confidence in the legal system. Barry Gold, Managing Director of The Carlyle Group, points out that project finance is a method for monetizing cash flows, providing security, and sharing or transferring risks. The Enron transactions had none of these characteristics. They were an attempt to arbitrage accounting, taxes, and disclosure.

In Lindenberg's view, traditional project finance is based on transparency, as opposed to the Enron partnerships, where outside investors did not have the opportunity to do the due diligence upon which any competent project finance investor or lender would have insisted. Those parties are interested in all the details that give rise to cash flows. As a result, there is a lot more disclosure in project finance than there is in most corporate deals.

Gold points out that, in traditional project finance, analysts and rating agencies do not have a problem with current disclosure standards; it is not hidden and it never has been. First, they know project financing is either with or without recourse and either on or off the balance sheet. For example, in the case of a joint venture where a company owns 50% of a project or less, the equity method of accounting is used. On the company's income statement, the company's share of earnings from the project are included below the line in the equity investment in unconsolidated subsidiaries and, on the balance sheet, its investment is included in equity investment in unconsolidated subsidiaries. The point to remember is that whether a project is financed on or off the balance sheet, analysts know where to look.

Lindenberg explains that off-balance-sheet treatment may not be the principal reason for most project financing. It usually is motivated more by considerations such as risk transfer or providing a way for parties with different credit ratings to jointly finance a project—whereas if all of those parties provided the financing on their own balance sheets, they would be providing unequal amounts of capital by virtue of their different borrowing costs. None of these considerations have anything to do with the Enron partnerships, where a 3% equity participation from a financial player with nothing at risk was used as a gimmick to get assets and related debt off the balance sheet.

Structured Project Finance

Even though pure project finance has not been affected very much by Enron, Lindenberg and Worenklein see some slowing of activity in the more innovative types of structured finance such as synthetic leasing, structured partnerships, and equity share trusts.[9]

---

[9] See Glenn McIsaac, Chris Beale, and Jonathan Lindenberg, "Financing in the New Merchant Power Generation Business," *Journal of Project Finance* 6 (Spring 2000), pp. 13–19, and David Fowkes and Nasir Kahn with Don Armstrong, "Leasing in Project Financing," *Journal of Project Finance* 6 (Spring 2000), pp. 21–32.

Lindenberg notes that synthetic leases are a mature product, understood by rating agencies and accountants, in which billions of dollars of deals have been done. But the problem is "headline risk." Since the Enron debacle, numerous other companies have had disclosure issues. Even though synthetic leases are transparent and well understood by financial experts, they have an off-balance-sheet element that is not understood by everyone in the market at large.

But Christoper Dymond of Greengate LLC cautions that the investor market has overreacted to anything that sounds "like Enron." Structured and project financing techniques have been developed for sound risk management reasons and, in his opinion, must be defended vigorously on those grounds. He believes a prejudice against "complexity" in financial structures could have a real economic and financial cost. Most sponsors and investors are sophisticated enough to make these distinctions. However, if sponsors fear that the wider market will punish them for using complex structures, they will stop using them. After the Enron crisis, several companies made public vows not to use any off-balance-sheet structures. But, rather than pandering to uninformed sentiment, Dymond believes that companies should make greater efforts to clearly delineate the difference between legitimate nonrecourse debt and the Enron structures.

Special Purpose Entities

By using corporate stock as collateral and by creating conflicts of interest, Feldman of Bingham McCutchen believes that Enron undermined the pristine nature of the special purpose, nonrecourse entity and caused all such structures to look suspect in some people's eyes. He stresses that in traditional project finance, a special purpose, nonrecourse entity must be clean and fully focused on the transaction concerned. In the aftermath of the Enron bankruptcy, project sponsors and the bankers and lawyers who support them have had to make special efforts to explain the legitimate business reasons for these entities.

Sources of Free Cash Flow

William Chew, Managing Director of Standard & Poor's recalls that immediately after Enron filed for bankruptcy protection, some questioned whether project and structured finance would survive in their current form. And indeed, some corporations with large amounts of off-balance-sheet financing and inadequate disclosure were subjected to increased scrutiny and sharply reduced valuations for both their equity and their debt. In response, a number of those companies expanded their liquidity and reduced their debt to the extent possible. But Chew believes that, as time progresses, that the main fallout from Enron and the other recent market shocks may be not so much a turning away from project finance but rather a greater stress on bottom-up evaluation of how companies generate recurring free cash flow and what might affect it over time. In this process, Chew believes that project finance and other types of structured finance probably will continue to play an important role. The change, in his view, is that the focus will be on not only the project structures, but also on how they may affect corporate-level cash flow and credit profiles—for example, through springing guarantees and potential debt acceleration, through contingent indemnification and performance guarantees, through negative pledges and their limits at both the project and the corporate holding company level, and through the potential for joint-venture and partnership dissolutions to create sudden changes in cash flows. Standard & Poor's reminds us in its project as well as its corporate credit analysis that there can be a big difference between generally accepted accounting principles (GAAP) and cash flow analysis.

Security Interests

Feldman notes that the power business, in part, has shifted from a contract business to a trading, cash flow kind of business where the counterparty becomes critical to the viability of a transaction. The security in the transaction is less the asset itself and more what the trading counterparty does with the asset. That asset has an option value in the hands of a counterparty, but a far different value if a bank has to foreclose on it—a value you would rather not find out.

In Feldman's opinion, Enron's alleged tendency to set its own rules for marking gas, electricity, and various other newer, thinly traded derivative contracts to market raises some interesting questions about collateral and security. Historically, the security in a power plant financing has consisted of contracts, counterparty arrangements, and assets. But if a lender's security depends on marking certain contracts to market, and there is some question as to the objectivity of the counterparty that is marking them to market, that raises additional questions as to what is an adequate sale, what is adequate collateral, how a lender takes an adequate security interest, how a lender monitors the value of its security interest, and what a lender needs to do to establish a sufficient prior lien in the cash flow associated with the transaction. In the case of a structured finance transaction, Mr. Feldman believes the key question remains just as it always has been: whether the security is real and whether you can get your hands on it.

How Companies Have Responded

Jacob Worenklein of U.S. Power Generating Company has seen affected companies respond to the post-Enron market environment rapidly and decisively to strengthen their liquidity through issuing new equity, canceling projects, selling assets, either unwinding structured finance deals or putting them on the balance sheet, and increased transparency and disclosure. Even though traditional project finance has little to do with the off-balance-sheet entities that brought Enron down, Dino Barajas of Paul, Hastings, Janovsky, and Walker, LLP fears a backlash that could affect project finance in the event of a credit crunch. If that happens, one possible solution could be, simply, to finance more projects on the corporate balance sheet. Some power companies have set up massive credit facilities for doing so based on their overall corporate cash flow and creditworthiness.

Another option for a company is to borrow against a basket of power projects, allowing the lenders to diversify their risks, although such a facility is still largely based on the credit fundamentals of the corporation. But Barajas believes that project financing on an individual plant basis can be preferable to either of these approaches for both project sponsors and lenders. For example, say a company is financing 10 projects and three run into trouble. The company can make a rational economic decision as to which of those projects are salvageable and which ones do not merit throwing in good money after bad. It might let one go into foreclosure and be restructured and sold. But if a company is financing ten projects together, its management may feel compelled to artificially bolster some of its projects so that the failure of one project does not bring the entire credit facility down. Making such an uneconomic decision for the near term would not be in the company's long-term interests.

Increased Transparency and Disclosure

Worenklein observes that after Enron major players started to release much more information than before about their businesses and financing arrangements. Similarly, Gold of The Carlyle Group saw an overriding aura of conservatism in disclosure, for example, in conference room discussions while drafting prospectuses for project finance deals. Bankers were making extra efforts to confirm that deals are being disclosed and explained the right way.

Going forward, Worenklein believes that strong management actions are needed to restore belief in honesty of numbers. A company's management needs to demonstrate the same passion for integrity as it had for growth in the past. It needs to get rid of gimmicks and consistently communicate and execute a simple, clear strategic vision. This involves cleaning up the balance sheet. Transactions that have significant recourse to the sponsor should be put back on the balance sheet. Only true nonrecourse deals should be left off the balance sheet. To convey an accurate, fair picture of the business, companies need to communicate—to the point of obsession—information and assumptions about how earnings are recognized, including mark-to-market transactions. In Worenklein's view, managing earnings is out and managing cash flow is in—and, as Chew of Standard & Poor's noted earlier, that is what the rating agencies are looking at anyway.

Regulatory Issues

Feldman of Bingham McCutchen brings up some regulatory issues. One of the reasons Enron was left to its own devices in valuing gas, electricity, and other types of contracts was that it became, in effect, the largest unregulated bank in the world. It was able to avoid regulation of its trading activities by the Commodity Futures Trading Commission (CFTC), partly as a result of its own lobbying efforts, and the Federal Energy Regulatory Commission (FERC) declined to get involved as well. Therefore, it was able to duck some of the scrutiny that regulators have directed toward commercial and investment banks dealing in derivatives. Of course, securities analysis had long complained about Enron's opaque financial reporting, only to be told in return that they just did not understand the business.

Other Lessons Learned

James Guidera of Calyon sees some general lessons from Enron in the field of structured finance:

- The transfer of assets, intangible and otherwise, into nonconsolidating vehicles controlled by a sponsor may mislead investors as to the extent of nonrecurring earnings or deferred losses, even in the absence of fraud.
- There is a risk of low recovery rates on structured transactions secured by intangible assets (investments, contracts, company stock) or by tangible assets whose values are not established on an arms-length basis.
- Having been badly burned by the Enron bankruptcy, banks and investors involved in structured and project financings, and in the energy sector generally, will be especially conservative, and this will limit credit and capital access for many clients in the sector, creating a general liquidity issue for these customers.

Dymond of Greengate LLC has several recommendations concerning accounting treatment and disclosure:

- An effort must be made by all in the project finance industry (and investor relations) to underscore the distinction between true nonrecourse structures and Enron's activities.
- The terms *nonrecourse* and *off-balance-sheet* should remain synonyms. Liabilities that truly have no recourse to a company's shareholders can justly be treated as off-balance-sheet. Enron appears to have violated this principle since the undisclosed liabilities in the off-balance sheet partnerships actually had significant recourse to Enron shareholders through share remarketing mechanisms.
- Many project finance structures are "limited" recourse rather than "non" recourse, and thus there is a potential gray area in which accounting rules allow off-balance sheet treatment but there is nonetheless some contingent liability to the parent company's shareholders. Full (footnote) disclosure of any potential shareholder recourse was advisable pre-Enron, and is absolutely necessary now.

To conclude, project finance today is alive and well as a form of structured finance. We may just need to remind some people of its basic fundamentals. Neither project finance nor sensible innovations in structured finance with sound, well explained business reasons have been shaken by Enron. The principal lessons learned from the Enron debacle have to do with transparency and disclosure. When some of your businesses or your financing structures become hard to explain, you may begin to question whether they make sense in the first place.

CONCLUSIONS

As we have highlighted in this chapter, structured finance is a term that covers a very wide range of financial market transactions and products. While a common definition of it seems to center on securitization, structured financial products also include complex instruments such as bonds with embedded exotic options and transactions such as project financing and leveraged leasing. We would suggest that securitization and the employment of SPV entities is a subset of structured finance, albeit a large subset.

In conclusion, it is probably best to say that there is no one definition of structured finance, and that the term can be used to describe any financial transaction or instrument that is not plain vanilla.

CHAPTER 2

Interest Rate Derivatives

A s we explained in Chapter 1, structured finance products are often linked to derivative instruments. As the name implies, a derivative instrument is one that derives its value from the value of some underlying variable or variables. Derivative instruments take the form of futures contracts, forward contracts, swap agreements, and option-type contracts. Derivative instruments are classified based on their underlying. They include interest rate derivatives, currency derivatives, equity derivatives, commodity derivatives, and credit derivatives. In this chapter and the one to follow, we will focus on two commonly used derivatives, interest rate derivatives (the subject of this chapter) and credit derivatives (the subject of Chapter 3). The forms of derivatives (futures/forwards, options, swaps) for currency, equity, and commodity derivatives are similar to those described for interest rate derivatives.

INTEREST RATE FORWARD AND FUTURES CONTRACTS

A *forward contract* is an over-the-counter agreement between two parties for the future delivery of the underlying at a specified price at the end of a designated time period. The designated date at which the parties must transact is called the *settlement* or *delivery date*. The party that assumes the long (short) position is obligated to buy (sell) the underlying at the specified price. The terms of the contract are the product of negotiation between the two parties. As such, a forward contract is specific to its two counterparties. Although we commonly refer to taking a long position as "buying a forward contract" and conversely taking a short position as "selling a forward contract," this is a misnomer. No money changes hands between the parties at the time the forward contract is established. Both sides are making a promise to engage in a transaction in the future according to terms negotiated upfront.

At the settlement date, the party with the long position pays the specified price called the *forward price* in exchange for delivery of the underlying from the party with the short position. The payoff of the forward contract for the long position on the settlement date is simply the difference between the price of the underlying minus the forward price. Conversely, the payoff of the forward contract for the short position on the settlement date is the difference between the forward price minus the price of the underlying. Clearly, a forward contract is a zero-sum game.

FUTURES CONTRACTS

A *futures contract* is a legal agreement between a buyer (seller) and an established exchange or its clearinghouse in which the buyer (seller) agrees to take (make) delivery of something at a specified price at the end of designated period. The price at which the parties agree to transact in the future is called the *futures price*. When a market participant takes a position by buying a futures contract, that individual is said to be in a *long futures position* or to be *long futures*. If, instead, the market participant's opening position is the sale of a futures contract, that investor is said to be in a *short position* or *short futures*.

As can be seen from the description, a futures contract is quite similar to a forward contract. They differ on four dimensions: First, futures contracts are standardized agreements as to the settlement date (or month) and quality of the deliverable. Moreover, because these contracts are standardized, they are traded on organized exchanges. In contrast, forward contracts are usually negotiated individually between buyer and seller and the secondary markets are often nonexistent or extremely thin. Second, an intermediary called a clearinghouse stands between the two counterparties to a futures contract and guarantees their performance. Both parties to a forward contract are subject to *counterparty risk*. Counterparty risk is the risk that the other party to the contract will fail to perform. Third, a futures contract is *marked-to-market* while a forward contract may or may not be marked-to-market. Last, although both a futures and forward contract set forth terms of delivery, futures contracts are not intended to be settled by delivery.

Interest rate futures contracts can be classified by the maturity of their underlying instruments. A short-term interest rate futures contract has an underlying instrument that matures in one year or less. Examples of this type are futures contracts in which the underlying instruments is a 3-

month Eurodollar certificate of deposit. The maturity of the underlying instrument of a long-term futures contract exceeds one year. An example is a futures contract in which the underlying is a coupon Treasury security.

Eurodollar CD Futures

Eurodollar CDs are U.S. dollar-denominated CDs issued primarily in London by U.S., Canadian, European, and Japanese banks. These CDs earn a fixed rate of interest related to dollar LIBOR. The term LIBOR comes from the London Interbank Offered Rate and is the interest rate at which one London bank offers funds to another London bank of acceptable credit quality in the form of a cash deposit. The rate is "fixed" by the British Bankers Association every business morning by the average of the rates supplied by member banks.

The 3-month (90-day) Eurodollar CD is the underlying instrument for the Eurodollar CD futures contract. The contracts are traded on the International Monetary Market of the Chicago Mercantile Exchange and the London International Financial Futures Exchange (LIFFE). This contract has a $1 million face value and is traded on an index price basis. The index price basis in which the contract is quoted is equal to 100 minus the annualized LIBOR futures. For example, a Eurodollar CD futures price of 98.23 means a 3-month LIBOR futures of 1.77%. The Eurodollar CD futures contract is a cash settlement contract. Specifically, the parties settle in cash for the value of a Eurodollar CD based on LIBOR at the settlement date. The Eurodollar CD futures contract is one of the most heavily traded futures contracts in the world. It is used frequently to trade the short end of the yield curve, and many hedgers believe this contract to be the best hedging vehicle for a wide range of hedging situations.

Treasury Bond and Note Futures

The Treasury bond futures contract is traded on the Chicago Board of Trade (CBOT). The underlying instrument for this contract is $100,000 par value of a hypothetical 20-year coupon. This hypothetical bond's coupon rate is called the *notional coupon*. The notional coupon is 6%. The underlying instrument is a hypothetical Treasury bond. While some interest rate futures contracts can only be settled in cash, the seller (the short) of a Treasury bond futures contract who chooses to make delivery rather than liquidate his/her position by buying back the contract prior to the settlement date must deliver some Treasury bond. This begs the question: "Which Treasury bond?" The CBOT allows the seller to deliver one of several Treasury bonds that the CBOT specifies are acceptable for delivery. These contracts have multiple deliverables to avoid having a single issue squeezed and to allow for varying schedules of new issues.[1] The set of all bonds that meet the delivery requirements for a particular contract is called the *deliverable basket*. We discuss this feature for credit default swaps in the next chapter.

The delivery process for the Treasury bond futures contract is innovative and has served as a model for bond futures contracts traded on various exchanges throughout the world. On the settlement date, the seller of the futures contract (the short) is required to deliver the buyer (the long) $100,000 par value of a 6%, 20-year Treasury bond. As noted, no such bond exists, so the seller must choose a bond from the deliverable basket to deliver to the long. To make delivery equitable to both parties, the CBOT uses conversion factors for adjusting the price of each Treasury issue that can be delivered to satisfy the Treasury bond futures contract. Within the deliverable basket, conversion factors are designed to make the cost of delivering each bond approximately the same assuming the yield curve is flat at 6%. Given the conversion factor for an issue and the futures price, the adjusted price is found by multiplying the conversion factor by the futures price. The adjusted price is called the *converted price*.

In selecting the issue to be delivered, the party with the short position will select from all the deliverable issues the one that will give the largest rate of return from a cash-and-carry trade. A *cash-and-carry trade* is one in which a cash bond that is acceptable for delivery is purchased with borrowed funds and simultaneously the Treasury bond futures contract is sold. The bond purchased can be delivered to satisfy the short futures position. Thus, by buying the Treasury issue that is acceptable for delivery and selling the futures, an investor has effectively sold the bond at the delivery price (i.e., the converted price). A rate of return can be calculated for this trade. This rate of return is referred to as the *implied repo rate*. The issue with the highest implied repo rate is call the *cheapest-to-deliver issue*. Again, we will the same concept when we discuss credit default swaps.

There are three Treasury note futures contracts: 10-year, 5-year, and 2-year. All three contracts are modeled after the Treasury bond futures contract and are traded on the CBOT.

INTEREST RATE SWAPS

An *interest rate swap* provides a vehicle for market participants to transform the nature of cash flows and the interest rate exposure of a portfolio, balance sheet, particular asset or liability, or structured transaction.

---

[1] The term "squeeze" is used to describe a shortage of the supply of a particular security relative to the demand. A trader who is short a particular security is always concerned with the risk of being unable to obtain sufficient securities to cover their position.

In an interest rate swap, two parties (called *counterparties*) agree to exchange periodic interest payments. The dollar amount of the interest payments exchanged is based on some predetermined dollar principal, which is called the *notional amount*. The dollar amount each counterparty pays to the other is the agreed-upon periodic interest rate times the notional amount. The only dollars that are exchanged between the parties are the interest payments, not the notional amount. Accordingly, the notional principal serves only as a scale factor to translate an interest rate into a cash flow. In the most common type of swap, one party agrees to pay the other party fixed interest payments at designated dates for the life of the contract. This party is referred to as the *fixed-rate payer*. The other party, who agrees to make interest rate payments that float with some reference rate, is referred to as the *fixed-rate receiver*.

The reference rates that have been used for the floating rate in an interest rate swap are various money market rates: Treasury bill rate, London interbank offered rate, commercial paper rate, bankers acceptances rate, certificates of deposit rate, federal funds rate, and prime rate. The most common is the *London Interbank Offered Rate* (LIBOR). LIBOR is the rate at which prime banks offer to pay on Eurodollar and other currency deposits available to other prime banks for a given maturity. There is not just one rate but a rate for different maturities. For example, there is a 1-month LIBOR, 3-month LIBOR, and 6-month LIBOR. Similarly, there are various Treasury bill rates, bankers acceptances rates, certificates of deposit rates, and so forth with different maturities quoted by different financial institutions. Interest rate swap agreements and other financial agreements define exactly which rates are used and how they are set.

An interest rate swap between two counterparties is illustrated in Exhibit 2.1. We assume that for the next five years party X agrees to pay party Y 10% per year, while party Y agrees to pay party X 6-month LIBOR (the reference rate). Party X is the fixed-rate payer, while party Y is the fixed-rate receiver. Assume that the notional amount is $50 million, and that payments are exchanged every six months for the next five years. This means that every six months, party X (the fixed-rate payer) will pay party Y $2.5 million (10% times $50 million divided by 2). The amount

EXHIBIT 2.1 Diagram of Interest Rate Swap Between Two Counterparties

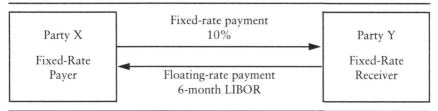

that party Y (fixed-rate receiver) will pay party X will be 6-month LIBOR times $50 million divided by 2. If 6-month LIBOR is 7%, party Y will pay party X $1.75 million (7% times $50 million divided by 2). Note that we divide by two because one-half year's interest is being paid.

Interest rate swaps are over-the-counter instruments. This means that they are not traded on an exchange. Consequently, the risks that each party takes when it enters into a swap is that the other party will fail to fulfill its obligations as set forth in the swap agreement. That is, each party faces default risk, known in this case as *counterparty risk*. In any agreement between two parties that must perform according to the terms of a contract, counterparty risk is the risk that the other party will default. With futures and exchange-traded options the counterparty risk is the risk that the clearinghouse will default. Market participants view this risk as small. In contrast, counterparty risk in a swap can be significant.

Interpreting a Swap Position

There are two ways that a swap position can be interpreted: (1) a package of forward/futures contracts and (2) a package of cash flows from buying and selling cash market instruments.

Package of Forward Contracts

Consider the hypothetical interest rate swap used earlier to illustrate a swap. Let's look at party X's position. Party X has agreed to pay 10% and receive 6-month LIBOR. More specifically, assuming a $50 million notional amount, X has agreed to buy a commodity called "6-month LIBOR" for $2.5 million. This is effectively a 6-month forward contract where X agrees to pay $2.5 million in exchange for delivery of 6-month LIBOR. The fixed-rate payer is effectively long a 6-month forward contract on 6-month LIBOR. The floating-rate payer is effectively short a 6-month forward contract on 6-month LIBOR. There is therefore an implicit forward contract corresponding to each exchange date.

Consequently, interest rate swaps can be viewed as a package of more basic interest rate derivative instruments—forwards.

Package of Cash Market Instruments

To understand why a swap can also be interpreted as a package of cash market instruments, consider an investor who enters into the transaction below:

■ Buy $50 million par value of a 5-year floating-rate bond that pays 6-month LIBOR every six months.

■ Finance the purchase by borrowing $50 million for five years at a 10% annual interest rate paid every six months.

The cash flows for this transaction are set forth in Exhibit 2.2. The second column of the exhibit shows the cash flows from purchasing the 5-year floating-rate bond. There is a $50 million cash outlay and then 10 cash inflows. The amount of the cash inflows is uncertain because they depend on future levels of 6-month LIBOR. The next column shows the cash flows from borrowing $50 million on a fixed-rate basis. The last column shows the net cash flows from the entire transaction. As the last column indicates, there is no initial cash flow (the cash inflow and cash outlay offset each other). In all 10 6-month periods, the net position results in a cash inflow of LIBOR and a cash outlay of $2.5 million. This net position, however, is identical to the position of a fixed-rate payer/floating-rate receiver.

It can be seen from the net cash flow in Exhibit 2.2 that a fixed-rate payer has a cash market position that is equivalent to a long position in a

EXHIBIT 2.2   Cash Flows for the Purchase of a 5-Year Floating-Rate Bond Financed by Borrowing on a Fixed-Rate Basis

Transaction:
   ■ Purchase for $50 million a 5-year floating-rate bond:
       Floating rate = LIBOR, semiannual pay
   ■ Borrow $50 million for five years:
       Fixed rate = 10%, semiannual payments

6-Month Period	Cash Flow (in millions of dollars) from:		
	Floating-Rate Bond[a]	Borrowing Cost	Net
0	−$50	+$50.0	$0
1	+ $(LIBOR_1/2) \times 50$	−2.5	+ $(LIBOR_1/2) \times 50 - 2.5$
2	+ $(LIBOR_2/2) \times 50$	−2.5	+ $(LIBOR_2/2) \times 50 - 2.5$
3	+ $(LIBOR_3/2) \times 50$	−2.5	+ $(LIBOR_3/2) \times 50 - 2.5$
4	+ $(LIBOR_4/2) \times 50$	−2.5	+ $(LIBOR_4/2) \times 50 - 2.5$
5	+ $(LIBOR_5/2) \times 50$	−2.5	+ $(LIBOR_5/2) \times 50 - 2.5$
6	+ $(LIBOR_6/2) \times 50$	−2.5	+ $(LIBOR_6/2) \times 50 - 2.5$
7	+ $(LIBOR_7/2) \times 50$	−2.5	+ $(LIBOR_7/2) \times 50 - 2.5$
8	+ $(LIBOR_8/2) \times 50$	−2.5	+ $(LIBOR_8/2) \times 50 - 2.5$
9	+ $(LIBOR_9/2) \times 50$	−2.5	+ $(LIBOR_9/2) \times 50 - 2.5$
10	+ $(LIBOR_{10}/2) \times 50 + 50$	−52.5	+ $(LIBOR_{10}/2) \times 50 - 2.5$

[a] The subscript for LIBOR indicates the 6-month LIBOR as per the terms of the floating-rate bond at time *t*.

floating-rate bond and a short position in a fixed-rate bond—the short position being the equivalent of borrowing by issuing a fixed-rate bond.

What about the position of a floating-rate payer? It can be easily demonstrated that the position of a floating-rate payer is equivalent to purchasing a fixed-rate bond and financing that purchase at a floating-rate, where the floating rate is the reference rate for the swap. That is, the position of a floating-rate payer is equivalent to a long position in a fixed-rate bond and a short position in a floating-rate bond.

Terminology, Conventions, and Market Quotes

Here we review some of the terminology used in the swaps market and explain how swaps are quoted. The *trade date* for a swap is the date on which the swap is transacted. The terms of the trade include the fixed interest rate, the maturity, the notional amount of the swap, and the payment bases of both legs of the swap. The date from which floating interest payments are determined is the *reset* or *setting date*, which may also be the trade date. The rate is fixed two business days before the interest period begins. The second (and subsequent) reset date will be two business days before the beginning of the second (and subsequent) swap periods. The *effective date* is the date from which interest on the swap is calculated, and this is typically two business days after the trade date. In a *forward-start swap* the effective date will be at some point in the future, specified in the swap terms. The floating interest rate for each period is fixed at the start of the period, so that the interest payment amount is known in advance by both parties (the fixed rate is known of course, throughout the swap by both parties).

While our illustrations assume that the timing of the cash flows for both the fixed-rate payer and floating-rate payer will be the same, this is rarely the case in a swap. An agreement may call for the fixed-rate payer to make payments annually but the floating-rate payer to make payments more frequently (semiannually or quarterly). Also, the way in which interest accrues on each leg of the transaction differs. Normally, the fixed interest payments are paid on the basis of a 30/360 day count. Floating-rate payments for dollar and euro-denominated swaps use an Actual/360 day count similar to other money market instruments in those currencies. Sterling-denominated swaps use an Actual/365 day count.

Accordingly, the fixed interest payments will differ slightly owing to the differences in the lengths of successive coupon periods. The floating payments will differ owing to day counts as well as movements in the reference rate.

The terminology used to describe the position of a party in the swap markets combines cash and futures market jargons, given that a swap position can be interpreted either as a position in a package of cash market instruments or a package of futures/forward positions. As we have said, the counterparty to an interest rate swap is either a fixed-rate payer or floating-rate payer.

The fixed-rate payer receives floating-rate interest and is said to be "long" or to have "bought" the swap. The long side has conceptually purchased a floating-rate note (because it receives floating-rate interest) and issued a fixed coupon bond (because it pays out fixed interest at periodic intervals). In essence, the fixed-rate payer is borrowing at fixed-rate and investing in a floating-rate asset. The fixed-rate receiver is said to be "short" or to have "sold" the swap. The short side has conceptually purchased a coupon bond (because it receives fixed-rate interest) and issued a floating-rate note (because it pays floating-rate interest). A fixed-rate receiver is borrowing at a floating rate and investing in a fixed-rate asset.

The convention that has evolved for quoting swaps is that a swap dealer sets the floating rate equal to the reference rate and then quotes the fixed rate that will apply. To illustrate this convention, consider the following 10-year swap terms available from a dealer:

- *Fixed-rate receiver:*
  Pay floating rate of 3-month LIBOR quarterly.
  Receive fixed rate of 8.75% semiannually.
- *Fixed-rate payer:*
  Pay fixed rate of 8.85% semiannually.
  Receive floating rate of 3-month LIBOR quarterly.

The offer price that the dealer would quote the fixed-rate payer would be to pay 8.85% and receive LIBOR "flat." (The word *flat* means with no spread.) The bid price that the dealer would quote the floating-rate payer would be to pay LIBOR flat and receive 8.75%. The bid offer spread is 10 bp.

The swap will specify the frequency of settlement for the fixed-rate payments. The frequency need not be the same as for the floating-rate payments.

Assume that the frequency of settlement is quarterly for the fixed-rate payments, the same as with the floating-rate payments. The day count convention is the same as for the floating-rate payment, "actual/360." The equation for determining the dollar amount of the fixed-rate payment for the period is

$$\text{Notional amount} \times (\text{Swap rate}) \times \frac{\text{No. of days in period}}{360}$$

It is the same equation as for determining the floating-rate payment except that the swap rate is used instead of the reference rate (3-month LIBOR in our illustration).

For example, suppose that the swap rate is 4.98% and the quarter has 90 days. Then the fixed-rate payment for the quarter is

$$\$100,000,000 \times 0.0498 \times \frac{90}{360} = \$1,245,000$$

If there are 92 days in a quarter, the fixed-rate payment for the quarter is

$$\$100,000,000 \times 0.0498 \times \frac{92}{360} = \$1,272,667$$

Note that the rate is fixed for each quarter but the dollar amount of the payment depends on the number of days in the period.

Application of an Interest Rate Swap: Creating a Synthetic Fixed- or Floating-Rate Security

Suppose Multinational Machine Corp., rated A by two rating agencies, is able to issue $100 million fixed-rate bonds for 10 years at 6% and Toys for Kids, lacking the size and credit rating to issue fixed-rate public debt other than high-yield debt at a very large spread over LIBOR, borrows $100 million from a syndicate of banks at 6-month LIBOR plus 2%. Multinational Machine sees an opportunity to lower its funding cost by swapping into floating rate debt. Toys for Kids would like fixed-rate exposure and sees an opportunity to swap floating for fixed at an advantageous rate.

Suppose that the interest rates that must be paid by the two corporations in the floating-rate and fixed-rate markets for a 10-year debt offering are as follows:

For Multinational Machine:
 Floating rate = 6-month LIBOR + 30 bp
 Fixed rate = 6.0%

For Toys for Kids:
 Floating rate = 6-month LIBOR + 200 bp
 Fixed rate = 10%.

Notice that Multinational Machine is able to borrow at cheaper rates in both the fixed and floating rate markets relative to Toys for Kids.

EXHIBIT 2.3   Diagram of the Interest Payments in an Interest Rate Swap

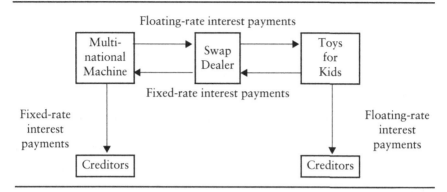

Suppose at the time Multinational Machines and Toys for Kids arrange their respective bond and bank financings so that both corporations enter into a 10-year interest rate swap with a $100 million notional amount with a swap dealer. The interest rate swap is diagrammed in Exhibit 2.3. Suppose the terms of the interest rate swap are as follows:[2]

For Multinational Machine:
  Pay floating rate of 6-month LIBOR
  Receive fixed rate of 6.2%

For Toys for Kids:
  Pay fixed rate of 6.45%
  Receive floating rate of 6-month LIBOR

The cost of the bond issue for Multinational Machine would then be as follows:

Interest paid
On fixed-rate bonds issued = 6%
On interest rate swap   = 6-month LIBOR
Total   = 6% + 6-month LIBOR

---

[2] Notice that on the floating-rate side, the swap dealer is paying and receiving 6-month LIBOR. However, on the fixed-rate side, the swap dealer is receiving 6.45% from Toys for Kids but paying only 6.2% to Multinational Machine. The 25 bp spread is earned by the swap dealer if the counterparties fulfill their obligations.

Interest received
    On interest rate swap   = 6.2%

Net cost
Interest paid	= 6% + 6-month LIBOR
Interest received	= 6.2%
Total	= 6-month LIBOR – 20 bp

Therefore, Multinational Machine has achieved its financing objective of floating-rate funding at an advantageous rate.

The cost of the syndicated bank loan for Toys for Kids would then be as follows:

Interest paid
On syndicated bank loan	= 6-month LIBOR + 200 bp
On interest rate swap	= 6.45%
Total	= 8.45% + 6-month LIBOR

Interest received
On interest rate swap	= 6-month LIBOR

Net cost
Interest paid	= 8.45% + 6-month LIBOR
Interest received	= 6-month LIBOR
Total	= 8.45%

As can be seen, by using the interest rate swap Toys for Kids is able to obtain the type of fixed-rate financing it sought at a rate it could not have achieved independently without the swap.

In fact, a closer examination of both transactions indicates that both firms were actually able to reduce their funding cost below what the cost would have been had they issued directly into the market for the type of coupon they sought. A comparison of the two costs for the two corporations is summarized below:

Multinational Machine:
    Floating-rate bond: 6-month LIBOR + 30 bp
    Fixed-rate bond + swap: 6-month LIBOR – 20 bp

Toys for Kids
    Fixed-rate high-yield bond: 10%
    Floating-rate bank loan + swap: 8.45%

While the magnitude of the reduction in funding costs that we have just illustrated is not likely to occur in real world markets, there are opportunities to reduce funding costs for the reasons described earlier in this chapter. In fact, the interest rate swaps market became the key vehicle for issuers in the United States to obtain lower funding cost in the Eurobond market in the early 1980s because of differences between the spreads demanded by fixed-rate and floating-rate investors in the U.S. bond market and in the Eurodollar bond market.

Nongeneric Interest Rate Swaps

The swap market is very flexible and instruments can be tailor-made to fit the requirements of a structured transaction. A wide variety of swap contracts are traded in the market. For example, the term of a swap need not be fixed; swaps may be *extendible* or *putable*. In an extendible swap, one of the parties has the right but not the obligation to extend the life of the swap beyond the fixed maturity date, while in a putable swap one party has the right to terminate the swap prior to its specified maturity date.

Other swaps that may be found in a structured financing transaction are described in the following sections.

Constant Maturity Swap

In a constant maturity swap, the parties exchange a LIBOR for a fixed swap rate. For example, the terms of the swap might state that 6-month LIBOR is exchanged for the 5-year swap rate or for the 5-year government bond rate on a semiannual basis for the next five years. In the U.S. market, the second type of constant maturity swap is known as a *constant maturity Treasury swap*.

Accreting and Amortizing Swaps

In a plain vanilla swap, the notional principal remains unchanged during the life of the swap. However, it is possible to trade a swap where the notional principal varies during its life. An accreting (or step-up) swap is one in which the principal starts off at one level and then increases in amount over time. The opposite, an amortizing swap, is one in which the notional reduces in size over time. An accreting swap would be useful where for instance, a funding liability that is being hedged increases over time. The amortizing swap might be employed by a borrower hedging a bond issue that featured sinking fund payments, where a part of the notional amount outstanding is paid off at set points during the life of the bond. If the principal fluctuates in amount, for example increasing in one year and then reducing in another, the swap is known as a *roller-*

coaster swap. Another application of an amortizing swap is as a hedge for a loan that is itself an amortizing one. Frequently this is combined with a forward-starting swap, to tie in with the cash flows payable on the loan. The pricing and valuation of an amortizing swap is no different in principle to a vanilla interest rate swap; a single swap rate is calculated using the relevant discount factors, and at this rate the net present value of the swap cash flows will equal zero at the start of the swap.

Basis Swap

In a conventional swap, one leg comprises fixed-rate payments and the other floating-rate payments. In a *basis swap* both legs are floating rate, but linked to different money market indices. One leg is normally linked to LIBOR, while the other might be linked to the CD rate or the commercial paper rate. This type of swap would be used by a bank in the United States that makes loans at a prime-based rate and funds its loans at LIBOR. A basis swap would eliminate the basis risk between the bank's income and interest expense. Other basis swaps are traded in which both legs are linked to LIBOR, but at different maturities; for instance one leg might be at 3-month LIBOR and the other at 6-month LIBOR. In such a swap, the basis is different as is the payment frequency: One leg pays out semiannually, while the other would be paying on a quarterly basis.

Swaptions

A *swaption* is an option to establish a position in an interest rate swap at some future date. The swaption contract specifies the swaption's expiration date as well as the fixed rate and tenor of the underlying swap. The swap's fixed rate is called the swaption's *strike rate.* There are two types of swaptions—pay fixed or receive fixed. A pay (receive) fixed swaption gives the buyer the right to establish a position in an interest rate swap where it will pay (receive) the fixed-rate cash flows and receive (pay) the floating-rate cash flows. Pay fixed swaptions are also known as *call swaptions* and receive fixed swaptions are also known as *put swaptions.*

OPTIONS

An *option* is a contract in which the writer of the option grants the buyer of the option the right, but not the obligation, to purchase from or sell to the writer something at a specified price within a specified period of time (or at a specified date). The *writer,* also referred to as the *seller,* grants this right to the buyer in exchange for a certain sum of money, which is called the *option price* or *option premium*. In effect, the writer is selling a promise in exchange for the option price. Conversely, the buyer pays the option price to obtain the writer's promise. The price at which the underlying may be bought or sold is called the *exercise* or *strike price*. The date after which an option is void is called the *expiration date*. Our focus in this chapter is on options where the "something" underlying the option is a interest rate instrument.

When an option grants the buyer the right to purchase the designated instrument from the writer (seller), it is referred to as a *call option*, or *call*. When the option buyer has the right to sell the designated instrument to the writer, the option is called a *put option*, or *put*.

An option is also categorized according to when the option buyer may exercise the option. There are options that may be exercised at any time up to and including the expiration date. Such an option is referred to as an *American option*. There are options that may be exercised only at the expiration date. An option with this feature is called a *European option*. There are also *Bermuda* option contracts that are hybrids between American and European option contracts. The distinguishing feature of a Bermuda option contract is that early exercise is possible but is restricted to certain dates in the option's life.

The maximum amount that an option buyer can lose is the option price. The maximum profit that the option writer can realize is the option price. The option buyer has substantial upside return potential, while the option writer faces substantial downside risk. We investigate the risk and reward profile for option positions later.

There are no margin requirements for the buyer of an option once the option price has been paid in full. Because the option price is the maximum amount that the investor can lose, no matter how adverse the price movement of the underlying instrument, there is no need for margin. Because the writer of an option has agreed to accept all of the risk (and none of the reward) of the position in the underlying instrument, the writer is generally required to put up the option price received as margin. In addition, as price changes occur that adversely affect the writer's position, the writer is required to deposit additional margin (with some exceptions) as the position is marked to market.

Notice that unlike in a futures contract, one party to an option contract is not obligated to transact. Specifically, the option buyer has the right but not the obligation to transact. The option writer does have the obligation to perform. In the case of a futures contract, both buyer and seller are obligated to perform. Of course, the buyer of a futures contract does not pay the seller to accept the obligation, while an option buyer pays the seller the option price.

Consequently, the risk and reward characteristics of the two contracts are also different. In the case of a futures contract, the buyer of the contract realizes a dollar-for-dollar gain when the price of the futures contract increases and suffers a dollar-for-dollar loss when the price of the futures contract drops. The opposite occurs for the seller of a futures contract. Options do not provide this symmetric risk and reward characteristic. The most that the buyer of an option can lose is the option price. While the buyer of an option retains all the potential benefits, the gain is always reduced by the amount of the option price. The maximum profit that the writer may realize is the option price; this is offset against substantial downside risk. This difference is extremely important because managers can use futures to protect against symmetric risk and options to protect against asymmetric risk.

Risk and Return Characteristics of Options

Here we illustrate the risk and return characteristics of the four basic option positions—(1) buying a call option, (2) writing a call option, (3) buying a put option, and (4) writing a put option. The discussion assumes that each option position is held to the expiration date and not exercised early. In our illustrations, we will use an option on a physical since the principles apply equally to futures options. To keep the illustration simple, we ignore transactions costs. The purchase of a call option creates a financial position referred to as a *long call position*. The maximum loss is the option price and there is substantial upside potential. The writer of a call option is said to be in a *short call position*. The maximum profit that the short call position can produce is the option price. The buying of a put option creates a financial position referred to as a *long put position*. As with all long option positions, the loss is limited to the option price. The profit potential, however, is substantial: the theoretical maximum profit is generated if the underlying's price falls to zero. Contrast this profit potential with that of the buyer of a call option. The theoretical maximum profit for a call buyer cannot be determined beforehand because it depends on the highest price that can be reached by the underlying's price before or at the option expiration date.

While the investor who takes a short position in Asset XYZ faces all the downside risk as well as the upside potential, the long put position limits the downside risk to the option price while still maintaining upside potential (reduced only by an amount equal to the option price).

Writing a put option creates a financial position referred to as a *short put position*. The profit and loss profile for a short put option is the mirror image of the long put option. The maximum profit from this position is the option price. The theoretical maximum loss can be substantial should the price of the underlying asset fall; at the outside, if the price were to fall all the way to zero, the loss would be as large as the strike price less the option price.

To summarize, buying calls or selling puts allows the investor to gain if the price of the underlying asset rises. Selling calls and buying puts allows the investor to gain if the price of the underlying asset falls.

Exchange-Traded versus OTC Options

There are exchange-traded options and over-the-counter options. Exchange-traded options have two advantages. First, the exercise price and expiration date of the contract are standardized. Second, as in the case of futures contracts, the direct link between buyer and seller is severed after the order is executed because of the interchangeability of exchange-traded options. The clearinghouse associated with the exchange where the option trades performs the same function in the options market that it does in the futures market.

OTC options are used in the many situations where an institutional investor needs to have a tailor-made option because the standardized exchange-traded option does not satisfy its investment objectives. Investment banking firms and commercial banks act as principals as well as brokers in the OTC options market.

OTC options can be customized in any manner sought by an institutional investor or other user. There are plain vanilla options such as options on a specific Treasury issue. The more complex OTC options created are called *exotic options*. Examples of OTC options are given in the next chapter. While an OTC option is less liquid than an exchange-traded option, this is typically not of concern since institutional investors who use OTC options as part of a hedging or asset/liability strategy intend to hold them to expiration.

In the absence of a clearinghouse, the parties to any over-the-counter contract are exposed to counterparty risk. In the case of a forward contract (an OTC contract) both parties face counterparty risk since both parties are obligated to perform. Thus, there is bilateral counterparty risk. In contrast, for an OTC option, once the option buyer pays the option price, it has satisfied its obligation. It is only the seller that must perform if the option is exercised. Thus, the option buyer is exposed to unilateral counterparty risk—the risk that the option seller will fail to perform.

The underlying for an interest rate option can be a fixed-income security or an interest rate futures contract. The former options are called *options on physicals*. In the United States, there are no actively exchange-traded options on physicals. Options on interest rate futures are called *futures options*. The actively traded interest rate options on exchanges are futures options.

A futures option gives the buyer the right to buy from or sell to the writer a designated futures contract at the strike price at any time during the life of the option. If the futures option is a call option, the buyer has the right to purchase one designated futures contract at the strike price. That is, the buyer has the right to acquire a long futures position in the designated futures contract. If the buyer exercises the call option, the writer acquires a corresponding short position in the futures contract. A put option on a futures contract grants the buyer the right to sell a designated futures contract to the writer at the strike price. That is, the option buyer has the right to acquire a short position in the designated futures contract. If the put option is exercised, the writer acquires a corresponding long position in the designated futures contract. Earlier we described several interest rate and bond futures contracts traded on various exchanges throughout the world. Options on these interest rate and bond futures contracts are also traded on these same exchanges.

In an attempt to compete with the OTC option market, the CBOT introduced in 1994 the *flexible Treasury futures options*. These futures options allow counterparties to customize options within certain limits. Specifically, the exercise price, expiration date, and type of exercise (American or European) can be customized subject to CBOT constraints.

Valuation of Options

The option value is a reflection of the option's *intrinsic value* and any additional amount over its intrinsic value. The premium over intrinsic value is often referred to as the *time value*. The intrinsic value of an option is its economic value if it is exercised immediately. If no positive economic value would result from exercising the option immediately, then the intrinsic value is zero.

For a call option, the intrinsic value is positive if the current price of the underlying security is greater than the strike price. The intrinsic value is then the difference between the two prices. If the strike price of a call option is greater than or equal to the current price of the security, the intrinsic value is zero. When an option has intrinsic value, it is said to be *in the money*. When the strike price of a call option exceeds the current price of the security, the call option is said to be *out of the money*; it has no intrinsic value. An option for which the strike price is equal to the current price of the security is said to be *at the money*. Both at-the-money and out-of-the-money options have an intrinsic value of zero because they will not generate a positive payoff if exercised. For a put option, the intrinsic value is equal to the amount by which the cur-

EXHIBIT 2.4 Relationship Between Security Price, Strike Price, and Intrinsic Value

If Security Price > Strike Price	Call Option	Put Option
Intrinsic value	Security price – Strike price	Zero
Jargon	In the money	Out of the money

If Security Price < Strike Price	Call Option	Put Option
Intrinsic value	Zero	Security price – Stock price
Jargon	Out of the money	In the money

If Security Price = Strike Price	Call Option	Put Option
Intrinsic value	Zero	Zero
Jargon	At the money	At the money

rent price of the security is below the strike price. The intrinsic value is zero if the strike price is less than or equal to the current market price. The relations above are summarized in Exhibit 2.4.

The time value of an option is the amount by which the option price exceeds its intrinsic value. The option buyer hopes that, at some time prior to expiration, changes in the market price of the underlying security will increase the value of the rights conveyed by the option. For this prospect, the option buyer is willing to pay a premium above the intrinsic value.

There are six factors that influence the value of an option in which the underlying is a fixed-income instrument:

1. current price of the underlying security;
2. strike price;
3. time to expiration of the option;
4. expected yield volatility over the life of the option;
5. short-term risk-free interest rate over the life of the option; and
6. coupon interest payment over the life of the option.

The impact of each of these factors may depend on whether (1) the option is a call or a put, and (2) the option is an American option or a European option. A summary of the effect of each factor on put and call option prices is presented in Exhibit 2.5.

At any time, the intrinsic value of an option can be determined. The question is, what is the time value of an option worth. To answer this question, option pricing models have been developed. The most popular model for the pricing of equity options is the Black-Scholes option pric-

EXHIBIT 2.5 Summary of Factors that Affect the Price of an Option on a
Fixed-Income Instrument

Increase in Factor with all Other Factors Held Constant	Effect on Call Option	Effect on Put Option
Current price of underlying security	increase	decrease
Strike price	decrease	increase
Time to expiration (American options)	increase	increase
Expected yield volatility	increase	increase
Short-term risk-free rate	increase	decrease
Coupon interest payments	decrease	increase

ing model.[3] By imposing certain assumptions and using arbitrage arguments, the Black-Scholes option pricing model computes the fair (or theoretical) price of a European call option on a nondividend-paying stock. There are problems with using the model to value an option on a fixed-income instrument and a futures option due to its underlying assumptions. The more commonly used model for valuing futures options is the Black model.[4] The model was developed to value European options on futures contracts.

Over-the-Counter Interest Rate Options

OTC interest rate options are created by commercial banks and investment banks for their clients. Dealers can customize the expiration date, the underlying, and the type of exercise. For example, the underlying could be a specific fixed-income security or a spread between yields in two sectors of the fixed-income market.

In addition to American- and European-type options, an OTC option can be created in which the buyer may exercise prior to the expiration date but only on designated dates. Such options are referred to as *Bermuda* options. With an OTC option, the buyer need not pay the option price at the time of purchase. Instead, the option price can be paid at the expiration or exercise date. For such options, the option writer is exposed to counterparty risk in addition to the option buyer.

In the OTC option market there are plain vanilla and exotic options. Plain vanilla options are options on specific securities or on the spread

---

[3] Fischer Black and Myron Scholes, "The Pricing of Corporate Liabilities," *Journal of Political Economy* 81 (May–June 1973), pp. 637–659.
[4] Fischer Black, "The Pricing of Commodity Contracts," *Journal of Financial Economics* 3 (March 1976), pp. 167–179.

between two sectors of the bond market. Exotic options have more complicated payoffs and we do not review these in this chapter.

CAPS AND FLOORS

Caps and floors are agreements between two parties, whereby one party for an upfront fee agrees to compensate the other if a designated interest rate (called the *reference rate*) is different from a predetermined level. The party that benefits, if the reference rate differs from a predetermined level, is called the *buyer,* and the party that must potentially make payments is called the *seller.* The predetermined interest rate level is called the *strike rate.* An interest rate cap specifies that the seller agrees to pay the buyer if the reference rate exceeds the strike rate. An interest rate floor specifies that the seller agrees to pay the buyer if the reference rate is below the strike rate.

The terms of an interest rate agreement include: (1) the reference rate; (2) the strike rate that sets the cap or floor; (3) the length of the agreement; (4) the frequency of reset; and (5) the notional amount (which determines the size of the payments). If a cap or a floor is in the money on the reset date, the payment by the seller is typically made in arrears.

Caps

A cap is essentially a strip of options. A borrower with an existing interest rate liability can protect against a rise in interest rates by purchasing a cap. If rates rise above the cap, the borrower will be compensated by the cap payout. Conversely, if rates fall the borrower gains from lower funding costs and the only expense is the upfront premium paid to purchase the cap. The payoff for the cap buyer at a reset date if the value of the reference rate exceeds the cap rate on that date is as follows:

Notional amount × (Value of the reference rate − Cap rate)
× (Number of days in settlement period/Number of days in year)

Naturally, if the reference rate is below the cap rate, the payoff is zero.

Floors

It is possible to protect against a drop in interest rates by purchasing a floor. This is exactly opposite of a cap in that a floor pays out when the reference rate falls below the strike rate. This would be used by an institution that wished to protect against a fall in income caused by a fall in interest rate—for example, a commercial bank with a large proportion of floating-rate assets. For the floor buyer, the payoff at a reset date is as follows if the value of the reference rate at the reset date is less than the floor rate:

Notional amount × (Floor rate – Value of the reference rate)
× (Number of days in settlement period/Number of days in a year)

The floor's payoff is zero if the reference rate is higher than the floor rate.

Collars

The combination of a cap and a floor creates a collar, which is a corridor that fixes interest payment or receipt levels. A collar is sometimes advantageous for borrowers because it has a lower cost than a straight cap. A collar protects against a rise in rates, and provides some gain if there is a fall down to the floor rate. The cheapest structure is a collar with a narrow spread between cap and floor rates.

CHAPTER 3

Credit Derivatives

The interest rate derivatives explained in the previous chapter are used in structured finance transactions to control interest rate risk with respect to changes in the level of interest rates. *Credit derivatives*, in contrast, allow the transfer of credit risk from parties in a structured finance transaction who want to shed credit risk to counterparties willing to accept credit risk.

The eight major credit derivatives according to the British Bankers Association are:[1]

- credit default swaps;
- index swaps such as credit default index swaps;
- basket default swaps;
- asset swaps;
- total return swaps;
- portfolio/synthetic collateralized debt obligations; and
- credit-linked notes.

We will discuss all but the last two credit derivatives in this chapter. Portfolio/synthetic collateralized debt obligations are discussed in Chapter 7 and credit-linked notes in Chapter 9.

DOCUMENTATION AND CREDIT DERIVATIVE TERMS

Before describing the various types of credit derivatives, we will discuss the documentation and key terms for credit derivatives. The International Swap and Derivatives Association (ISDA) first developed in 1998

---

[1] British Bankers Association, *Credit Derivatives Report* 2003/2004.

a standard contract that could be used by parties for trades in credit derivatives contracts. While the documentation is primarily designed for credit default swaps and total return swaps, the contract form is sufficiently flexible so that it can be used for the other credit derivatives described in this chapter as well.

Reference Entity and Reference Obligation

The documentation will identify the reference entity and/or the reference obligation. The *reference entity*, also referred to as the *reference issuer*, is the issuer of the debt instrument. The *reference obligation*, also referred to as the *reference asset*, is the particular debt issue for which the credit protection is being sought. For example, a reference entity could be Viacom. The reference obligation would be a specific Viacom bond issue.

Credit Events

A credit derivative has a payout that is contingent upon a *credit event* occurring. The *1999 ISDA Credit Derivatives Definitions* (referred to as the "1999 Definitions") provides a list of eight credit events that seek to capture every type of situation that could cause the credit quality of the reference entity to deteriorate or cause the value of the reference obligation to decline:

1. bankruptcy;
2. credit event upon merger;
3. cross acceleration;
4. cross default;
5. downgrade;
6. failure to pay;
7. repudiation/moratorium; and
8. restructuring.

Bankruptcy is defined as a variety of acts that are associated with bankruptcy or insolvency laws. *Failure to pay* results when a reference entity fails to make one or more required payments when due. When a reference entity breaches a covenant, it has defaulted on its obligation. When a default occurs, the obligation becomes due and payable prior to the original scheduled due date (had the reference entity not defaulted). This is referred to as an *obligation acceleration*. A reference entity may disaffirm or challenge the validity of its obligation. This is a credit event that is covered by *repudiation/moratorium*.

The most controversial credit event that may be included in dealing with credit derivatives is restructuring of an obligation. A *restructuring* occurs when the terms of the obligation are altered so as to make the new terms less attractive to the debt holder than the original terms.The terms that can be changed typically include, but are not limited to, one or more of the following:

- a reduction in the interest rate;
- a reduction in the principal;
- a rescheduling of the principal repayment schedule (e.g., lengthening the maturity of the obligations) or postponement of an interest payment; and
- a change in the level of seniority in the reference entity's debt structure.

The reason why restructuring is so controversial is that a protection buyer benefits from the inclusion of restructuring as a credit event and feels that eliminating restructuring as a credit event will erode its credit protection. The protection seller, in contrast, would prefer not to include restructuring since even routine modifications of obligations that occur in lending arrangements may trigger a payout to the protection buyer. Moreover, if the reference obligation is a loan and the protection buyer is the lender, there is a dual benefit for the protection buyer to restructure a loan. The first benefit is that the protection buyer receives a payment from the protection seller. Second, the accommodating restructuring fosters a relationship between the lender (who is the protection buyer) and its customer (the corporate entity that is the obligor of the reference obligation).

Because of this problem, the *Restructuring Supplement to the 1999 ISDA Credit Derivatives Definitions* (the "Supplement Definition") issued in April 2001 provided a modified definition for restructuring. There is a provision for the limitation on reference obligations in connection with restructuring of loans made by the protection buyer to the borrower that is the obligor of the reference obligation. In addition, the supplement limits the maturity of reference obligations that are physically deliverable when restructuring results in a payout triggered by the protection buyer.

In January 2003, the ISDA published its revised credit events definitions in the *2003 ISDA Credit Derivative Definitions* (referred to as the "2003 Definitions").The revised definitions reflected amendments to several of the definitions for credit events set forth in the 1999 Definitions. Specifically, there were amendments for bankruptcy, repudiation, and restructuring. The major change was to restructuring, whereby the ISDA allows parties to a given trade to select from among the following four definitions:

1. no restructuring,
2. "full" or "old" restructuring, which is based on the 1998 Definitions;
3. "modified restructuring," which is based on the Supplement Definition; and
4. "modified modified restructuring."

CREDIT DEFAULT SWAPS[2]

By far, credit default swaps are the largest sector of the credit derivatives market. A credit default swap has a single reference entity and is therefore referred to as a single-name credit default swap. In a credit default swap, the protection buyer pays a fee to the protection seller in exchange for the right to receive a payment conditioned upon the occurrence of a credit event by the reference entity. Should a credit event occur, the protection seller must make a payment and the contract terminates. If no credit event occurs by the maturity of the swap, both sides terminate the swap agreement and no further obligations are incurred. The tenor, or length of time of a credit default swap, is typically three to five years.

In a typical credit default swap, the protection buyer pays for the protection premium over several settlement dates rather than upfront. A standard credit default swap specifies quarterly payments. The quarterly payment is determined using one of the day-count conventions in the bond market. The day-count convention used for credit default swaps is actual/360, the same convention used in the U.S. dollar interest rate swap market. A day convention of actual/360 means that to determine the payment in a quarter, the actual number of days in the quarter are used and 360 days are assumed for the year. Consequently, the swap premium payment for a quarter is

$$
\begin{aligned}
&\text{Quarterly swap premium payment} \\
&= \text{Notional amount} \times \text{Swap rate (in decimal)} \\
&\quad \times \left(\frac{\text{Actual no. of days in quarter}}{360} \right)
\end{aligned}
$$

Credit default swaps can be settled in cash or physically. Physical delivery means that if a credit event as defined by the documentation

---

[2] For a further discussion of credit default swaps, see Chapter 3 in Mark J. P. Anson, Frank J. Fabozzi, Moorad Choudhry, and Ren-Raw Chen, *Credit Derivatives: Instruments, Applications, and Pricing* (Hoboken, NJ: John Wiley & Sons, 2003).

occurs, a bond issue of the reference entity is delivered by the protection buyer to the protection seller in exchange for a cash payment. Because physical delivery does not rely upon obtaining market prices for the reference obligation in determining the amount of the payment in a credit default swap, this method of delivery is more efficient in terms of determining the protection payout.

To illustrate the mechanics of a credit default swap, we assume that the reference entity is Corporation W and the underlying is $10 million par value of the bonds of Corporation W. The $10 million is the notional amount of the contract. The swap premium—the payment made by the protection buyer to the protection seller—is 250 bp per annum. Suppose that there are 91 actual days in a quarter. Then the quarterly swap premium payment made by the protection buyer would be

$$\$10,000,000 \times 0.025\left(\frac{91}{360}\right) = \$63,194.44$$

In the absence of a credit event, the protection buyer will make a quarterly swap premium payment over the life of the swap. If a credit event occurs, two things happen:

1. The protection buyer pays out the accrued premium from the last payment date to time of credit event, on a days fraction basis. After that payment, there are no further payments of the swap premium by the protection buyer to the protection seller.
2. A *termination value* is determined for the swap.

The procedure for computing the termination value depends on the settlement terms provided by the swap. Settlement will be either physical or cash. As noted above, the market practice for credit default swaps is physical settlement. With physical settlement the protection buyer delivers a specified amount of the face value of bonds of the reference entity to the protection seller. The protection seller pays the protection buyer the face value of the bonds.

Since all reference entities that are the subject of credit default swaps have many issues outstanding, there will be a number of alternative issues of the reference entity that the protection buyer can deliver to the protection seller. These issues are known as *deliverable obligations*. The swap documentation will set forth the characteristics necessary for an issue to qualify as a deliverable obligation. The short will select the cheapest-to-deliver issue and the choice granted to the short is effectively an embedded option. From the list of deliverable obligations, the protection buyer will select for delivery to the protection seller the cheapest-to-deliver issue.[3]

With *cash settlement*, the termination value is equal to the difference between the nominal amount of the reference obligation for which a credit event has occurred and its market value at the time of the credit event. The termination value is then the amount of the payment made by the protection seller to the protection buyer No bonds are delivered by the protection buyer to the protection seller. The documentation for the basket default swap, explained in the next section, sets forth how the market value at the time of the credit event is determined.

CREDIT DEFAULT SWAP INDEX

In a *credit default swap index*, the credit risk of a standardized basket of reference entities is transferred between the protection buyer and protection seller. As of year end 2005, the only standardized indexes are those compiled and managed by Dow Jones. For the corporate bond indexes, there are separate indexes for investment-grade and high-yield names. The most actively traded contract as of year end 2005 is the one based on the North American Investment Grade Index (denoted by DJ.CDX.NA.IG). As the name suggests, the reference entities in this index are those with an investment-grade rating. The index includes 125 corporate names in North America. The index is an equally weighted index. That is, each corporate name (i.e., reference entity) comprising the index has a weight of 0.8%. The index is updated semiannually by Dow Jones.

The mechanics of a credit default swap index are slightly different from those of a single-name credit default swap. As with a single-name credit default swap, a swap premium is paid. However, if a credit event occurs, the swap premium payment ceases in the case of a single-name credit default swap. In contrast, for a credit default swap index the swap payment continues to be made by the protection buyer. However, the amount of the quarterly swap premium payment is reduced. This is because the notional amount is reduced as result of a credit event for a reference entity.

For example, suppose that a portfolio manager is the protection buyer for a DJ.CDX.NA.IG and the notional amount is $100 million. Using the formula above for computing the quarterly swap premium payment, the payment before a credit event occurs would be

---

[3] While we did not cover Treasury bond and note futures contracts because they are not prevalent in structured financial transaction, the notion of a cheapest-to-deliver issue exists in that market because the short has the choice of which Treasury issue to deliver among the issues that the exchange specifies as acceptable for delivery.

$$\$100,000,000 \times \text{Swap rate (in decimal)}\left(\frac{\text{Actual no. of days in quarter}}{360}\right)$$

After a credit event occurs for one reference entity, the notional amount declines from $100 million to $99,200,000. The reduced notional amount is equal to 99.2% of the $100 million because each reference entity for the DJ.CDX.NA.IG is 0.8%. Thus, the revised quarterly swap premium payment until the maturity date or until another credit event occurs for one of the other 124 reference entities is

$$\$99,200,000 \times \text{Swap rate (in decimal)}\left(\frac{\text{Actual no. of days in quarter}}{360}\right)$$

As of this writing, the settlement term for a credit default swap index is physical settlement. However, the market is considering moving to cash settlement. The reason is because of the cost of delivering an odd lot in the case of a credit event for a reference entity. For example, in our hypothetical credit default swap index if there is a credit event, the protection buyer would have to deliver to the protection seller bonds of the reference entity with a face value of $80,000. Neither the protection buyer nor the protection seller would like to deal with such a small position.

BASKET DEFAULT SWAPS

As explained in Chapter 1, a collateralized debt obligation (CDO) is a structured portfolio credit. The major growth in this sector of the market is the synthetic CDO sector. This structure relies on the use of basket default swaps. Unlike a single-name CDS, in a *basket default swap*, there is more than one reference entity. There are different types of basket default swaps. They are classified as follows:

- Nth-to-default swaps;
- subordinate basket default swaps; and
- senior basket default swaps.

Nth-to-Default Swaps

In an *Nth-to-default swap*, the protection seller makes a payment to the protection buyer only after there has been a default for the Nth reference entity and no payment for default of the first $(N-1)$ reference entities. Once there is a payout for the Nth reference entity, the credit default swap terminates. That is, if the other reference entities that have not defaulted subsequently do default, the protection seller does not make any payout.

Let us begin with an illustration of a *first-to-default basket swap*. We will assume that there are five reference entities. The payout for a first-to-default basket swap is triggered after there is a default for only one of the reference entities. For any subsequent defaults for the four remaining reference entities, there is no payment made by the protection.

In a *second-to-default basket swap,* a payout is triggered only after there is a second default from among the reference entities. Again, assuming there are five reference entities, in a second-to-default swap, if there is only one reference entity that a defaults over the tenor of the swap, no payment is made by the protection seller. However, if there is a default for a second reference entity during the swap's tenor, there is a payout by the protection seller. After that payment, the swap terminates and the protection seller does not make any payment for a default that may occur for the three remaining reference entities.

Subordinate Basket Default Swaps

In a *subordinate basket default swap* the two key elements are:

1. a maximum payout for each defaulted reference entity; and
2. a maximum aggregate payout over the tenor of the swap for the basket of reference entities.

To illustrate a subordinate basket default swap, we will assume that there are five reference entities and that (1) the maximum payout is $10 million for a reference entity and (2) the maximum aggregate payout is $15 million. We will also assume that defaults result in the following losses over the tenor of the swap:

Loss Resulting from Default:	Amount
First reference entity	$6 million
Second reference entity	$10 million
Third reference entity	$16 million
Fourth reference entity	$12 million
Fifth reference entity	$15 million

The mechanics of a subordinate basket default swap are then as follows:

- Should there be a default for the first reference entity, there is a $6 million payout.
- The remaining amount that can be paid out on any subsequent defaults for the other four reference entities is $9 million.
- Should there be a default for the second reference entity of $10 million, only $9 million will be paid out.
- The swap terminates.

Senior Basket Default Swap

In a *senior basket default swap* there is a maximum payout for each reference entity, but the payout is not triggered until after a specified dollar loss threshold is reached. To illustrate this type of swap, we once again assume that there are five reference entities and the maximum payout for an individual reference entity is $10 million. We also assume that there is no payout until the first $40 million of default losses. This amount is the *threshold*.

Using the hypothetical losses listed above for the subordinate basket default swap, the payout by the protection seller would be as follows. The losses for the first three defaults total $32 million. However, because of the maximum payout for a reference entity, only $10 million of the $16 million loss on the third reference entity is applied to the $40 million threshold. Consequently, after the third default, $26 million ($6 million + $10 million + $10 million) is applied toward the threshold. When the fourth reference entity defaults, only $10 million is applied to the $40 million threshold. At this point, $36 million is applied to the $40 million threshold. When the fifth reference entity defaults in our illustration, only $10 million is relevant since the maximum payout for a reference entity is $10 million. The first $4 million of the $10 million is applied to cover the threshold, bringing the the total payment by the protection seller to $40 million.

Comparison of Riskiness of Different Default Swaps[4]

Let's compare the riskiness of each type of default swap from the perspective of the protection seller. This will also help reinforce an understanding of the different types of swaps.

We will assume that for the basket default swaps there are the same five reference entities. The following four credit default swaps are ranked from highest to lowest risk for the reasons explained:

---

[4] The illustration and discussion in this section draws from "*Nth* to Default Swaps and Notes: All About Default Correlation," *CDO Insight* (May 30, 2003) UBS Warburg.

1. *Subordinate basket default swap*: The maximum for each reference entity is $10 million with a maximum aggregate payout of $10 million.
2. *First-to-default swap*: The maximum payout is $10 million for the first reference entity to default.
3. *Fifth-to-default swap*: The maximum payout for the fifth reference entity to default is $10 million.
4. *Senior basket default swap*: There is a maximum payout for each reference entity of $10 million, but there is no payout until a threshold of $40 million is reached.

All but the senior basket default swap will definitely require the protection seller to make a payout by the time the fifth loss reference entity defaults (subject to the maximum payout on the loss for the individual reference entities). Consequently, the senior basket default swap exposes the protection seller to the least risk.

Now look at the relative risk of the other three default swaps with a $10 million maximum payout: subordinate basket default swap, first-to-default swap, and fifth-to-default swap. Consider first the subordinate basket default swap versus first-to-default swap. Suppose that the loss for the first reference entity to default is $8 million. In the first-to-default swap the payout required by the protection seller is $8 million and then the swap terminates (i.e., there are no further payouts that must be made by the protection seller). For the subordinate basket swap, after the payout of $8 million of the first reference entity to default, the swap does not terminate. Instead, the protection seller is still exposed to $2 million for any default loss resulting from the other four reference entities. Consequently, the subordinate basket default swap has greater risk than the first-to-default swap. Finally, the first-to-default has greater risk for the protection seller than the fifth-to-default swap because the protection seller must make a payout on the first reference entity to default.

ASSET SWAPS

An investor who seeks to earn a credit spread on a fixed-rate credit-risky bond but also wants to minimize interest rate risk by converting a fixed-rate exposure to a floating-rate exposure can do so by using an *asset swap*. In an asset swap, the investor enters into the following two transactions simultaneously: buys the fixed-rate, credit-risky bond and enters into an interest rate swap. We discussed interest rate swaps in Chapter 2.

While an asset swap is not a true credit derivative, it is closely associated with the credit derivatives market because it explicitly sets out the price of credit as a spread over an investor's funding cost, typically the London interbank offered rate (LIBOR). Although it allows the acquiring of credit risk while minimizing interest rate risk, it does not allow an investor to protect against or transfer credit risk. It is because of this shortcoming of an asset swap that other types of derivative instruments and structured products, particularly credit default swaps, were created.

Investor Structured Asset Swap

An investor creates this structure by entering into the following terms in an interest rate swap:

- The investor will agree to be the fixed-rate payer.
- The term of the swap selected by the investor will match the maturity of the credit-risky bond purchased.
- The timing of the swap payments will match the timing of the cash flow of the credit-risky bond purchased.

If the issuer defaults on the issue, the investor must continue to make payments to the dealer and is therefore still exposed to interest rate risk.

Let us now illustrate a basic asset swap. Suppose that an investor purchases $20 million par value of a 6.85%, 5-year bond for a single A rated telecom company at par value. The coupon payments are semiannual. At the same time, the investor enters into a 5-year interest rate swap with a dealer where the investor is the fixed-rate payer and the payments are made semiannually. Suppose that the swap rate is 6.00% and the investor receives 6-month LIBOR plus 45 bp.

Let's look at the cash flow for the investor every six months for the next five years:

Receive from telecom bonds:	6.85%
− Payment to dealer on swap:	6.00%
+ Payment from dealer on swap:	6-month LIBOR
Net received by investor:	0.85% + 6-month LIBOR

Thus, regardless of how interest rates change, if the telecom issuer does not default on the issue, the investor earns a 85 bp over 6-month LIBOR. Effectively, the investor has converted a fixed-rate, single-A, 5-year bond into a 5-year floating-rate bond with a spread over 6-month LIBOR. Thus, the investor has created a synthetic floating-rate bond.

This transaction has some similarities to an unfunded total return swap (TRS), although the dealer is not paying the total return of the bond. Rather it pays a floating LIBOR-based rate. Hence this deal lies between a pure asset swap and a TRS. As a matter of terminology, we should note that in a pure asset swap, the investor in a fixed-rate bond would pay the exact coupon on that bond to a counterparty in return for a floating-rate payment such as LIBOR, flat or plus or minus a spread. If the fixed-rate payment is different from the bond coupon, then in correct technical terms the investor simply owns a fixed-rate bond and enters into an interest rate swap, although the economics of the transaction are similar to those of a pure asset swap.

While our illustration has demonstrated how an asset swap can convert a fixed-rate bond into a synthetic floating-rate bond, an asset swap can also be used to convert a floating-rate bond into a synthetic fixed-rate bond.

Asset Swap Structure (Package) Created by a Dealer

In our description of an asset swap, the investor bought the credit-risky bond and entered into an interest rate swap with a dealer. Typically, an asset swap combines the sale of a credit-risky asset owned by an investor to a counterparty, at par and with no interest accrued, with an interest rate swap. This type of asset swap structure or package is referred to as a *par asset swap*. If there is a default by the issuer on the credit-risky bond, the asset swap transaction is terminated and the defaulted bonds are returned to the investor plus or minus any mark-to-market on the asset swap transaction. Hence, the investor is still exposed to the bond issuer's credit risk.

The coupon on the bond in the par asset swap is paid in return for LIBOR, plus a spread if necessary. This spread is the *asset swap spread* and is the price of the asset swap. In effect the asset swap allows investors that are LIBOR funded to receive the asset swap spread. This spread is a function of the credit risk of the underlying credit-risky bond. The asset swap spread may be viewed as equivalent to the price payable on a credit default swap written on that asset.

To illustrate this asset swap structure, suppose that in our previous illustration the swap rate prevailing in the market is 6.30% rather than 6.00%. The investor owns the telecom bonds and sells them to a dealer at par with no accrued interest. The asset swap agreement between the dealer and the investor is as follows:

- The term is five years.
- The investor agrees to pay the dealer 6.30% semiannually.
- The dealer agrees to pay the investor every six months 6-month LIBOR plus an asset-swap spread of 30 bp.
- Having sold the telecom bonds to the dealer, the investor no longer receives interest on them.

In our first illustration of an asset swap given earlier, the investor is creating a synthetic floater without a dealer. The investor owns the bonds. The only involvement of the dealer is as a counterparty to the interest rate swap. In the second structure, the dealer is the counterparty to the asset swap structure and the dealer owns the underlying credit-risky bonds. If there is a default, the dealer returns the bonds to the investor. This transaction in effect amounts to an unfunded total return swap (TRS). Normally, in an unfunded TRS, the bond is moved off the balance sheet to the dealer, and the dealer pays the floating rate (in this case, six-month LIBOR + 30 bp) and receives the prevailing swap rate (in this case 6.30% fixed), but the investor still receives the bond coupon. In a true-sale asset swap, however, the investor does not receive the coupon.

Using Swaptions to Remove Unwanted Structural Features

There are variations of the basic asset swap structure to remove unwanted noncredit structural features of the underlying credit-risky bond. The simplest example of an asset swap variation to remove an unwanted noncredit structural feature is when the bond is callable. If the bond is callable, then the future cash flows of the bond are uncertain because the issue can be called. Moreover, the issue is likely to be called if interest rates decline below the bond's coupon rate.

This problem can be addressed in a transaction where the investor buys the bond and enters into an interest rate swap. The tenor of the interest rate swap would still be for the term of the bond. However, the investor would also enter into a swaption in which the investor has the right to effectively terminate the swap from the time of the first call date for the bond to the maturity date of the bond. In the swaption, since the investor is paying fixed and receiving floating, the swaption must be one in which the investor receives fixed and pays floating. Specifically, the investor will enter into a receive fixed swaption.

In an asset swap that is structured with a dealer, this is simpler to do. The transaction can be structured such that the asset swap is terminated if the bonds are called.

TOTAL RETURN SWAPS

A *total return swap* is a swap in which one party makes periodic floating-rate payments to a counterparty in exchange for the total return realized on a reference asset (or underlying asset). The reference asset could be one of the following:

■ credit-risky bond;
■ a loan;
■ a reference portfolio consisting of bonds or loans;
■ an index representing a sector of the bond market; or
■ an equity index.

Our focus in this section is on total return swaps where the reference asset is one of the first four types listed above. We first explain how a total return swap can be used when the reference asset is a credit-risky bond and a loan. While these types of total return swaps are more aptly referred to as total return *credit* swaps, we will simply refer to them as total return swaps. When the bond index consists of a credit risk sector of the bond market, the total return swap is referred to as a *total return bond index swap* or in this chapter as simply a *total return index swap*. We will explain how a total return index swap offers asset managers and hedge fund managers increased flexibility in managing a bond portfolio. In the appendix to this chapter we explain the pricing of total return swaps.

ECONOMICS OF A TOTAL RETURN SWAP

The total return on a reference asset includes all cash flows as well as the capital appreciation or depreciation of that reference asset. The floating rate is a reference interest rate (typically LIBOR) plus or minus a spread. The party that agrees to make the floating rate payments and receive the total return is referred to as the *total return receiver* or the *swap buyer*; the party that agrees to receive the floating rate payments and pay the total return is referred to as the *total return payer* or *swap seller*. Total return swaps are viewed as unfunded credit derivatives, because there is no up-front payment required.

If the total return payer owns the underlying asset, it has transferred its economic exposure to the total return receiver. Effectively then, the total return payer has a neutral position that typically will earn LIBOR plus a spread. However, the total return payer has only transferred the economic exposure to the total return receiver; it has not transferred the actual asset. The total return payer must continue to fund the underlying asset at its marginal cost of borrowing or at the opportunity cost of investing elsewhere the capital tied up by the reference assets.

The total return payer may not initially own the reference asset before the swap is transacted. Instead, after the swap is negotiated, the total return payer will purchase the reference asset to hedge its obligations to pay the total return to the total return receiver. In order to purchase the reference asset, the total return payer must borrow capital. This borrowing cost is factored into the floating rate that the total return receiver must pay to the swap seller. Exhibit 3.1 diagrams how a total return credit swap works.

In the exhibit the dealer raises cash from the capital markets at a funding cost of straight LIBOR. The cash that flows into the dealer from the capital markets flows right out again to purchase the reference asset. The asset provides both interest income and capital gain or loss depending on its price fluctuation. This total return is passed through in its entirety to the investor according to the terms of the total return swap. The investor, in turn, pays the dealer LIBOR plus a spread to fulfill its obligations under the swap.

From the dealer's perspective, all of the cash flows in Exhibit 3.1 net out to the spread over LIBOR that the dealer receives from the investor. Therefore, the dealer's profit is the spread times the notional amount of the total return swap. Furthermore, the dealer is perfectly hedged. It has no risk position except for the counterparty risk of the investor. Effectively, the dealer receives a spread on a riskless position.

In fact, if the dealer already owns the reference asset on its balance sheet, the total return swap may be viewed as a form of credit protection that offers more risk reduction than a credit default swap. A credit default swap has only one purpose: to protect the investor against default risk. If the issuer of the reference asset defaults, the credit default swap provides a payment. However, if the underlying asset declines in value but no default occurs, the credit protection buyer receives no payment. In contrast, under a total return swap, the reference asset owned by the dealer is protected from declines in value. In effect, the investor acts as a "first loss" position for the dealer because any decline in value of the reference asset must be reimbursed by the investor.

The investor, on the other hand, receives the total return on a desired asset in a convenient format. There are several other benefits in

EXHIBIT 3.1   Total Return Swaps

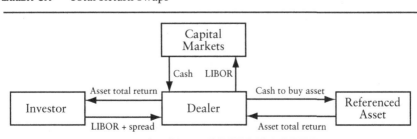

using a total return swap as opposed to purchasing a reference asset itself. First, the total return receiver does not have to finance the purchase of the reference asset itself. Instead, the total return receiver pays a fee to the total return payer in return for receiving the total return on the reference asset. Second, the investor can take advantage of the dealer's "best execution" in acquiring the reference asset. Third, the total return receiver can achieve the same economic exposure to a diversified basket of assets in one swap transaction that would otherwise take several cash market transactions to achieve. In this way a total return swap is much more efficient means for transacting than the cash market is. Finally, an investor who wants to short a credit-risky asset such as a corporate bond will find it difficult to do so in the market. An investor can do so efficiently by using a total return swap. In this case the investor will use a total return swap in which it is a total return payer.

There is a drawback of a total return swap if an asset manager employs it to obtain credit protection. In a total return swap, the total return receiver is exposed to both credit risk and interest rate risk. For example, the credit spread can decline (resulting in a favorable price movement for the reference asset), but this gain can be offset by a decline in the price of the reference asset resulting from a rise in the level of interest rates.

Total Return Swap Compared to an Interest Rate Swap

It is worthwhile comparing market conventions for a total return swap to those of an interest rate swap. A plain vanilla or generic interest rate swap involves the exchange of a fixed-rate payment for a floating-rate payment. A *basis swap* is a special type of interest rate swap in which both parties exchange floating-rate payments based on different reference interest rates. For example, one party's payments may be based on 3-month LIBOR, while the other party's payments are based on the 6-month Treasury rate. In a total return swap, both parties pay a floating rate.

The quotation conventions for a generic interest rate swap and a total return swap differ. In a generic interest rate swap, the fixed-rate payer pays a spread to a Treasury security with the same tenor as the swap (i.e., the swap spread) and the fixed-rate receiver pays the reference rate flat (i.e., no spread or margin). The payment by the fixed-rate receiver (i.e., floating-rate payer) is referred to as the *funding leg*. For example, suppose an interest rate swap quote for the swap spread of a 5-year, 3-month, LIBOR-based swap is 50 bp. This means that the fixed-rate payer agrees to pay the 5-year Treasury rate that exists at the inception of the swap plus 50 bp and the fixed-rate receiver agrees to pay 3-month LIBOR. In contrast, the quote convention for a total return swap is that the total return receiver receives the total return flat and pays the total return payer an interest rate based on a reference rate (typically LIBOR) plus or minus a spread. That is, the funding leg (i.e., what the total return receiver pays) includes a spread.

Illustration

Let's illustrate a total return swap where the reference asset is a corporate bond. Consider an asset manager who believes that the fortunes of XYZ Corporation will improve over the next year so that the company's credit spread relative to U.S. Treasury securities will decline. The company has issued a 10-year bond at par with a coupon rate of 9% and therefore the yield is 9%. Suppose at the time of issuance, the 10-year Treasury yield is 6.2%. This means that the credit spread is 280 bp and the asset manager believes it will decrease over the year to less than 280 bp.

The asset manager can express this view by entering into a total return swap that matures in one year as a total return receiver with the reference asset being the 10-year, 9% XYZ Corporation bond issue. For simplicity, assume that the total return swap calls for an exchange of payments semiannually. Suppose the terms of the swap are that the total return receiver pays the 6-month Treasury rate plus 160 bp in order to receive the total return on the reference asset. The notional amount for the contract is $10 million.

Suppose that over the course of the swap's 1-year term the following occurs:

- The 6-month Treasury rate for computing the first semiannual payment is 4.8%.
- The 6-month Treasury rate for computing the second semiannual payment is 5.4%.
- At the end of one year the 9-year Treasury rate is 7.6%.
- At the end of one year the credit spread for the reference asset is 180 bp.

First let's look at the payments that must be made by the asset manager. The first swap payment made by the asset manager is 3.2% (4.8% plus 160 bp divided by two) multiplied by the $10 million notional amount. The second swap payment made is 3.5% (5.4% plus 160 bp divided by two) multiplied by the $10 million notional amount. Thus,

First swap payment paid: $10 million × 3.2% = $320,000
Second swap payment paid: $10 million × 3.5% = $350,000
Total payments: $670,000

The payments that will be received by the asset manager are the two coupon payments plus the change in the value of the reference asset. There will be two coupon payments. Since the coupon rate is 9% the amount received for the coupon payments is $900,000.

Finally, the change in the value of the reference asset must be determined. At the end of one year, the reference asset has a maturity of nine years. Since the 9-year Treasury rate is assumed to be 7.6% and the credit spread is assumed to decline from 280 bp to 180 bp, the reference asset will sell to yield 9.4%. The price of a 9%, 9-year bond selling to yield 9.4% is 97.61. Since the par value is $10 million, the price is $9,761,000. The capital loss is therefore $239,000. The payment to the total return receiver is then:

Coupon payment = $900,000
Capital loss = $239,000
Swap payment = $661,000

Netting the swap payment made and the swap payment received, the asset manager must make a payment of $9,000 ($661,000 – $670,000).

Notice that even though the asset manager's expectations were realized (i.e., a decline in the credit spread), the asset manager had to make a net outlay. This illustration highlights one of the disadvantages of a total return swap noted earlier: The return to the investor is dependent on both credit risk (declining or increasing credit spreads) and market risk (declining or increasing market rates). Two types of market interest rate risk can affect the price of a fixed-income asset. *Credit independent market risk* is the risk that the general level of interest rates will change over the term of the swap. This type of risk has nothing to do with the credit deterioration of the reference asset. *Credit dependent market interest rate risk* is the risk that the discount rate applied to the value of an asset will change based on either perceived or actual default risk.

In the illustration, the reference asset was adversely affected by market interest rate risk, but positively rewarded for accepting credit dependent market interest rate risk. To remedy this problem, a total return receiver can customize the total return swap transaction. For example, the asset manager could negotiate to receive the coupon income on the reference asset plus any change in value due to changes in the credit spread. Now the asset manager has expressed a view exclusively on credit risk; credit independent market risk does not affect the swap value. In this case, in addition to the coupon income, the asset manager would receive the difference between the present value of the reference asset at a current spread of 280 bp and the present value of the reference asset at a credit spread of 180 bp.

Total Return Index Swaps

Thus far our focus has been on a single reference asset. Total return index swaps are swaps where the reference asset is the return on a market index. The market index can be an equity index or a bond index. Our focus will be on bond indexes.

Broad-based bond market indexes such as the Lehman, Salomon Smith Barney, and Merrill Lynch indexes have subindexes that represent major sectors of the bond market. For example, there is the Treasury and agency sector, the credit sector (i.e., investment-grade corporate bonds, at one time referred to as the corporate sector), the mortgage sector (consisting of agency residential mortgage-backed securities), the commercial mortgage-backed securities (CMBS) sector, and the asset-backed securities (ABS) sector. The non-Treasury sectors offer a spread to Treasuries and are hence referred to as "spread sectors." The spread in the mortgage sector is primarily compensation for the prepayment risk associated with investing in this sector. Spread to compensate for credit risk is offered in the credit spread sector, of course, and the CMBS and ABS sectors. There are also indexes available for other credit spread sectors of the bond market such as the high-yield corporate bond sector and the emerging market bond sector. Thus, a total return index swap in which the underlying index is a credit spread sector allows an asset manager to gain or reduce exposure to that sector.

CHAPTER 4

Basic Principles of Securitization

Securitization is a well-established practice in the global debt capital markets. It refers to the sale of assets, which generate cash flows, from the entity that owns them to another entity that has been specifically set up for the purpose, and the issuing of notes by this second entity. These notes, backed by the cash flows from the original assets sold to the second entity, are referred to as *asset-backed securities*. The technique was introduced initially as a means of funding for U.S. depository institutions starting in 1969 and is the major reason for the development of the strong U.S. housing finance market. Subsequently, the technique was applied to other assets such as credit card payments and auto loan receivables. It has also been employed as part of asset/liability management in order to manage balance sheet risk for financial institutions.

Securitization allows institutions such as banks, other financial entities such as insurance companies and finance companies, and nonfinancial corporations to convert assets that are not readily marketable—such as residential mortgages, car loans, or lease receivables—into rated securities that are tradeable in the secondary market. The investors that buy these securities gain an exposure to these types of original assets that they would not otherwise have access to.

In this chapter, we discuss the motivation for securitization from the issuer's perspective, the basic mechanics of a securitization, and a description of the collateral. In the next chapter our focus is on securitization structures. Our primary focus in this and the next chapter will be on what is referred to as *cash securitizations*. In Appendix B, however, we discuss a relatively new type of securitization, *synthetic securitizations*.

While our focus in this chapter and the next is on securitizations used by corporations, it should be noted that some municipal governments use this form of financing rather than issuing municipal bonds and several European central governments use this form for financing. The securitization technology that we describe in this chapter and the next has been applied to create *collateralized debt obligations*, which we cover in Chapters 6 and 7.

WHAT IS A SECURITIZED TRANSACTION?

The key element of securitization is that the obligation of the issuer to repay lenders is backed by the value of a financial asset or credit support provided by a third party to the transaction. When we say the value of a "financial asset," we mean a loan, an account receivable or a note receivable. Keep in mind that a loan or a receivable is a financial asset to the lender but a liability to the borrower. So, in a securitization, the lender is using a pool of loans or receivables it owns as collateral for debt instruments that it issues. The financial assets included in the collateral for a securitization are referred to as *securitized assets*. To obtain a desired credit rating sought by a corporation for the asset-backed securities created in a securitization, both the value of the financial assets and third-party credit support may be needed.

A corporation issues a secured debt instrument whose credit standing is supported by a lien on specific assets (i.e., a mortgage bond or collateral trust bond) or by a third-party guarantee. However, with traditional secured bonds, it is the ability of the issuer to generate sufficient earnings to repay the debt obligation that is necessary for the issuer to repay the debt. So, if a manufacturer of farm equipment issues a mortgage bond in which the bondholders have a first mortgage lien on one of its plants, those bondholders still rely primarily on the ability of the manufacturer to generate cash flow from all of its operations is required to pay off the bonds.

In a securitization, the source of repayment shifts from the cash flow of the issuer to the cash flow of the pool of financial assets and/or a third party that guarantees the payments if the pool of financial assets does not generate sufficient cash flow. If the manufacturer of farm equipment has receivables from installment sales contracts to customers (i.e., a financial asset for the farm equipment company) and uses these receivables as collateral in a securitization as described in this chapter, payment to the buyers of the bonds backed by these receivables depends only on the ability to collect the receivables. That is, it does not depend on the ability of the corporation to generate cash flow from operations.

The financial assets included in the collateral for an asset securitization are referred to as *securitized assets*.

The issuers of asset-backed securities include:

- captive finance companies of manufacturing firms that provide financing only for their parent company's products;
- financing subsidiaries of major industrial corporations;
- independent finance companies; and
- domestic and foreign commercial banks.

An example of the first type of issuer is the captive finance companies of automobile manufacturers. For example, Ford Motor Credit Co. is a captive finance company of Ford Motor Company. It provides financing for individuals who want to purchase a motor vehicle or commercial financing for companies that want to purchase a fleet of motor vehicles manufactured by Ford Motor Company.

Financing subsidiaries of major industrial corporations provide financing for not only their parent company's products but products of other vendors. Three examples are General Electric Capital Corporation (known as GE Capital), IBM Global Financing, and Caterpillar Financial Services Corporation (known as Cat Financial). GE Capital, a wholly-owned subsidiary of General Electric, is a diversified financial servicing company. IBM Global Financing is a wholly-owned subsidiary of IBM that provides financing for both IBM and non-IBM equipment. Cat Financial, the financial arm of Caterpillar Inc. (the world's largest manufacturer of construction and mining equipment, natural gas and diesel engines, and industrial gas turbines), offers a wide range of financing alternatives for Caterpillar equipment, Solar gas turbines, products equipped with Caterpillar components, fork lift trucks manufactured by Mitsubishi Caterpillar Forklift of America, Inc., and related products sold through Caterpillar dealers.

ILLUSTRATION OF A SECURITIZATION

Let's use an illustration to describe a securitization. In our illustrations throughout this chapter, we use a hypothetical firm, Farm Equip Corporation. This company is assumed to manufacturer farm equipment. Some of its sales are for cash, but the bulk of its sales are from installment sales contracts. Effectively, an installment sale contract is a loan to the buyer of the farm equipment who agrees to repay Farm Equip Corporation over a specified period of time. For simplicity we assume that the loans are typically for four years. The collateral for the loan is the farm equipment purchased by the borrower. The loan specifies an interest rate that the buyer pays.

The credit department of Farm Equip Corporation makes the decision as to whether or not to extend credit to a customer. That is, the credit department receives a credit application from a customer and, based on criteria established by the firm, decide on whether to extend a loan and the amount. The criteria for extending credit or a loan are referred to as *underwriting standards*. Because Farm Equip Corporation is extending the loan, it is referred to as the *originator* of the loan.

Moreover, Farm Equip Corporation may have a department that is responsible for servicing the loan. *Servicing* involves collecting payments from borrowers, notifying borrowers who may be delinquent, and, when necessary, recovering and disposing of the collateral (i.e., farm equipment in our illustration) if the borrower does not make loan repayments by a specified time. While the servicer of the loans need not be the originator of the loans, in our illustration we assume that Farm Equip Corporation is the servicer.

Now let's see how these loans can be used in a structured finance transaction. We assume that Farm Equip Corporation has more than $200 million of installment sales contracts. This amount is shown on the corporation's balance sheet as an asset. We further assume that Farm Equip Corporation wants to raise $200 million. Rather than issuing corporate bonds for $200 million (for the reasons explained in the next section), the treasurer of the corporation decides to raise the funds via a structured financing.

To do so, the Farm Equip Corporation sets up a legal entity referred to as a special purpose vehicle (SPV). At this point, we will not explain the purpose of this legal entity, but it will be made clearer later that the SPV is critical in a structured finance transaction. In our illustration, the SPV that is set up is called FE Asset Trust (FEAT). Farm Equip Corporation will then sell to FEAT $200 million of the loans. Farm Equip Corporation will receive from FEAT $200 million in cash, the amount it wanted to raise. But where does FEAT get $200 million? It obtains those funds by selling securities that are backed by the $200 million of loans. The securities are the asset-backed securities we discussed earlier. These asset-backed securities issued in a structured finance transaction are also referred to as bond classes or *tranches*.

The structure is diagrammed in Exhibit 4.1.

A simple transaction can involve the sale of just one bond class with a par value of $200 million. We will call this Bond Class A. Suppose that 200,000 certificates are issued for Bond Class A with a par value of $1,000 per certificate. Then, each certificate holder would be entitled to 1/200,000 of the payment from the collateral. Each payment made by the borrowers (i.e., the buyers of the farm equipment) consists of principal repayment and interest.

EXHIBIT 4.1 Basic Securitization Structure

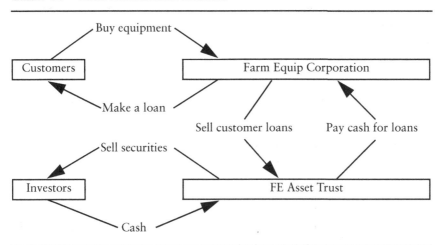

A structure can be more complicated. There can be rules for distribution of principal and interest other than on a pro rata basis to different bond classes. It may be difficult at this introductory stage to understand why such a structure should be created. What is important to understand is that there are institutional investors who have needs for bonds with different maturity, risk, and price-volatility characteristics. A securitization can be designed to create bond classes with investment characteristics that satisfy the needs of different institutional investors.

An example of a more complicated transaction is one in which two bond classes are created, Bond Class A1 and Bond Class A2. The par value for Bond Class A1 is $90 million and for Bond Class A2 is $110 million. The priority rule can simply specify that Bond Class A1 receives all the principal that is paid by the borrowers (i.e., the buyers of the farm equipment) until all of Bond Class A1 has paid off its $90 million and then Bond Class A2 begins to receive principal. Bond Class A1 is then a shorter term bond than Bond Class A2.

As will be explained later, there are structures where there is more than one bond class but the two bond classes differ as to how they will share any losses resulting from defaults of the borrowers. In such a structure, the bond classes are classified as *senior bond classes* and *subordinate bond classes*. This structure is called a *senor-subordinate structure*. Losses are realized by the subordinate bond classes before there are any losses realized by the senior bond classes. For example, suppose that FEAT issued $180 million par value of Bond Class A, the senior bond class, and $20 million par value of Bond Class B, the subordinate bond class. As

EXHIBIT 4.2 The Securitization Process

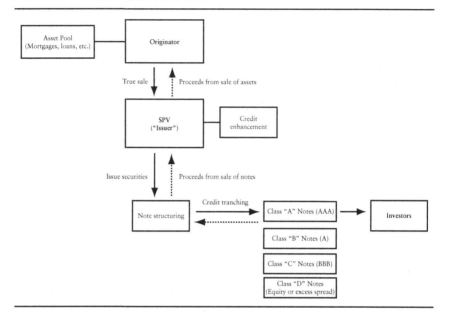

long as there are no defaults by the borrower greater than $20 million, then Bond Class A will be fully repaid its $180 million.

The general securitization process is depicted in Exhibit 4.2. In this case, there are four classes of notes, the first three having credit ratings that range from AAA to BBB. These classes are also known as *tranches* and the process of creating such a structure is sometimes called *tranching*.

REASONS WHY ENTITIES SECURITIZE ASSETS

The principal reasons why a nonbank corporation may elect to issue an asset-backed security rather than a corporate bond are (1) to potentially reduce funding costs, (2) to diversify funding sources, and (3) to accelerate earnings for financial reporting purposes. For banks, there are additional reasons. We first discuss the reasons for nonbank corporations and then describe the reasons for banks.

The Potential for Reducing Funding Costs

To understand the potential for reducing funding costs by issuing an asset-backed security rather than a corporate bond, suppose that Farm Equip Corporation has a triple-B credit rating. If it wants to raise funds equal to $200 million and it issues a corporate bond, its funding cost would be whatever the benchmark Treasury yield is plus a yield spread for triple-B issuers. Suppose, instead, that Farm Equip Corporation uses $200 million of its installment sales contracts (i.e., the loans it has made to customers) as collateral for a bond issue. What is its funding cost? It probably is the same as if it issued a corporate bond. The reason is that if Farm Equip Corporation defaults on any of its outstanding debt, the creditors will go after all of its assets, including the loans to its customers.

However, suppose that Farm Equip Corporation can create another legal entity and sell the loans to that entity. That entity is the special purpose vehicle that we described earlier in our hypothetical securitization transaction. In our illustration, it is Farm Equipment Asset Trust (FEAT). If the sale of the loans by Farm Equip Corporation to FEAT is done properly—that is, the sale is at the fair market value of the loans—FEAT, not Farm Equip Corporation, then *legally* owns the receivables. This means that if Farm Equip Corporation is forced into bankruptcy, its creditors *cannot* try to recover the loans (sold to FEAT) because they are legally owned by FEAT. What is the implication of structuring a transaction in this way?

When FEAT sells bonds backed by the loans, those interested in buying the bonds will evaluate the credit risk associated with collecting the payments due on the loans independent of the credit rating of Farm Equip Corporation. What credit rating will be received for the bonds issued by FEAT? Whatever FEAT wants the credit rating to be! It may seem strange that the issuer (the SPV, FEAT) can get any credit rating it wants, but that is the case. The reason is that FEAT will show the characteristics of the collateral for the asset-backed securities (i.e., the loans to Farm Equip's customers) to a rating agency. In turn, the rating agency will evaluate the credit quality of the collateral and inform the issuer what must be done to obtain a desired credit rating.

More specifically, the issuer may be asked to "credit enhance" the structure. There are various forms of credit enhancement that we review later. Basically, the rating agencies looks at the potential losses from the collateral and make a determination of how much credit enhancement is needed for the bond classes issued to achieve the ratings targeted by the issuer. The higher the credit rating sought by the issuer, the more credit enhancement a rating agency will require. Thus, Farm Equip Corporation, which is triple-B rated, can obtain funding using its loans to its customers as collateral to obtain a better credit rating for the bonds issued (i.e., asset-backed securities) than its own credit rating. In fact, with enough credit enhancement, it can issue a bond of the highest credit rating, triple A.

The key to a corporation issuing bonds with a higher credit rating than the corporation's own credit rating is the SPV. Its role is critical because it is the SPV (FEAT in our illustration) that separates the assets used as collateral from the corporation that is seeking financing (Farm Equip Corporation in our illustration).

Why doesn't a corporation always seek the highest credit rating (triple A) for the bonds backed by the collateral in a securitization transaction? The answer is that credit enhancement does not come without a cost. As described later, there are various credit enhancement mechanisms, all of which increase the costs associated with securitized borrowing via an asset-backed security. So, when it is seeking a higher rating, the corporation must assess the tradeoff between the additional cost of credit enhancing the bonds versus the reduction in funding cost by issuing a bond with a higher credit rating.

It is important to realize that if a bankruptcy of the corporation seeking funds occurs (Farm Equip Corporation in our example), a bankruptcy judge may decide that the assets of the SPV are among the assets available to the creditors of the bankrupt corporation. This is an unresolved legal issue in the United States. Legal experts have argued that this is unlikely. In the prospectus of an asset-backed security, there will be a legal opinion addressing this issue. This is the reason why special purpose vehicles in the United States are referred to as "bankruptcy remote" entities.

Diversifying Funding Sources

An issuer seeking to raise funds via a securitization must establish itself as an issuer in the asset-backed securities market. Among other things, this requires selling enough securities to get the issuer's name established and to create a reasonably liquid after-market for trading those securities. Once an issuer establishes itself in the market, it can look at both the corporate bond market and the asset-backed securities market to determine the better funding source. That is, it will compare the all-in-cost of funds in the corporate bond market and the asset-backed securities market and select the one with the lower cost.

Accelerating Earnings for Financial Reporting Purposes

Generally accepted accounting principles (GAAP) permit a corporation to use a portfolio of its receivables or assets to accelerate earnings for shareholder reporting purposes. This reason is best described by means of an illustration.

Consider again Farm Equip Corporation, the manufacturer of farm equipment. Suppose that this firm has $200 million in installment sales contracts. For financial reporting purposes, the installment sales contracts are not realized as revenue until the installment payments are received. Suppose that the agreement with the buyer of the farm equipment requires that the buyer pay 8% interest per annum. Suppose further that the treasurer of Farm Equip Corporation approaches the firm's investment banker and is told that it can sell an asset-backed security backed by the installment sales contracts at a cost of 5%. This means that Farm Equip Corporation is receiving from the installment sales contracts 8% and would pay investors in the asset-backed securities 5%. The difference between what Farm Equip Corporation is receiving and paying is 3% or 300 bp. Part of that difference represents a cost to Farm Equip Corporation for "servicing" the installment sales contracts. For now, assume that the servicing fee is 1%.

After reducing the 300 bp margin by the 100 bp servicing fee, there are 200 bp remaining. This is referred to as the *net interest spread*. This is a profit to Farm Equip Corporation that will be realized by the sale of the asset-backed securities and it can be booked as income immediately. The income is effectively in the form of an asset referred to as *interest-only strip*. How much of that income will be realized by Farm Equip Corporation for financial reporting purposes? Or equivalently, what is the value of the interest-only strip? We can apply the basic principle of valuation to determine it. This is done as follows. First, Farm Equip Corporation's treasurer must determine the dollar amount of the 200 bp for each year over the expected life of the asset-backed security. Then the present value of this dollar amount for each period is computed.

For example, suppose that the $200 million in installment sales contracts call for principal repayment of $50 million per year for the next four years. Then assuming that none of the borrowers default on their contractual obligation or pay off their loans earlier than the scheduled principal repayment date (referred to as a "prepayment"), this means that each year the dollar net interest based on the net interest spread of 200 bp is as follows:

Beginning of Year	Balance Outstanding	Dollar Net Interest
1	$200,000,000	$4,000,000
2	150,000,000	3,000,000
3	100,000,000	2,000,000
4	50,000,000	1,000,000

The next step is to compute the present value of the dollar net interest. The question is: What is the appropriate discount rate? The discount rate should reflect the uncertainty of realizing the projected dollar net interest over the next four years. Let's suppose that a fair market rate is 12%. Then the present value of the dollar net interest discounted at 12% is $8,022,088.78 as shown below:[1]

Beginning of Year	Balance Outstanding	Dollar Net Interest	PV Factor at 12%	Present Value ($)
1	$200,000,000	$4,000,000	0.89286	$3,571,428.57
2	150,000,000	3,000,000	0.79719	2,391,581.63
3	100,000,000	2,000,000	0.71178	1,423,560.50
4	50,000,000	1,000,000	0.63552	635,518.08
	Value of interest-only strip			$8,022,088.78

The $8,022,088.78 value of the interest-only strip would be reported as income in the year that the asset-backed securities are issued.

The key in the valuation of the interest-only strip is determining the dollar net interest spread each year and the appropriate interest rate at which to discount the dollar amount for each year. Consider first the dollar net interest each year. In the analysis above, it is assumed that the $200 million in installment sales contracts will be paid—that is, no defaults are assumed. Suppose instead that, due to defaults, the treasurer projects that the balances outstanding after defaults are as follows:

Beginning of Year	Balance Outstanding	Dollar Net Interest
1	$199,000,000	$3,980,000
2	147,000,000	2,940,000
3	95,000,000	1,900,000
4	42,000,000	840,000

Then the dollar net interest and the present value at 12% each year are shown below, along with the value of the interest-only strip:

Beginning of Year	Balance Outstanding	Dollar Net Interest	PV Factor at 12%	Present Value ($)
1	$199,000,000	$3,980,000	0.89286	$3,553,571.43
2	147,000,000	2,940,000	0.79719	2,343,750.00
3	95,000,000	1,900,000	0.71178	1,352,382.47
4	42,000,000	840,000	0.63552	533,835.19
	Value of interest-only strip			$7,783,539.09

---

[1] Notice that calculations have been simplified by assuming that all of the dollar net interest spread is received at the end of the year.

Thus, based on this, the reported income due to the securitization would be $7,783,539.09 (the value of the interest-only strip) versus $8,022,088.78, in the case where no defaults are assumed. If a more appropriate discount rate is higher than 12%, then the value of the interest-only strip is reduced. For example, at a 15% rate, the value of the interest-only strip is $7,633,477.58, assuming no defaults and $7,413,485.51, assuming the defaults in the table above.

If there are prepayments, the value of the interest-only strip is reduced. This is because when a borrower repays a loan, the loan balance is reduced. The issuer receives the dollar net interest only on the outstanding loan balance. For example, suppose that there are no defaults but that the borrowers prepay their loans such that the balance outstanding each year is as follows:

Beginning of Year	Balance Outstanding	Dollar Net Interest
1	$200,000,000	$4,000,000
2	70,000,000	1,400,000
3	20,000,000	400,000
4	10,000,000	200,000

It can be shown that the present value of the interest-only strip in this case is $5,099,315.71. When discounted at a 12% rate, the value is even less than the case above, where there are defaults.

It is not a simple task to determine the defaults and therefore the dollar net interest and the appropriate interest rate for discounting. Consequently, the firm's independent auditors must assess the assumptions made by management in determining income resulting from a securitization. There are shareholder suits against management and its independent auditors in cases where shareholders have challenged income generated from a securitization for a firm that has faced financial difficulties. The issue is whether reasonable assumptions were made regarding defaults and whether the appropriate discount rate was used.

It is important to understand that a corporation can use a financing via securitization to achieve a target income. Stock analysts project a consensus earnings for a corporation. Suppose that management in the absence of securitization needs $0.10 per share to achieve the target earnings. Management may be able to utilize all or part of its receivables or loans to achieve the targeted amount via securitization.

One more advantage should be noted. Our discussion here deals with realization of income for financial reporting purposes. How about the tax treatment? Under the tax code, the sale of the assets to the SPV and the resulting income need not be recognized for this purpose. That is, income realized for financial reporting purposes need not be realized for tax purposes. So, income can be accelerated for financial reporting purposes by selling financial assets but taxes on that income can be postponed.

Motivation for Banks

The driving force behind securitization has been the need for banks to realize value from the assets on their balance sheet. Typically these assets are residential mortgages, corporate loans, and retail loans such as credit card debt. Here are the factors that might lead a bank to securitize a part of its balance sheet:

- *To increase ROE:* If revenues received from assets remain roughly unchanged after a securitization, but that securitization decreases the size of the assets, the securitization will lead to an increase in the return on equity ratio.
- *To reduce capital requirements:* The level of capital required to support the balance sheet can be reduced by a securitization, which again can lead to cost savings or allows the bank to allocate capital to other, perhaps more profitable, businesses.
- *To obtain cheaper funding:* Frequently the interest payable on ABS securities is considerably below the level payable on the underlying loans. This creates a profit margin for the originating entity.

In other words, the main reasons that a bank securitizes part of its balance sheet is for one or all of the following reasons:

- funding the assets it owns;
- balance sheet capital management; and
- risk management and credit risk transfer.

We consider each of these in turn.

Funding

Banks can use securitization to (1) support asset growth, (2) diversify their funding mix and reduce cost of funding, and (3) reduce maturity mismatches. The market for asset-backed securities is large and therefore access to this source of funding will enable a bank to grow its loan books at a faster pace than if it were reliant on traditional funding sources alone. For example, in the United Kingdom a former building society-turned-bank, Northern Rock plc, took advantage of securitization to back its growing share of the U.K. residential mortgage market.

Securitizing assets also allows a bank to diversify its funding mix. All banks will not wish to be reliant on only a single or a few sources of funding, as this can be high-risk in times of market difficulty. Banks aim to optimize their funding among a mix of retail, interbank, and wholesale sources. Securitization has a key role to play in this mix. It also enables a bank to reduce its funding costs. This is because the securitization process delinks the credit rating of the originating institution from the credit rating of the issued notes. Typically most of the notes issued by SPVs will be higher rated than the bonds issued directly by the originating bank itself. While the liquidity of the secondary market in ABS is frequently lower than that of the corporate bond market, and this adds to the yield payable by an ABS, it is frequently the case that the cost to the originating institution of issuing debt is still lower in the ABS market because of the its higher rating.

Finally, there is the issue of maturity mismatches. The business of bank asset-liability management (ALM) is inherently one of maturity mismatch, since a bank often funds long-term assets such as residential mortgages with shorter-term liabilities such as bank account deposits or interbank funding. Such a maturity mismatch can be removed via securitization, as the originating bank receives funding from the sale of the assets, and the economic maturity of the issued notes frequently matches that of the bank's assets.

Balance Sheet Capital Management

Banks use securitization to improve balance sheet capital management. This provides (1) regulatory capital relief, (2) economic capital relief, and (3) diversified sources of capital. As stipulated in the Bank for International Settlements (BIS) capital rules, also known as the *Basel rules*, banks must maintain a minimum capital level for their assets in relation to the risk of these assets. Under Basel I, for every $100 of risk-weighted assets a bank must hold at least $8 of capital; however, the designation of each asset's risk-weighting is restrictive. For example with the exception of mortgages, customer loans are 100% risk-weighted regardless of the underlying rating of the borrower or the quality of the security held.

The anomalies that this raises, which need not concern us here, are addressed by the Basel II rules, which become effective in 2007 (explained in Appendix A). However the Basel I rules, which became effective in 1992, are another driver of securitization. As an SPV is not a bank, it is not subject to Basel rules and needs only the amount of capital that is economically required by the nature of the assets it contains. This is not a set amount, but is significantly below the 8% level required by banks in all cases. Although an originating bank does not obtain 100% regulatory capital relief when it sells assets off its balance sheet to an SPV, because it often retains a "first-loss" piece (to be discussed shortly) out of the issued notes, its regulatory capital requirement will be significantly reduced after the securitization.

EXHIBIT 4.3   Impact on Originating Bank's Balance Sheet from a Securitization

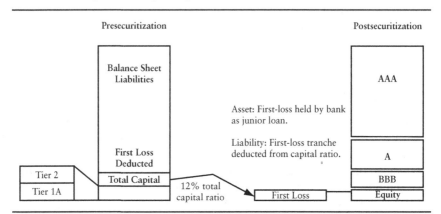

To the extent that securitization provides regulatory capital relief, it can be thought of as an alternative to capital raising, compared with the traditional sources of Tier 1 (equity), preferred shares, and perpetual loan notes with step-up coupon features. By reducing the amount of capital that has to be used to support the asset pool, a bank can also improve its return-on-equity (ROE). This will be received favorably by shareholders.

Exhibit 4.3 illustrates using a hypothetical example the effect on the liability side of an originating bank's balance sheet from a securitization transaction. Following the process, selected assets have been removed from the balance sheet, although the originating bank usually retains the first-loss piece. With regard to the regulatory capital impact, this first-loss amount is deducted from the bank's total capital position. For example, assume a bank has $100 million of risk-weighted assets and a target Basel ratio of 12%, and securitizes all $100 million of these assets. Under the Basel rules, 8% capital in relation to risk-weighted assets is a minimum; regulators prefer to see capital ratios above the minimum and banks generally try to keep such ratios consistent with those of their peer groups. The bank retains the first-loss tranche, which forms 1.5% of the total issue. The remaining 98.5% is sold on to the market. The bank will still have to set aside 1.5% of capital as a buffer against future losses, but it has been able to free itself of the remaining 10.5% of capital.

Risk Management

Once assets have been securitized, the credit risk exposure on these assets for the originating bank is reduced considerably and, if the bank does not retain a first-loss capital piece (the most junior of the issued notes), it is removed entirely. This is because assets have been sold to the SPV. Securitization can also be used to remove nonperforming assets from banks' balance sheets. This has the dual advantage of removing credit risk and improving the value of the bank in investors' perception by reducing the ratio of nonperforming loans to total loans, as well as freeing up regulatory capital as before. Further, there is a potential upside from securitizing such assets: if any of them start performing again, or there is a recovery value obtained from defaulted assets, the originator will receive any surplus profit made by the SPV.

BENEFITS OF SECURITIZATION TO INVESTORS

Investor interest in the ABS market has been considerable from its inception. This is because investors perceive asset-backed securities as possessing a number of benefits. Investors can:

■ diversify sectors of interest;
■ access different (and sometimes superior) risk-reward profiles; and
■ access sectors that are otherwise not open to them.

A key benefit of securitizing ABS is the ability to tailor risk-return profiles. If there is a lack of assets of any specific credit rating, these can be created via securitization. ABS frequently offer better risk-reward performance than corporate bonds of the same rating and maturity. While it might seem peculiar that, for example, the credit performance for one AA-rated bond is better than for another just because it is asset-backed, this often occurs because the originator holds the first-loss piece in the structure.

A holding in an ABS also diversifies an investor's risk exposure. For example, rather than invest $100 million in an AA-rated corporate bond and be exposed to "event risk" associated with the issuer, investors can gain exposure to, for instance, 100 pooled assets. These pooled assets clearly have lower concentration risk.

WHAT RATING AGENCIES LOOK AT IN RATING ASSET-BACKED SECURITIES

In this chapter, we review the factors that the rating agencies—Moody's Investors Service, Standard & Poor's, and FitchRatings—consider in assigning a credit rating to an asset-backed security. In analyzing credit risk, the rating agencies focus on (1) credit quality of the collateral, (2) the quality of the seller/servicer, and (3) cash flow stress and payment structure. We discuss each below.

Credit Quality of the Collateral

Analysis of the credit quality of the collateral depends on the asset type. The rating agencies look at the underlying borrower's ability to pay and the borrower's equity in the asset. By the "borrower" we mean the individual or business entity that is the obligor for the financial asset that is used as the collateral for the securitization. In our Farm Equipment Corporation illustration, the borrowers are the entities that purchased the farm equipment via installment sales contracts. The borrower's equity will be a key determinant as to whether a borrower has an economic incentive to default or to sell the asset and pay off a loan.

For example, suppose three years ago a farmer purchased equipment that currently has a market value of $200,000 and the outstanding balance of the installment sales contract is $30,000. The farmer's equity in the equipment is $170,000 ($200,000 minus $30,000). It is highly unlikely that the farmer will default on the installment sales contract. It would be expected that the farmer would sell the equipment to realize the equity of $170,000 rather than default and have the equipment repossessed. In contrast, if the equipment has a market value of $200,000 but the outstanding balance of the installment sales contract is $320,000, it is likely that the farmer will default if the farmer does not have the ability to pay.

The rating agencies also look at the experience of the originators of the underlying loans and assess whether the loans underlying a specific transaction have the same characteristics as the experience reported by the issuer. That is, the originator of the loan or installment sales contract—Farm Equip Corporation in our illustration—has a credit department that assesses whether to extend credit to a customer. If the underwriting standards are lax, then this is reflected in high default rates; tough underwriting standards are reflected in low default rates. Rating agencies also assess the underwriting standards by looking at historical default rates of an originator and monitor the default rates over time to determine if there has been a deterioration or an improvement in underwriting standards.

In addition to default rates, rating agencies look at historical recovery rates. It is the default rates combined with recovery rates that determine what the potential loss will be. For example, suppose that the historical recovery rate is 40% and that the historical default rate for the collateral is 2%. This means that for every $100 of collateral, there will be defaults of about $2. Of the $2 of defaults, $0.80 will be recovered and therefore $1.20 will be lost. This is a rate of 1.2% and is referred to as the *loss rate*.

The concentration of loans is also examined by rating agencies. The underlying principle of asset securitization is that the large number of borrowers in the collateral pool will reduce the credit risk via diversification. If there are a few borrowers included in the collateral pool that are significant in size relative to the entire pool balance, this diversification benefit can be lost, resulting in a higher level of default risk. This risk is called *concentration risk*. Rating agencies will set concentration limits on the amount or percentage of loans or receivables from any one borrower. If the concentration limit at issuance is exceeded, the issue receives a lower credit rating than if the concentration limit was not exceeded. If after issuance the concentration limit is exceeded, the bonds may be downgraded.

Quality of the Seller/Servicer

All loans and receivables must be serviced. These responsibilities are fulfilled by a third party to an asset-backed securities transaction called a *servicer*. While viewed as a "third party," in many asset-backed securities transactions, the servicer is effectively the originator of the loans used as the collateral for the corporation seeking funding.

The servicer may also be responsible for advancing payments when there are delinquencies in payments (that are likely to be collected in the future) resulting in a temporary shortfall in the payments that must be made to the investors in the securities issued in a securitization transaction.

The role of the servicer is critical in a securitization transaction. Therefore, rating agencies look at the ability of a servicer to perform all the activities for which a servicer will be responsible before they assign a credit rating to the bonds issued. For example, the following factors are reviewed when evaluating servicers: servicing history, experience and capabilities, human resources, financial condition, growth, competition, and business environment.

Based on its analysis, a rating agency determines whether the servicer is acceptable or unacceptable. If a servicer is unacceptable, a securitization transaction is not rated. The rating agency may require a "backup" servicer if there is a concern about the ability of a servicer to perform.

Remember that the issuer of an asset-backed security, the special purpose vehicle, is not a corporation with employees. It simply has loans and receivables. The servicer therefore plays an important role in assuring that the payments are collected from the borrowers.

Cash Flow Stress and Payment Structure

The rating agencies analyze the extent to which the cash flow from the collateral can satisfy all of the obligations of the asset-backed securities transaction. The cash flow of the collateral consists of interest and principal repayment. The cash flow payments that must be made are interest and principal to investors, servicing fees, and any other expenses for which the issuer is liable. The rating agencies analyze the structure to test whether the collateral's cash flows match the payments that must be made to satisfy the issuer's obligations. This requires that the rating company make assumptions about losses and delinquencies under various interest rate scenarios.

Based on its analysis of the collateral and the stress testing of the structure to assess the risk that the bondholders will not be repaid in full, a rating agency determines the amount of credit enhancement necessary for an issue to receive a particular credit rating.

DESCRIPTION OF THE COLLATERAL

The cash flows of the pool of assets (i.e., collateral) backing a securitization transaction are used to make the payments to the bond classes. Investors want to estimate the cash flow of that will be distributed to them and therefore must make projections about prepayments and defaults. In doing so, investors use the information provided in the prospectus, prospectus supplement, investor marketing material that contains computations, and remittance reports.

Subsequent to issuance, information is reported in Form S-3 that provides performance information (including delinquencies and losses) since origination and is referred to as *static pool information.* In this section, we will discuss measures to describe a pool of assets and for quantifying actual and projected prepayments and defaults. The term "static pool" is often used in the ABS market to refer to a group of loans or other receivables originated or acquired at approximately the same time on the basis of similar criteria, the performance of which is tracked as a group over time.[2]

Amortizing versus Revolving Structures

In our illustration of securitization thus far, the collateral has been a pool of amortizing assets. That is, there is a schedule of principal repayment

---

[2] Edward E. Gainor, "Preparing to Comply with the SEC's New Rules Governing Offerings of Asset-Backed Securities," *Journal of Structured Finance* 10, no. 3 (Fall 2004), p. 19.

and the outstanding balance declines over the life the of the structure. No additional loans are added to the pool and the securitization is said to be an amortizing structure. The schedule for the repayment of the principal is called an *amortization schedule*. Any excess payment over the scheduled principal payment is called a *prepayment*. Prepayments can be made to pay off the entire balance; a partial prepayment is called a *curtailment*.

There are securitizations where the assets are nonamortizing. With nonamortizing assets only minimum periodic payments are required and there is no scheduled principal repayment. If the payment from the pool of assets into the SPV is less than the interest on the outstanding loan balance due to investors in the ABS, the shortfall is added to the outstanding loan balance. If the periodic payment is greater than the interest on the outstanding loan balance, then the difference is either (1) applied to the reduction of the outstanding loan balance or (2) used to purchase additional assets for the pool. Whether (1) or (2) occur depends on the time period. In such structures, there is a *lockout period* wherein any principal payment received is used to purchase additional assets. After the lockout period, the principal payments received are used to pay down the principal to the bond classes. This period is called the *principal amortization period*. Securitizations of this type are referred to as *revolving structures*. Since there is no schedule of principal payments (i.e., no amortization schedule) for a nonamortizing asset, the concept of a prepayment does not apply.

Some securitizations are backed by amortizing assets but are a blend of the two structures. That is, during a lockout period any principal repayments (regularly scheduled and prepayments) are reinvested in additional assets but after the lockout period the principal payments are distributed to the bond classes.

Information Used In Underwriting Process

To understand the information about the pool of assets backing a securitization, it is necessary to understand the information used in the underwriting process. The most important information used by a lender in making the decision to lend funds for any consumer loan are the loan-to-value ratio, the payment-to-income ratio, and the credit score.[3] We discuss each next.

Loan-to-Value Ratio

The ratio of the principal balance of the loan relative to the value of the asset is called the *loan-to-value ratio* (LTV). The value of the asset in the

---

[3] In the case of residential mortgage loans, the type of documentation provided by the borrower and the reason for the loan are also important factors.

LTV ratio can be a market value obtained from the sale or an appraised or an estimated value. A ratio of 0.8, for example, means that the principal balance of the loan obtained to purchase the asset is 80% of the market value. This is a commonly computed ratio for securitized products backed by residential and commercial mortgage loans.

The difference between the value of an asset and the principal balance of the loan is called the *borrower's equity*. When the LTV is less than 1, the borrower has positive equity in the asset and there is an incentive for the borrower not to default. Instead of defaulting, it would be an economic advantage for the borrower to sell the asset and pay off the loan, pocketing the residual proceeds. A ratio greater than 1 means that the amount borrowed exceeds the value of the asset and there is an incentive for the borrower to default. All studies of defaults have found that LTV is one of the most important variables in predicting the default of the borrower. The higher the ratio, the greater the likelihood that the borrower will default.

A concept that is similar to the LTV for ABS backed by auto loans is the *advance rate*. The advance rate is computed differently for used and new cars. For the former, the advance rate is the amount borrowed as a percentage of the car's *wholesale* price. For new cars, it is the amount borrowed as a percentage of the manufacturer's suggested retail price (MSRP). The advance rate can exceed 100% on a new car because taxes, accessories, and extended warranties that are financed are not considered part of the MSRP.

Payment-to-Income Ratio

The *payment-to-income ratio* (PTI) is the ratio of the amount of the monthly loan payment to the income available each month to satisfy the loan payment. The higher the PTI, the greater the amount of the borrower's income must be applied to service the loan.

In the case of loans for residential mortgages, two PTI ratios are typically calculated: "front" ratio and "back" ratio. The front ratio is calculated by dividing the total monthly payments on the property (including principal, interest, property taxes, and homeowners insurance) by the pretax monthly income. The back ratio is similar, but adds other debt payments (including auto loan and credit card payments) to the total payments.

In the case of commercial mortgage loans, an analogous measure is the *debt service coverage ratio* (DSCR). This is the ratio of the property's net operating income (NOI) divided by the debt service. The NOI is defined as the rental income reduced by cash operating expenses (adjusted for a replacement reserve). A ratio greater than 1 means that the cash flow from the property is sufficient to cover debt servicing. The higher the ratio, the more likely that the borrower will be able to meet debt servicing from the property's cash flow.

Credit Score

Probably the most important measure for assessing credit risk is a *credit score*. A credit score seeks to summarize a borrower's credit history into a single number—a numerical grade of the borrower's credit history. This is done by using scoring models that assign points for different variables that have been historically found to best predict future credit performance based on studies of large samples of borrowers. The variables that have been found to be useful in predicting future credit performance include the number of late payments of loans within a specified time period, the amount of time credit has been established, the amount of credit used compared to the amount of credit available, the length of time at the current residence, the employment history, and negative credit information such as bankruptcies, charge-offs, and collections.

There are several credit scoring models that are currently in use: the Fair Isaacs model, the Emperica model, and the Beacon model. There are three different credit-reporting firms that calculate credit scores using these models. Experian uses the Fair Isaacs model, Transunion supports the Emperica model, and Equifax uses the Beacon model. Despite the fact that the credit scores have different underlying methodologies, the scores are generically referred to as "FICO" scores. Typically, lenders get more than one score in order to minimize the impact of variations in credit scores across providers. When a lender obtains all three scores, generally the middle score is used, while the convention is to use the lower score when only two are available. The general rule of thumb is that a borrower needs a credit score of 660 or higher to qualify as a "prime" credit.

Attributes of the Pool of Assets

In describing the composition and characteristics of the pool of assets, an issuer typically stratifies the assets into different categories by attribute. Attributes, discussed in the sections below, are typically expressed in terms of ranges. The view in categorizing assets is that a particular category within an attribute will share the same characteristics that will affect the cash flow (prepayments and defaults).

Weighted Average Contract Rate

Not all of the loans that are included in a pool of loans that are securitized have the same interest rate. The loan rate is called the *contract rate.* The *gross weighted average contract rate,* or gross WAC, is found by weighting the contract rate of for each loan in the pool by the percentage of the outstanding loan balance relative to the outstanding loan balance of all the loans in the pool.[4] Another name for the gross weighted average contract rate is the *weighted average contract rate.*

Letting

r_i = the contract rate for loan i,
w_i = outstanding balance of loan i/outstanding loan balance of all loans in the pool, and
N = total number of loans,

then the gross WAC is computed as follows:

$$\text{gross WAC} = r_1 w_1 + r_2 w_2 + \ldots + r_N w_N$$

Suppose a pool of assets has just seven loans and the outstanding loan balance, contract rate, and months remaining to maturity of each loan as shown in Exhibit 4.4.

The WAC for this loan pool is

$$0.1750(7.0\%) + 0.1312(6.80\%) + 0.2105(7.10\%) + 0.1017(6.60\%)$$
$$+ 0.0929(7.25\%) + 11.59\%(7.20\%) + 17.28\%(6.75\%) = 6.96\%$$

The gross WAC at any given point in time multiplied by the outstanding mortgage balance is the potential dollar interest (ignoring defaults) that is available to pay interest to the bond classes in the structure before the payment of any fees.

EXHIBIT 4.4 Illustration of Calculation of Gross WAC

Loan	Outstanding Loan Balance ($)	Weight in Pool(%)	Contract Rate (%)
1	320,000	17.50	7.00
2	240,000	13.12	6.80
3	385,000	21.05	7.10
4	186,000	10.17	6.60
5	170,000	9.29	7.25
6	212,000	11.59	7.20
7	316,000	17.28	6.75
Total	1,829,000	100.00	

---

[4] For the auto loan ABS the loan rate is called the annual percentage rate (APR).

In a describing a securitization, another important measure is the *net WAC*. This measure is computed by subtracting from the gross WAC the (1) servicing fee, (2) trustee fees, and (3) any payments for credit enhancement. The net WAC multiplied by the outstanding loan balance of the pool indicates how much is available to pay interest to the bond classes in the structure assuming the payments are realized. In many structures, the net WAC is established as the rate that will be paid to some bond classes.

Excess Spread

The amount available *after* paying the holders of all bond classes and all fees ignoring any potential losses and the allocation of some proceeds in a securitization for credit enhancement is called the *gross excess spread*. The gross excess spread reduced by the amount necessary to cover losses is called the *net excess spread*. Depending upon the structure, a portion of the excess spread may have to be retained by the SPV to build up credit support over time. The net excess spread after the amount that must be retained by the SPV is called the *free excess spread* and this amount can be distributed to the issuer.

Weighted Average Maturity

A *weighted average maturity*, or WAM, is found by weighting the remaining number of months to maturity for each loan in the pool by that loan's percentage weight in the total pool. Letting L_i equal the number of months remaining for loan i, then the WAM is computed as follows:

$$WAM = r_1L_1 + r_2L_2 + \ldots + r_NL_N$$

The WAM for this loan pool whose loans are shown in Exhibit 4.4 is

$17.50\%(165) + 0.1312(158) + 0.2105(173) + 0.1017(189)$
$+0.0929(170)+11.59\%(163)+17.28\%(174) = 168$ months (rounded)

PREPAYMENTS MEASURES

As explained earlier, for amortizing assets there can be prepayments (i.e., any payment toward the repayment of principal that is in excess of the scheduled principal payment). In describing prepayments for a pool of assets, market participants refer to the *prepayment rate* or *prepayment speed*.

Single Monthly Mortality Rate

The most commonly used monthly prepayment rate measure is the *single monthly mortality rate* (SMM). To compute this measure, the amount available in the loan pool to prepay that month must first be computed. The amount available in the loan pool to prepay in a month, say month t, is the beginning loan balance in the in month t reduced by the scheduled principal payment in month t. The SMM for a month t is then computed as follows:

$$SMM_t = \frac{\text{Prepayment in month } t}{\left[\begin{array}{cc}\text{Beginning balance} & \text{Scheduled principal payment} \\ \text{for month } t & \text{in month } t\end{array}\right]}$$

To illustrate, assume the following in month t:

beginning balance in month t	= \$179,163,383
scheduled principal payment in month t	= \$920,674
prepayments in month t	= \$148,913

The SMM for month t is then

$$SMM_t = \frac{\$148,913}{(\$179,163,383 - \$920,674)} = 0.0005143 = 0.5143\%$$

An SMM_t of 0.5143% is interpreted as follows: In month t, 0.5143% of the outstanding mortgage balance available to prepay in month t prepaid.

While the calculation above showed how the SMM is computed for a month, the prepayment for a month will then be used to determine the cash flow of a mortgage pool for the month. Given a projected SMM for month t, the projected prepayment for month t is found as follows:

Prepayment for month t = SMM
$\times$ (Beginning balance for month t
$-$ Scheduled principal payment in month t)

Suppose the remaining mortgage balance at the beginning of some month is \$145 million and the scheduled principal payment for that month is \$1.5 million. The projected SMM for the month is 0.5143%. Then the projected prepayment for the month is

$$0.005143 \times (\$145,000,000 - \$1,500,000) = \$738,021$$

Conditional Prepayment Rate

The SMM is a monthly rate. Annualizing the SMM gives the *conditional prepayment rate* (CPR) which is also referred to as the *constant prepayment rate*. Given the SMM for a given month, the CPR is found using the following formula:

$$CPR = 1 - (1 - SMM)^{12}$$

For example, suppose that the SMM is 0.005143. Then the CPR is

$$CPR = 1 - (1 - 0.005143)^{12}$$
$$= 1 - (0.994857)^{12} = 0.06 = 6\%$$

A CPR of 6% means that, ignoring scheduled principal payments, approximately 6% of the pool's outstanding loan balance at the beginning of the year will be prepaid by the end of the year.

This measure is referred to as a "conditional" prepayment rate because the prepayments in one year depend upon (i.e., are conditional upon) the amount available to prepay in the previous year.

Given a CPR, an SMM can be derived using the following formula:

$$SMM = 1 - (1 - CPR)^{1/12}$$

Prepayments for Auto-Loan-Backed Deals

Prepayments for auto-loan-backed securities are measured in terms of the *absolute prepayment rate*, denoted *not* by APR but by ABS.[5] The ABS is the monthly prepayment expressed as a percentage of the *original* collateral amount. Recall that the SMM expresses prepayments based on the prior month's balance.

There is a mathematical relationship between the ABS and SMM. Given the SMM (expressed as a decimal), the ABS (expressed as a decimal) is obtained as follows:

$$ABS = \frac{SMM}{1 + [SMM \times (M - 1)]}$$

where M is the number of months after origination (i.e., loan age).

---

[5] ABS was probably used because it was the first prepayment measure used for asset-backed securities.

Suppose that the SMM is 2.1%, or 0.021, in month 32. Then the ABS is

$$\text{ABS} = \frac{0.021}{1 + [0.021 \times (32 - 1)]} = 0.0127 = 1.27\%$$

Given the ABS, the SMM is obtained as follows:

$$\text{SMM} = \frac{\text{ABS}}{1 - [\text{ABS} \times (M - 1)]}$$

The SMM can then be converted to a CPR using the formula above.

To illustrate the formula, suppose that the ABS is 1.5%, or 0.015, in month 26. Then the SMM is

$$\text{SMM} = \frac{0.015}{1 - [0.015 \times (26 - 1)]} = 0.024 = 2.4\%$$

DEFAULTS AND DELINQUENCIES

Delinquency Measures

When a borrower fails to make one or more timely payments, the loan is said to be *delinquent*. Delinquency measures are designed to gauge whether borrowers are current on their loan payment as well as stratifying unpaid loans according to the seriousness of the delinquency. The method used is determined by the servicer. When the underlying pool of assets is mortgage loans, the two commonly used methods for classifying delinquencies are those recommended by the Office of Thrift Supervision (OTS) and the Mortgage Bankers Association (MBA).

The OTS method uses the following loan delinquency classifications:

- payment due date to 30 days late: *Current*;
- 30–60 days late: *30 days delinquent*;
- 60–90 days late: *60 days delinquent*; and
- more than 90 days late: *90+ Days delinquent*.

The MBA method is a somewhat more stringent classification method, classifying a loan as 30 days delinquent once payments are not received after the due date. Thus, a loan classified as "current" under the OTS method would be listed be as "30 days delinquent" under the

MBA method. To further illustrate the inconsistencies between the two methods, a June 9, 2000 report by Moody's titled, "Contradictions in Terms: Variations in Terminology in the Mortgage Market," shows how the reported delinquencies can differ dramatically.

Default Measures

The conditions that result in classification of some loans as delinquent (such as the loss of a job or illness) may change, resulting in the resumption of timely principal and interest payments. However, some portion of the loans classified as delinquent may end up in default. By definition, default is the point where the borrower loses title to the property in question. Default generally occurs for loans that are 90+ days delinquent.[6]

Three measures for quantifying default are the conditional default rate, the cumulative default rate, and the charge-off rate. The *conditional default rate* (CDR) is the annualized value of the unpaid principal balance of newly defaulted loans over the course of a month as a percentage of the unpaid balance of the pool (before scheduled principal payment) at the beginning of the month. It is computed by first calculating the default rate for the month as shown:

$$\text{Default rate for month } t$$
$$= \frac{\text{Defaulted loan balance in month } t}{\left[\begin{array}{c}\text{Beginning balance} \\ \text{for month } t\end{array} - \begin{array}{c}\text{Scheduled principal payment} \\ \text{in month } t\end{array}\right]}$$

This is annualized as follows to get the CDR:

$$\text{CDR}_t = 1 - (1 - \text{Default rate for month } t)^{12}$$

The second default measure is the *cumulative default rate,* which is denoted by CDX in order to avoid confusion with CDR. CDX is the proportion of the total face value of loans in the pool that have gone into default as a percentage of the total face value of the pool.

The *charge-off rate* (COR) is the annualized rate of loan liquidations.[7] The calculation begins with the following for the month:

---

[6] Loans where the borrower becomes bankrupt may be classified as having defaulted at an earlier point in time.

[7] See Joel W. Brown and William M. Wadden, "Mortgage Credit Analysis," Chapter 18 in Frank J. Fabozzi (ed.), *Investing in Asset-Backed Securities* (Hoboken, NJ: John Wiley & Sons, 2000).

Liquidation rate for month t

$$= \frac{\text{Liquidated loan balance in month } t}{\left[\begin{array}{cc} \text{Beginning balance} & \text{Scheduled principal payment} \\ \text{for month } t & \text{in month } t \end{array}\right]}$$

and then annualized as follows:

$$\text{COR}_t = 1 - (1 - \text{Liquidation rate for month } t)^{12}$$

Loss Severity Measures

Where the lender has a lien on the property, a portion of the value of the loan can be recovered through the legal recovery process (foreclosure/repossession) and subsequent sale of the asset. The difference between the proceeds received from the recovery process (after all transaction costs) and principal balance of the loss is the loss in dollars. The *loss severity rate* is equal to

$$\text{Loss severity rate} = \frac{(\text{Liquidation balance in month } t - \text{Liquidation proceeds})}{\text{Liquidation balance in month } t}$$

The loss severity rate ranges from 0 to 1. If the loss severity rate is zero, then liquidation proceeds are equal to the liquidated loan balance. A loss severity rate of 1 means that there are no liquidation proceeds.

The *loss rate* is equal to the COR multiplied by the loss severity rate.

Monthly Payment Rate for Credit Card Receivable ABS

For a pool of credit card receivables, the cash flow consists of finance charges collected, fees, and principal. Finance charges collected represent the periodic interest the credit card borrower is charged based on the unpaid balance after the grace period. Fees include late payment fees and any annual membership fees.

The *monthly payment rate* (MPR) expresses the monthly payment (which includes finance charges, fees, and any principal repayment) of a credit card receivable portfolio as a percentage of the credit card debt outstanding in the pool. That is, for month t

$$\text{MPR}_t = \frac{\text{Payments in month } t \text{ for finance charges, fees, and principal}}{\text{Credit card debt outstanding in month } t - 1}$$

For example, suppose a $500 million credit card receivable portfolio in January realized $50 million of payments in February. The MPR would then be 10% ($50 million divided by $500 million).

There are two reasons why the MPR is important. First, if the MPR reaches an extremely low level, there is a chance that there will be extension risk with respect to the principal payments on the bonds. Second, if the MPR is very low, then there is a chance that there will not be sufficient cash flows to pay off the principal. This is one of the events that could trigger early amortization of the principal in a credit-card-backed deal.

CHAPTER 5

Securitization Structures

We provided the basics of securitization in the previous chapter. In this chapter, we discuss securitization structures and the use of interest rate derivatives in a securitization.

USE OF INTEREST RATE DERIVATIVES IN SECURITIZATION TRANSACTIONS[1]

Chapter 2 reviewed derivative instruments. In this section, we explain the use of interest rate derivatives in securitization transactions for hedging and yield enhancement. Three types of over-the-counter interest rate derivatives commonly used in securitizations are interest rate swaps, interest rate caps, and interest rate corridors. Because they are over-the-counter instruments, they expose the trust (the special-purpose vehicle (SPV)) to counterparty risk.

Interest Rate Swaps

An interest rate swap can be used to alter the cash flow characteristics of the assets (liabilities) to match the characteristics of the liabilities (assets). For example, suppose a transaction has a pool of fixed-rate, monthly payment loans but the bond classes that are supported by the collateral have floating rate, monthly payment characteristics. A generic or plain vanilla swap can be used to convert the monthly, fixed-rate cash flows to monthly, floating-rate cash flows based on the reference rate and margin

---

[1] This section draws from Frank J. Fabozzi, Raymond Morel, and Brian D. Grow, "Use of Interest Rate Derivatives in Securitization Transactions," *Journal of Structured Finance* 11 (Summer 2005), pp. 22–27.

owed to the covered classes of bonds. For example, the prospectus supplement of the Toyota Auto Receivables 2003-B Owner Trust, $554,000,000 Floating Rate Asset Backed Notes, Class A-3 states:

> In order to issue the Class A-3 Notes bearing interest at a floating rate when the Receivables bear fixed interest rates, the Trust will enter into the Swap Agreement with the Swap Counterparty. Pursuant to the Swap Agreement, on each Payment Date the Trust is obligated to pay to the Swap Counterparty in respect of the Class A-3 Notes an amount equal to the amount deemed to accrue on a notional amount equal to the outstanding principal balance of the Class A-3 Notes as of the preceding Payment Date at a fixed rate of interest of 2.295% (the "Class A-3 Notional Rate") calculated on an 30/360 basis (the "Class A-3 Swap Interest Amount"). The amount to be paid by the Swap Counterparty in respect of the Class A-3 Notes on any Payment Date will be the amount of interest that accrued thereon at the related floating interest rate from the preceding Payment Date to such current Payment Date (the "Class A-3 Interest Amount").
>
> Any net amounts payable by the Trust to the Swap Counterparty on any Payment Date will be deducted from Collections for the related Collection Period prior to making any payments of interest or principal of the Notes.

In the above example, the trust pays a fixed rate to the counterparty in exchange for a floating rate. In other securitizations, the payments are reversed and the trust pays a floating rate to the counterparty in exchange for a fixed rate. For example, in the Citibank Credit Card Issuance Trust, $500,000,000, 4.75%, Class 2003-A10 Notes of December 2013 transaction, the class A notes are paid a fixed rate of interest, but the assets (credit card receivables in this example) generate a floating rate of interest. This mismatch is hedged through the use of an amortizing swap where the trust pays LIBOR plus a margin to the counterparty in exchange for a fixed rate that is passed on to the ABS noteholders. The following language is taken from the related prospectus supplement:

> Under the interest rate swap, the issuer will pay interest monthly to the swap counterparty on the notional amount based on a floating rate of interest equal to one-month LIBOR plus a margin not greater than 0.21% per annum

and the swap counterparty will pay interest monthly to the issuer on the notional amount based on the rate of interest applicable to these Class A notes.

The issuer's net swap payments will be paid out of funds available in the interest funding subaccount for these Class A notes. Net swap receipts from the swap counterparty will be deposited into the interest funding subaccount for these Class A notes and will be available to pay interest on these Class A notes.

As explained in Chapter 2, amortizing swap is a swap in which the notional amount declines over time based on a predetermined amortization schedule, actual collateral balance, or the actual bond balance. This type of swap is used in certain types of securitizations when the collateral amortizes over time. Hence, the fixed notional amount for a plain vanilla swap when a hedge is initially placed will become overhedged as the pool pays down and an amortizing swap mitigates this exposure. For example, the notional amount depends on the actual collateral balance in the KeyCorp Student Loan Trust 2003-A, Asset-Backed Notes transaction. The related prospectus supplement states:

> In accordance with the terms of the Group I Interest Rate Swap, on each Distribution Date, the Trust will owe the Swap Counterparty the sum of the following amounts for each of the monthly periods in the related Collection Period, beginning with the monthly period commencing September 1, 2003 (each, a "Net Trust Swap Payment"): (I) the product of:
>
> 1. the Commercial Paper Rate as determined as of the first day of the related monthly period;
> 2. the aggregate principal balance of the Commercial Paper Rate Loans as determined as of the first day of the related monthly period; and
> 3. a fraction, the numerator of which is the actual number of days in the related monthly period and the denominator of which is 360.
>
> And, in accordance with the terms of the Group I Interest Rate Swap, on each Distribution Date, the Swap Counterparty will owe the Trust an amount equal to the sum of the following amounts for each of the monthly periods in the related Collection Period beginning with the monthly

period commencing September 1, 2003 (each, a "Net Trust Swap Receipt"): (II) the product of:

1. Three-Month LIBOR (calculated in the same manner and on such dates as such index is calculated for the Notes for the related interest period) less 0.15%;
2. the aggregate principal balance of the Commercial Paper Rate Loans as determined as of the first day of the related monthly period; and
3. a fraction, the numerator of which is the actual number of days in the related monthly period and the denominator of which is 360.

Payments will be made on a net basis with respect to each of the Group I Interest Rate Swap between the Trust and the Swap Counterparty, in an amount equal to the excess of (I) over (II) above for the related Collection Period, in the case of a Net Trust Swap Payment, or the excess of (II) over (I) above for the related Collection Period, in the case of a Net Trust Swap Receipt.

Similarly, issuers of notes backed by credit card receivables use amortizing swaps where the notional amount is tied to the principal amount of the liability. The following excerpt taken from the prospectus supplement related to the Citibank Credit Card Issuance Trust, $500,000,000, 4.75%, Class 2003-A10 Notes of December 2013 issue, demonstrates this feature:

The interest rate swap will have a notional amount equal to the outstanding dollar principal amount of these Class A notes and will terminate on the expected principal payment date of these Class A notes.

Basis Risk and Use of Proceeds

Interest rate derivatives are also used in securitizations to hedge against interest rate scenarios where the benchmark index for the liabilities may rise more rapidly than the asset benchmark index. This mismatch in indexes is called "basis risk." The trust's interest liability to bondholders, subject to credit enhancement, is limited to the amount of interest generated by the collateral. This basis risk shortfall is a risk to investors that can be mitigated by incorporating interest rate derivatives into the transactions.

Transactions can mitigate interest rate and basis risk for different collateral payment characteristics by utilizing multiple interest rate derivatives. For example, the prospectus of the GE Commercial Equipment Financing LLC, Series 2003-1, $376,946,000 Asset-Backed Notes states:

> The DB Swap Agreement will include confirmations for three separate swap transactions, under which the Issuer will receive amounts based on LIBOR and pay amounts based upon a fixed rate of interest, an index based upon commercial paper rates ("CP"), and a constant treasury maturity index ("CMT"), as applicable.
>
> The GECS Swap Agreement will include one confirmation for a swap transaction under which the Issuer will receive amounts based on LIBOR and pay amounts based on an index based upon the interest rate on the Hybrid Loans.
>
> Under each Swap Agreement only the net amount due by the Issuer or by the applicable Swap Counterparty, will be remitted on each Payment Date. All net amounts received by the Issuer will be included in the Available Amounts on the Payment Date such net amounts are received.
>
> "CMT Rate" means, with respect to any Interest Accrual Period, a rate based upon the one-year constant treasury maturity index applicable to the CMT Loans.
>
> "CP Rate" means, with respect to any Interest Accrual Period, a rate based upon the rate listed for "1-Month" Commercial Paper (Non-Financial) as stated in the Federal Reserve Statistical Release H.15 (519).
>
> "Hybrid Rate" means, with respect to any Interest Accrual Period, a rate based upon a weighted average of the interest rate index applicable to the Hybrid Loans.

The proceeds from interest rate derivatives are utilized in the waterfall for one or more of the following three purposes:

1. cover losses on the collateral;
2. build overcollateralization by paying off bond principal;[2] and
3. cover basis risk shortfall.

---

[2] Using interest to pay down the principal of a bonds prior to the scheduled repayment date is referred to as "turboing" bonds.

Proceeds are directed to these purposes in the waterfall and can be prioritized in any order. It is important to understand the use of the proceeds when analyzing the impact of the derivative on bond cash flows.

In securitizations backed by residential mortgage loans that utilize excess interest and overcollateralization as credit support, proceeds from the typical swap will be used to cover losses and build overcollateralization prior to being applied to basis risk shortfall (the difference between the certificate coupon and the available funds cap).[3] Following is an example from the Structured Asset Investment Loan Trust Mortgage Pass-Through Certificates, Series 2005-4 issue, which demonstrates this priority of payments:

> (1) to the Swap Counterparty, any Net Swap Payment owed to the Swap Counterparty pursuant to the Swap Agreement for such Distribution Date;
>
> (2) to the Swap Counterparty, any unpaid Swap Termination Payment not due to a Swap Counterparty Trigger Event owed to the Swap Counterparty pursuant to the Swap Agreement;
>
> (3) to the Offered Certificates, Current Interest and any Carryforward Interest for each such class for such Distribution Date, for application in accordance with the same priorities set forth in clauses A(ii) through (iv) and B(ii) through (iv) under "—Interest Payment Priorities" above, to the extent unpaid pursuant to such clauses;
>
> (4) to the Offered Certificates, any amount necessary to maintain the Targeted Overcollateralization Amount specified in clauses (1) and (2) under "—Credit Enhancement—Application of Monthly Excess Cashflow" above for such Distribution Date, for application pursuant to the priorities set forth in such clauses, after giving effect to distributions pursuant to such clauses;
>
> (5) to the Offered Certificates, any Basis Risk Shortfalls and Unpaid Basis Risk Shortfalls for each such class and for such Distribution Date, for application pursuant to the priorities set forth in clauses (3)(a) and (b) under "—

---

[3] An available funds cap is included in transactions backed by adjustable-rate residential mortgage loans because the loans are typically benchmarked to 6-month LIBOR and the securities issued by the SPV are benchmarked to 1-month LIBOR (hence there is basis risk). Hence, for any month the available interest from the loans may be less than the amount due the bondholders. The available funds cap restricts the amount due to the bondholders to the interest available.

Credit Enhancement—Application of Monthly Excess Cashflow" above, to the extent unpaid pursuant to such clauses;

On the other hand, some securitization transactions backed by residential mortgage loans use the swap proceeds to cover basis risk shortfall prior to covering losses and building overcollateralization. This type of waterfall is a deviation from the distribution waterfall that caps certificate interest payments at the available funds cap. Since the total swap proceeds is reduced by the basis risk shortfall payment prior to covering losses and building overcollateralization in this structure, the swap will provide less credit enhancement for the certificates, but will help reduce basis risk. Following is an excerpt from the prospectus supplement for the Bear Stearns Asset Backed Securities I Trust 2005-HE5 Asset-Backed Certificates, Series 2005-HE5 issue, which demonstrates this type of structure:

> ...the Swap Administrator will withdraw the following amounts from the Swap Account to remit to the trustee for distribution to the certificates in the following order of priority:

> first, to each class of Class A Certificates, on a pro rata basis, to pay accrued interest and any Interest Carry Forward Amount to the extent due to the interest portion of a Realized Loss with respect to the related mortgage loans, in each case to the extent not fully paid as described under "Description of the Certificates — Distributions on the Certificates —Interest Distributions" above;

> second, sequentially to the Class M-1, Class M-2, Class M-3, Class M-4, Class M-5, Class M-6, Class M-7 and Class M-8 Certificates, in that order, to pay accrued interest, in each case to the extent not fully paid as described under "Description of the Certificates—Distributions on the Certificates—Interest Distributions" above, and any Interest Carry Forward Amount to the extent due to the interest portion of a Realized Loss with respect to the related mortgage loans;

> third, to pay, first to the Class A Certificates, on a pro rata basis, and second, sequentially to the Class M-1, Class M-2, Class M-3, Class M-4, Class M-5, Class M-6, Class M-

7 and Class M-8 Certificates, in that order, any Basis Risk Shortfall Carry Forward Amounts for such distribution date; and

fourth, to pay as principal to the Class A Certificates and Class M Certificates to be applied as part of the Extra Principal Distribution Amount to the extent that the Overcollateralization Amount is reduced below the Overcollateralization Target Amount as a result of Realized Losses and to the extent not covered by Excess Spread distributed in the same manner and priority as the Principal Distribution Amount; and as described under "Description of the Certificates—Excess Spread and Overcollateralization Provisions" above.

Interest Rate Caps And Corridors

An interest rate cap can be used to hedge against a rise in interest rates. The buyer of the cap pays the seller of the cap an upfront fee for this right at closing. An interest rate corridor is an interest rate cap where the liability of the seller is limited to a specified maximum rate (ceiling) and naturally the cost to the buyer is reduced accordingly. As with an interest rate cap, the seller is compensated via a single up-front fee. For example, the prospectus of the Park Place Securities Inc., Asset-Backed Pass Through Certificates, Series 2004-WCW2 states:

> The following Certificates will have the benefit of an interest rate corridor: (i) the Class A-1 Certificates; (ii) the Group II Certificates; and (iii) the Mezzanine Certificates (collectively, the "Cap Contracts"). Pursuant to the Cap Contracts, Swiss Re Financial Products Corporation (together with any successor, the "Counterparty" or "Cap Provider") will agree to pay to the Trust a monthly payment in an amount equal to the product of: (1) for the Distribution Date in November 2004 through the Distribution Date in July 2008, the excess, if any, of one-month LIBOR over the rate set forth in the related Cap Contract, up to a maximum rate set forth in the related Cap Contract; (2) the lesser of (i) the notional amount for such interest accrual period set forth in the related Cap Contract and (ii) the aggregate Certificate Principal Balance of the related Certificates; and (3) a fraction, the numerator of which is the actual number of days in the related Interest Accrual Period, and the denominator of

which is 360. The notional amount declines in accordance with a schedule set forth in the related Cap Contract. The Cap Contracts will terminate after the final Distribution Date set forth above.

Another use for an interest rate cap or corridor is yield maintenance. This is seen quite often in mortgage-backed securities (MBS) net interest margin (NIM) transactions. NIM securities, discussed later in this chapter, are bonds structured to receive cash flows from excess spreads to the extent there are any. A typical MBS NIM transaction is a short-term principal and interest instrument with three primary sources of funds, including any prepayment penalties, residual released from an underlying MBS transaction (usually certificated as class X and class P), and payments from a cap or corridor (also called a *Yield Maintenance Agreement*). The NIM usually pays a fixed or floating interest rate, which is paid first in the NIM distribution waterfall, and all remaining funds are applied to principal. Prepayment penalty and residual cash flow are not extremely stable sources of funds. Since the NIM trust must pay interest to the NIM noteholders each month, the structure will typically include a cap or corridor to help stabilize the cash flow and ensure that timely interest will be paid to NIM noteholders.

Counterparty Risk

The use of derivative instruments introduces counterparty risk for the trust, and therefore the way counterparty risk is managed in securitizations should be understood.

The risk of counterparty default can be partially mitigated by entering into swaps with highly rated counterparties and using commonly developed methods in the derivatives market for doing so (e.g., margin, netting, and overcollateralization). The majority of the swaps in securitizations involving investment-grade-rated notes contain rating triggers specifying certain steps that must be taken by the counterparty if its debt rating migrates below a certain level. Typically, the counterparty must, at its own cost and within a specified time period, usually 30 days, either (i) find a replacement counterparty with a rating higher than the rating specified in the trigger, (ii) post a specified amount of collateral, or (iii) obtain a guarantee from an entity with a rating higher than the rating specified in the trigger. The counterparty may also need to receive confirmation from the specified rating agencies that the rating of the notes will not move downward as a result of these actions. If the counterparty does not satisfy these requirements, then depending on the swap documents, either (1) the swap is terminated automatically or (2) the trust may have the option of terminating the swap. Upon a termination of the swap, it is probable that there would be a swap termination payment due by the trust to the swap counterparty or from the counterparty to the trust.

The rating trigger decreases but does not eliminate the trust's potential exposure to interest rate and counterparty risk. To illustrate, if the swap counterparty is downgraded below its rating trigger, it may decide to pursue (i), (ii), or (iii) described above. Since there is a finite number of swap providers to the marketplace, a downgrade below a rating trigger could require a swap provider to pursue these remedies for a very large number of swaps. This would translate to a very high cost to the counterparty at a time when its credit situation is already deteriorating. Alternatively, the counterparty may not pursue the remedies described above, thereby either automatically terminating the swap or leaving the decision to the trustee (noteholders) whether or not to terminate the swap.

If the trustee does not terminate the swap, then the transaction is exposed to a counterparty in a deteriorating credit situation for the future payments due under the swap agreement. If the swap is terminated, the trust may owe a sizeable termination payment to the counterparty. The method for determining the swap termination payment is specified in the swap documents for each transaction but typically it is based on the mark-to-market value of the swap. At the time of termination, the swap has a value based on its specified fixed and floating rates, the current and anticipated future interest rate environment, and remaining term of the swap. Depending on how interest rates have moved since the swap was initially settled, one of the parties will be in the money and one will be out of the money. The party that is out of the money will owe the value of its position to the party that is in the money. Therefore, if the swap is terminated, the trust will be exposed to the interest rate risk that it was trying to hedge and it may owe the counterparty a termination payment. Depending on where it is specified in the distribution waterfall, the termination payment could be senior to interest or principal that is due to the transaction's noteholders. When evaluating a transaction, one should consider the interest rate risk to which the trust is exposed without the hedge, the counterparty risk of rating downgrade or default, and the possibility of a potential termination payment being paid senior to current interest and principal due noteholders.

CREDIT ENHANCEMENT

The way credit enhancement works is some third party is either paid a fee (or an insurance premium) or earns extra yield on a security in the structure to assume credit risk. There are two forms of credit enhance-ment—external and internal. *External credit enhancement* involves third-party guarantees such as insurance or a letter of credit. *Internal credit enhancement* includes overcollateralization, senior-subordinate structures, and reserves. Deals often have more than one form of credit enhancement. The rating agencies specify the amount of credit enhance-ment required to obtain a specific credit rating. The issuer decides on what mechanisms to use.

It is critical for the issuer to examine each form of credit enhance-ment prior to issuance to determine the enhancement mechanism or combination of credit enhancement mechanisms that is most cost effec-tive. Due to changing market conditions, the least expensive form of credit enhancement today may not be the least expensive in a subse-quent securitization transaction.

As explained earlier, the reason why an issuer does not simply seek a triple-A rating for all the securities in the structure is that there is a cost to doing so. The issuer must examine the cost of credit-enhancing a structure to obtain a triple-A rating versus the reduction in the yield (i.e., the increase in price) at which it can offer the securities due to a triple-A rating. In general the issuer, in deciding to improve the credit rating on some securities in a structure, will evaluate the tradeoff associ-ated with the cost of enhancement versus the reduction in yield required to sell the security.

Below we describe the various forms of credit enhancement mecha-nisms.

External Credit Enhancements

External credit enhancements come in the form of third-party guarantees that provide for first-loss protection against losses up to a specified amount. Historically, the most common forms of external credit enhance-ments have been letters of credit and bond insurance. A structure with external credit support is subject to the credit risk of the third-party guar-antor. Should the third-party guarantor be downgraded, the bond classes of a transaction guaranteed by that entity could be subject to downgrade depending on the historical performance of the collateral. This is the chief disadvantage of third-party guarantees.

External credit enhancements do not materially alter the cash-flow characteristics of a structure except in the form of prepayment. In case of a default resulting in credit losses within the guarantee level, inves-tors will receive the principal amount as if a prepayment has occurred. If the credit losses exceed the guarantee level, investors may realize a shortfall in the cash flow.

Letter of Credit

A bank letter of credit (LOC), one of the oldest forms of credit enhancement but one that has been rarely used in recent years, is a financial guarantee by the issuing bank.[4] The financial guarantee specifies that the issuing bank is committed to reimburse credit losses up to a predetermined amount.

Two are two reasons for the decline in the popularity of LOCs for credit enhancing in securitization transactions. First, there are few banks that have retained triple-A ratings and even for those that have, there is the risk that they will be downgraded in the future. As noted above, a downgrading may result in the downgrading of the affected bond classes. Second, risk-based capital requirements have changed since this form of credit enhancement was first popular. These requirements have made it more expensive for banks to issue standby letters of credit, thereby increasing the cost to entities seeking to use them as a form of credit enhancement.

Bond Insurance[5]

Bond insurance, also called a *surety bond*, is a financial guarantee from an insurance company, usually a so-called monoline insurance company that specializes in one line of insurance—in this case financial guarantees. The guarantee is for the timely payments of principal and interest if these payments cannot be satisfied from the cash flow from the underlying loan pool. The principal payments will be made without acceleration, except if the insurer elects to do so. The most prominent monoline insurers in this field are Ambac Assurance Corporation (Ambac), Financial Guaranty Insurance Corporation (FGIC), Financial Security Assurance (FSA), Municipal Bond Insurance Corporation (MBIA), and XL Capital Assurance, while the most prominent reinsurers are ACE Guaranty Re, AXA Re Finance, Enhance Re, and RAM Re.

Based on historical experience with financial guarantees by monoline insurers, capital market participants have a high degree of confidence in bond insurance because no investor in any bond-insured

---

[4] A bank letter of credit issued as a guarantee, sometimes known as a standby letter of credit, is different from a commercial letter of credit used in international trade transactions, which an importer opens through a bank in favor of an exporter. The exporter is assured of payment after merchandise is shipped and documents specified in the letter of credit are presented to the bank.

[5] For a more detailed discussion of bond insurance, see Mahesh K. Kotecha, "The Role of Financial Guarantees in Asset-Backed Securities," Chapter 6 in Frank J. Fabozzi (ed.), *Issuer Perspectives on Securitization* (Hoboken, NJ: John Wiley & Sons, 1998).

security has failed to receive a single timely payment of principal or interest. Moreover, downgrade risk is viewed as minimal because no U.S. financial guarantee company has been downgraded. Investors realize another benefit from bond insurance. While rating agencies face reputational risk when assigning a rating to a security, monoline insurers are placing their own capital and credit rating at risk. Hence, investors can correctly expect that the transaction structure is inherently safe and that is will remain so over the life of the securities guaranteed.

Internal Credit Enhancements

Internal credit enhancements come in more complicated forms than external credit enhancements and may alter cash flow characteristics of loans even in the absence of default. Credit enhancement levels (i.e., the amount of subordination for each form of enhancement utilized within a deal) are determined by the rating agencies from which the issuer seeks a rating for the bond classes. This is referred to as "sizing" the transaction, and is based on the rating agencies' expectations for the performance of the loans collateralizing the deal in question. Typically, a triple-A or double-A rating is sought for the deal's most senior bond classes. The type and amount of credit enhancement utilized in a deal represents the intersection of the issuer's need to maximize deal proceeds and the rating agencies' judgment with respect to how much credit enhancement is required in order to bestow the desired rating on the senior bond classes.

The most common forms of internal credit enhancements are senior/subordinate structures, overcollateralization, and reserve funds. The credit enhancement forms are used both individually and in combination, depending on the loan types in question. Typically, securitizations where underlying credit performance is historically strong utilize senior/subordinate structures, since the credit enhancement required is relatively small and the senior/subordinate structure offers efficient execution. Deals backed by lower-quality loans require higher levels of enhancement, and typically utilize a combination of the above-referenced credit enhancement forms.

Most securitization transactions that employ internal credit enhancements follow a predetermined schedule that prioritizes the manner in which principal and interest generated by the underlying collateral must be used. This schedule, which is set down in the deal's prospectus, is known as the *cash flow waterfall*, or simply the *waterfall*. At the top of the waterfall would be cash flows due to senior bondholders (interest and principal, depending upon the principal payment schedule) as well as some standard fees and expenses (e.g., the servicing fee). After the cash flow obligations at the top of the waterfall are met, cash flows down to lower priority classes (AA, A, BBB bond classes and so on).

The cash flow that remains after all of the scheduled periodic payment obligations are met is the excess spread. In a sense, therefore, this excess spread is the first line of defense against collateral losses, since deals that are structured to have a large amount of excess spread can absorb relatively large levels of collateral losses. If the excess spread is fully absorbed by losses, the bondholders, starting with the most junior, subordinate class and working up to the more senior classes, will begin to be negatively affected by credit losses.

In discussing internal credit enhancement, we should emphasize that the goal is to optimize the conflicting needs to create protection for the higher-rated bond classes in the deal while maximizing deal proceeds. The market has developed certain structuring conventions for different products and sectors. An important point of note is that these conventions are not dictated by regulatory fiat, but are created where credit protection and economic efficiency intersect.

Senior-Subordinate Structure

The senior-subordinate structure involves the subordination of some bond classes for the benefit of attaining a high investment-grade rating for other bond classes in the structure. Based on an analysis of the collateral, a rating agency will decide how many triple-A bonds can be issued, how many double-A bonds, and so forth down to nonrated bonds. A structure can have simply two bond classes, a senior bond class and a subordinate bond class. Or it can have several subordinate bond classes in addition to the senior bond class.

For example, suppose that a senior-subordinate structure for $200 million of collateral is as follows:

Bond Class	Rating	Percent of Structure	Par Value
A	AAA	65%	$130 million
B	AA	20%	$40 million
C	BBB	10%	$20 million
D	Not rated	5%	$10 million

Bond class A is the senior bond class. The subordinate bond classes are B, C, and D.

The rule for recognizing losses is as follows. As a $1 of loss on the collateral is realized, that loss is first applied to bond class D. When bond class D has no balance, the next dollar of loss is applied to bond class C, and then bond class B. After all the subordinate bond classes are wiped out due to losses, the losses are realized by the senior bond class.

The cost of this form of credit enhancement is based on the proceeds for selling the bonds which is, in turn, determined by the demand for the bonds. The yields that must be offered on the bond classes are subject to investor demands. The lower the credit rating of the bond class (i.e., the more likely the bond class is to realize a loss), the more yield that investors will demand and the lower the proceeds that will be received from the sale of the bonds for that bond class. The proceeds for the sale of all the bond classes have to be compared to the cost of the collateral pool.

One of the perceived advantages of internal credit enhancements such as overcollateralization and the senior-subordinate structures is the relative lack of event risk that accompanies external credit enhancement (i.e., a third-party guarantee). The assets in the collateral pool are intended to provide all the required credit support and investors are at risk only with regard to the performance of those assets.

Senior/Subordinate Structure with Shifting Interest Mechanism for Mortgage Deals Almost all existing senior/subordinate structures backed by residential mortgage loans also incorporate a *shifting interest structure*. This structure redirects principal prepayments disproportionately from the subordinate bond class to the senior bond class according to a specified schedule. The rationale for the shifting interest structure is to have enough subordinate bond classes outstanding to cover future credit losses.

The basic credit concern that investors in the senior bond class have is that while the subordinate bond classes provides a certain level of credit protection for the senior bond class at the closing of the deal, the level of protection may deteriorate over time due to prepayments and certain liquidation proceeds. The objective is to distribute these payments of principal such that the credit protection for the senior bond class does not deteriorate over time.

The percentage of the mortgage balance of the subordinate bond class to that of the mortgage balance for the entire deal is called the *level of subordination* or the *subordinate interest*. The higher the percentage, the greater the level of protection for the senior bond class. The subordinate interest changes after the deal is closed due to prepayments. That is, the subordinate interest shifts (hence the term "shifting interest"). The purpose of a shifting interest mechanism is to allocate prepayments and certain liquidation proceeds so that the subordinate interest is maintained at an acceptable level to protect the senior bond class.

Now let's be more specific about how the shifting interest mechanism works. The *senior percentage* is defined as the ratio of the balance of the senior bond class to the balance of the entire deal. It is also called the *senior interest* and is equal to 100% minus the subordinate interest. The prospectus specifies how different scheduled principal payments and prepayments will be allocated between the senior bond class and the subordinate bond class.

The scheduled principal payments are allocated based on the senior percentage. So, if in some month the senior percentage is 82% and the scheduled principal payment is $1 million, then the senior bond class will get $820,000 and the subordinate bond class $180,000.

Allocation of the prepayments is based on the *senior prepayment percentage*.[6] This is defined as follows:

Senior percentage + (Shifting interest percentage × Subordinate interest)

The "shifting interest percentage" in the formula above is specified in the prospectus, and we provide an illustration shortly. To illustrate the formula, suppose that in some month the senior interest is 82%, the subordinate interest is 18%, and the shifting interest percentage is 70%. The senior prepayment percentage for that month is:

$$82\% + (0.70 \times 18\%) = 94.6\%$$

Thus, if prepayments for the month are $100,000, then $94,600 is allocated to the senior bond class and $5,400 to the subordinate bond class.

The prospectus will provide the shifting interest percentage schedule for calculating the senior prepayment percentage. For fixed-rate mortgages, a commonly used shifting interest percentage schedule is as follows:

Year after Issuance	Shifting Interest Percentage
1–5	100
6	70
7	60
8	40
9	20
After year 9	0

The shifting interest percentage schedule given in the prospectus is the "base" schedule. The schedule can change over time depending on the performance of the collateral. If the performance is such that the credit protection is deteriorating or may deteriorate, the base shifting

---

[6] In some deals it is called the *accelerated distribution percentage*.

interest percentages are overridden and a higher allocation of prepayments is made to the senior bond class. The trustee undertakes performance analysis to determine whether to override the base schedule. The performance analysis is concerned with whether the collateral or structure fails certain tests, thus triggering an override of the base schedule. We discuss these provisions later.

While the shifting interest structure is beneficial to the senior bond class holder from a credit standpoint, it also alters the cash-flow characteristics of the senior bond class even in the absence of defaults. The size of the subordination also matters. A larger subordinate class redirects a higher proportion of prepayments to the senior bond class, thereby shortening the average life of the senior bond class even further.

Overcollateralization

The total par value of the bond classes is the liability of the structure. So, if a structure has two bond classes with a total par value of $400 million, then that is the amount of the liability. The amount of the collateral backing the structure must be at least equal to the amount of the liability. If the amount of the collateral exceeds the amount of the liability of the structure, the deal is said to be *overcollateralized*. The amount of overcollateralization represents a form of internal credit enhancement because it can be used to absorb losses. For example, if the liability of the structure is $400 million and the collateral's value is $410 million, then the structure is overcollateralized by $10 million. Thus, the first $10 million of losses will not result in a loss to any of the bond classes in the structure.

Overcollateralization can be generated after the transaction *closes* through excess spread which we discuss below. In addition, the collateral in a transaction may be divided into separate groups, each supporting a separate class of bonds. An example occurs in the securitization of home equity loan transactions where one class of bonds may be supported by fixed-rate loans and another class of bonds may be supported by adjustable-rate loans. As explained next, each group of financial assets will have excess spread. The excess spread will be used first to support the class of bonds created from the same group of loans. Any remaining excess spread can be used to support other bond classes. This feature is called a cross-support provision and this type of enhancement is known as *cross collateralization*. The manner and conditions for applying a cross-support provision is explained in the prospectus supplement.

After all the bonds in a transaction have been retired, the remaining funds in the reserve account and any remaining collateral are distributed to the originator (assuming the originator has not sold its interest in the collateral).

The cost of an overcollateralization as a form of credit enhancement is implicit in the price paid of tying up collateral.

Reserve Funds

Reserve funds come in two forms: cash reserve funds and excess spread. *Cash reserve funds* are straight deposits of cash generated from issuance proceeds. In this case, part of the underwriting proceeds from the deal are deposited into a hypothecated fund, which typically invests in money market instruments.

Excess spread accounts involve the monthly allocation of excess spread or cash into a separate reserve account after paying out the net coupon, servicing fee, and all other expenses. For example, suppose that (1) the gross weighted average contract rate (gross WAC rate) for the collateral is 7.75%; (2) the servicing and other fees are 0.25%; and (3) the net weighted average contract rate (net WAC rate) of the bond classes issued is 7.25%. This means that there is excess servicing of 0.25% (7.75% minus 0.25% minus 7.25%). The amount in the reserve account will gradually increase and can be used to cover possible future losses.

The excess spread is a form of self-insurance. As described previously, excess spread acts as the first line of credit support for the deal. This form of credit enhancement relies on the assumption that defaults occur infrequently in the very early life of the loans but gradually increase over time.

If losses on a deal are low, the excess spread will increase. At this point, the excess spread can be deployed within the deal in a number of ways. In some deals, some of the excess spread may be used to pay additional principal to bonds within the deal. Generally speaking, however, the excess spread is part of the "equity" of a deal. At some point, excess spread will be released to either the owner of the deal's "residual" bond class (i.e., the equity interest in the deal) or to bonds in the deal that are structured to receive these cash flows. As mentioned above, such bonds are referred to as Net Interest Margin (NIM) securities.

An important feature to note in the analysis of senior/subordinate bond classes is the deal's *step-down* provisions. These provisions allow for the reduction in credit support over time. As noted above, investors in the senior bond class will be concerned about whether, if the collateral performance is deteriorating, step-down provisions should be altered. The provisions that prevent the credit support from stepping down are called "triggers."[7] Principal payments from the subordinate

---

[7] The term "trigger" also has other meanings in the field of finance, for example a provision in a loan agreement that puts the borrower in default if the borrower's credit rating falls below a certain defined level.

bond classes are diverted to the senior bond class if a trigger is reached. The diversion of principal varies from issuer to issuer. The most conservative approach is to stop all principal payments from being distributed to the subordinate bond classes. Alternatively, some issuers allow the subordinate bond classes to receive regularly scheduled principal (amortization) on a pro rata basis but divert all prepayments to the senior bond class.

There are two triggers based on the level of credit performance that must be passed before the credit support can be reduced: a delinquency trigger and loss trigger. The triggers are expressed in the form of a test that is applied in each period. The *delinquency test*, in its most common form, prevents any step-down from taking place as long as the current over 60-day delinquency rate exceeds a specified percentage of the then-current pool balance. The *principal loss test* prevents a step-down from occurring if cumulative losses exceed a certain limit (which changes over time) of the original balance of the mortgage pool.

In addition to triggers based on the performance of the collateral, there is a *balance test*, which measures the change in the senior interest from the closing to the current month. If the senior interest has increased (in other words, if the subordinate interest has decreased, reducing the level of protection for the senior bond class), the balance test has failed, triggering a revision of the base schedule for the allocation of principal payments from the subordinate bond classes to the senior bond class. Unlike a trigger that will increase the allocation to the senior bond class, there are balance tests that will increase the allocation to the subordinate bond class. This can occur where the subordinate interest improved by a significant amount. That amount is set forth in the prospectus. For example, the prospectus may set forth that if the subordinate interest doubles, the base schedule is overridden such that more is allocated to the subordinate bond class.

MORE DETAILED ILLUSTRATION OF A SECURITIZATION

We conclude this chapter with an illustration of a hypothetical securitization where the collateral is a future flow. The illustration will show the issues that will be considered by the investment bank that is structuring the deal. To illustrate, we assume a hypothetical airline ticket receivables transaction that is being originated by the fictitious ABC Airways plc, a U.K. airline, and arranged by the equally fictitious XYZ Securities Limited. We have:

Originator   ABC Airways plc

Issuer   "Airways No. 1 Ltd"

Transaction   Ticket receivables airline future flow securitization bonds,
                €200 million three-tranche floating rate notes, legal maturity 2010,
                Average life 4.1 years

Tranches   Class "A" note (AA), LIBOR plus [ ] bp
                Class "B" note (A), LIBOR plus [ ] bp
                Class "E" note (BBB), LIBOR plus [ ] bp

Arranger   XYZ Securities plc

XYZ Securities undertakes due diligence on the assets to be securitized. For this case, it examines the airline performance figures over the last five years as well as model future projected figures, including:

- total passenger sales;
- total ticket sales;
- total credit card receivables; and
- geographical split of ticket sales.

It is the future flow of receivables, in this case credit card purchases of airline tickets, that is being securitized. The nature of the underlying assets is always very important, and is the key driver behind why notes of the same credit rating and average maturity, and in the same order of seniority in a capital structure (and so theoretically identical credit risk) offer different yields at issuance. In this case, credit card receivables are a higher-risk asset class than, say, residential mortgages. Also, even though the source of repayment for the securitized notes is credit card payments from airline passengers, the financial strength of the issuer has an important bearing on the success of the securitization, as explained in the rest of this chapter.

The present and all future credit card ticket receivables generated by the airline will be transferred to an SPV. The investment bank's syndication desk will seek to place the notes with institutional investors across Europe. The notes are first given an indicative pricing ahead of the issue, to gauge investor sentiment. The notes will be "benchmarked" against recent issues with similar asset classes, as well as the spread level in the unsecured market of comparable issuer names.

The deal structure is shown at Exhibit 5.1. The process leading to issue of notes is as follows:

- ABC Airways plc sells its future flow ticket receivables to an offshore SPV set up for this deal, incorporated as Airways No. 1 Ltd;
- the SPV issues notes in order to fund its purchase of the receivables;
- the SPV pledges its right to the receivables to a fiduciary agent, the Security Trustee, for the benefit of the bondholders;
- the Trustee accumulates funds as they are received by the SPV; and
- the bondholders receive interest and principal payments, in the order of priority of the notes, on a quarterly basis.

In the event of default, the trustee acts on behalf of the bondholders to safeguard their interests.

The investment bank considers if an insurance company, a monoline insurer, should be approached to "wrap" the deal by providing a guarantee of backing for the SPV in the event of default. This insurance is provided in return for a fee.

EXHIBIT 5.1 Airways No. 1 Limited Deal Structure

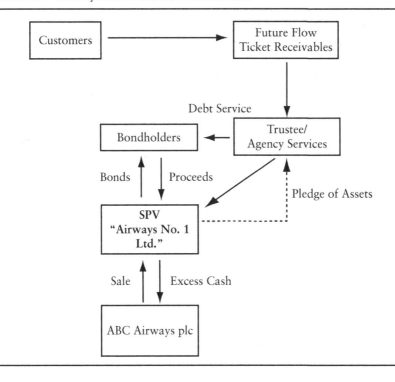

XYZ Securities constructs a cash flow model to estimate the size of the issued notes. This financial model considers historical sales volume, any seasonal variation in sales, credit card cash flows, and so on. Certain assumptions are made when constructing the model, for example, growth projections, inflation levels, tax levels, and so on. The model considers a number of different scenarios and also calculates the minimum asset coverage levels required to service the issued debt. Among those scenarios might be a slowdown in the airline's sales, which in the case of a future flow transaction, and therefore a revolving pool of assets, could lead to a shortage of assets and in turn to a paydown in waterfall order. The model then calculates the amount of notes that can be issued against the assets while maintaining the minimum asset coverage.

It would be easier for XYZ Securities to place the notes with investors if those notes have a formal credit rating. It is common for securitization deals to be rated by one or more of the three major rating agencies. As explained in the previous chapter, the methodology employed by the rating agencies takes into account both qualitative and quantitative factors, and differs according to the asset class being securitized. The main issues in a deal such as our hypothetical Airway No. 1 deal would be expected to include:

■ *Corporate credit quality*: These are risks associated with the originator, and are factors that affect its ability to continue operations, meet its financial obligations, and provide a stable foundation for generating future receivables. This might be analyzed according to the following: (1) ABC Airways' historical financial performance, including its liquidity and debt structure; (2) its status within its domicile country, for example, whether it is state owned; (3) the general economic conditions for industry and for airlines; and (4) the historical record and current state of the airline, for instance its safety record and age of its aircraft.
■ *Competition and industry trends*: ABC Airways' market share, the competition on its network.
■ *Regulatory issues*: Such as need for ABC Airways to comply with forthcoming legislation that would impact its cash flows.
■ *Legal structure*: That is of the SPV and transfer of assets.
■ *Cash flow analysis*.

Based on the findings of the ratings agency, the arranger may redesign some aspect of the deal structure so that the issued notes are rated at the required level.

This is a selection of the key issues involved in the process of securitization. Depending on investor sentiment, market conditions and legal issues, the process from inception to closure of the deal may take anything from 3 to 12 months or more. After the notes have been issued, the arranging bank no longer has anything to do with the issue. However, the notes themselves require a number of agency services for their remaining life until they mature or are paid off. These agency service roles include paying agent, cash manager, and custodian.

CHAPTER 6

Cash Flow Collateralized Debt Obligations

The *collateralized debt obligation* (CDO) was a natural advancement of securitization technology, first introduced in 1988. A CDO is essentially a structured finance product in which a distinct legal entity, a special purpose vehicle (SPV), issues bonds or notes against an investment in cash flows of an underlying pool of assets. These assets include one or more of the following types of debt obligations:

- investment-grade and high-yield corporate bonds;
- emerging market bonds;
- residential mortgage-backed securities (RMBS);
- commercial mortgage-backed securities (CMBS);
- asset-backed securities (ABS);
- real estate investment trusts (REIT) debt;
- bank loans;
- special-situation loans and distressed debt; and
- other CDOs.

When the underlying pool of debt obligations consists of bond-type instruments, a CDO is referred to as a *collateralized bond obligation* (CBO). These CDOs are classified as *corporate bond-backed CDOs, emerging market-backed CDOs,* and *structured finance-backed CDOs.* The collateral for the latter includes RMBS, CMBS, ABS, and REIT debt. When the underlying pool of debt obligations is bank loans, a CDO is referred to as a *collateralized loan obligation* (CLO).

Originally CDOs were developed as repackaging structures for high-yield corporate bonds and illiquid instruments such as certain convertible bonds, but they have developed into sophisticated investment management vehicles in their own right. Through the 1990s, CDOs were the fastest growing asset class in the ABS market, due to a number of features that made them attractive to issuers and investors alike. A subsequent development was the synthetic CDO, a structure that uses credit derivatives in its construction and is therefore called a *structured credit product.*

In this chapter we explain the basic CDO structure, the types of CDOs, and the motivation for creating a portfolio of CDOs. Our focus in this chapter is on cash flow CDOs. In the next chapter, we cover synthetic CDOs.

FAMILY OF CDOs

The CDO family is shown in Exhibit 6.1. The first distinction in the CDO family is between cash CDOs and synthetic CDOs. A *cash CDO* is backed by a pool of cash-market debt instruments. These were the original types of CDOs issued.

A *synthetic CDO* is a CDO where the investor has economic exposure to a pool of debt instruments, but this exposure is realized via a credit derivative rather than the purchase of the cash-market instruments.

Both a cash CDO and a synthetic CDO are further divided based on the motivation of the sponsor. The motivation is either "balance sheet" or "arbitrage." As explained below, in a *balance sheet CDO*, the motivation of the sponsor is to remove assets from its balance sheet. In an *arbitrage CDO,* the motivations of the sponsor are (1) to gain a fee for managing the underlying pool of assets of the CDOs and (2) to capture a spread between the return realized on the collateral underlying the CDO and the cost of borrowing funds to purchase that collateral (i.e., the interest rate paid on the CDOs' debt).

Cash arbitrage CDOs are further divided into cash flow and market value CDOs depending on the credit protection mechanism that ensures repayment of the CDO's debt. In a *cash flow CDO,* the after-default interest, maturing principal, and default recoveries from the underlying assets provide CDO debt with credit protection. In a *market value CDO,* the ability of the CDO to realize sufficient proceeds from the sale of its assets to repay its debt provides the CDO debt with credit protection. There has been little issuance of market value CDOs since the 1980s. This is because sponsors who were motivated to use them for balance sheet management purposes generally stopped using them after a change in accounting rules in the 1990s. Our focus in this chapter is therefore on cash flow CDOs.

EXHIBIT 6.1 The CDO Family

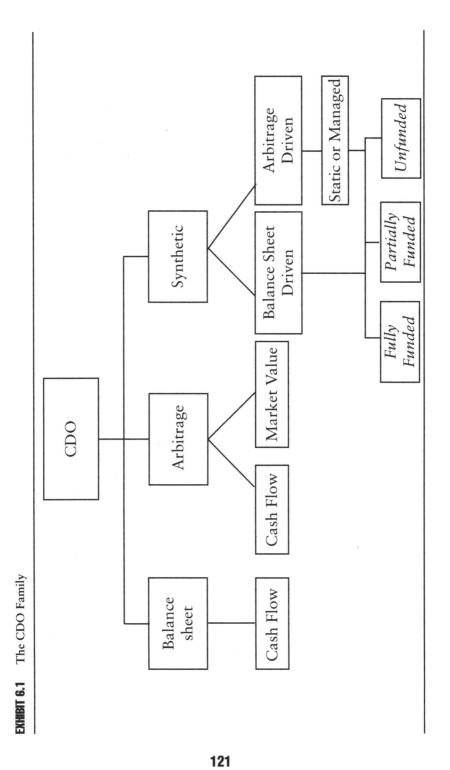

BASIC STRUCTURE OF A CASH FLOW CDO

In a CDO, there is an *asset manager* responsible for managing the portfolio. The manager is referred to as the "CDO manager" or the "collateral manager." There are restrictions imposed (i.e., restrictive covenants) as to what the CDO manager may do and certain tests that must be satisfied for the CDO securities to maintain the credit rating assigned at the time of issuance. We'll discuss some of these requirements later.

The funds to purchase the underlying assets or collateral (i.e., the bonds and loans) are obtained from the issuance of debt obligations. The total debt obligations for a given CDO are generally divided into several different classes or "tranches" (from the French word for "slice"), each with a different risk profile to suit different investor preferences. The tranches are generally ranked by seniority as follows:

- senior tranches;
- mezzanine tranches; and
- subordinate/equity tranche.

A rating will be sought for all but the subordinate/equity tranche. Senior tranches typically are rated AAA or AA. Mezzanine tranches typically are rated A through B. Since the subordinate/equity tranche receives the residual cash flow, no rating is sought for this tranche.

The ability of the CDO to make the interest payments to the tranches and pay off the tranches as they mature depends on the performance of the underlying assets. The proceeds to meet the obligations to the CDO tranches (interest and principal repayment) can come from (1) coupon interest payments from the underlying assets, (2) maturing assets in the underlying pool, and (3) sale of assets in the underlying pool.

To maintain the credit quality of the CDO's portfolio, trading restrictions are imposed to constrain the CDO manager's authority to buy and sell bonds. The conditions for disposing of assets are specified and usually are driven by credit-risk considerations. We will discuss these considerations later. Also, in assembling the portfolio, the CDO manager must meet certain requirements set forth by the agencies that rate the transaction.

There are three distinct periods in the life of a CDO. The first is the *ramp-up period*. This period usually begins two to six months before the closing date of the transaction and usually ends fewer than six months afterwards when the CDO manager completes the purchase of the CDO's initial portfolio. The *reinvestment period* or revolving period is when principal proceeds are reinvested in new collateral assets and usually is five to seven years long. In the *final period*, the portfolio assets mature or are sold, and the note holders are paid off as described next.

Distribution of Income

Income is derived from interest income and capital appreciation on underlying assets. The income is then used as follows: Payments are first made to the trustee and administrators and then for the CDO manager's senior fee. Once these fees are paid, the senior tranches are paid their interest. At this point, before any other payments are made, certain compliance tests must be passed. These tests are will be discussed later. If the compliance tests are passed, then interest is paid to the mezzanine tranches. Once the mezzanine tranches are paid, another set of compliance tests is conducted. If these compliance tests are passed, interest is paid to the subordinate/equity tranche. Such a distribution schedule is often called a *waterfall*.

In contrast, if either senior or mezzanine compliance tests are failed, then, depending on the CDO's structure and how severely those tests are failed, available income is used either to pay down senior tranche principal or purchase more collateral assets. If the senior tranches are paid off fully but mezzanine compliance tests are failed, then any remaining income after paying interest to the mezzanine tranche is used to redeem the mezzanine tranches. Only after senior debt and mezzanine debt are paid interest and any principal that is due as a result of the failure of the compliance test does any remaining CDO income flow to the subordinate/equity tranche.

During the life of the CDO transaction, a portfolio administrator will produce a periodic report detailing the quality of the collateral pool. This report is known as an investor or *trustee report* and also shows the results of the compliance tests that are required to affirm that the tranches of the CDO have maintained their credit ratings.

Distribution of Principal Cash Flow

Principal cash flow from CDO assets is distributed as follows after the payment of the fees to the trustees, administrators, and senior managers. If there is a shortfall in interest paid to the senior tranches, principal proceeds are used to make up the shortfall. Assuming that the compliance tests are satisfied during the reinvestment period, principal is reinvested. After the reinvestment period or if the compliance tests are failed, principal cash flow is used to pay down the senior tranches until the compliance tests are satisfied. If all the senior tranches are paid down, then the mezzanine tranches are paid off, and then the subordinate/equity tranche is paid off.

After all the debt obligations are satisfied in full, the subordinate/equity investors are paid. Typically, there are also incentive fees paid to management based on performance. Usually, a target return for the subordinate/equity investors is established at the inception of the transaction. Management is then permitted to share on some *pro rata* basis once the target return is achieved.

CDOs AND SPONSOR MOTIVATION

As can be seen in Exhibit 6.1, cash flow CDOs are categorized according to the motivation of their sponsors: balance sheet CDOs and arbitrage CDOs.

Balance Sheet CDOs

Cash flow CDOs are similar to other asset-backed securitizations involving SPVs. Bonds or loans are pooled together, and the cash flows from these assets are used to back the liabilities of the notes issued by the SPV into the market. As the underlying assets are sold to the SPV, they are removed from the originator's balance sheet; hence the credit risk associated with these assets is transferred to the holders of the issued notes

Banks and other financial institutions are the primary originators of *balance sheet CDOs*. These are deals securitizing banking assets such as commercial loans of investment-grade or subinvestment-grade rating. The main motivations for entering into this arrangement are:

- to obtain regulatory relief;
- to increase return on capital via the removal of lower yielding assets from the balance sheet;
- to secure alternative and/or cheaper sources of funding; and
- to free up lending capacity with respect to an industry or other category of borrowers.

Investors are often attracted to balance sheet CDOs because they are perceived as offering a higher return than say, credit card ABS, at a similar level of risk exposure. They also represent a diversification away from traditional ABS investments. The asset pool in a balance sheet CDO is static, that is, it is not traded or actively managed by a portfolio manager. For this reason the structure is similar to more traditional ABS or repackaging vehicles.

Arbitrage Motivated CDOs

A *cash flow arbitrage* CDO has certain similarities with a balance sheet CDO, and if it is a static pool CDO, it is also conceptually similar to an ABS deal.[1] The priority of payments is similar, starting from expenses, Trustee and servicing fees, senior noteholders, and so on down to the most junior noteholder.

---

[1] Except that in a typical ABS deal such as a consumer or trade receivables deal, or a residential MBS deal, there are a large number of individual underlying assets, whereas with a CBO or CLO there may be as few as 20 underlying loans or bonds.

The key as to whether it is economically feasible to create an arbitrage CDO is whether a structure can offer a competitive return to the equity tranche.

To understand how the equity tranche generates cash flows, consider the following basic $100 million CDO structure with the coupon rate to be offered at the time of issuance as follows:

Tranche	Par Value	Coupon Type	Coupon Rate
Senior	$80,000,000	Floating	LIBOR + 70 bp
Mezzanine	10,000,000	Fixed	Treasury rate + 200 bp
Equity	10,000,000	—	—

Suppose that the collateral consists of high-yield bonds that all mature in 10 years and the coupon rate for every bond is the 10-year Treasury rate plus 400 bp. The CDO enters into an interest rate swap agreement with another party with a notional principal of $80 million in which the CDO agrees to do the following:

- Pay a fixed rate each year equal to the 10-year Treasury rate plus 100 bp
- Receive LIBOR

Keep in mind, the goal is to show how the equity tranche can be expected to generate a return.

Let's assume that the 10-year Treasury rate at the time the CDO is issued is 7%. Now we can walk through the cash flows for each year. Look first at the collateral. The collateral will pay interest each year (assuming no defaults) equal to the 10-year Treasury rate of 7% plus 400 bp. So the interest will be

Interest from collateral: $11\% \times \$100,000,000 = \$11,000,000$

Now let's determine the interest that must be paid to the senior and mezzanine tranches. For the senior tranche, the interest payment will be

Interest to senior tranche: $\$80,000,000 \times (\text{LIBOR} + 70 \text{ bp})$

The coupon rate for the mezzanine tranche is 7% plus 200 bp. So, the coupon rate is 9% and the interest is

Interest to mezzanine tranche: $9\% \times \$10,000,000 = \$900,000$

Finally, let's look at the interest rate swap. In this agreement, the CDO manager is agreeing to the swap counterparty 7% each year (the 10-year Treasury rate) plus 100 bp, or 8%. In our illustration because the notional principal is $80 million, the CDO manager selected the $80 million because this is the amount of principal for the senior tranche. So, the CDO manager pays to the swap counterparty:

Interest to swap counterparty: $8\% \times \$80,000,000 = \$6,400,000$

The interest payment received from the swap counterparty is LIBOR based on a notional amount of $80 million. That is,

Interest from swap counterparty: $\$80,000,000 \times LIBOR$

Now we can put this all together. Let's look at the interest coming into the CDO:

Interest from collateral	= $11,000,000
Interest from swap counterparty	= $80,000,000 × LIBOR
Total interest received	= $11,000,000 + [$80,000,000 × LIBOR]

The interest to be paid out to the senior and mezzanine tranches and to the swap counterparty are:

Interest to senior tranche	= $80,000,000 × (LIBOR + 70 bp)
Interest to mezzanine tranche	= $900,000
Interest to swap counterparty	= $6,400,000
Total interest paid	= $7,300,000 + [$80,000,000 × (LIBOR + 70 bp)]

Netting the interest payments coming in and going out we have:

Total interest received	= $11,000,000 + [$80,000,000 × LIBOR]
−Total interest paid	= $7,300,000 + [$80,000,000 × (LIBOR + 70 bp)]
Net interest	= $3,700,000 − [$80,000,000 × (70 bp)]

Since 70 bp times $80 million is $560,000, the net interest remaining is $3,140,000 (= $3,700,000 − $560,000). From this amount, any fees (including the asset management fee) must be paid. The balance is then the amount available to pay the subordinate/equity tranche. Suppose that these fees are $614,000. Then the cash flow available to the equity tranche is $2.5 million. Since the tranche has a par value of $10 million and is assumed to be sold at par, this means that the potential return is 25%.

Obviously, some simplifying assumptions have been made. For example, it is assumed that there are no defaults. It is assumed that all of the issues purchased by the CDO manager are noncallable (or not prepayable) and therefore the coupon rate would not decline because issues are called. Moreover, after some period the CDO must begin repaying principal to the senior and mezzanine tranches. Consequently, the interest swap must be structured to take this into account since the entire amount of the senior tranche is not outstanding for the life of the collateral.

In fact, the poor collateral performance of CBOs backed by high-yield corporate bonds from 2000 to 2003 was further compounded by their interest rate hedging strategy. Collateral managers of CBOs entered into agreements to pay fixed and receive floating on interest rate swaps. As interest rates fell during the period, CBO collateral managers were net payers on these swaps. Such an interest rate hedging strategy would not have been a problem if the CDO portfolios and liabilities were still intact. The collateral manager would have used fixed-rate payments from their portfolios to pay the fixed rate on the swap, and used the floating-rate payment coming from the swap to pay the floating-rate bondholders on their liabilities. But bond defaults on high-yield corporate bonds had reduced CBO portfolios and the working of overcollateralization triggers (discussed later) had accelerated the principal paydown of CBO liabilities. This caused the notional amount of the interest rate swap to be greater than the amount of the assets and liabilities in CBOs. As a result, many CBOs were overhedged, resulting in losses on their hedge positions.[2]

Despite the simplifying assumptions, the illustration above does demonstrate the basic economics of the CDO, the need for the use of an interest rate swap, and how the equity tranche realizes a return.

COMPLIANCE TESTS

The basic CDO structure is designed to split the aggregate credit risk of the collateral pool into various tranches, which are the overlying notes, each of which has a different credit exposure from the other. As a result each note exhibits a different risk/reward profile, and so will attract itself to different classes of investors.

The notes issued have different risk profiles as a result of their relative subordination, that is, the notes are structured in descending order of seniority. In addition, the structure makes use of *credit enhancements* to varying degrees, which may include:

---

[2] Douglas Lucas, Laurie S. Goodman, and Frank J. Fabozzi, *Collateralized Debt Obligations: Structures and Analysis* (Hoboken, NJ: John Wiley & Sons, 2006).

- *Overcollateralization:* The overlying notes are lower in value compared to the underlying pool; for example, $250 million nominal of assets are used as backing for $170 million nominal of issued bonds.
- *Cash reserve accounts:* A reserve is maintained in a cash account and used to cover initial losses; the funds may be sourced from part of the debt proceeds.
- *Excess spread:* Cash inflows from assets exceed the interest service requirements of liabilities.
- *Insurance wraps:* Losses suffered by the asset pool are covered by insurance, for which an insurance premium is paid as long as the cover is needed.

The quality of the collateral pool is monitored regularly and reported on by the portfolio administrator, who produces the investor report. This report details the results of various *compliance tests*, which are undertaken at individual asset level as well as the aggregate level.

Compliance tests are specified as part of the process leading up to the issue of notes, in discussion between the originator and the rating agency or rating agencies. The ratings analysis is comprehensive and focuses on the quality of the collateral, individual asset default probabilities, the structure of the deal, and the track record and reputation of the originator. If a CDO fails an important compliance test such as the coverage tests described below, the portfolio administrator will inform the deal originator (or collateral manager). Upon this occurrence, an immediate restriction is placed on any further trading by the vehicle and the originator has 30 days to rectify the position. After this date, the only trading that is permitted is that required on a credit risk basis (to mitigate credit risk and possible further loss due to say, defaults in the portfolio). At the next coupon date, known as the determination date, if the collateral manager still fails the compliance test, then principal on the notes will begin to be paid off, in order of priority. During this phase, the CDO is also likely to be put on "credit watch" by the credit rating agency, with a view to possible downgrade, because the underlying portfolio will be viewed as having deteriorated in quality from the time of its original rating analysis.

There are two types of compliance tests, quality tests and coverage tests.

Quality Tests

Quality tests include a (1) minimum collateral diversification score, (2) minimum weighted-average rating, and (3) minimum weighted-average coupon, and weighted-average spread. These tests are calculated on a regular basis and also each time the composition of the assets changes—

for example, because certain assets have been sold, new assets purchased, or because bonds have paid off ahead of their legal maturity date. If the test results fall below the required minimum, trading activity is restricted to only those trades that will improve the test results.

A *collateral diversification score* is used to gauge the diversity of the collateral's assets. All rating agencies have diversity scores. The greater the score value, the more diverse is the CDO portfolio across industries. Every time the composition of the collateral changes, a diversity measure is computed. The most well-known diversity score is the one developed by Moody's.

A measure is also needed to gauge the credit quality of the collateral. Certainly one can describe the distribution of the credit ratings of the collateral in terms of the percentage of the collateral's assets in each credit rating. However, such a measure would be awkward in establishing tests for a minimum credit rating for the collateral. There is a need to have one figure that summarizes the rating distribution test.

Moody's and Fitch have developed a measure to summarize the rating distribution. This is commonly called the *weighted-average rating factor* (WARF) for the collateral. This involves assigning a numerical value to each rating. These numerical values are called *rating factors*. The CDO manager must maintain a minimum average rating score. Unlike Moody's and Fitch, S&P uses a different system. S&P specifies required rating percentages that the collateral must maintain. Specifically, S&P requires strict percentage limits for lower-rated assets in the collateral portfolio.

Coverage Tests

The other type of compliance tests, coverage tests, are viewed as more important than quality tests, since if any of them are "failed," the cash flows will be diverted from the normal waterfall as described earlier and will be used to begin paying off the senior notes until the test results improve. These include the overcollateralization test and the interest coverage test. We will be described each below.

Overcollateralization Tests

The *overcollateralization ratio* (OC ratio) for a tranche is found by computing the ratio of the principal balance of the collateral portfolio divided by the principal balance of that tranche plus all tranches senior to it. That is,

$$\text{OC ratio for a tranche}$$
$$= \frac{\text{Principal (par) value of collateral}}{\text{Principal for tranche} + \text{Principal for all tranches senior to it}}$$

The higher the ratio, the greater protection there is for the note holders. Note that the OC ratio is based on the principal or par value of the assets. (Hence an overcollateralization test is also called a *par value test.*) An OC ratio is computed for specified tranches subject to the overcollateralization test. The overcollateralization test for a tranche involves comparing the tranche's OC ratio with the tranche's required minimum ratio as specified in the guidelines. The required minimum ratio is called the *overcollateralization trigger.* The overcollateralization test for a tranche is passed if the OC ratio is greater than or equal to its respective overcollateralization trigger.

For example, suppose that a cash flow CDO has two rated tranches that are subject to the overcollateralization test—classes A and B. Therefore, two overcollateralization ratios are computed for this deal. For each tranche, the overcollateralization test involves first computing the OC ratio as follows:

$$\text{OC ratio for Class A} = \frac{\text{Principal (par) value of collateral portfolio}}{\text{Principal for Class A}}$$

$$\text{OC ratio for Class B} = \frac{\text{Principal (par) value of collateral portfolio}}{\text{Principal for Class A} + \text{Principal for Class B}}$$

Once the OC ratio for a tranche is computed, it is then compared with the overcollateralization trigger for the tranche as specified in the guidelines. If the computed OC ratio is greater than or equal to the overcollateralization trigger for the tranche, then the test is passed with respect to that tranche.

Suppose that the overcollateralization trigger is 113% for class A and 101% for class B. Note that the lower is the seniority, the lower is the overcollateralization trigger. The class A overcollateralization test is failed if the ratio falls below 113%, and the class B overcollateralization test is failed if the ratio falls below 101%.

Interest Coverage Tests

The *interest coverage ratio* (IC ratio) for a tranche is the ratio of scheduled interest due on the underlying collateral portfolio to scheduled interest to be paid to that tranche and all tranches senior to it. That is,

IC ratio for a tranche

$$= \frac{\text{Scheduled interest due on underlying collateral portfolio}}{\text{Scheduled interest for tranche} + \text{Scheduled interest for all tranches senior}}$$

The higher the IC ratio, the greater is the protection. An IC ratio is computed for specified tranches subject to the interest coverage test. The interest coverage test for a tranche involves comparing the tranche's IC ratio with the tranche's *interest coverage trigger* (i.e., the required minimum ratio as specified in the guidelines). The interest coverage test for a tranche is passed if the computed IC ratio is greater than or equal to its respective interest coverage trigger.

Consider once again our hypothetical cash flow CDO where classes A and B are subject to the interest coverage test. The following two IC ratios therefore are computed:

IC ratio for Class A

$$= \frac{\text{Scheduled interest due on underlying collateral portfolio}}{\text{Scheduled interest to Class A}}$$

IC ratio for Class B

$$= \frac{\text{Scheduled interest due on underlying collateral portfolio}}{\text{Scheduled interest to Class A} + \text{Scheduled interest to Class B}}$$

CHAPTER 7

Synthetic Collateralized Debt
Obligation Structures

The ongoing development of securitization technology has resulted in more complex structured finance products, as illustrated by the synthetic collateralized debt obligation (CDO). This structured credit product was introduced to meet differing needs of originators, where credit risk transfer is of more importance than funding considerations. Compared with cash CDO deals, which feature an actual transfer of ownership or *true sale* of the underlying assets to a separately incorporated legal entity, a synthetic securitization structure is engineered so that the credit risk of the assets is transferred by the sponsor or originator of the transaction, from itself, to the investors by means of credit derivative instruments. The originator is therefore the credit protection buyer and investors are the credit protection sellers. This credit risk transfer may be undertaken either directly or via an SPV. Using this approach, underlying or *reference* assets are not necessarily moved off the originator's balance sheet, so it is adopted whenever the primary objective is to achieve risk transfer rather than balance sheet funding. The synthetic structure enables removal of credit exposure without asset transfer, so it may be preferred for risk management and regulatory capital relief purposes. For banking institutions, it also enables loan risk to be transferred without selling the loans themselves, thereby allowing customer relationships to remain unaffected.

In this chapter we discuss synthetic CDOs, explaining the motivation for their issuance, the mechanics of this structure, funding mechanics, investor risks, the advantages and disadvantages of these structures, variations in synthetic CDOs, and factors an investor should consider in the analysis of synthetic CDOs. A case study of a synthetic CDO transaction is presented.

MOTIVATIONS FOR SYNTHETIC CDOs

Differences between synthetic and cash CDOs are perhaps best reflected in the different cost-benefit economics of issuing each type. The motivations behind the issue of each type usually also differ.

Synthetic deals can be unfunded, partially funded, or fully funded. An *unfunded* CDO structure would be comprised wholly of credit default swaps, while *fully funded CDO structures* would be arranged so that the entire credit risk of the reference portfolio was transferred through the issue of credit-linked notes. We discuss these shortly.

The originators of the first synthetic deals were banks that wished to manage the credit risk exposure of their loan books without having to resort to the administrative burden of true-sale cash securitization. They are a natural progression in the development of credit derivative structures, with single-name credit default swaps being replaced by portfolio default swaps. Synthetic CDOs can be "delinked" from the sponsoring institution, so that investors do not have any credit exposure to the sponsor itself. The first deals in Europe were introduced in 1998 at a time when widening credit spreads and the worsening of credit quality among originating firms meant that investors were sellers of cash CDOs that had retained a credit linkage to the sponsor. A synthetic arrangement also means that the credit risk of assets that are otherwise not suited to conventional securitization may be transferred, while the actual assets are retained on the balance sheet. Such assets include bank guarantees, letters of credit, or cash loans that have some legal or other restriction on being securitized. For this reason, synthetic CDOs are more appropriate than cash CDOs for assets that are originated in multiple legal jurisdictions.

The economic advantage of issuing a synthetic versus a cash CDO can be significant. Put simply, the net benefit to the originator is the gain in regulatory capital cost, minus the cost of paying for credit protection on the credit default swap side. In a fully funded structure, a sponsoring bank will obtain full capital relief when note proceeds are invested in 0% risk-weighted collateral such as U.S. Treasuries or U.K. gilts. In a *partially funded* structure, the majority of the credit risk of the pool of reference assets is transferred by means of the *super-senior swap*, which is a credit default swap. The remaining credit risk is transferred using credit-linked notes, which represent the "funded" element. The reason the swap is called "super-senior" is because the CDO is structured so that the most senior credit-linked note is always rated AAA; the swap is rated senior to this, hence "super senior." It represents catastrophe risk, because it would only expose the investor to a loss if the AAA piece below it experienced default—statistically a very low probability. The super-senior swap portion will carry a 20% risk weighting.[1] In fact, a moment's thought should make clear to us that a synthetic deal would be cheaper: Where credit default swaps are used, the sponsor pays a basis point fee, which for a AAA security might be in the range of 10 to 30 bp, depending on the stage of the credit cycle. In a cash structure where bonds are issued, the cost to the sponsor would be the benchmark yield plus the credit spread, which would be considerably higher compared to the default swap premium. This is illustrated in the example shown in Exhibit 7.1, where we assume certain spreads and premiums in comparing a partially funded synthetic deal with a cash deal. The assumptions are:

■ That the super-senior credit swap cost is 15 bp, and carries a 20% risk weight.
■ The equity piece retains a 100% risk weighting.
■ the synthetic CDO invests note proceeds in sovereign collateral that pays sub-LIBOR.

Of course, the economic benefits of cash versus synthetic securitization will differ according to originator requirement.

EXHIBIT 7.1   Cost Structure: Synthetic versus Cash Flow CDO

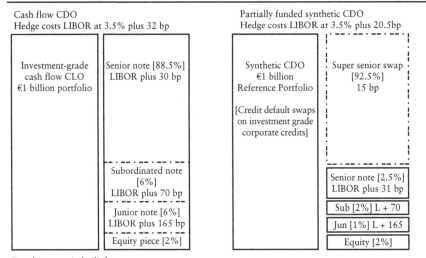

Regulatory capital relief
Cash CDO
Capital charge on assets reduces from 8% (100% RW) to 2% (equity piece only now 100% RW)
Regulatory capital relief is 6%
Synthetic CDO
Capital charge on assets reduces from 8% (100% RW) to 3.48% (equity piece plus super senior swap at 20% RW)
Regulatory capital relief is 4.52%

---

[1] This is as long as the counterparty is an OECD bank, which is invariably the case.

MECHANICS

A synthetic CDO is so called because the transfer of credit risk is achieved "synthetically" via a credit derivative, rather than by a "true sale" to an SPV. Thus, in a synthetic CDO, the credit risk of the underlying loans or bonds is transferred to the SPV using credit default swaps and/or total return swaps (TRS). However the assets themselves are not legally transferred to the SPV, and they remain on the originator's balance sheet. Using a synthetic CDO, the originator can obtain regulatory capital relief and manage the credit risk on its balance sheet, but does not receive any funding.[2] In other words, a synthetic CDO structure enables originators to separate credit risk exposure and asset funding requirements.

The credit risk of the asset portfolio, now known as the *reference portfolio*, is transferred, directly or to an SPV, through credit derivatives. The most common credit contracts used are credit default swaps. A portion of the credit risk may be sold on as credit-linked notes. Typically a large majority of the credit risk is transferred via the super-senior credit default swap, which is transacted with a swap counterparty, but usually sold to monoline insurance companies at a significantly lower spread over LIBOR compared with the senior AAA-rated tranche of cash flow CDOs. This is a key attraction of synthetic deals for originators. Most deals are structured with mezzanine notes sold to a wider set of investors, the proceeds of which are invested in risk-free collateral such as Treasury bonds or Pfandbriefe securities. The most junior note, known as the "first-loss" piece, may be retained by the originator. On occurrence of a credit event among the reference assets, the originating bank receives funds remaining from the collateral after they have been used to pay the principal on the issued notes, less the value of the junior note.

A generic synthetic CDO structure is shown in Exhibit 7.2. In this generic structure, the credit risk of the reference assets is transferred to the issuer SPV and ultimately to the investors by means of the credit default swap and an issue of credit-linked notes. In the default swap arrangement, the risk transfer is undertaken in return for the default swap premium, which is then paid to investors by the issuer. The note issue is invested in risk-free collateral rather than passed on to the originator. This is done in order to delink the credit ratings of the notes from the rating of the originator. If the collateral pool was not established, a downgrade of the sponsor could result in a downgrade of the issued notes. Investors in the notes expose themselves to the credit risk of the reference assets, and if there are

---

[2] This is because reference assets that are protected by credit derivative contracts, and which remain on the balance sheet, will, under Basel rules, be subject to a lower regulatory capital charge.

EXHIBIT 7.2 Synthetic CDO Structure

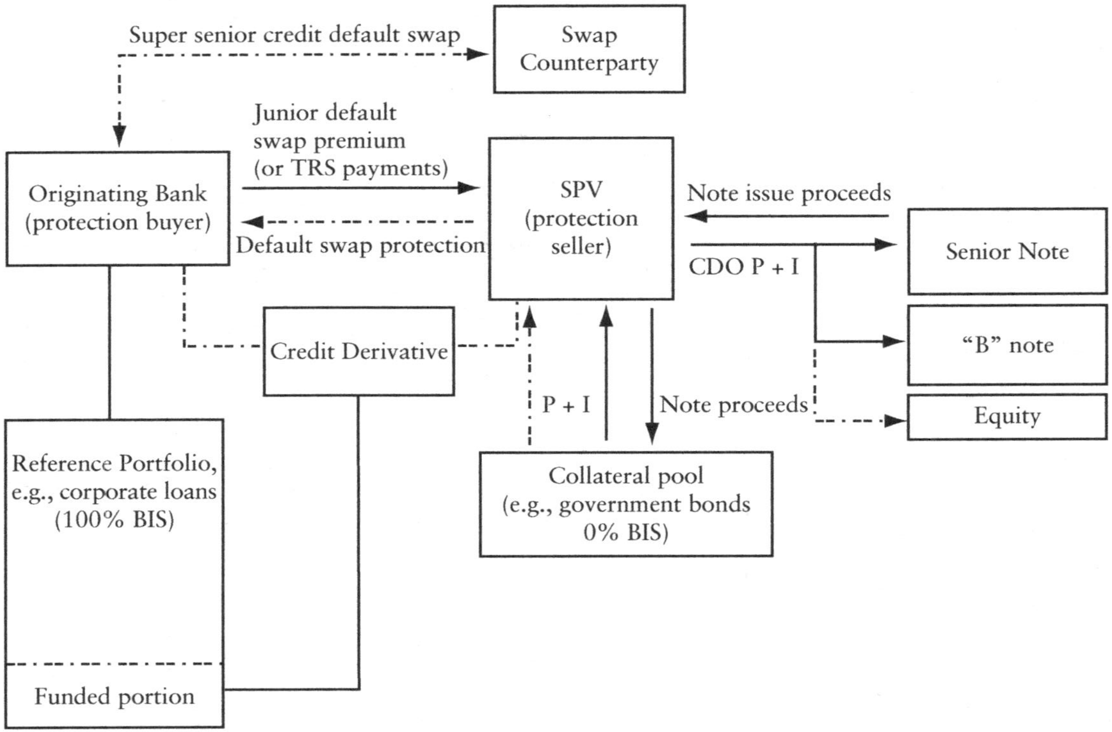

no credit events, they will earn returns at least the equal of the collateral assets and the default swap premium. If the notes are credit-linked, they will also earn excess returns based on the performance of the reference portfolio. If there are credit events, the issuer SPV will deliver the assets to the swap counterparty and pay the nominal value of the assets to the originator out of the collateral pool. Credit default swaps are unfunded credit derivatives, while credit-linked notes (CLNs), the subject matter of Chapter 9, are funded credit derivatives where the protection seller (the investors) funds the value of the reference assets upfront, and receives a reduced return on occurrence of a credit event.

FUNDING MECHANICS

As the super-senior piece in a synthetic CDO does not need to be funded, this provides the key advantage of the synthetic mechanism compared to a cash flow arbitrage CDO. For example, during the first half of 2002, the yield spread for the AAA-note piece averaged 45 to 50 bp over LIBOR,[3] while the cost of the super-senior swap was around 10 to 12 bp. This means that if the CDO collateral manager can reinvest in the collateral pool risk-free assets at LIBOR minus, say, 5 bp, it is able to gain from a savings of 28 to 35 bp on each nominal $100 of the structure that is not funded. This is a considerable gain. If we assume that a synthetic CDO is 95% unfunded and 5% funded, this is equivalent to the reference assets trading at approximately 26 to 33 bp cheaper in the market. There is also an improvement to the return-on-capital measure for the CDO collateral manager. Since typically the manager retains the equity piece, if this is 2% of the structure and the gain is 33 bp, the return on equity will be improved by 0.33/0.02 or 16.5%. In fact the deal economics that are modelled during the structuring of the transaction will play a part on how the deal is tranched: If there is investor appetite for more funded investments, a greater proportion of the deal will be in the form of CLNs. The manager's share of equity will also depend on market appetite for CDO equity.[4]

---

[3] Averaged from the yield spread on seven synthetic deals closed during January–June 2002, yield spread at issue, rate data from Bloomberg.

[4] There are pros and cons in the debate as to whether or not it is better for the CDO originator to retain some or all of the equity. One argument for the originator to retain an equity interest is that it motivates the originator to prudently manage the vehicle as it has an interest in its performance. The other side holds that as the equity piece return is variable and dependent on the surplus cash generated by the vehicle, it may tempt managers who hold no equity stake to trade recklessly with other people's money.

Another benefit of structuring CDOs as synthetic deals is their potentially greater attraction for investors (protection sellers). Often, selling credit default swap protection on a particular reference credit generates a higher return than going long on the underlying cash bond. In general, this is because the credit default swap price is greater than the asset swap price for the same name, for a number of reasons. For instance, during the first half of 2002 the average spread of the synthetic price over the cash price as reported by Bloomberg was over 40 bp in the 5-year maturity area for BBB-rated credits. The reasons why default swap spreads tend to be above cash spreads include:

- The credit risk covered by the default swap includes trigger events that are not pure default scenarios, such as restructuring.
- On occurrence of a credit event, the amount of loss is calculated assuming that the reference security was at an initial price of par, whereas in the cash market that security may have been bought at a discount to par. Assume we buy a security at a price discount to par of x, and that the obligor defaults: the physical security can be sold at the new defaulted price of y, where $x > y$, resulting in a loss of $(x - y)$. If the investor had instead sold a credit default swap on the same name, the investor would pay the difference between par and y, which is a greater loss. Therefore the default swap price is higher to compensate for this.
- The bondholder is aware of the exact issue that it is holding in the event of default; however default swap sellers may receive potentially any bond from a basket of deliverable instruments that rank *pari passu* with the cash asset; this is the delivery option afforded the long swap holder. This applies to physically-settled default swaps and means the protection buyer will deliver the *cheapest-to-deliver* asset.
- The borrowing rate for a cash bond in the repo market may differ from LIBOR if the bond is to any extent *special*; this does not impact the default swap price which is fixed at inception.
- Certain bonds rated AAA (such as U.S. agency securities) sometimes trade below LIBOR in the asset swap market; however, a bank writing protection on such a bond will expect a premium (positive spread over LIBOR) for selling protection on the bond.
- Depending on the precise reference credit, the default swap may be more liquid than the cash bond, resulting in a lower default swap price, or less liquid than the bond, resulting in a higher price.
- Default swaps may be required to pay out on credit events that are technical defaults, and not the full default that impacts a cash bond-holder; protection sellers may demand a premium for this additional risk.

Note however the existence of ongoing counterparty risk for the seller of a default swap is a factor that suggests that its price should be below the cash price!

INVESTOR RISKS IN SYNTHETIC TRANSACTIONS

The key structural differences between a synthetic and conventional securitization are the absence of a true sale of assets and the use of credit derivatives. Investors must therefore focus on different aspects of risk that the synthetic CDO represents. Although it might be said that each securitization—irrespective of it being cash or synthetic—is a unique transaction with its own characteristics, synthetic deals are very transaction-specific because they can be tailor-made to meet very specific requirements. Such requirements can be with regard to reference asset type, currency, underlying cash flows, credit derivative instrument, and so on.

Investor risk in a synthetic deal centers on (1) the credit risk inherent in the reference assets and (2) the legal issues associated with the definition of credit events. Also, to a smaller extent, there is the counterparty credit risk associated with the credit default swap that transfers the credit risk to the CDO structure. The first risk is closely associated with securitization in general but synthetic securitization in particular. Remember that the essence of the transaction is credit risk transfer, and investors (protection sellers) desire exposure to the credit performance of reference assets. So investors are taking on the credit risk of these assets, be they conventional bonds, structured products such as asset-backed securities (ABS) and mortgage-backed securities (MBS), loans, or other assets. The primary measure of this risk is the credit rating of the assets, taken together with any credit enhancements, as well as their historical ratings performance.

The second risk is more problematic and open to translation issues. In a number of deals the sponsor of the transaction is also tasked with determining when a credit event has taken place; as the sponsor is also buying protection there is scope for conflict of interest here. The more critical concern, and one that has given rise to litigation in past cases, is what exactly constitutes a credit event. A lack of clear legal definition can lead to conflict when the protection buyer believes that a particular occurrence is indeed a credit event and therefore the trigger for a protection payout, but this is disputed by the protection seller. Generally, the broader the definition of "credit event," the greater the risk there is of dispute. Trigger events should therefore be defined in the governing legal documentation as closely as possible.

This is of course key: Most descriptions of events defined as trigger events include those listed in the International Swaps and Derivatives Association (ISDA) *Credit Derivatives Definitions* that were described in

Chapter 3. They include circumstances that fall short of a general default, so that payouts can be enforced when the reference asset obligor is not in default. This means that the risk taken on by investors in a synthetic CDO deal is higher than that taken on in a cash CDO deal because the hurdle for a credit event may be lower than that for outright default. It is important for investors to be aware of this: Credit ratings for a bond issue will not reflect all the credit events that are defined by ISDA. This means that the probability of loss for a synthetic note of a specific rating may be higher than for a conventional note of the same reference name.

VARIATIONS IN SYNTHETIC CDOS

Synthetic CDOs have been issued in a variety of forms, labeled generically form as arbitrage CDOs or balance sheet CDOs. Structures can differ to a considerable degree from one another, having only the basics in common with each other. Another development is the *managed synthetic* CDO.

A synthetic arbitrage CDO is originated generally by collateral managers who wish to exploit the difference in yield between that obtained on the underlying assets and that payable on the CDO, both in note interest and servicing fees. The generic structure is as follows: A specially created SPV, the protection seller, enters into a total return swap with the originating bank, the protection buyer, or financial institution, referencing the bank's underlying portfolio (the reference portfolio). The portfolio is actively managed and is funded on the balance sheet by the originating bank. The SPV receives the "total return" from the reference portfolio, and in return it pays LIBOR plus a spread to the originating bank. The SPV also issues notes that are sold into the market to CDO investors, and these notes can be rated as high as AAA as they are backed by high-quality collateral, which is purchased using the note proceeds. A typical structure is shown in Exhibit 7.3.

A balance sheet synthetic CDO is employed by banks that wish to manage regulatory capital. As before, the underlying assets are bonds, loans, and credit facilities originated by the issuing bank. In a balance sheet CDO, the SPV enters into a credit default swap agreement with the originator, with the specific collateral pool designated as the reference portfolio. The SPV receives the premium payable on the default swap, and thereby provides credit protection on the reference portfolio.

There are three types of CDO within this structure. A fully synthetic CDO is a completely *unfunded* structure that uses credit default swaps to transfer the entire credit risk of the reference assets to investors who are protection sellers. In a *partially funded* CDO, only the highest credit

EXHIBIT 7.3 Generic Synthetic Arbitrage CDO Structure

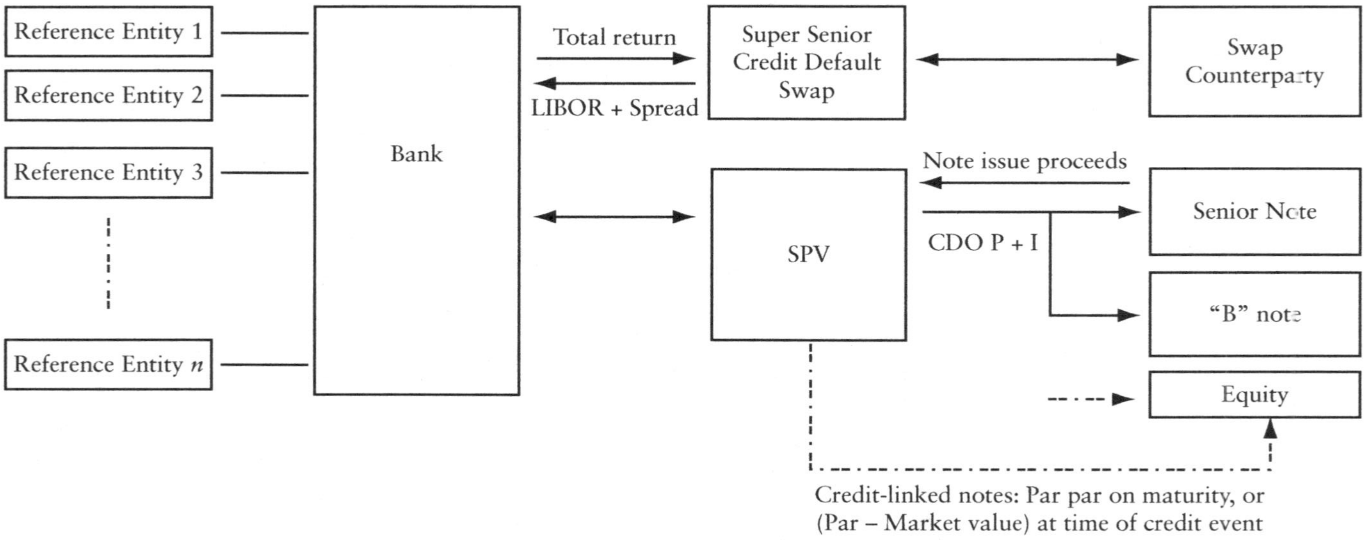

Reference Entity 1
Reference Entity 2
Reference Entity 3
Reference Entity n

Bank

Total return
LIBOR + Spread

Super Senior Credit Default Swap

Swap Counterparty

SPV

Note issue proceeds
CDO P + I

Senior Note
"B" note
Equity

Credit-linked notes: Par par on maturity, or (Par – Market value) at time of credit event risk segment of the portfolio is transferred. The cash flow that would be needed to service the synthetic CDO overlying liability is received from the AAA-rated collateral that is purchased by the SPV with the proceeds of an overlying note issue. An originating bank obtains maximum regulatory capital relief by means of a partially funded structure, through a combination of the synthetic CDO and what is known as a *super senior swap* arrangement with an OECD banking counterparty. A super senior swap provides additional protection to that part of the portfolio, the senior segment, that is already protected by the funded portion of the transaction. The sponsor may retain the super senior element or may sell it to a monoline insurance firm or credit default swap provider.

Some commentators have categorized synthetic deals using slightly different terms. For instance Boggiano, Waterson, and Stein define the following types:[5]

- balance sheet static synthetic CDO;
- managed static synthetic CDO;
- balance sheet variable synthetic CDO; and
- managed variable synthetic CDO.

The basic structure described by Boggiano, Waterson, and Stein is the same as we described earlier for a partially funded synthetic CDO. In fact there is essentially little difference between the first two types of deals; in the latter a collateral manager rather than the credit swap counterparty selects the portfolio. However, the reference assets remain static for the life of the deal in both cases. For the last two deal types, the main difference would appear to be that a collateral manager, rather than the originator bank, trades the portfolio of credit swaps under specified guidelines. In our view, this is not a structural difference, and so in this chapter we will consider them both as managed CDOs, which are described later.

A generic, partially funded synthetic transaction is shown in Exhibit 7.4. It shows an arrangement whereby the issuer enters into two credit default swaps. The first swap with an SPV provides protection for losses up to a specified amount of the reference pool,[6] while the second swap is set up with the OECD bank or, occasionally, an insurance company.[7]

---

[5] Kenneth Boggiano, David Waterson, and Craig Stein, "Four Forms of Synthetic CDOs," *Derivatives Week* 11, no. 23 (June 10, 2002).

[6] In practice, to date this portion has been between 5% and 15% of the reference pool.

[7] Under Basel I, if the swap counterparty is an OECD bank it in effect transforms the assets being protected into 20% risk-weighted assets, as if they were bank risk (which, in effect, the assets now are). Under Basel II, the bank counterparty will need to be AA rated or better, otherwise the capital treatment may, under certain circumstances, be 50%.

EXHIBIT 7.4 Partially Funded Synthetic CDO Structure

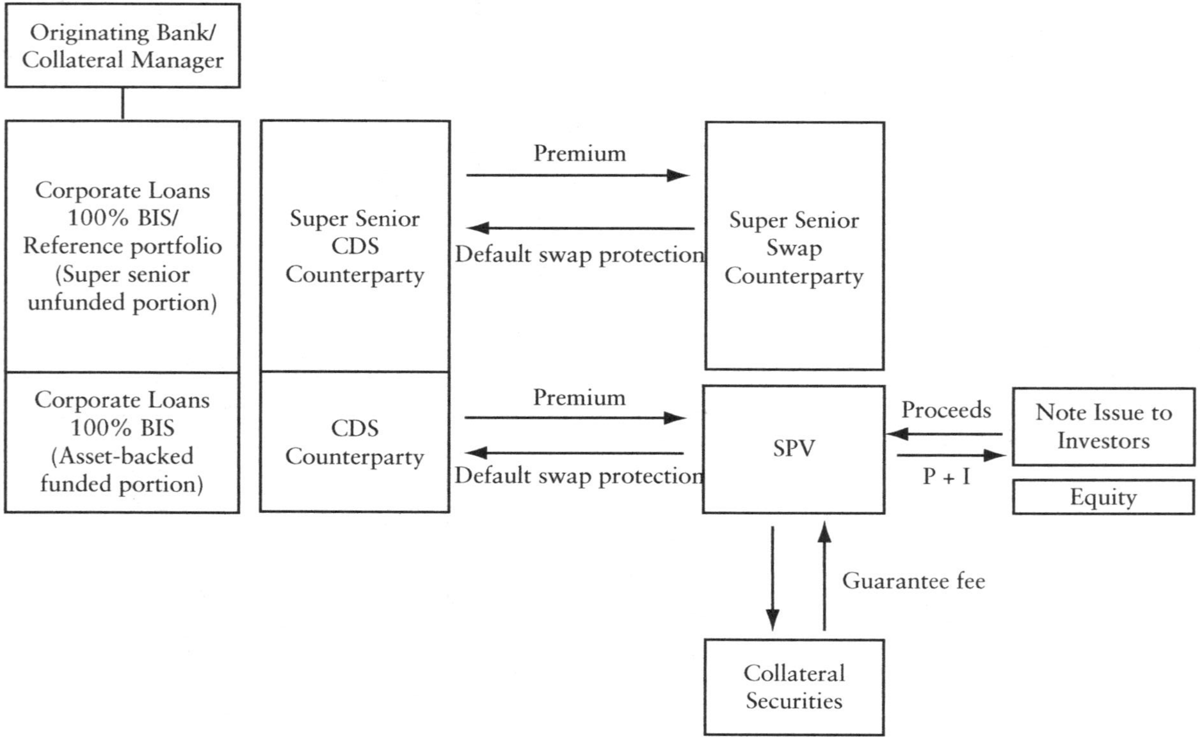

EXHIBIT 7.5 Fully Funded Synthetic Balance Sheet CDO Structure

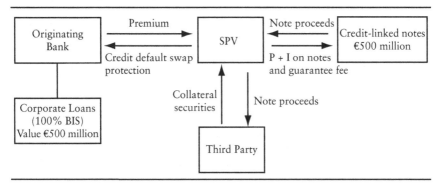

A *fully funded* CDO is a structure where the credit risk of the entire portfolio is transferred to the SPV via a credit default swap. In a fully funded (or just "funded") synthetic CDO, the issuer enters into the credit default swap with the SPV, which itself issues credit-linked notes equal to the entire value of the assets on which the risk has been transferred. The proceeds from the notes are invested in risk-free government or agency debt such as U.S. Treasuries, U.K. gilts, German Bunds or Pfandbriefe, or in senior unsecured bank debt. Should there be a default on one or more of the underlying assets, the required amount of the collateral is sold and the proceeds from the sale are paid to the issuer to recompense for the losses. The premium paid on the credit default swap must be sufficiently high to ensure that it covers the difference in yield between that on the collateral and that on the notes issued by the SPV. The generic structure is illustrated at Exhibit 7.5.

Fully funded CDOs are relatively uncommon. One of the advantages of the partially funded arrangement is that the issuer will pay a lower premium compared to a fully funded synthetic CDO, because it is not required to pay the difference between the yield on the collateral and the coupon on the note issue (the unfunded part of the transaction). The downside is that the issuer will receive a reduction in risk weighting for capital purposes to 20% for the risk transferred via the super senior default swap.

The *fully unfunded* CDO uses only credit derivatives in its structure. The swaps are rated in a similar fashion to notes, and there is usually an "equity" piece that is retained by the originator. The reference portfolio will again be commercial loans, usually 100% risk-weighted, or other assets. The credit rating of the swap tranches is based on the rating of the reference assets, as well as other factors such as the diversity of the assets and ratings performance correlation. The typical structure is illus-

EXHIBIT 7.6   The Fully Synthetic or Unfunded CDO

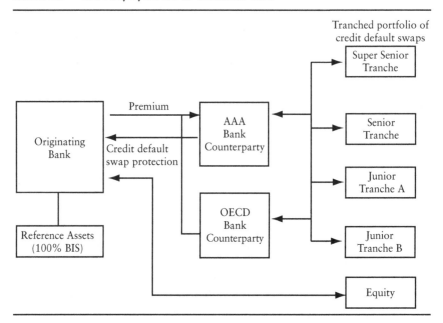

trated in Exhibit 7.6. As well as the equity tranche, there will be one or more junior tranches, one or more senior tranches, and a super-senior tranche. The senior tranches are sold on to AAA-rated banks as a portfolio credit default swap, while the junior tranche is usually sold to an OECD bank. The ratings of the tranches typically are:

- super senior AAA;
- senior AA to AAA;
- junior BB to A; and
- equity, unrated.

The credit default swaps are not single-name swaps, but are written on a class of debt. The advantage for the originator is that it can name the reference asset class to investors without having to disclose the name of specific loans. Default swaps are usually cash settled and not physically settled so that the reference assets can be replaced with other assets if desired by the sponsor.

Within the European market, static synthetic balance sheet CDOs are the most common structure. The reasons that banks originate them are twofold:

■ *Capital relief:* Banks can obtain regulatory capital relief by transferring lower-yield corporate credit risk such as corporate bank loans off their balance sheets. Under Basel I rules, all corporate debt carries an identical 100% risk-weighting; therefore with banks having to assign 8% of capital for such loans, higher-rated (and hence lower-yielding) corporate assets will require the same amount of capital, but will generate a lower return on that capital. A bank may wish to transfer such higher-rated, lower-yield assets from its balance sheet, and this can be achieved via a CDO transaction. The capital requirements for a synthetic CDO are lower than for corporate assets. For example, the funded segment of the deal is supported by high-quality collateral such as government bonds and via a repo arrangement with an OECD bank that would carry a 20% risk weighting, as would the super-senior element.

■ *Transfer of credit risk:* The cost of servicing a fully funded CDO, and the premium payable on the associated credit default swap, can be prohibitive. With a partially funded structure, the issue amount is typically a relatively small share of the asset portfolio. This substantially lowers the default swap premium. Also, as the CDO investors suffer the first-loss element of the portfolio, the super senior default swap can be arranged at a considerably lower cost than on a fully funded CDO can.

Synthetic deals may be either static or managed. Static deals hold the following advantages:

■ There are no ongoing management fees to be borne by the vehicle.
■ The investor can review and grant approval to credits that are to make up the reference portfolio.

The disadvantage is that if there is a deterioration in credit quality of one or more names, then there is no ability to remove or offset those names from the pool and the vehicle continues to suffer from them. For example, during 2001 a number of high-profile defaults in the market caused static pool CDOs to perform below expectation. This partly explains the rise in popularity of the deal, which we discuss later.

THE SINGLE-TRANCHE SYNTHETIC CDO

The flexibility of the synthetic CDO, enabling deal types to be structured to meet the needs of a wide range of investors and issuers, is well illustrated with the tailor-made or "single-tranche CDO" structure.

The single-tranche CDO has been developed in response to investor demand for exposure to a specific part of a pool of reference credits. With this structure, an arranging bank creates a tailored portfolio that meets specific investor requirements with regard to:

- portfolio size and asset class;
- portfolio concentration, geographical and industry variation;
- portfolio diversity and rating; and
- investment term-to-maturity.

The structure is illustrated in Exhibits 7.7 and 7.8, respectively, without and with an SPV issuer. Under this arrangement, there is only one note tranche. The reference portfolio, made up of credit default swaps, is dynamically hedged by the originating bank itself. The deal has been arranged to create a risk/reward profile for one investor only, who buys the single tranche note. This also creates an added advantage that the deal can be brought to market very quickly. The key difference between single-tranche and traditional synthetic CDOs is that the arranging bank does not transfer the remainder of the credit risk of the reference pool. Instead, this risk is dynamically managed, and hedged in the market using derivatives.

EXHIBIT 7.7 Single Tranche 1 Issue Direct from Arranging Bank

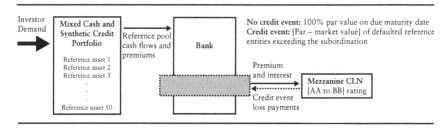

EXHIBIT 7.8 Single Tranche 2 Issue via SPV

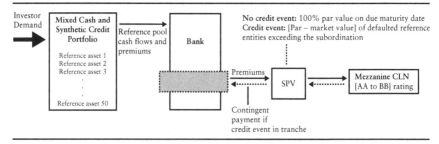

SUMMARY OF THE ADVANTAGES OF SYNTHETIC STRUCTURES

The introduction of synthetic securitization vehicles was in response to specific demands of sponsoring institutions, and they present certain advantages over traditional cash flow structures. These advantages include:

- A synthetic transaction can, in theory, be placed in the market sooner than a cash deal, and the time from inception to closure can be as low as four weeks, with average execution time of six to eight weeks compared to three to four months for the equivalent cash deal; this reflects the shorter ramp-up period noted above.
- There is no requirement to fund the super-senior element.
- For many reference names the credit default swap is frequently cheaper than the same-name underlying cash bond.
- Transaction costs such as legal fees can be lower as there is no necessity to set up an SPV.
- Banking relationships can be maintained with clients whose loans need not be actually sold off the sponsoring entity's balance sheet.
- The range of reference assets that can be covered is wider, and includes undrawn lines of credit, bank guarantees, and derivative instruments that would give rise to legal and true-sale issues in a cash transaction.
- The use of credit derivatives introduces greater flexibility to provide tailor-made solutions for credit risk requirements.
- The cost of buying protection is usually lower as there is little or no funding element and the credit protection price is below the equivalent-rate note liability.

This does not mean that the cash CDO transaction is now an endangered species. It retains certain advantages of its own over synthetic deals, which include:

- No requirement for an OECD bank (the 20% BIS risk-weighted entity) to act as the swap counterparty to meet capital relief requirements.
- Lower capital relief available compared to the 20% risk weighting on the OECD bank counterparty.
- Larger potential investor base, as the number of counterparties is potentially greater (certain financial and investing institutions have limitations on the degree of usage of credit derivatives).
- Lower degree of counterparty exposure for the originating entity. In a synthetic deal the default of a swap counterparty would mean cessation of premium payments or more critically a credit event protection payment, and termination of the credit default swap.

Investment banking advisors will structure the arrangement that best meets their sponsoring client's requirements. Depending on the nature of those requirements, the arrangement may be either a synthetic or cash deal.

FACTORS TO CONSIDER IN CDO ANALYSIS

There are four key issues that investors should consider when analyzing synthetic CDO tranches. We discuss each next.

Analysis for CDOs
The return analysis for CDOs performed by potential investors is necessarily different from that undertaken for other securitized asset classes. For CDOs, the three key factors to consider are:

- default probabilities and cumulative default rates;
- default correlations; and
- recovery rates.

Analysts make assumptions about each of these with regard to individual reference assets, usually with recourse to historical data. We consider each factor in turn.

Default Probability Rates
The level of default probability rates will vary with each deal. Rating-agency and other analysts will use a number of methods to estimate default probabilities, such as individual reference credit ratings and historical probability rates. Since there may be as many as 150 or more reference names in a CDO's collateral pool, a common approach is to use the average rating of the reference portfolio. Rating agencies such as Moody's provide data on the default rates for different ratings as an "average" class, which can be used in the analysis.

Correlation
The correlation among assets in the reference portfolio of a CDO is an important factor in CDO returns analysis. A problem arises with what precise correlation value to use; these can be correlation among default probabilities, correlation among timings of defaults, and correlation among spreads. The *diversity score* value of the CDO plays a part in this: it represents the number of uncorrelated bonds with identical par value and the same default probability.

Recovery Rates

Recovery rates for individual obligors differ by issuer and industry classification. Rating agencies publish data on the average prices of all defaulted bonds, and generally analysts will construct a database of recovery rates by industry and credit rating for use in modeling the expected recovery rates of assets in the collateral pool. Note that for synthetic CDOs with credit default swaps as assets in the portfolio, this factor is not relevant.

Analysts undertake simulation modeling to generate scenarios of default and expected return. For instance they may model the number of defaults up to maturity, as well as the recovery rates and the timing of these defaults. All of these are viewed as random variables, so they are modeled using a stochastic process. It is important to note that the rating agencies estimate average recovery rates. The actual recovery rate can vary widely depending upon the current macroeconomic environment.

CDO Yield Spreads

Fund managers consider investing in CDO-type products because they represent a diversification in the fixed-income markets with yields that are comparable to credit card or auto loan ABS. A cash CDO also gives investors exposure to sectors in the market that may not otherwise be accessible to them—for example, credits such as small- or medium-sized corporate entities that rely entirely on bank financing. Also, because of the extent of its credit enhancement and note tranching, a CDO may show a better risk/reward profile than straight conventional debt, with a higher yield but incorporating asset and insurance backing. In cash and synthetic CDOs, the notes issued are often bullet bonds, with fixed term to maturity, whereas other ABS and MBS products are amortizing securities with only average (expected life) maturities. This may suit certain longer-dated investors.

An incidental perceived advantage of cash CDOs is that they are typically issued by financial institutions such as higher-rated banks. This usually provides comfort on the credit side, but also on the underlying administration and servicing side with regard to underlying assets, compared to consumer receivables securitizations.

CASE STUDY

We conclude this chapter by looking at a deal issued in 2002 in the Asian market, ALCO 1 Limited. The deal discussed is an innovative structure and a creative combination of securitization technology and credit derivatives. It shows how a portfolio manager can utilize vehicles of this kind to exploit its expertise in credit trading as well as provide attractive returns for investors.

According to Moody's, ALCO 1 CDO is the first rated synthetic balance sheet CDO from a non-Japanese bank. It is a S$2.8 billion structure sponsored and managed by the Development Bank of Singapore (DBS). A summary of terms follows:

Name	ALCO 1 Limited
Originator	Development Bank of Singapore Ltd.
Arrangers	JPMorgan Chase Bank
	DBS Ltd.
Trustee	Bank of New York
Closing date	December 15, 2001
Maturity	March 2009
Portfolio	S$2.8 billion of credit default swaps (Singapore dollars)
Reference assets	199 reference obligations (136 obligors)
Portfolio administrator	JPMorgan Chase Bank Institutional Trust Services

The structure allows DBS to shift the credit risk on a S$2.8 billion reference portfolio of mainly Singapore corporate loans to a special purpose vehicle, ALCO 1, using credit default swaps. As a result DBS can reduce the risk capital it has to hold on the reference loans, without physically moving the assets from its balance sheet. The structure is S$2.45 billion super senior tranche—an unfunded credit default swap—with a S$224 million notes issue and a S$126 million first-loss piece retained by DBS. The notes are issued in six classes, collateralized by Singapore government Treasury bills and a reserve bank account known as a "GIC" account. There is also a currency and interest-rate swap structure in place for risk hedging, and a put option that covers purchase of assets by the arranger if the deal terminates before expected maturity date. The issuer enters into credit default swaps with a specified list of counterparties. The default swap pool is static, but there is a substitution facility for up to 10% of the portfolio. This means that under certain specified conditions, up to 10% of the reference loan portfolio may be replaced by loans from outside the vehicle. Other than this though, the reference portfolio is static.

Since ALCO-1, the first rated synthetic balance sheet deal in Asia, similar structures have been adopted by other commercial banks in the region. The principal innovation of the vehicle is the method by which the reference credits are selected. The choice of reference credits on which swaps are written must, as expected with a CDO, follow a number of criteria set by the rating agency, including diversity score, rating factor, weighted average spread, geographical and industry concentration, among others.

Structure and Mechanics

The deal structure and note tranching are shown at Exhibit 7.9. The issuer enters into a portfolio credit default swap with DBS as the CDS

EXHIBIT 7.9   ALCO 1 Structure and Tranching

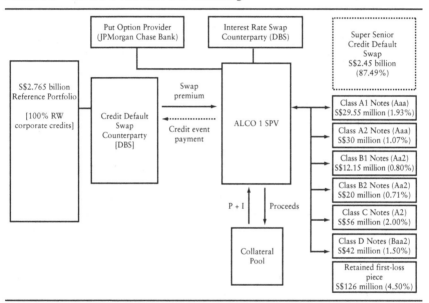

Source: Moody's Pre-Sale Report, November 12, 2001. Used with permission.

Class	Amount	Percent	Rating	Interest Rate
Super senior swap	S$2.450m	87.49%	NR	N/A
Class A1	US$29.55m	1.93%	Aaa	3m USD LIBOR + 50 bp
Class A2	S$30m	1.07%	Aaa	3m SOR + 45 bp
Class B1	US$12.15m	0.80%	Aa2	3m USD LIBOR + 85 bp
Class B2	S$30m	0.71%	Aa2	3m SOR + 80 bp
Class C	S$56m	2.00%	A2	5.20%
Class D	S$42m	1.50%	Baa2	6.70%

Source: Note: S$ = Singapore dollars; US$ = United States dollars.
Source: Moody's.

counterparty to provide credit protection against losses in the reference portfolio. The credit default swaps are cash settled. In return for protection premium payments, after aggregate losses exceeding the S$126 million "threshold" amount, the issuer is obliged to make protection payments to DBS. The maximum obligation is the S$224 million note proceeds value. In standard fashion associated with securitized notes, further losses above the threshold amount will be allocated to overlying notes in their reverse order of seniority. The note proceeds are invested in a collateral pool comprised initially of Singapore Treasury bills.

During the term of the transaction, DBS as the CDS counterparty is permitted to remove any eliminated reference obligations that are fully paid, terminated early, or otherwise no longer eligible. In addition DBS has the option to remove up to 10% of the initial aggregate amount of the reference portfolio, and substitute new or existing reference names.

For this structure, credit events are defined specifically as:

- failure to pay; and
- bankruptcy.

Note how this differs from European-market CDOs where the list of defined credit events is invariably longer, frequently including restructuring and credit rating downgrade.

The reference portfolio is an Asian corporate portfolio, but with a small percentage of loans originated in Australia. The portfolio is concentrated in Singapore (80%). The weighted average credit quality is Baa3/Ba1, with an average life of three years. The Moody's diversity score is low (20), reflecting the concentration of loans in Singapore. There is a high industrial concentration. The total portfolio at inception was 199 reference obligations among 136 reference entities (obligors). By structuring the deal in this way, DBS obtains capital relief on the funded portion of the assets, but at lower cost and less administrative burden than a traditional cash flow securitization, and without the need for a true sale of the assets.

CHAPTER **8**

Securitized and Synthetic Funding Structures

The accessibility of securitization techniques, together with greater liquidity in the credit derivative market, has given rise to new types of money market funding structures. These vehicles have enabled a wider range of market participants to tap the markets, often with illiquid or untradeable assets being used as synthetic collateral. They also provide a diversified funding source for banks, other financial institutions, and corporations. In this chapter we discuss funding vehicles that are structured as synthetic securitizations in the commercial paper and medium-term note markets. We also discuss a basic funding instrument, the basket total return swap, which is traded under an International Swap and Derivatives Association (ISDA) agreement and termed a credit derivative, but in practice works exactly as a repurchase agreement. We begin with a discussion of commercial paper and asset-backed commercial paper program.

COMMERICAL PAPER

Companies' short-term capital and *working capital* requirements are usually sourced directly from banks in the form of bank loans. An alternative short-term funding instrument is *commercial paper* (CP), which is available to corporations that have sufficiently strong credit ratings. CP is a short-term unsecured promissory note. The issuer of the note promises to pay its holder a specified amount on a specified maturity date. CP normally has a zero coupon and therefore trades at a discount to its face value. The discount represents interest to the investor in the period to maturity.

Originally, the CP market was restricted to borrowers with high credit ratings, and although lower-rated borrowers do now issue CP, sometimes by obtaining credit enhancements or setting up collateral arrangements, issuance in the market is still dominated by highly-rated companies. The majority of issues are very short-term, from 30 to 90 days in maturity; it is extremely rare to observe paper with a maturity of more than 270 days or nine months. This is because of regulatory requirements in the United States, which state that debt instruments with a maturity of less than 270 days need not be registered with the Securities and Exchange Commission (SEC). Corporations therefore issue CP with a maturity less than nine months and thereby avoid the costs associated with registering issues with the SEC.

There are two major markets, the U.S. dollar market and the Eurocommercial paper market. CP markets are wholesale markets and transactions are typically very large in size. Although there is a secondary market in CP, very little trading activity takes place since investors generally hold CP until maturity.

The issuers of CP are often divided into two categories of companies, banking and financial institutions and non-financial companies. The majority of CP issues are by financial companies. Financial companies include not only banks but the financing arms of corporations such as General Motors Acceptance Corporation, Ford Motor Credit Co., and Daimler-Chrysler Financial. As noted above, most of the issuers have strong credit ratings, but lower-rated borrowers have tapped the market, often after arranging credit support from higher-rated companies such as letters of credit from banks, or by arranging collateral for the issue in the form of high-quality assets such as Treasury bonds. CP issued with credit support is known as *credit-supported commercial paper*, while paper backed with assets is known naturally enough, as *asset-backed commercial paper*. Paper that is backed by a bank letter of credit is termed *LOC paper*. Although banks charge a fee for issuing letters of credit, borrowers are often happy to pay it, since by so doing they are able to tap the CP market. The yield paid on an issue of CP is lower than on a commercial bank loan.

Although CP is a short-dated security, it is issued within a longer term program—usually for three to five years for Eurocommercial paper; U.S. CP programs are often open ended. For example a company might arrange a five-year CP program with a limit of $100 million. Once the program is established the company can issue CP up to this amount, say for maturities of 30 or 60 days. The program is continuous and new CP can be issued at any time—daily if required. The total amount in issue cannot exceed the limit set for the program. A CP program can be used by a company to manage its short-term liquidity—that is, its working capital requirements. New paper can be issued whenever a need for cash arises, and for an appropriate maturity.

Issuers often roll over their funding and use funds from a new issue of CP to redeem a maturing issue. There is a risk that an issuer might be unable to roll over the paper where there is a lack of investor interest in the new issue. To provide protection against this risk an issuer often arranges a standby line of credit from a bank, normally for all of the CP program, to draw against in the event that it cannot place a new issue. Bank lines of credit are generally reviewed on a yearly basis. Unlike revolving credit facilities, they are not legally binding commitments and can be withdrawn if a borrower's creditworthiness deteriorates.

There are two methods by which CP is issued, known as *direct-issued* or *direct paper* and *dealer-issued* or *dealer paper*. Direct paper is sold by the issuing firm directly to investors, and no agent bank or securities house is involved. It is common for financial companies to issue CP directly to their customers, often because they have continuous programs and constantly rollover their paper. It is therefore cost-effective for them to have their own sales arm and sell their CP direct. The treasury arms of certain nonfinancial companies also issue direct paper. Dealer paper is sold using a banking or securities house intermediary. Some large companies issue CP both directly and through dealers.

We refer to CP programs as described above as *conventional CP programs* to distinguish them from the next type of CP programs we discuss, asset-backed commercial paper.

ASSET-BACKED COMMERCIAL PAPER

The rise in securitization has led to the growth of short-term instruments backed by the cash flows from other assets, known as *asset-backed commercial paper* (ABCP). As explained in Chapter 4, securitization is the practice of using the cash flows from a specified asset, such as residential mortgages, car loans, or commercial bank loans, as backing for an issue of bonds. The assets themselves are transferred from the original owner (the originator) to a special purpose vehicle (SPV) that is a specially created legal entity created to make them separate and bankruptcy-remote from the originator. In the meantime, the originator is able to benefit from capital market financing, often charged at a lower rate of interest than that paid by the originator on its own debt.

Generally, securitization is used as a funding instrument by companies for three main reasons: (1) it offers lower-cost funding compared with than traditional bank loan or bond financing; (2) it is a mechanism by which assets such as corporate loans or mortgages can be removed from the balance sheet, thus improving the lender's return on assets or return-on-equity ratios; and (3) it increases a borrower's funding options. When entering into a securitization, an entity may issue term securities against assets into the public or private market, or it may issue commercial paper via a special vehicle known as a *conduit*. These conduits are usually sponsored by commercial banks.

Corporations access the commercial paper market for normal short-term funding requirements and also as an interim step toward permanent financing, rolling over individual issues as part of a longer-term program and using interest-rate swaps to arrange a fixed-rate if required. Conventional CP issues discussed in the previous section are a form of direct borrowing based on the borrower's balance sheet and creditworthiness. By borrowing directly from the investor and eliminating the bank as an intermediary (except possibly as selling agent), a corporation can fund at a cheaper rate than by borrowing from a commercial bank. CP is a well-known example of disintermediation that has significantly reduced the role of commercial banks in financing large corporations and led commercial banks to move in the direction of investment banking to serve their large corporate customers. (In the case of the United States, after a long but ultimately successful battle to remove the legislative barriers that had separated commercial banking and investment banking since the depression in the 1930s.) Issuing ABCP enables an originator to benefit from money market financing to which it might otherwise not have access because its credit rating is not sufficiently strong. A bank may also issue ABCP for balance sheet or funding reasons. ABCP trades, however, exactly as conventional CP. However, the administration and legal treatment is more onerous because of the need to establish the CP trust structure and issuing SPV. The servicing of an ABCP program follows that of conventional CP and is carried out by the same entities, such as the "trust" arms of banks such as JPMorgan Chase, Deutsche Bank, and Bank of New York.

Exhibit 8.1 details a hypothetical ABCP issue and typical structure.

Basic Characteristics

ABCP programs are invariably issued via SPVs, which in the money markets are known as conduits. They are typically established by commercial banks and finance companies to enable them to access LIBOR-based funding, at close to LIBOR, and to obtain regulatory capital relief. This can be done for the bank or a corporate customer.

An ABCP conduit has the following features:

EXHIBIT 8.1   Hypothetical ABCP Issue and Typical Structure

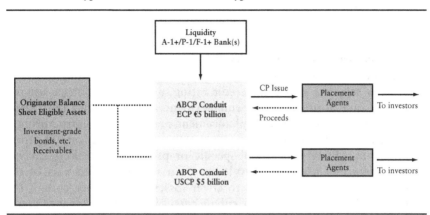

- It is a bankruptcy-remote legal entity that issues CP to finance the purchase of assets from a seller of assets.
- The interest on the CP issued by the conduit, and its principal on maturity, will be paid out of the receipts on the assets purchased by the conduit.
- Conduits have also been set up to exploit credit arbitrage opportunities, such as raising finance at LIBOR to invest in high-quality assets such as investment-grade rated structured finance securities that pay above LIBOR.

The assets that can be funded via a conduit program are many and varied. To date they have included:

- trade receivables and equipment lease receivables;
- credit card receivables;
- auto loans and leases;
- corporate loans, franchise loans, mortgage loans;
- real estate leases;
- investment-grade rated structured finance bonds such as ABS, MBS and CDO notes; and
- future (expected) cash flows.

Conduits are classified into "program types," which refer to the make-up of the underlying asset portfolio. They can be single-seller or multiseller, which indicates how many institutions or entities are selling assets to the conduit. They are also designated as funding or securities credit arbitrage vehicles. A special class of conduit known as a *struc-*

tured investment vehicle (SIV, sometimes called a special investment vehicle) exist that issue both CP and medium-term notes (MTNs), and which are usually credit arbitrage vehicles.

Credit Enhancement and Liquidity Support

To make the issue of liabilities from a conduit more appealing to investors or to secure a particular credit rating, a program sponsor usually arranges some form of credit enhancement and/or backup borrowing facility. (We discussed credit enhancement mechanisms in structuring a securitization in Chapter 5.) Two types of credit enhancement are generally used in ABCP: either pool-specific or program-wide. *Pool-specific credit enhancement* covers only losses on a specific named part of the asset pool and cannot be used to cover losses in any other part of the asset pool. *Program-wide credit enhancement* is a fungible layer of credit protection that can be drawn on to cover losses from the start or if any pool-specific facility has been used up.

Pool-specific credit enhancement instruments include the following:

- over-collateralization, where the nominal value of the underlying assets exceeds that of the issued paper;
- surety bond: a guarantee of repayment from a sponsor or other bank;
- letter of credit: a standby facility from which the issuer can draw funds;
- irrevocable loan facility; and
- excess cash invested in eligible instruments such as U.S. Treasury bills.

The size of a pool-specific credit enhancement facility is quoted as a fixed percentage of the asset pool.

Program-wide credit enhancement is in the same form as pool-specific enhancement, and acts as a second layer of credit protection. It may be provided by a third party such as a commercial bank as well as by the sponsor.

Liquidity support is separate from credit enhancement. While credit enhancement facilities cover losses due to asset default, liquidity providers undertake to make available funds should they be required for reasons other than asset default. A liquidity line is drawn on, if required, to ensure timely repayment of maturing CP. This might occur because of market disruption (such that the issuer could not place new CP), an inability of the issuer to roll maturing CP, or because of asset and liability mismatches. This last item is the least serious situation, and reflects that in many cases long-dated assets are used to back short-dated liabilities, and cash flow dates often do not match. The availability of a liquidity arrangement provides comfort to investors that CP will be repaid in full and on time, and is usually arranged with a commercial bank. It is usually provided as a loan agreement for an amount equal to 100% of the face amount of CP issued, under which the liquidity provider agrees to lend funds to the conduit as required. The security for the liquidity line comes from the underlying assets.

Exhibit 8.1 illustrates a typical ABC structure issuing to the U.S. CP and Euro CP markets. Exhibit 8.2 shows a multiseller conduit set up to issue in the ECP market.

Illustration of an ABCP Structure

In Exhibit 8.3 we illustrate an hypothetical example of a securitization of bank loans in an ABCP structure. The loans, denominated in sterling, have been made by ABC Bank and are secured on borrowers' specified assets, for example liens on property, cash flows of the borrowers' businesses, or other assets. The bank makes a "true sale" of the loans to a SPV, named Claremont Finance. This has the effect of removing the loans from the bank's balance sheet, reducing the bank's regulatory capital requirements, and also protecting those loans in the event of bankruptcy or liquidation of the bank. The SPV raises finance by issuing commercial paper, via its appointed CP dealer(s), which is the treasury desk of MC Investment Bank. The paper is rated A-1/P-1 by the rating agencies and is issued in U.S. dollars. The liability of the CP is met by the cash flow from the original ABC Bank loans.

ABC manager is the SPV manager for Claremont Finance, a subsidiary of ABC Bank. Liquidity for Claremont Finance is provided by ABC Bank, which also acts as the hedge provider. Hedging, to the extent

EXHIBIT 8.2 Multiseller EABCP Conduit

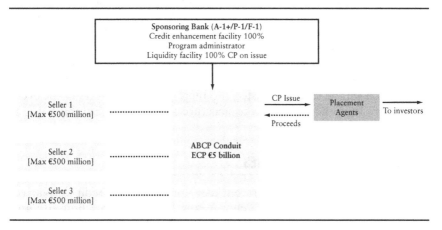

EXHIBIT 8.3 Claremont Finance ABCP Structure

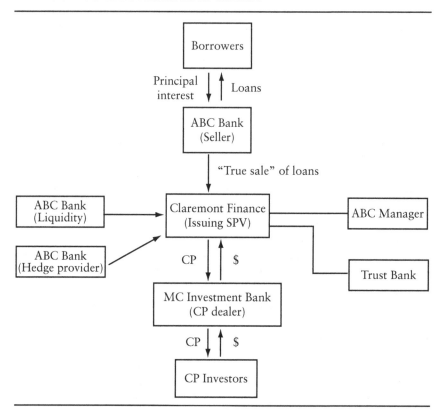

required, is effected by means of an interest rate swap agreement, and in cases where some of the loans are foreign-currency denominated, a currency swap agreement between Claremont Finance and ABC Bank. Depending on its own interest rate and currency positions and risk management strategies, ABC Bank may further hedge its positions in all or parts of those swaps. The trustee for the transaction is Trust Bank Limited, which acts as security trustee and represent the investors in the event of default. The other terms of the structure are shown in Exhibit 8.4.

SYNTHETIC FUNDING STRUCTURES

In this section, we discuss recent developments in credit-derivative-based synthetic structures, which are now being used for liquidity and balance sheet asset-liability management. These combine total return

EXHIBIT 8.4   Terms of the Hypothetical Claremont Finance ABCP Structure

Program facility limit:	US$500 million
Facility term:	The facility is available on an uncommitted basis renewable annually by the agreement of the SPV manager and the security trustee. It has a final termination date five years from first issue.
Tenor of paper:	Seven days to 270 days
Prepayment guarantee:	In the event of prepayment of a loan, the seller will provide Claremont Finance with a guaranteed rate of interest for the relevant interest period.
Hedge agreement:	Claremont Finance will enter into currency and interest-rate swaps with the hedge provider to hedge any interest-rate or currency risk that arises.
Events of default:	Under event of default the issuance program will cease and in certain events will lead to Claremont Finance to pay loan collections into a segregated specific collection account. Events of default can include nonpayment by Claremont Finance under the transaction documentation, insolvency or ranking of charge where the charge ceases to be a first ranking charge over the assets of Claremont Finance.
Loans guarantee:	Loans purchased by Claremont Finance will meet a range of eligibility criteria specified in the transaction offering circular. These criteria will include requirements on currency of the loans, their term to maturity, confirmation that they can be assigned, that they are not in arrears, and so on.

swaps (discussed in Chapter 3) with commercial paper and medium-term note issuance vehicles, and enable originators to raise LIBOR-based funding from wholesale interbank markets. To begin, we consider the simplest arrangement, the funded basket total return swap.

The Basket Total Return Swap

The total return swap (TRS) may be used as a funding tool to secure off-balance-sheet financing for assets held (for example) on a market making book. It is most commonly used in this capacity by broker-dealers and securities houses that have little or no access to unsecured or LIBOR-flat funding. When used for this purpose, the TRS is similar to a repurchase agreement (repo) transaction, although there are detail differences. (A repo is an agreement to sell a security for a specified price and buy it back later at another specified price. It is essentially a secured loan. The party that sells the securities and agrees to buy them bank is the party that needs financing; the party that buys the securities and agrees to sell them bank is the party that provides the financing.) Often a TRS approach is used instead of a classic repo when the assets that require funding are less liquid or not really tradable. These assets can include lower-rated bonds, illiquid bonds (such as certain asset-backed securities (ABS), mortgage-backed securities (MBS), and collateralized debt obligations (CDOs) and assets such as hedge fund interests.

Bonds that are taken on by the TRS provider must be acceptable to it in terms of credit quality. If no independent price source is available, the TRS provider may insist on pricing the assets itself.

As a funding tool the TRS is transacted as follows:

- The broker-dealer swaps out a bond or basket of bonds that it owns to the TRS counterparty (usually a bank), who pays the market price for the security or securities.
- The maturity of the TRS can be for anything from one week to one year or even longer. For longer-dated contracts, a weekly or monthly reset is usually employed, so that the TRS is repriced and cash flows exchanged each week or month.
- The funds that are passed over by the TRS counterparty to the broker-dealer have the economic effect of being a loan to cover the financing of the underlying bonds. This loan is charged at LIBOR plus a spread.
- At the maturity of the TRS, the broker-dealer owes interest on funds to the swap counterparty, while the swap counterparty owes the market performance of the bonds to the broker-dealer if they have increased in price. The two cash flows are netted out.
- For a longer-dated TRS that is reset at weekly or monthly intervals, the broker-dealer owes the loan interest plus any decrease in basket value to the swap counterparty at the reset date. The swap counterparty will owe any increase in value.

By entering into this transaction the broker-dealer obtains LIBOR-based funding for a pool of assets it already owns, while the swap counterparty earns LIBOR plus a spread on funds are effectively secured by a pool of assets. This transaction takes the original assets off the balance sheet of the broker-dealer during the term of the trade, which might also be desirable.

The broker-dealer can add or remove bonds from or to the basket at each reset date. When this happens, the swap counterparty revalues the basket and provides more funds or receives funds as required. Bonds are removed from the basket if they have been sold by the broker-dealer, while new acquisitions can be funded by being placed in the TRS basket.

We illustrate a funding TRS trade using an example. Exhibit 8.5 shows a portfolio of five hypothetical convertible bonds on the balance sheet of a broker-dealer. The exhibit also shows market prices. This portfolio has been swapped out to a TRS provider in a six-month, weekly reset TRS contract. The TRS bank has paid over the combined market value of the portfolio at a lending rate of 1.14125%. This represents one-week LIBOR plus 7 bp. We assume the broker-dealer usually funds at above this level, and that this rate is an improvement on its normal funding. It is not unusual for this type of trade to be undertaken even if the funding rate is not an improvement, however, for diversification reasons.

We see from Exhibit 8.5 that the portfolio has a current market value of approximately $151,080,000. This value is lent to the broker-dealer in return for the bonds.

One week later the TRS is reset. We see from Exhibit 8.6 that the portfolio has increased in market value since the last reset. Therefore, the swap counterparty pays this difference over to the broker-dealer. This payment is netted out with the interest payment due from the broker-dealer to the swap counterparty. The interest payment is shown as $33,526.

Exhibit 8.7 shows the basket after the addition of a new bonds, and the resulting change in portfolio value.

Synthetic ABCP Conduit

The latest development in ABCP conduits is the synthetic structure. As with synthetic structured credit products, this structure uses credit derivatives to effect an economic transfer of risk and exposure between the originator and the issuer, so that there is not necessarily a sale of assets from the originator to the issuer. We will describe synthetic conduits by means of an hypothetical transaction, which is a total return, swap-backed ABCP structure.

Exhibit 8.8 is a structure diagram for a synthetic ABCP vehicle that uses total return swaps in its structure. It illustrates a hypothetical conduit, Golden Claw Funding, which issues paper into both the U.S. CP market and the Euro CP market. It has been set up as a funding vehicle, with the originator accessing the CP market to fund assets that it holds on its balance sheet. The originator can be a bank, non-bank financial institution such as a hedge fund, or a corporation. In our case study the originator is a hedge fund called ABC Fund Limited.

The structure shown in Exhibit 8.8 has the following features:

■ The CP issuance vehicle and the Purchase Company (PC) are based off-shore at a location such as Jersey, Ireland, or Cayman Islands.

EXHIBIT 8.5 Funding TRS Trade

Market Rates

EUR/USD FX Rate	1.266550
USD 1W LIBOR	1.4055

Name	Currency	Nominal Value	Price	Accrued	Amount	FX Rate	ISIN/ CUSIP Code	Market Price	Accrued Interest
ABC Telecom	EUR	16,000,000	111.671%	0.8169%	22,795,534.57	1.2666		111.6713875	0.81693989
XYZ Bank	USD	17,000,000	128.113%	1.7472%	22,076,259.03	1.0000		128.113125	1.74722222
XTC Utility	EUR	45,000,000	102.334%	0.3135%	58,845,000.00	1.2666		102.3337875	0.31352459
SPG Corporation	EUR	30,000,000	100.32500		30,000,325.00	1.2666		100.325	0
Watty Exploited	USD	15,000,000	114.997%	0.7594%	17,363,503.13	1.0000		114.9973125	0.759375
					151,080,621.72				

166

EXHIBIT 8.5　(Continued)

Payments

Interest ($)

Rate	0.000000%
Principle	151,080,000.00
Interest Payable	+0.00

Performance ($)

New Portfolio Value	151,080,621.72
Old Portfolio Value	n/a
Performance Payment	n/a

Net Payment ($)

Broker-Dealer receives from swap counterparty	+0.00

New Loan

Portfolio Additions ($)	0.00	
New Loan Amount ($)	151,080,621.72	
New Interest Rate	1.141250%	1w LIBOR + 7 bp

EXHIBIT 8.6 Spreadsheet Showing Basket of Bonds at TRS Reset Date Plus Performance and Interest Payments Due from Each TRS Counterparty

EUR/USD   1.2431

Bond	Curr	Nominal Value	Price	Accrued	Amount	FX	ISIN/ CUSIP	Market Price	Accrued
ABC Telecom	EUR	16,000,000	111.5000%	0.78%	22,331,239	1.2431		111.5	0.77595628
XYZ Bank	USD	17,000,000	125.0000%	1.58%	21,518,931	1		125	1.58194444
XTC Utility	EUR	45,000,000	113.0000000%	0.28%	63,369,825	1.2431		113	0.23278689
SPG Corporation	EUR	30,000,000	100.75		30,225,000	1.2431		100.75	
Watty Exploited	USD	15,000,000	113.0620%	0.63%	17,053,518.2	1		113.0619965	0.628125
					154,498,511.95				

EXHIBIT 8.6 (Continued)

Payments

Interest
Rate	1.14125%	1W LIBOR + 7 bp
Amount	151,080,000.00	151,113,526.12
Interest payable	33,526.12	

Old portfolio value	+151,080,951.67 USD
Interest rate	1.14125%
Interest payable by broker-dealer	+33,526.33 USD

Performance
Old portfolio value	151,080,000.00
New portfolio value	154,498,511.95
Performance payment	−3,418,511.95

New portfolio value	+154,498,511 USD
Performance	3,418,511 USD

Swap ctpy pays	−3,384,985.83 [if negative, swap counterparty pays, if positive, broker-dealer pays]
	Net payment

New loan
Additions	—
New loan amount	154,498,511.95
New interest rate	1.14875%

EXHIBIT 8.7 TRS Basket Value After Addition of New Bond

EUR/USD   1.228

Name	Curr	Nominal	Price	Accrued	Amount	Fx	Isin	Price	Accrued
ABC Telecom	EUR	16,000,000	111.5000%	0.78%	22,331,239	1.2431		111.5	0.77595628
XYZ Bank	USD	17,000,000	125.0000%	1.58%	21,518,931	1		125	1.58194444
XTC Utility	EUR	45,000,000	113.0000000%	0.28%	63,369,825	1.2431		113	0.28278689
SPG Corporation	EUR	30,000,000	100.75		30,225,000	1.2431		100.75	
Watty Exploited	USD	15,000,000	113.0620%	0.00628125	17,053,518	1		113.0619965	0.628125
Lloyd Cole Funding	USD	15,000,000	112.0923%	0.57%	16,899,628.1	1		112.0923125	0.571875
					171,398,140.07				

EXHIBIT 8.7 (Continued)

Payments		
Interest		
Rate	1.14875%	1W LIBOR + 7 bp
Amount	154,498,511.95	
Interest payable	34,510.03	
Performance		
Old portfolio value	154,498,511.95	
New portfolio value	171,398,140.07	
Performance payment	−16,899,628.13	
Swap ctpy pays	−16,865,118.09	
New loan		
Additions	16,899,628.13	
New loan amount	171,398,140.07	
New interest rate	1.22750%	

- The conduit issues CP in the U.S. dollar market via a co-issuer based in Delaware. It also issues Euro-CP via an offshore SPV.
- Proceeds of the CP issue are loaned to the PC, which uses these funds to purchase assets from the originator. As well as purchasing assets directly, the vehicle may also acquire an "interest" in assets that are held by ABC Fund Limited via a note referenced to a basket of assets. If assets are purchased and put directly onto the balance sheet of the PC, this is akin to what happens in a conventional ABCP structure. If interests in the assets are acquired via referenced note, then they are not actually sold to the PC, and remain on the balance sheet of ABC Fund Limited. Assets can be bonds, structured finance bonds, equities, mutual funds, hedge fund shares, convertible bonds, synthetic products, and private equity.
- Simultaneously, as it purchases assets or a note linked to assets, the PC enters into a TRS contract with ABC Fund Limited under which it pays the performance on the assets and receives interest on the CP proceeds it has used to purchase assets and referenced notes. The TRS is the means by which ABC Fund retains the economic interest in the assets it is funding, and the means by which the PC receives the interest it needs to pay back to Golden Claw as CP matures.

EXHIBIT 8.8   Synthetic ABCP Conduit, Hypothetical Deal "Golden Claw Funding"

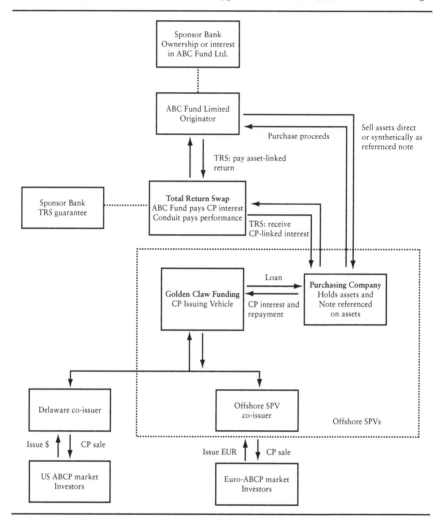

■ The issue vehicle itself may also purchase assets and referenced notes, so we show in Exhibit 8.8 that it also has a TRS between itself and ABC Fund Limited.

The Golden Claw structure is a means by which funds can be raised without a true sale structure. The TRS is guaranteed by the sponsor bank, which will ensure that the conduit is rated at the short-term rating of that sponsor bank. As CP matures, it will be repaid with a rollover issue of CP, with interest received via the TRS contract. If CP cannot rolled over, then the PC or the issuer will need to sell assets or referenced notes to repay principal, or otherwise the TRS guarantor will need to cover the repayment.

Essentially, the TRS is the means by which the conduit can be used to secure LIBOR-flat based funding for the originator, as long as payments under it are guaranteed by a sponsor or guarantor bank. Alternatively, the originator can arrange for a banking institution to provide a standby liquidity backup for the TRS in the event that it cannot roll over maturing CP. This service would be provided for a fee.

To show how the conduit cash flow mechanics would work, consider this example. Assume the first issue of CP by the Golden Claw structure. The vehicle issues $100 nominal of one-month CP at an all-in price of $99.50. These funds are lent by the vehicle to its purchase company, which uses these funds to buy $99.50 worth of assets synthetically from ABC Fund in the form of par-priced options referenced to these assets. Simultaneously it enters into a TRS with ABC Fund for a nominal amount of $100.

On the maturity of the CP, assume that the reference assets are valued at $103. This represents an increase in value of $3. ABC Fund will pay this increase in value to the purchase company, which will then pay this, under the terms of the TRS, back to ABC Fund. (In practice, this cash flow nets to zero, so no money actually moves.) Also under the terms of the TRS, ABC Fund pays the maturing CP interest of $0.50, plus any expenses and costs of Golden Claw itself, to the purchase company, which in turn pays this to Golden Claw, enabling it to repay CP interest to investors. The actual nominal amount of the CP issue is repaid by rolling it over (reissuing it).

If for any reason CP cannot be rolled over on maturity, the full nominal value of the CP must be paid under the terms of the TRS by ABC Fund to the purchase company.

Offshore Synthetic Funding Structures

Investment banks are increasingly turning to offshore synthetic structured solutions for their funding, regulatory capital, and accounting treatment requirements. We saw earlier how total return swaps could be used to obtain off-balance-sheet funding of assets at close to LIBOR, and how synthetic conduit structures can be used to access the ABCP market at LIBOR or close to LIBOR. Below we discuss synthetic structures that issue in both the CP and the MTN market, and are set up to provide funding for investment bank portfolios or reference portfolios of their clients. There are a number of ways to structure these deals, some using multiple SPVs, and new variations are being introduced all the time.

We illustrate the approach taken when setting up these structures by describing two different hypothetical funding vehicles.

Offshore Synthetic Funding Vehicle

A commercial bank or an investment bank can set up an offshore SPV that issues both CP and MTNs to fund underlying assets that are acquired synthetically. We describe this with an illustration.

Assume an investment bank wishes to access the CP and MTN markets to borrow funds at close to LIBOR. It sets up an offshore SPV, Long-Term Funding Limited, which has the freedom to issue the following liabilities as required: CP, MTN, repo agreements, and guaranteed investment contracts (GICs). GICs are deposit contracts that pay either a fixed coupon to lenders or a fixed spread over LIBOR.

These liabilities are used to fund the purchase of assets that are held by the investment bank. These assets are purchased synthetically via TRS contracts or sometimes in cash form as a reverse repo trade. The vehicle is illustrated in Exhibit 8.9.

The vehicle is structured in such a way that the liabilities it issues are rated at A-1/F-1 and Aaa/AAA. It enables the originating bank to access the money and capital markets at rates that are lower than it would oth-

EXHIBIT 8.9   Long-Term Funding Limited: Offshore Synthetic Funding Vehicle

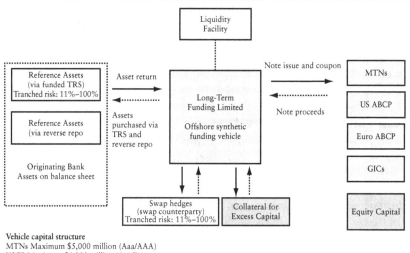

Vehicle capital structure
MTNs Maximum $5,000 million (Aaa/AAA)
USCP Maximum $4,000 million (A-1/F-1)
ECP Maximum $1,000 million (A-1/F-1)

erwise obtain in the interbank (unsecured) market. The originator invests its own capital in the structure in the form of an equity piece. At the same time, a liquidity facility is also put in place, to be used in the event that the vehicle is not able to pay maturing CP and MTNs. The liquidity facility is an additional factor that provides comfort to the rating agencies.

The vehicle's asset structure is composed of mainly synthetic securities, accessed using funded TRS contracts. However, to retain flexibility, the vehicle is also able to bring in assets in cash form in the form of reverse repo transactions. Possible types of assets that can be "acquired" by Long-Term Funding Ltd. include short-term money market instruments rated AAA, bullet corporate bonds rated from AAA to BB, structured finance securities (including ABS, RMBS, and CMBS securities rated from AAA to BB), government agency securities such as those issued by Ginnie Mae and Pfandbriefe securities, securities issued by government-sponsored entities (Fannie Mae and Freddie Mac), and secondary-market bank loans and syndicated loans rated at AAA to BBB. Reference assets can be denominated in any currency, and currency swaps are arranged to hedge the currency mismatch that results from the vehicle issuing in U.S. dollars and euros. In addition to the quality of the underlying reference assets, the credit rating of the TRS and repo counterparties is also taken into consideration when the liabilities are rated.

As for the liability structure, Long-Term Funding Ltd. finances the purchase of TRS and reverse repos by issuing CP, MTNs, and GICs. The interest-rate risk that arises from issuing GICs is hedged using interest-rate swaps. The ability of Long-Term Funding Ltd. to issue different types of liabilities allows the originating bank to access funding at any maturity from one-month to very long-term, and across a variety of sources. For instance, CP may be bought by banks, corporations, money market funds, and supranational institutions such as the World Bank; GIC contracts are frequently purchased by insurance companies.

Multi-SPV Synthetic Conduit Funding Structure

One of the main drivers behind the growth of synthetic funding structures has been the need for banks to reduce regulatory capital charges. While banks have achieved this by setting up offshore SPVs that issue liabilities and references assets synthetically, recent proposals on changing accounting treatment for SPVs means that this approach may not be sufficient for some institutions. The structure we describe here can reference an entire existing SPV synthetically, in effect a synthetic transfer of assets that have already been synthetically transferred. The vehicle would be used by banks or fund managers to obtain funding and capital relief for an entire existing portfolio without having to move any of the assets themselves.

EXHIBIT 8.10   Multi-SPV Offshore Synthetic Conduit Funding Structure

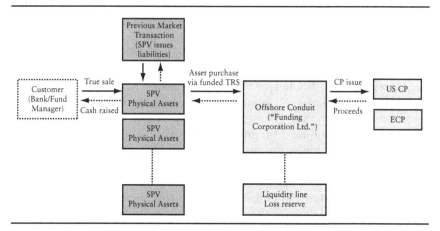

The key to the synthetic multi-SPV conduit is the CP and MTN issuance vehicle, which is a standalone vehicle established by a commercial or investment bank. Such a vehicle provides funding to an existing SPV or SPVs, and acquires the assets synthetically. The assets are deemed as being held within the structure and as such attract a 0% risk-weighting under Basel I.

The structure is illustrated in Exhibit 8.10. This structure has the following features:

- An offshore SPV issues CP into the U.S. and Euro markets.
- The offshore conduit, Funding Corporation Ltd., purchases the entire balance sheet of an existing SPV synthetically. The funds issued in the CP market are used to provide a funded TRS contract to the SPV whose assets are being funded.
- The customer gains a funding source and also retains the return on the assets; however it benefits from a reduced capital charge and no longer needs to mark the assets to market.
- The investment bank, originator, and CP investors (in that order) offer to bear any losses on the reference portfolio due to credit events or default, and earn a fee income for setting up this facility.
- Assets and additional SPVs can be added at any time.
- A liquidity facility is in place in the event that CP cannot be issued.

This structure is yet another example of the flexibility and popularity of credit derivatives, and structured credit products created from credit derivatives, in the debt capital markets today.

Combined Referenced Note and TRS Funding Structure

For a number of reasons, entities such as hedge funds or other investment companies, whether they are independent companies or parts of banking or bancassurance conglomerates, are not able to obtain funding from mainstream banks directly. Hedge funds, for example, are commonly funded via prime brokerage facilities set up with banks. Put simply, under a prime brokerage, the provider of the facility holds the assets of the hedge fund in custody, and these assets act as security collateral against which funds are advanced. (A prime broker acts in a similar capacity for a hedge fund in its foreign-exchange trading operations, confirming and settling trades with counterparties on behalf of the hedge fund and in effect substituting the credit of the prime broker for that of the hedge fund. Prime brokers also provide securities clearance and custody services to hedge funds.) These funds are used by the hedge funds to pay for the assets they have purchased and are then lent by the primer broker at a spread over LIBOR, typically 50 to 70 bp. The prime broker also lends assets to cover short positions.

Many investment companies hold positions in illiquid assets, such as hedge fund-of-funds shares, or other difficult-to-trade assets. It is more difficult to raise funds in the wholesale markets using such assets as collateral because of the problem associated with transferring them to the custody of the cash lender. The advent of credit derivatives and financial engineering has enabled companies to get around this problem by setting up tailor-made structures for funding purposes. Here we describe an example of a funding or liquidity structure that raises cash in the wholesale market via a note and TRS structure that references a basket of illiquid assets.

Assume two entities that are part of a bancassurance group: a regulated broker-dealer ("Smith Securities") and a hedge fund derivative investment house ("Smith Investments Company"). The investment house raises funds primarily from its parent banking group; however for diversity purposes, it also wishes to raise funds from other sources. One such source is the wholesale markets via a note and TRS structure as illustrated in Exhibit 8.11.

The lender is an investment bank ("ABC Bank") that is willing to advance funds to the investment company, secured by its assets, at a rate of LIBOR plus 20 bp. This is a considerable saving on the investment company's cost of funds with a prime broker, and comparable with its parent group funding rate. However its assets cannot be transferred as they are untradeable assets, and so they cannot act as collateral in the normal way one observes in, for example, repo trades.

Instead we can create the following structure that will enable the funding to be raised:

EXHIBIT 8.11   Combined Note and TRS Funding Structure

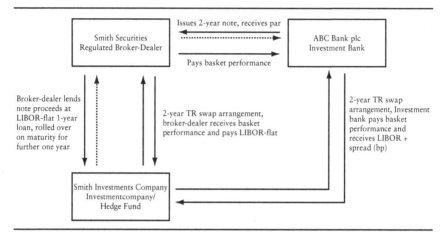

■ ABC Bank plc does not lend funds directly; instead it purchases a two-year note at a price of par. The return on this note is linked to the performance of a basket of assets held by Smith Investment Company. Because Smith Investment Company is an unregulated entity, it cannot issue a note into the wholesale markets. Consequently, the note is issued by its sister company, Smith Securities.

■ The funds raised by the sale of the note are transferred, in the form of a loan, from Smith Securities to Smith Investment Company at LIBOR-flat.

■ Simultaneously the two companies enter into a TRS arrangement wherein the start and maturity dates matching that of the note. Under this TRS, Smith Securities receives the performance of the basket of assets and pays LIBOR-flat.

■ Also simultaneously, Smith Investment Company and ABC Bank plc enter into a TRS arrangement whereby the bank pays the performance of the basket of assets and receives LIBOR plus 20 bp.

The net cash flow of this structure is such that Smith Investment Company pays ABC Bank plc LIBOR plus 20 bp, and raises funds via the proceeds of the note issue by Smith Securities. The economic effect is that of a two-year loan from ABC Bank to Smith Investment Company, but because of legal, regulatory, operational, and administrative restrictions we need to have the structure described above to effect this.

Note that under some jurisdictions, it is not possible for group companies to make inter-company loans, particularly if the two companies are incorporated in different countries, without attracting withholding tax on the loans. For example, the maximum permissible maturity for inter-company loans may be one year. To get around this, in Exhibit 8.11 we have shown the loan from Smith Securities to be a 1-year loan, which is then rolled over for another year on maturity.

CHAPTER 9

Credit-Linked Notes

Credit derivatives are grouped into *funded* and *unfunded* variants. In an unfunded credit derivative, typified by a credit default swap, the protection seller does not make an upfront payment to the protection buyer. In a funded credit derivative, typified by a credit-linked note (CLN), the investor in the note is the credit protection seller and is making an upfront payment to the protection buyer when buying the note. Thus, the protection buyer is the issuer of the note. If no credit event occurs during the life of the note, the redemption value of the note is paid to the investor on maturity. If a credit event does occur, then on maturity a value less than par will be paid out to the investor. This value will be reduced by the nominal value of the reference asset to which the CLN is linked. In this chapter, we discuss CLNs.

DESCRIPTION OF CLNs

Credit-linked notes exist in a number of forms, but all of them contain a link between the return they pay and the credit-related performance of the underlying asset. A standard CLN is a security, usually issued by an investment-grade-rated entity, that has an interest payment and fixed maturity structure similar to a vanilla bond. The performance of the CLN, however, including the maturity value, is linked to the performance of a specified underlying asset or assets as well as that of the issuing entity. CLNs are usually issued at par. They are often used as a financing vehicle by borrowers in order to hedge against credit risk; CLNs are purchased by investors to enhance the yield received on their holdings. Hence, the issuer of the CLN is the protection buyer and the buyer of the note is the protection seller.

Essentially CLNs are hybrid instruments that combine a pure credit risk exposure with a vanilla bond. The CLN pays regular coupons; however the credit derivative element is usually set to allow the issuer to decrease the principal amount, and/or the coupon interest, if a specified credit event occurs.

ILLUSTRATION OF A CLN

To illustrate a CLN, consider a bank issuer of credit cards that wants to fund its credit card loan portfolio via an issue of debt. The bank is rated AA–. In order to reduce the credit risk of the loans, it issues a two-year CLN. The principal amount of the bond is 100 (par) as usual, and it pays a coupon of 7.50%, which is 200 bp above the 2-year benchmark. The equivalent spread for a vanilla bond issued by a bank of this rating would be of the order of 120 bp. With the CLN though, if the incidence of bad debt among credit card holders exceeds 10% then the terms state that note holders will only receive back 85 per 100 par. The credit card issuer has in effect purchased a credit option that lowers its liability in the event that it suffers from a specified credit event, which in this case is an above-expected incidence of bad debts. The cost of this credit option to the credit protection buyer is paid in the form of a higher-coupon payment on the CLN. The credit card bank has issued the CLN to reduce its credit exposure, in the form of this particular type of credit insurance. If the incidence of bad debts is low, the CLN is redeemed at par. However, if there a high incidence of such debt, the bank will only have to repay a part of its loan liability.

INVESTOR MOTIVATION

Investors may wish purchase the CLN because the coupon paid on it will be above what the credit card bank would pay on a vanilla bond it issued, and higher than other comparable investments in the market. In addition such notes are usually priced below par on issue. Assuming the notes are eventually redeemed at par, investors will also realize a substantial capital gain.

SETTLEMENT

As with credit default swaps, CLNs may be cash settled or physically settled. However, there are differences associated with the funded nature of CLNs and also with the specific type of CLN that is being considered.

The true credit derivative CLN is a note issued by one party that references another party as the credit reference name. But certain bonds have been labeled as "CLNs" despite being issued by the same companies that are the credit references. For these bonds, the occurrence of a credit event signifies immediate termination of the bond. However, there is no settlement process as such because the protection seller is already holding the bond. In this respect, such CLNs are more akin to vanilla cash bonds of the same issuer.[1]

For true CLNs, the settlement process is similar to that for CDS contracts. Consider a CLN issued by ABC Securities that references XYZ Automotive plc. Specifically:

- Under cash settlement, upon occurrence of a credit event the note is terminated. The protection buyer will pay the default value, or recovery value (RR), of the reference name to the protection seller. This is equivalent to the [100 − RR] payout under a CDS contract.
- Under physical settlement, upon occurrence of a credit event the note is terminated. The protection buyer will deliver a XYZ Automotive plc bond—out of a deliverable basket of XYZ bonds—to the protection seller. The protection seller of course retains the original CLN bond, issued by ABC Securities.

Note that the protection buyer may well be ABC Securities, but does not have to be.

The value of the reference asset at the time of the credit event determines the payout under the terms of the CLN. This is known as the recovery value. In practice, a process of administration must be undertaken, in some cases lasting years, before the ultimate recovery value for the various classes of debtors can be realized. To assist payout under a credit derivative contract, a third-party calculation agent may be appointed at the inception of the contract. The role of the calculation agent is to determine the market value of the defaulted reference asset at, or shortly after, the credit event has occurred, so that the CLN may be matured and the redemption proceeds calculated. This would apply under cash or physical settlement.

Exhibit 9.1 illustrates a cash-settled CLN.

---

[1] The reason such bonds are termed "CLNs" is that their payoff is linked to a credit-related performance of the issuer such as a change in the credit rating.

EXHIBIT 9.1 Credit-Linked Note

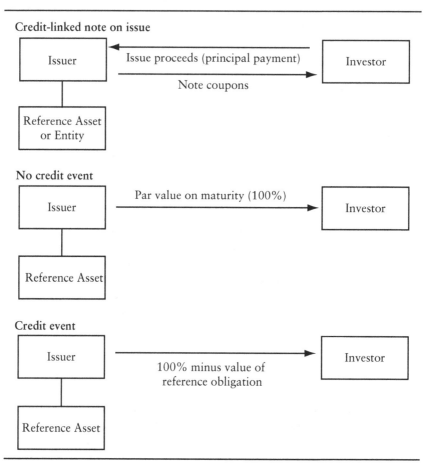

Credit-linked note on issue

Issuer — Issue proceeds (principal payment) / Note coupons — Investor

Reference Asset or Entity

No credit event

Issuer — Par value on maturity (100%) → Investor

Reference Asset

Credit event

Issuer → 100% minus value of reference obligation — Investor

Reference Asset

FORMS OF CREDIT LINKING

CLNs may be issued directly by a financial or corporate entity or via a special purpose vehicle (SPV). They have been issued with several different forms of credit-linking. For instance, a CLN may have its return performance linked to the issuer's, or a specified reference entity's, credit rating, risk exposure, financial performance or circumstance of default. Exhibit 9.2 shows a page from Bloomberg screen "CLN" with a list of the various types of CLN issue that have been made. Exhibit 9.3 shows another page

EXHIBIT 9.2 Bloomberg Screen CLN

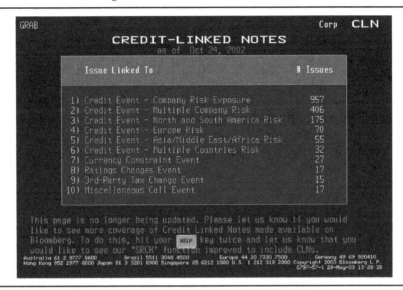

Source: © Bloomberg L.P. Used with permission.

EXHIBIT 9.3 Bloomberg Screen Showing a Sample of CLNs Impacted by Change in Reference Entity Credit Rating, October 2002

GRAB				Corp	CLN

Page 1/ 1

RATINGS CHANGES EVENT

Issuer	Settle Date	Cpn	Crncy	Maturity Date	Rating Changes Exposure
1) BHFBK	04/28/1998	6.25	DEM	04/28/2006	Govt of Ukraine
2) BSPIR	03/21/2000	7.00	EUR	02/20/2010	B-Spires
3) CATTLE	10/21/1999	8.63	GBP	12/07/2007	Cattle PLC
4) CNTCNZ	09/14/2000	FRN	AUD	09/14/2007	Contact Energy
5) CNTCNZ	09/14/2000	FRN	USD	09/14/2007	Contact Energy
6) HI	11/13/1997	FRN	USD	11/13/2013	Household Fin Co
7) IFCTF	08/04/1997	7.88	USD	08/04/2002	Indust Fin Corp
8) IFCTF	08/04/1997	7.75	USD	08/04/2007	Indust Fin Corp
9) KPN	06/13/2000	FRN	EUR	06/13/2002	KPN NV
10) KPN	06/13/2000	FRN	EUR	06/13/2002	KPN NV
11) KPN	06/13/2000	6.05	EUR	06/13/2003	KPN NV
12) METALF	07/25/2000	6.75	EUR	07/25/2005	MetallGesell Fin
13) METALF	07/25/2000	6.75	EUR	07/25/2005	MetallGesell Fin
14) OSTDRA	02/16/2000	Var	EUR	02/16/2007	Oester Draukraft
15) SIRSTR	06/25/1998	FRN	USD	10/06/2006	Bk Tokyo-Mitsub
16) SOWLN	03/26/1998	6.89	GBP	03/26/2008	Southern Water
17) SPIRES	01/26/1998	FRN	DEM	10/24/2007	Greece

Australia 61 2 9777 8600   Brazil 5511 3048 4500   Europe 44 20 7330 7500   Germany 49 69 920410
Hong Kong 852 2977 6000 Japan 81 3 3201 8900 Singapore 65 6212 1000 U.S. 1 212 318 2000 Copyright 2003 Bloomberg L.P.
G797-57-1 29-May-03 13:29:32

Source: © Bloomberg L.P. Used with permission.

accessed from Bloomberg screen CLN with a list of CLNs whose coupons have been affected by a change in the reference entity's credit rating.

Many CLNs are issued directly by banks and corporate borrowers in the same way as conventional bonds. An example of such a bond is shown at Exhibit 9.4. This shows Bloomberg screen DES for a CLN issued by British Telecom plc, the 8.125% note due in December 2010. The terms of this note state that the coupon will increase by 25 bp for each one-notch rating downgrade below A–/A3 suffered by the issuer during the life of the note. The coupon will decrease by 25 bp for each ratings upgrade, with a minimum coupon set at 8.125%. In other words, this note allows investors to take on a credit play on the fortunes of the issuer.

Exhibit 9.5 shows Bloomberg screen YA for this note as of May 29, 2003. We see that a rating downgrade meant that the coupon on the note was now 8.375%.

Exhibit 9.6 is the Bloomberg DES page for a U.S. dollar denominated CLN issued directly by Household Finance Corporation (HFC).[2] Like the British Telecom bond, the return of this CLN is linked to the credit risk of the issuer, but in a different way. The coupon of the HFC

EXHIBIT 9.4   Bloomberg Screen DES for British Telecom plc 8.125% 2010 Credit-Linked Note Issued on December 5, 2000

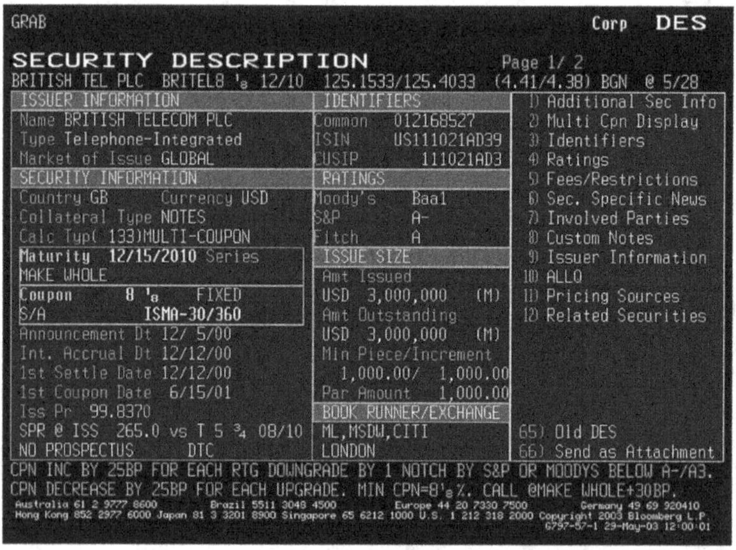

Source: © Bloomberg L.P. Used with permission.

---

[2] HFC was subsequently acquired by HSBC.

EXHIBIT 9.5   Bloomberg Screen YA for British Telecom CLN, May 29, 2003

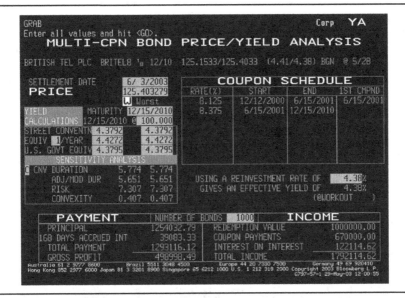

Source: © Bloomberg L.P. Used with permission.

EXHIBIT 9.6   Bloomberg DES Screen for Household Finance Corporation CLN

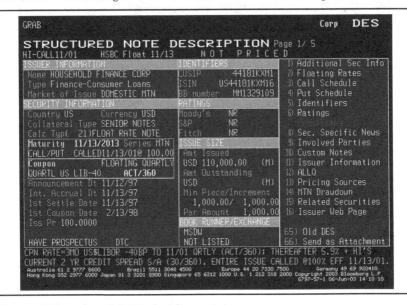

Source: © Bloomberg L.P. Used with permission.

bond was issued as floating USD-LIBOR, but the bond was not called by November 2001, the coupon would be the issuer's two-year "credit spread" over a fixed rate of 5.9%.[3] In fact, the issuer called the bond with effect from the coupon change date. Exhibit 9.7 shows the Bloomberg screen YA for the bond and how its coupon remained as at first issue until the call date.

Another type of credit-linking is evidenced from Exhibit 9.8, the Ford CLN Bloomberg DES page. This is a Japanese-yen-denominated bond issued by Alpha-Spires, which is a medium-term note program vehicle (a SPV) set up by Merrill Lynch. The note itself is linked to the credit quality of Ford Motor Credit Co. In the event of a default of the reference name, the note will be called immediately. Exhibit 9.9 shows the rate fixing for this note as of the last coupon date. The screen snapshot was taken on June 6, 2003.

Structured products such as synthetic collateralized debt obligations (CDOs) described in Chapter 7 may combine both CLNs and credit

EXHIBIT 9.7   Bloomberg YA Screen for Household Finance Corporation CLN, June 6, 2003

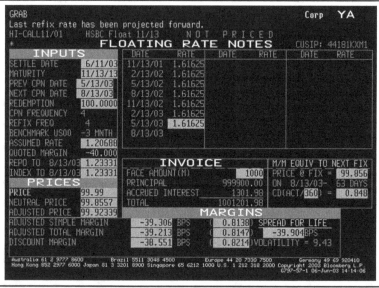

Source: © Bloomberg L.P. Used with permission.

---

[3] Exactly how to calculate the credit spread would be specified in the CLN issue's offering circular. For example, it could be the difference between current LIBOR and the current yield on one of HFC's other bond issues or the average of current yields on several of its other issues.

EXHIBIT 9.8   Bloomberg DES Screen for Ford CLN

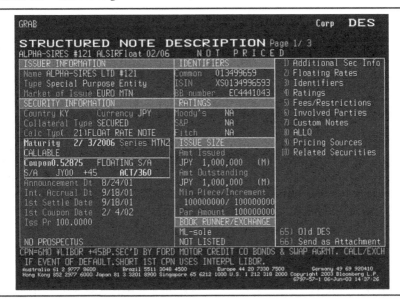

Source: © Bloomberg L.P. Used with permission.

EXHIBIT 9.9   Bloomberg YA Screen for Ford CLN, June 6, 2003

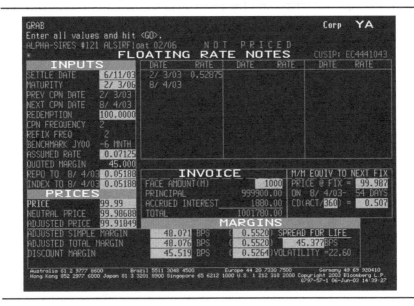

Source: © Bloomberg L.P. Used with permission.

EXHIBIT 9.10   CLN and Credit Default Swap Structure on Single Reference Name

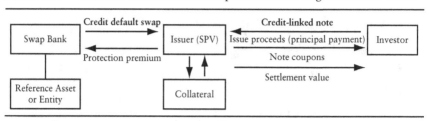

default swaps to meet issuer and investor requirements. For instance, Exhibit 9.10 shows a credit structure designed to provide a higher return for an investor on comparable risk to the cash market. An issuing entity is set up in the form of a special purpose vehicle (SPV) that issues CLNs to the market. The structure is engineered so that the SPV has a neutral position on a reference asset. It has bought protection on a single reference name by issuing a funded credit derivative, the CLN, and simultaneously sold protection on this name by selling a credit default swap on this name. The proceeds of the CLN are invested in risk-free collateral such as Treasury bills or a Treasury bank account. The coupon on the CLN will be a spread over LIBOR. It is backed by the collateral account and the fee generated by the SPV in selling protection with the credit default swap. Investors in the CLN will have exposure to the reference asset or entity, and the repayment of the CLN is linked to the performance of the reference entity. If a credit event occurs, the maturity date of the CLN is brought forward and the note is settled as par minus the value of the reference asset or entity.

THE FIRST-TO-DEFAULT CREDIT-LINKED NOTE

A standard CLN is issued in reference to one specific bond or loan. An investor purchasing such a note is writing credit protection on a specific reference credit. A CLN that is linked to more than one reference credit is known as a *basket credit-linked note.* A development of the CLN as a structured product is the First-to-Default CLN (FtD), which is a CLN that is linked to a basket of reference assets. The investor in the CLN is selling protection on the first credit to default.[4] Exhibit 9.11 shows this progression in the development of CLNs as structured products, with the *fully funded synthetic CDO,* described in Chapter 7, being the vehicle that uses CLNs tied to a large basket of reference assets.

---

[4] "Default" here meaning a credit event as defined in the ISDA definitions.

EXHIBIT 9.11   Progression of CLN Development

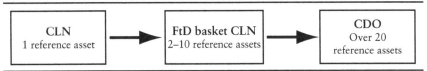

An FtD CLN is a funded credit derivative in which the investor sells protection on one reference in a basket of assets, whichever is the first to default. The return on the CLN is a multiple of the average spread of the basket. The CLN will mature early on occurrence of a credit event relating to any of the reference assets. Settlement on the CLN can be either of the following:

- Physical settlement, with the defaulted asset(s) being delivered to the noteholder.
- Cash settlement, in which the CLN issuer pays redemption proceeds to the noteholder calculated as:

Principal amount × Reference asset recovery value

In practice, it is not the "recovery value" that is used but the market value of the reference asset at the time the credit event is verified. Recovery of a defaulted asset follows a legal process of administration and/or liquidation that can take some years, and so the final recovery value may not be known with certainty for some time. Because the computation of recovery value is so difficult, holders of a CLN may prefer physical settlement where they take delivery of the defaulted asset.

Exhibit 9.12 shows a generic FtD credit-linked note.

To illustrate, consider an FtD CLN issued at par, with a term-to-maturity of five years, that is linked to a basket of five reference assets with a face value (issued nominal amount) of $10 million. An investor purchasing this note will pay $10 million to the issuer. If no credit event occurs during the life of the note, the investor will receive the face value of the note on maturity. If a credit event occurs on any of the assets in the basket, the note will redeem early and the issuer will deliver a deliverable obligation of the reference entity, or a portfolio of such obligations, for a $10 million nominal amount. An FtD CLN carries a similar amount of risk exposure on default to a standard CLN, namely the recovery rate of the defaulted credit. However, its risk exposure prior to default is theoretically lower than a standard CLN, as it can reduce default probability through diversification. The investor can obtain exposure to a basket of reference entities that differ by industrial sector and by credit rating.

EXHIBIT 9.12 First-to-Default CLN Structure

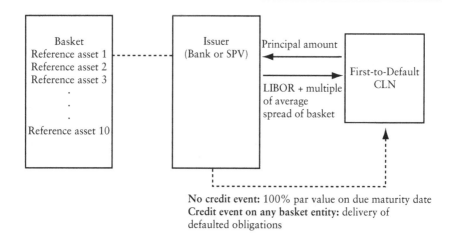

No credit event: 100% par value on due maturity date
Credit event on any basket entity: delivery of
defaulted obligations

EXHIBIT 9.13 Diversified Credit Exposure to Basket of Reference Assets:
Hypothetical Reference Asset Mix

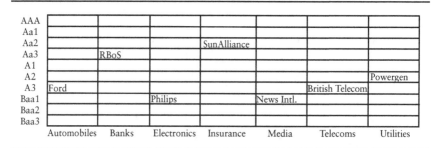

The matrix shown in Exhibit 9.13 illustrates how an investor can select a credit mix in the basket that diversifies risk exposure across a wide range; we show a hypothetical mix of reference assets to which an issued FtD could be linked. The precise selection of names will reflect an investor's own risk/return profile requirements.

The FtD CLN creates a synthetic credit entity that features a note return with enhanced spread. Investors receive a spread over LIBOR that is the average return of all the reference assets in the basket. This structure serves to diversify credit risk exposure while benefiting from a higher average return. If the pool of reference assets is sufficiently large, the structure becomes similar to a single-tranche CDO. This is discussed in Chapter 6.

CHAPTER 10

Structured Notes

For a plain vanilla bond structure, the (1) coupon interest rate is either fixed over the life of the security or floating at a fixed spread to reference rate; and (2) the principal is a fixed amount that is due on a specified date. There are bonds that have slight variations that are common in the marketplace. A callable bond may have a redemption date that is prior to the scheduled maturity date. The option to call the bond prior to the maturity date resides with the issuer; the benefit of calling the issue depends on the market interest rate at which the callable bond issue can be refinanced. Similarly, a putable bond has a maturity date that can be shortened, but in this case the option resides with the bondholder; if the market rate on comparable bonds exceeds the coupon rate, the bondholder will exercise. A convertible bond typically has at least two embedded options. The first is the bondholder's right to convert the bond into common stock. The second is the issuer's right to call the bond. Some convertible bonds are also putable.

Callable, putable, and convertible bonds are considered traditional securities, as are other similar structures such as extendible and tractable bonds.[1] There are bonds with embedded options that have much more complicated provisions for one or more of the following: interest rate payable, redemption amount, and timing of principal repayment. The interest or redemption amount can be tied to the performance or the level of one or more interest rates or noninterest rate benchmarks. As a result, the potential performance (return and risk) of such securities will be substantially different than those offered by plain vanilla bond structures. These securities are popularly referred to as *structured notes*.

---

[1] An extendible bond grants the issuer the right to extend the redemption date beyond the stated maturity date. A retractable bond grants the bondholder the right to redeem on a date prior to the original maturity date.

Historically, the problem with structured notes has been that they have been purchased by some entities that are unfamiliar with their investment risks. As a result, their have been major losses for some financial institutions and some large corporations as well. For example, in 1994 a large number of banks experienced losses from investing in certain types of structured notes.

In this chapter, we discuss structured notes, including the investor motivation for investing in such notes, issuer motivation for creating them, the design of structured notes, and provide examples.

STRUCTURED NOTES DEFINED

In a 1994 report by the Federal Reserve Bank of Chicago, the following description of structured notes appears:

> Unlike straight derivatives whose entire value is dependent on some underlying security, index or rate, structured securities are hybrids, having components of straight debt instruments and derivatives intertwined. Rather than paying a straight fixed or floating coupon, these instruments' interest payments are tailored to a myriad of possible indices or rates. The Federal Home Loan Bank (FHLB), one of the United States' largest issuers of such products, has *more than* 175 indices or index combinations against which cash flows are calculated. In addition to the interest payments, the securities' redemption value and final maturity can also be affected by the derivatives embedded in structured notes. Most structures contain embedded options, generally sold by the investor to the issuer. These options are primarily in the form of caps, floors, or call features. The identification, pricing and analysis of these options give structured notes their complexity.[2]

---

[2] Karen McCann and Joseph Cilia, "Product Summary: Structured Notes," Federal Reserve Bank of Chicago, The Financial Markets Unit, Supervision and Regulation, November 1994, p. 6. This type of definition is one used by regulators of depository institutions. For example, in the instructions for Call Reports for banks, structured notes are defined as "debt securities, including all asset-backed securities except mortgage-backed securities and inflation-indexed Treasuries, whose cash flow characteristics (coupon rate, redemption amount, or stated maturity) depend upon one or more indices and/or that have embedded forwards or options or are otherwise commonly known as 'structured notes.'"

The key to structured notes is that derivatives are involved. In the previous definition, the authors state that "straight debt instruments and derivatives are intertwined." Moreover, in this definition, the derivatives such as options are generally sold to the investor. What the definition suggests is that the issuer of a structured note may be exposed to the risk associated with having sold a derivative. For example, a structured note can have an interest rate that is tied to the performance of the S&P 500. The issuer of such a structured note is therefore exposed to the risk of a substantial interest expense if the S&P performs extremely well.

However, the above definition is not shared by all market participants. Consider the following two definitions. In a survey article of structured notes, Telpner defines structured notes as "fixed-income securities—sometimes referred to as hybrid securities that present the appearance of fixed-income securities—that combine derivative elements and do not necessarily reflect the risk of the issuer."[3] Here the key element is that the issuer is not necessarily taking on the opposite risk of the investors.

In their book on the structured notes market, Peng and Dattatreya write, "Structured notes are fixed income debentures linked to derivatives."[4] They go on to say:

> A key feature of structured notes is that they are created by an underlying swap transaction. The issuer rarely retains any of the risks embedded in the structured note and is almost hedged out of the risks of the note by performing a swap transaction with a swap counterparty. This feature permits issuers to produce notes of almost any specification, as long as they are satisfied that the hedging swap will perform for the life of the structured note. To the investor, this swap transaction is totally transparent since the only credit risk to which the investor is exposed is that of the issuer.[5]

In this definition, the focus is not on the issuer selling a debt instrument with derivative-type payoffs to investors, but the issuer protecting itself against the risks associated with the potential payoffs it must make to investors by hedging those risks. That is, the upside potential available to investors in a structured note do not reflect the risk to the issuer. While

[3] Joel S. Telpner, "A Survey of Structured Notes," *The Journal of Structured and Project Finance* 9 (Winter 2004), pp. 6–19.

[4] Scott Y. Peng and Ravi Dattatreya, *The Structured Note Market* (Chicago: Probus, 1995), p. 2.

[5] Peng and Dattatreya, *The Structured Note Market*, p. 2.

Peng and Dattatreya say that this can be done with a swap transaction, any other derivative can be employed to hedge the risk faced by an issuer.

MOTIVATION FOR INVESTORS AND ISSUERS

The motivation for the purchase of structured notes by investors includes (1) the potential for enhancing yield; (2) acquiring a view on the bond market; (3) obtaining exposure to alternative asset classes; (4) acquiring exposure to a particular market but not a particular aspect of it;[6] and (5) controlling risks.

The potential for yield enhancement was the motivation behind the popularity of structured notes in the sustained low-interest-rate environment in the late 1980s. After the high interest rates (double digits) that prevailed in the early 1980s, institutional investors faced interest rates that were not sufficient to satisfy the liabilities for the financial products they created during the high-interest-rate environment. Local governments had come to rely on interest income from higher interest rates in order to fund operations and avoid raising property and personal taxes. Structured notes offered the opportunity to provide a higher return than that prevailing in the market for plain vanilla debt obligations if certain market scenarios occurred.

The ability of issuers to hedge risk using derivatives allowed them to create securities for investors who had a view on the bond market. For example, a structured note could be created that allowed exposure to a change in the yield curve, the change in the spread between two reference interest rates, or the direction of interest rates (e.g., a leveraged payoff if interest rates declined).

Structured notes that have payoffs based on the performance of asset classes other than bonds allow investors to take views on other markets in which they may be prohibited from investing by regulatory or client constraint. For example, suppose that an investor who must restrict portfolio holdings to investment-grade bonds has a view on the equity market. The investor would not be permitted to invest in equities. However, by investing in an investment-grade bond whose payoff is based on the performance of the equity market, the investor has obtained exposure to the equity market. For this reason, some market participants refer to structured notes as "rule busters."

---

[6] For example, a U.S. investor may want exposure to Japanese equities but not yen assets, so the investor can buy U.S. dollar-denominated bonds that have a payoff linked to the Japanese stock market index.

Finally, a structured note can be used to hedge exposure that an investor may not be able to hedge more efficiently using derivative products. For example, suppose that an investor is concerned with exposure in its current portfolio to changes in credit spreads. While there are currently credit derivatives that would allow the investor to hedge this exposure, suppose that the investor is not permitted to utilize them. An investor can have an issuer create a structured note that has a payoff based on a particular credit spread. The issuer can protect itself by taking a position in the credit derivatives market.

But what is the benefit of all this customization for the issuer? By creating a customized product for an investor, the issuer seeks a lower funding cost than if it had issued a bond with a plain vanilla structure.

How do borrowers or their agents find investors who are willing to buy structured notes? In a typical plain vanilla bond offering, the sales force of the underwriting firm solicits interest in the issue from its customer base. That is, the sales forces will make an inquiry to investors about their needs and preferences. In the structured note market, the process is often quite different. Because of the small size of an offering and the flexibility to customize the offering in the swap market, investors can approach an issuer through its agent about designing a security for their needs. This process of customers inquiring of issuers or their agents to design a security is called a *reverse inquiry*. For example, the World Bank, a major issuer of structured notes, indicates that to propose a new issue, an investor can contact an underwriter or the World Bank directly. The criteria the World Bank will use in deciding to proceed with the transaction will be based on a minimum size of USD 10 million or equivalent in other currencies, a minimum maturity of one year, the complexity of the transaction, and the suitability of the proposed structured note for the issuer as well as the investor.

ISSUANCE FORM AND ISSUERS

A structured note can be issued in the public market or as a private placement or a 144A security. It can take the form of either commercial paper, a medium-term note, a certificate of deposit, or a corporate bond. A medium-term note (MTN) differs from a corporate bond in the manner in which it is distributed to investors when initially sold. Although some investment-grade corporate bond issues are sold on a best-efforts basis, typically they are underwritten by investment bankers. MTNs have been traditionally distributed on a best-efforts basis by either an investment banking firm or other broker/dealers acting as agents.

Another difference between corporate bonds and MTNs is that when MTNs are offered, they are usually sold in relatively small amounts on a continuous or an intermittent basis as part of a continuous rolling program, while plain vanilla bonds are sold in large discrete offerings.[7]

The issuer must be of high credit quality so that credit risk is minimal in order to accomplish the objectives that motivated the creation of the structured note. Issuers include highly rated corporations, banks, and U.S. government agencies. Because credit risk increases over time, the type of issuer and the form of the security are tied to the investor's planned holding period of the investor. Exhibit 10.1 provides a summary of the relationships among the maturity profile of the investor, the typical form of the debt instrument, and the typical issuer.

CREATING STRUCTURED NOTES

Peng and Dattatreya describe the three main steps in creating a structured note:[8]

- conceptual stage;

EXHIBIT 10.1 Maturity Profile Factor, Typical Form of Instrument, and Typical Issuer

Maturity	Typical Form of Instrument	Typical Issuer
Under 1 year	Commercial paper	A1/P1 rated corporations
1 to 3 years	Commercial paper, Bank note, MTN	Banks, corporations
Greater than 3 years	Corporate bond, MTN	U.S. government agencies

Adapted from Scott Y. Peng and Ravi Dattatreya, *The Structured Note Market* (Chicago: Probus, 1995), p. 303.

---

[7] In the United States, a corporation that wants an MTN program will file a shelf registration with the SEC for the offering of securities. While the SEC registration for MTN offerings is between $100 million and $1 billion, once the total is sold, the issuer can file another shelf registration. The registration includes a list of the investment banking firms, usually two to four, that the corporation has arranged to act as agents to distribute the MTNs. The issuer posts rates over a range of maturities, typically as a spread over a benchmark such as a Treasury security of comparable maturity. The agents then make the offering rate schedule available to their investor base interested in MTNs.

[8] Chapter 8 in Peng and Dattatreya, *The Structured Note Market.*

■ identification process; and
■ structuring or construction stage.

In customizing a structured note for a client, the investment banker must understand the client's motivation. This is the conceptual stage of the process. We described earlier why investors look to the structured note market for customization. The investor will provide the motivation through reverse inquiry.

In the identification process, the investment banker identifies the underlying components that will be packaged to create the structured note based on the requirements identified in the conceptual stage. This process begins with specifying five customization factors: nationality, rate profile, risk/return, maturity, and credit. The nationality factor specifies the country where the client would like to have some investment exposure. In the case of structured notes where the underlying is an interest rate, the rate factor determines the directional play (e.g., rising or falling interest rates, flattening or steepening yield curve) that is to be embedded in the structure. The amount of risk to be embedded in the structured note is the risk/return customization factor. Both the maturity and credit customization factors determine the instrument that will be used and the type of issuer as described in Exhibit 10.1.

In the structuring or construction stage, the investment banker gathers the pertinent market data and issuer-specific information. This information includes the target funding cost for the issuer (after underwriting fees) and the desired coupon and principal structure based on information from the conceptual and identification stages. In determining the cost of the structure, recognition must be given to the hedging cost that will be incurred when using the derivative instrument or instruments. Other specifications of the structured note that may have to be determined will depend on the complexity of the structure. For example, a structure may require that the correlation of the factors driving the price of the underlying instruments in the structure be estimated.

EXAMPLES OF STRUCTURED NOTES

A wide range of structured notes have been created in the market. Here we will discuss only two types: interest-rate structured notes and equity-linked structured notes.

Interest Rate Linked Structured Notes

The general coupon formula for a floating-rate security is

Reference interest rate ⅰ Quoted margin

A structured note whose coupon rate is linked to a reference interest rate has a coupon reset formula that differs from the one above. Examples include leveraged/deleveraged floaters, step-up notes, dual indexed, floaters, range notes, and inverse floaters. We discuss each below and in our discussion of inverse floaters, we describe how they are created with the use of interest rate swaps.

Leveraged/Deleveraged Floaters

A coupon reset formula could be as follows:

$$L \times (\text{Reference interest rate}) + \text{Quoted margin}$$

where L is a positive value that is different from 1. Depending on the value of L, the structured note is either a leveraged or deleveraged floater.

When L exceeds 1 in the coupon reset formula, the structured note is referred to as a *leveraged floater*. When L is less than 1, the structured note is called a *deleveraged floater*. That is, the coupon rate for a deleveraged floater is computed as a fraction of the reference rate plus the quoted margin. Bankers Trust issued such a floater in April 1992 that matured in March 2003. This issue delivered quarterly coupon payments according to the following formula: 0.40 × (10-year Constant Maturity Treasury rate) + 2.65% with a floor of 6%.

Step-Up Notes

Step-up notes are securities that have a have coupon rates that increase over time. These securities are called *step-up notes* because the coupon rates "step up" over time. For example, a 5-year step-up note might have a coupon rate that is 5% for the first two years and 6% for the last three years. Or, the step-up note could call for a 5% coupon rate for the first two years, 5.5% for the third and fourth years, and 6% for the fifth year. When there is only one change (or step up), as in our first example, the issue is referred to as a *single step-up note*. When there is more than one change, as in our second example, the issue is referred to as a *multiple step-up note*.

An example of an actual multiple step-up note is a 5-year issue of the Student Loan Marketing Association (Sallie Mae) issued in May 1994. The coupon schedule is as follows:

6.05% from 5/3/94 to 5/2/95

6.50% from 5/3/95 to 5/2/96
7.00% from 5/3/96 to 5/2/97
7.75% from 5/3/97 to 5/2/98
8.50% from 5/3/98 to 5/2/99

Dual-Indexed Floaters

The coupon rate for a *dual-indexed floater* is typically a fixed percentage plus the difference between two reference rates. For example, the Federal Home Loan Bank System issued a floater in July 1993 that matured in July 1996 whose coupon rate was the difference between the 10-year Constant Maturity Treasury rate and 3-month LIBOR plus 160 bp. This issue reset and paid quarterly.

Range Notes

For a *range note*, the coupon rate is equal to the reference rate as long as the reference rate is within a certain range at the reset date. If the reference rate is outside of the range, the coupon rate is zero for that period.

For example, a 3-year range note might specify that the reference rate is 1-year LIBOR and that the coupon rate resets every year. The coupon rate for the year will be 1-year LIBOR as long as 1-year LIBOR at the coupon reset date falls within the range as specified below:

	Year 1	Year 2	Year 3
Lower limit of range	4.5%	5.25%	6.00%
Upper limit of range	5.5%	6.75%	7.50%

If 1-year LIBOR is outside of the range, the coupon rate is zero. For example, if in Year 1 1-year LIBOR is 5% at the coupon reset date, the coupon rate for the year is 5%. However, if 1-year LIBOR is 6%, the coupon rate for the year is zero since 1-year LIBOR is greater than the upper limit for Year 1 of 5.5%.

Consider a range note issued by Sallie Mae in August 1996 that matured in August 2003. This issue made coupon payments quarterly. The investor received 3-month LIBOR plus 155 bp for every day during the quarter that 3-month LIBOR was between 3% and 9%. Interest accrued at 0% for each day that 3-month LIBOR was outside this range. As a result, this range note had a floor of 0%.

Inverse Floaters

Typically, the coupon formula on floaters is such that the coupon rate increases when the reference rate increases, and decreases when the reference rate decreases. However, there are issues whose coupon rates move in the opposite direction from the change in the reference rates. Such issues are called *inverse floaters* or *reverse floaters*.[9]

The coupon reset formula for an inverse floater is

$$K - L \times (\text{Reference interest rate})$$

When L is greater than 1, the security is referred to as a leveraged inverse floater.

For example, suppose that for a particular inverse floater K is 12% and L is 1. Then the coupon reset formula would be

$$12\% - (\text{Reference rate})$$

Suppose the reference rate is 1-month LIBOR, then the coupon formula would be

$$12\% - (\text{1-month LIBOR})$$

If in some month 1-month LIBOR at the coupon reset date is 5%, the coupon rate for the period is 7%. If in the next month 1-month LIBOR declines to 4.5%, the coupon rate increases to 7.5%.

Notice that if 1-month LIBOR exceeded 12%, then the coupon reset formula would produce a negative coupon rate. To prevent this, there is a floor imposed on the coupon rate. Typically, the floor is zero. There is also a cap on the inverse floater. This occurs if 1-month LIBOR is zero. In that unlikely event, the maximum coupon rate is 12% for our hypothetical inverse floater. In general, it will be the value of K in the coupon reset formula for an inverse floater.

Suppose instead that the coupon formula for an inverse floater whose reference rate is 1-month LIBOR is as follows:

$$28\% - 3 \times (\text{1-month LIBOR})$$

If 1-month LIBOR at a reset date is 5%, then the coupon rate for that month is 13%. If in the next month 1-month LIBOR declines to 4%, the coupon rate increases to 16%. Thus, a decline in 1-month LIBOR of 100 bp increases the coupon rate by 300 bp. This is because the value for L in the coupon reset formula is 3. Assuming neither the cap nor the

---

[9] Inverse floaters in the mortgage-backed securities market are common and are created without the use of a derivative instrument by simply dividing a bond class into a floater and inverse floater at the time the deal is structured.

floor is reached, for each 1 bp change in 1-month LIBOR the coupon rate changes by 3 bp.

As an example, consider an inverse floater issued by the Federal Home Loan Bank System in April 1999. This issue matured in April 2002 and delivered quarterly payments according to the following formula:

$$18\% - 2.5 \times (3\text{-month LIBOR})$$

This inverse floater had a floor of 3% and a cap of 15.5%.

How Inverse Floaters are Created Using Interest Rate Swaps   An inverse floater can also be created when an investment banking firm underwrites a fixed-rate bond (corporates, agencies, and municipalities) and simultaneously enters into an interest rate swap for a time that is generally less than the bond's tenor. The investor owns an inverse floater for the swap's tenor, which then converts to a fixed-rate bond (the underlying collateral) when the swap contract expires. An inverse floater created using a swap is called an *indexed inverse floater.*

To see how this can be accomplished, let us assume the following. An issuer wants to issue $200 million on a fixed-rate basis for 20 years. An investment bank suggests two simultaneous transactions.

Transaction 1: Issue a $200 million, a 20-year bond in which the coupon rate is determined by the following rules for a specific reference rate:

For years 1 through 5:   14% – Reference rate
For years 6 through 10:   5%

Transaction 2: Enter into a 5-year interest rate swap with the investment bank with a notional principal amount of $200 million in which semiannual payments are exchanged as follows using the same reference rate:

Issuer pays the reference rate
Issuer receives 6%

Note that for the first five years, the investor owns an inverse floater because as the reference rate increases (decreases) the coupon rate decreases (increases). However, even though the security issued pays an inverse floating rate, the combination of the two transactions results in fixed-rate financing for the issuer:

Rate issuer receives
From the investment bank via the swap: 6%

Rate issuer pays
To security holders: 14% − Reference rate
To the investment bank via the swap: Reference rate

Net payments
(14% − Reference rate) + Reference rate − 6% = 8%

Equity-Linked Structured Notes

An equity swap can be used to design a bond issue with a coupon rate tied to the performance of an equity index.

To illustrate how this is done, suppose the Universal Information Technology Company (UIT) seeks to raise $100 million for the next five years on a fixed-rate basis. UIT's investment banker indicates that if bonds with a maturity of five years were issued, the interest rate on the issue would have to be 8.4%. At the same time, there are institutional investors seeking to purchase bonds but are interested in making a play (i.e., betting on) on the future performance of the stock market. These investors are willing to purchase a bond whose annual interest rate is based on the actual performance of the S&P 500 stock market index.

The banker recommends to UIT's management that it consider issuing a 5-year bond whose annual interest rate is based on the actual performance of the S&P 500. The risk with issuing such a bond is that UIT's annual interest cost is uncertain since it depends on the performance of the S&P 500. However, suppose that the following two transactions are arranged:

1. On January 1, UIT agrees to issue, using the banker as the underwriter, a $100 million 5-year bond whose annual interest rate is the actual performance of the S&P 500 that year minus 300 bp. The minimum interest rate, however, is set at zero. The annual interest payments are made on December 31.
2. UIT enters into a 5-year, $100 million notional amount equity swap with the banker in which each year for the next five years UIT agrees to pay 7.9% to the banker, and the banker agrees to pay the actual performance of the S&P 500 that year minus 300 bp. The terms of the swap call for the payments to be made on December 31 of each year. Thus, the swap payments coincide with the payments that must be made on the bond issue. Also as part of the swap agreement, if the S&P 500 minus 300 bp results in a negative value, the banker pays nothing to

UIT and this risk is usually hedged with a basis swap that pays a fixed or floating cash flow in return for receiving the return on the S&P.

Exhibit 10.2 diagrams the payment flows for this swap. Consider what has been accomplished with these two transactions from the perspective of UIT. Specifically, focus on the payments that must be made by UIT on the bond issue and the swap and the payments that it will receive from the swap. These are summarized as follows:

Interest payments on bond issue:	S&P 500 return – 300 bp
Swap payment from the banker:	S&P 500 return – 300 bp
Swap payment to the banker:	7.9%
Net interest cost:	7.9%

EXHIBIT 10.2   Bond Structure: Conventional versus S&P Linked Note

a. Conventional Bond Issue

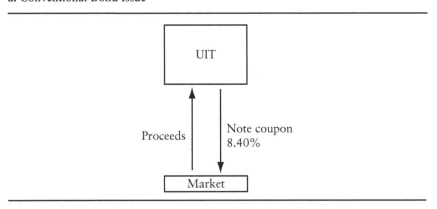

b. S&P Linked Note

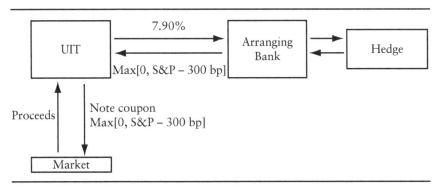

Thus, the net interest cost is a fixed rate despite the bond issue paying an interest rate tied to the S&P 500. This was accomplished with the equity swap.

There are several questions that should be addressed. First, what was the advantage to UIT to entering into this transaction? Recall that if UIT issued a bond, the banker estimated that UIT would have to pay 8.4% annually. Thus, UIT has saved 50 bp (8.4% minus 7.9%) per year. Second, why would investors purchase this bond issue? In real world markets, there are restrictions imposed on institutional investors as to types of investment or by other portfolio guidelines. For example, an institutional investor may be prohibited by a client or by other portfolio guidelines from purchasing common stock. However, it may be permitted to purchase a bond of an issuer such as UIT despite the fact that the interest rate is tied to the performance of common stocks. Third, is the banker exposed to the risk of the performance of the S&P 500? In the swap market, there are ways for the banker to protect itself.

CHAPTER 11

Large Ticket Leasing: Leasing Fundamentals

A lease is a contract over the term of which the owner of the equipment permits another entity to use it in exchange for a promise by the latter to make a series of payments. The owner of the equipment is referred to as the *lessor.* The entity that is being granted permission to use the equipment is referred to as the *lessee.*

Most corporate financial executives recognize that earnings are derived from the use of an asset, not its ownership, and that leasing is simply an alternative financing method. More equipment is financed today by equipment leases than by bank loans, private placements, or any other method of equipment financing. Nearly any asset that can be purchased can also be leased, from aircraft, ships, satellites, computers, refineries, and steam-generating plants, on one hand, to typewriters, duplicating equipment, automobiles, and dairy cattle, on the other hand.

In order to compare leasing with other methods of financing, it is necessary to understand the basics of how leasing works and the differences among the general categories of equipment leases. This will be explained in this chapter, along with the reasons often cited for leasing, the types of lessors, and tax and financial reporting requirements. Understanding leasing is also important for understanding lease securitization. In the next chapter, we discuss leveraged leases.

HOW LEASING WORKS

A typical leasing transaction works as follows: The lessee first decides on the equipment needed. The lessee then decides on the manufacturer, the make, and the model. The lessee specifies any special features desired, the terms of warranties, guaranties, delivery, installation, and services. The lessee also negotiates the price. After the equipment and terms have been specified and the sales contract negotiated, the lessee enters into a lease agreement with the lessor. The lessee negotiates with the lessor on the length of the lease; the rental; whether sales tax, delivery, and installation charges should be included in the lease; and other optional considerations.

After the lease has been signed, the lessee assigns its purchase rights to the lessor, which then buys the equipment exactly as specified by the lessee. When the equipment is delivered, the lessee formally accepts the equipment to make sure it gets exactly what was ordered. The lessor then pays for the equipment, and the lease goes into effect.

When all costs associated with the use of the equipment are to be paid by the lessee and not included in the lease payments, the lease is called a *net lease* or *triple-net lease*. Examples of such costs are property taxes, insurance, and maintenance. These costs are paid directly by the lessee and may not be deducted from the lease payments.

At the end of the lease term, the lessee usually has the option to renew the lease, to buy the equipment, or to terminate the agreement and return the equipment. As we shall see later in this chapter, the options available to the lessee at the end of the lease are very significant in that the dimensions of such options determine the nature of the lease for tax purposes and the classification of the lease for financial accounting purposes.

TYPES OF EQUIPMENT LEASES

Equipment leases fall into the following two general categories: (1) nontax-oriented leases and (2) tax-oriented true leases. We discuss each type of lease in the following sections.[1]

Nontax-Oriented Leases

Nontax-oriented leases, most commonly referred to as a *conditional sale leases*, transfer substantially all of the benefits and risks incidental to ownership of the leased property to the lessee and usually give the lessee a fixed-price bargain purchase option or renewal option not based on fair market value at the time of exercise.

We discuss the guidelines under the Internal Revenue Code for a lease to be classified as a conditional sale leases for tax purposes later in

---

[1] There is a third type of specialized lease that is not discussed, a *tax-oriented TRAC lease for over-the-road vehicles.*

this chapter. If a lease is classified as a conditional sale lease, the lessee treats the property as owned thereby entitling the lessee to depreciate the property for tax purposes, claim any tax credit that may be available, and deduct as an expense the imputed interest portion of the lease payments. The lessor under a conditional sale lease treats the transaction as a loan and cannot offer the low lease rates associated with a true lease because the lessor does not retain the tax benefits available to the owner of the equipment.

Tax-Oriented True Leases

The *true lease* offers all of the primary benefits commonly attributed to leasing. Substantial cost savings can often be achieved through the use of tax-oriented true leases in which the lessor claims and retains the tax benefits of ownership and passes through to the lessee a portion of such tax benefits in the form of reduced lease payments. The lessor claims tax benefits resulting from equipment ownership such as tax depreciation deductions, and the lessee deducts the full lease payment as an expense. The lessor in a true lease owns the leased equipment at the end of the lease term. A tax-oriented true lease (also sometimes called a *guideline lease*) either contains no purchase option or has a purchase option based on fair market value.

The principal advantage to a lessee of using a true lease to finance an equipment acquisition is the economic benefit that comes from the indirect realization of tax benefits that might otherwise be lost because the lessee cannot use the tax benefits. This occurs when the lessee neither has a sufficient tax liability, nor expects to be able to fully use the tax benefits in the future if those benefits are carried forward.

If the lessee is unable to generate a sufficient tax liability to currently use all tax benefits, the cost of owning new equipment will effectively be higher than leasing the equipment under a true lease. Under these conditions, leasing is usually a less costly alternative than borrowing to buy because the lessor uses the tax benefits from the acquisition and passes on a portion of these benefits to the lessee through a lower lease payment.

The lower cost of leasing realized by a lessee throughout the lease term in a true lease must be weighed against the loss of the leased equipment's market value at the end of the lease term, referred to as the *residual value*. A framework for evaluating the tax and timing effects is presented later in this chapter.

The Internal Revenue Service is well aware that parties to a leasing transaction may find it more advantageous from a tax point of view to characterize an agreement as a "lease" rather than as a conditional sale agreement. Therefore, guidelines have been established by the IRS to distinguish between a true lease and a conditional sales agreement. These guidelines are discussed later.

Single-Investor Leases versus Leveraged Leases

There are two categories of true leases: single-investor leases (or direct leases) and leveraged leases. *Single-investor leases* are essentially two-party transactions, with the lessor purchasing the leased equipment with its own funds and being at risk for 100% of the funds used to purchase the equipment.

The leveraged form of a true lease of equipment is the ultimate form of lease financing. The most attractive feature of a *leveraged lease,* from the standpoint of a lessee unable to use tax benefits of depreciation, is its low cost as compared to alternative methods of financing. Leveraged leasing also satisfies a need for lease financing of especially large capital equipment projects with economic lives of up to 25 or more years, although leveraged leases are also used where the life of the equipment is considerably shorter. The leveraged lease can be a most advantageous financing device when used for the right kinds of projects and structured correctly.

A leveraged lease of equipment is conceptually similar to a single-investor lease. The lessee selects the equipment and negotiates the lease in much the same manner. Also, the terms for rentals, options, and responsibility for taxes, insurance, and maintenance are similar. However, a leveraged lease is appreciably more complex in size, documentation, legal involvement, and, most importantly, the number of parties involved and the unique advantages that each party gains.

Leveraged leases of equipment are generally offered only by corporations and financial institutions acting as lessors. This is because in a leveraged lease the tax benefits available to individual lessors are much more limited than those available to a corporation.

The lessor in a leveraged lease of equipment becomes the owner of the leased equipment by providing only a percentage (20% to 30%) of the capital necessary to purchase the equipment. The remainder of the capital (70% to 80%) is borrowed from institutional investors on a nonrecourse basis to the lessor. Such a loan is secured by a first lien on the equipment, an assignment of the lease, and an assignment of the lease payments. The cost of the nonrecourse borrowing is a function of the credit standing of the lessee. The lease rate varies with prevailing interest rates and with the risk of the transaction.

A "leveraged lease" is always a true lease. The lessor in a leveraged lease can claim all of the tax benefits incidental to ownership of the equipment even though the lessor provides only 20% to 30% of the capital needed to purchase the equipment. This ability to claim the tax benefits attributable to the entire cost of the leased equipment and the right to 100% of the residual value provided by the lease, while providing and being at risk for only a portion of the cost of the equipment, is the "leverage" in a leveraged lease. This leverage enables the lessor in a leveraged lease to offer the lessee much lower lease rates than the lessor could provide under a single-investor nonleveraged lease.

Single-investor nonleveraged leases are basically two-party transactions with a lessee and a lessor. However, leveraged leases by their nature involve a minimum of three parties with diverse interests: a lessee, a lessor, and a nonrecourse lender. Indeed, leveraged leases are sometimes called *three-party transactions*. We will discuss leveraged leases in more detail in the next chapter.

FULL PAYOUT LEASES VERSUS OPERATING LEASES

Thus far, the leases we have discussed are comparable to equipment financing transactions in that the lease term is for a substantial portion of the economic life of the leased equipment. In these leases the lessor expects to recover its entire investment plus (1) a targeted return on its investment from the lease payments received; (2) any tax benefits the lessor is entitled to receive; and (3) the residual value anticipated when the lease terminates. These types of leases are called *full payout leases*. Such leases are essentially financing transactions.

Other types of leases called *operating leases*, in contrast to full payout lease, are not financing transactions. Operating leases may be for only a fraction of the life of the asset. An operating lease is always a true lease for tax purposes. That is, the lessor is entitled to all the tax benefits associated with ownership, and the lessee is entitled to deduct the lease payments.

We shall explain later in this chapter the special meaning of the term "operating lease" for financial accounting purposes. Transactions classified as operating leases are not disclosed in the body of the balance sheet as financial obligations. Instead, they are shown in the footnotes to the financial statement as fixed obligations. This classification may arise despite the fact that the transaction, for all intents and purposes, is a financing transaction.

REASONS FOR LEASING

Leasing is an alternative to purchasing. Because the lessee is obligated to make a series of payments, a lease arrangement resembles a debt contract. Thus, the advantages cited for leasing are often based on a comparison between leasing and purchasing using borrowed funds.

Cost

Many lessees find true leasing attractive because of its apparent low cost. This is particularly evident where a lessee cannot currently use tax benefits associated with equipment ownership due to such factors as lack of currently taxable income or net operating loss carryforwards.

If it were not for the different tax treatment for owning and leasing equipment, the costs would be identical in an efficient capital market. However, due to the different tax treatment as well as the diverse abilities of taxable entities to currently utilize the tax benefits associated with ownership, no set rule can be offered as to whether borrowing to buy or a true lease is the cheaper form of financing.

The cost of a true lease depends on the size of the transaction and whether the lease is tax-oriented or nontax-oriented. The equipment leasing market can be classified into the following three market sectors: (1) a small-ticket retail market with transactions in the $5,000 to $100,000 range; (2) a middle market with large-ticket items covering transactions between $100,000 and $5 million; and (3) a special products market involving equipment cost in excess of $5 million.

Tax-oriented leases generally fall into the second and third markets. Most of the leveraged lease transactions are found in the third market and the upper range of the second market. The effective interest cost implied by these lease arrangements is considerably below prevailing interest rates that the same lessee would pay on borrowed funds. Even so, the potential lessee must weigh the lost economic benefits from owning the equipment against the economic benefits to be obtained from leasing.

Nontax-oriented leases fall primarily into the small-ticket retail market and the lower range of the second market. There is no real cost savings associated with these leases compared to traditional borrowing arrangements. In most cases, however, cost is not the dominant motive of the firm that employs this method of financing.

From a tax perspective, leasing has advantages that lead to a reduction in cost for a company that is in a tax-loss-carryforward position and is consequently unable to claim tax benefits associated with equipment ownership currently or for several years in the future.

Conservation of Working Capital

The most frequent advantage of leasing cited by leasing company representatives and lessees is that it conserves working capital. The reasoning is as follows: When a firm borrows money to purchase equipment, the lending institution rarely provides an amount equal to the entire price of the equipment to be financed. Instead, the lender requires the borrowing firm to take an equity position in the equipment by making a down payment. The amount of the down payment will depend on such factors as the type of equipment, the creditworthiness of the borrower, and prevailing economic conditions. Leasing, in contrast, typically provides 100% financing since it does not require the firm to make a down payment. Moreover, costs incurred to acquire the equipment, such as delivery and installation charges, are not usually covered by a loan agreement. They may, however, be structured into a lease agreement.

The validity of this argument for financially sound firms during normal economic conditions is questionable. Such firms can simply obtain a loan for 100% of the equipment or borrow the down payment from another source that provides unsecured credit. On the other hand, there is doubt that the funds needed by a small firm for a down payment can be borrowed, particularly during tight money periods. Also, some leases do, in fact, require a down payment in the form of advance lease payments or security deposits at the beginning of the lease term.

Preservation of Credit Capacity by Avoiding Capitalization

Current financial reporting standards for leases require a leasing obligation classified as a capital lease (discussed later) be capitalized as a liability and the equipment recorded as an asset on the balance sheet. According to Financial Accounting Standards Board (FASB) Statement No. 13, the principle for classifying a lease as a capital lease for financial reporting purposes is as follows:

> A lease that transfers substantially all of the benefits and risks incident to ownership of property should be accounted for as the acquisition of an asset and the incurrence of an obligation by the lessee.

FASB Statement No. 13 specifies four criteria for classifying a lease as a capital lease. We will discuss these four criteria later in this chapter. Leases not classified as capital leases are considered operating leases. Unlike a capital lease, an operating lease is not capitalized. Instead, certain information regarding such leases must be disclosed in a footnote to the financial statement.

Many chief financial officers are of the opinion that avoiding capitalization of leases will enhance the financial image of their corporations. By allowing a company to avoid capitalization, an operating lease preserves credit capacity. An operating lease—and particularly a leveraged lease, discussed in the next chapter enables a lessee to utilize institutional (lessor) equity as a source of funding somewhat like subordinated debt. Because there is generally ample room for designing lease arrangements so as to avoid having a lease classified as a capital lease, chief financial officers generally prefer that lease agreements be structured as operating leases.

As a practical matter, most long-term true leases (payout type leases for the lessors) are structured to qualify as operating leases for financial accounting purposes for the lessees at the request of the lessees.

Risk of Obsolescence and Disposal of Equipment

When a firm owns equipment, it faces the possibility that at some future time the equipment may not be as efficient as more recently manufactured equipment. The owner may then elect to sell the original equipment and purchase the newer, more technologically efficient version. The sale of the equipment, however, may produce only a small fraction of its book value. By leasing, it is argued, the firm may avoid the risk of obsolescence and the problems of disposal of the equipment. The validity of this argument depends on the type of lease and the provisions therein.

With a *cancelable* operating lease, the lessee can avoid the risk of obsolescence by terminating the contract. However, the avoidance of risk is not without a cost since the lease payments under such lease arrangements reflect the risk of obsolescence perceived by the lessor. At the end of the lease term, the disposal of the obsolete equipment becomes the problem of the lessor. The risk of loss in residual value that the lessee passes on to the lessor is embodied in the cost of the lease.

The risk of disposal faced by some lessors, however, may not be as great as the risk that would be encountered by the lessee. Some lessors, for example, specialize in short-term operating leases of particular types of equipment, such as computers or construction equipment, and have the expertise to release or sell equipment coming off lease with substantial remaining useful life. A manufacturer-lessor has less investment exposure since its manufacturing costs will be significantly less than the retail price. Also, it is often equipped to handle reconditioning and redesigning due to technological improvements. Moreover, the manufacturer-lessor will be more active in the resale market for the equipment and thus be in a better position to find users for equipment that may be obsolete to one firm but still satisfactory to another. IBM is the best example of a manufacturer-lessor that has combined its financing, manufacturing, and marketing talents to reduce the risk of disposal. This reduced risk of disposal, compared with that faced by the lessee, is presumably passed along to the lessee in the form of a reduced lease cost.

Nonetheless, financial institutions and other lessors are financing ever larger, more complex, and longer-lived assets, and uncertainty over the residual value of those assets is one of the biggest risks for lessors. A steel plant, for example, could have an estimated useful life of 30 years, but its actual useful life could be as short as 25 years or as long as 40 years. If the useful life of the plant turns out to be less than the lessor has projected, the lessor could suffer a loss on a lease that appeared profitable in the original analysis. For some types of assets there are abundant data to support estimates of residual value and for other types of assets there are very little data—particularly for new, unique, complex, or infrequently traded assets. The primary factors that affect residual value are the three components of depreciation: useful life (deterioration), economic obsolescence, and technological obsolescence. Rode, Fishbeck, and Dean suggest that lessors use the best information available to simulate the behavior of these three factors as well as the correlation among the three factors, based on probabilistic ranges of outcomes, to produce distributions of useful life curves, estimated values, and confidence intervals.[2] Because conditions inevitably change over time, lessors should update their modeling frequently during the life of the equipment.

Restrictions on Management

When a lender provides funds to a firm for an extended period of time, provisions to protect the lender are included in the loan agreement. The purpose of protective provisions, or protective covenants, is to ensure that the borrower remains creditworthy during the period over which the funds are borrowed. Protective provisions impose restrictions on the borrower. Failure to satisfy such a protective covenant usually creates an event of default that, if not cured upon notice, gives the lenders certain additional rights and remedies under the loan agreement, including the right to perfect a security agreement or to demand the immediate repayment of the principal. In practice, the remedy and ability to cure vary with the seriousness of the event of default.

An advantage of leasing is that a lease agreement typically does not impose financial covenants and restrictions on management as does a loan agreement used to finance the purchase of equipment. The historical reason for this in true leases is that the Internal Revenue Service discouraged true leases from having attributes of loan agreements. Leases, however, may contain restrictions as to location of the property and

---

[2] David C. Rode, Paul S. Fishbeck, and Steve R. Dean, "Residual Risk and the Valuation of Leases under Uncertainty and Limited Information," *Journal of Structured and Project Finance* 7 (Winter 2002), pp. 37–49.

additional investments by the lessee in the leased equipment in order to ensure compliance with tax laws.

Impact on Cash Flow and Book Earnings

In a properly structured true lease arrangement, the lower lease payment from leasing rather than borrowing can provide a lessee with a superior cash flow. Whether the cash flow on an after-tax basis after taking the residual value of the equipment into account is superior on a present value basis must be ascertained.

Leasing versus buying has a different effect on book earnings. Lease payments under a true lease will usually have less impact on book earnings during the early years of the lease than will depreciation and interest payments associated with the purchase of the same equipment.

TYPES OF LESSORS

Corporate lessors may be generally categorized as commercial banks or their subsidiaries, independent leasing companies, captive leasing subsidiary companies of nonfinance companies, finance companies or their subsidiaries, investment banking firms, and subsidiaries of life or casualty insurance companies.

Many banks and bank holding companies or their subsidiaries participate indirectly in leasing through working relationships with independent and captive leasing companies. Independent leasing companies engage in equipment leasing in the same way as banks. After purchasing and taking title to the equipment requested by the lessee, most such companies lease the equipment to lessees as full-payout-type leases. However, some independent leasing companies may specialize in short-term operating leases. Specialized leasing companies provide leasing and servicing of specific equipment in a particular industry. For example, many independent leasing companies concentrate on data processing equipment.

Captive leasing or finance companies are generally subsidiaries of equipment manufacturers, and their primary purpose is to secure financing for the customers of the parent company. Captives may also be involved in the lease financing of equipment other than that manufactured by their parent company.

In recent years, many nonfinance industrial and service companies without a need to finance their own products have established captive leasing companies to engage in tax-oriented leasing of equipment. These companies have become important participants in the market.

LEASE BROKERS AND FINANCIAL ADVISERS

The growth of the leasing industry has produced a demand for intermediaries to assist lessors in servicing lessees. Lease brokers and financial advisers serve as architects or packagers of lease transactions by bringing together lessors, lessees, and, in the case of a leveraged lease, third-party lenders. Leasing subsidiaries of banks and bank holding companies, investment bankers, commercial banks, and small independent leasing companies have all played an important role as lease brokers and financial advisers.

Lease brokers and financial advisers can perform a useful service for both lessees and lessors in arranging equipment leases. They can be especially helpful to a lessee by obtaining attractive pricing from a legitimate investor and advising the lessee in structuring and negotiating the transaction. While lease brokers and financial advisers typically represent lessees, they also can be helpful to a lessor in finding solutions to negotiating issues.

For its services as an intermediary, the lease broker or financial adviser receives a brokerage commission. The amount of the remuneration can vary widely, depending on the complexity of the deal and the attractiveness of the deal to the lessor in the prevailing economic environment. The standard fee usually ranges from ½% to 4% of the cost of the equipment, depending on the services provided by the broker and the size and difficulty of the transaction. In some brokered transactions, the lease broker or financial adviser also may receive at least a portion of its compensation in the form of a share participation in the residual value of the leased equipment. And, in still other situations, the broker or financial adviser will work for a flat fee.

LEASE PROGRAMS

Lessors can structure lease transactions to suit the needs of most companies. Examples of various lease programs available are described below.

A *standard lease* provides 100% long-term financing with level payments over the term of the lease. Standard documentation facilitates quick handling and closing of the lease transaction. Installation costs, delivery charges, transportation expense, and taxes applicable to the purchase of the equipment may be included as part of the lease financing package.

A *custom lease* contains special provisions designed to meet particular needs of a lessee. It may, for example, schedule lease payments to fit cash flow. Such a lease can be particularly helpful to a seasonal business.

A master lease, as discussed earlier, works like a line of credit. It is an agreement that allows the lessee to acquire, during a fixed period of time, equipment as needed without having to renegotiate a new lease contract for each item. With this arrangement, the lessee and lessor agree to the fixed terms and conditions that will apply for various classifications of equipment for a specified period, usually six months to one year. At any time within that period, the lessee can add equipment to the lease up to an agreed maximum, knowing in advance the rate to be paid and the leasing conditions.

Designed as a sales tool for equipment manufacturers or distributors, a *vendor lease* program permits suppliers to offer financing in the form of true or conditional sale leases. Vendor leases may be structured as tax-oriented or nontax-oriented leases. They may be either short-term operating leases or full payout leases. Vendor lease programs can be offered directly by manufacturers and distributors or in conjunction with a third-party leasing company.

An *offshore lease* is an agreement to lease equipment to be used outside the United States. Offshore lease programs offer leases calling for payments to U.S. lessors in U.S. dollars or local currencies for equipment used abroad. Both true leases and conditional sale leases can be arranged for firms requiring equipment in overseas operations. However, the tax benefits to U.S. lessors are insignificant since little depreciation is available on equipment located outside of the United States.

Sale-and-leaseback transactions can be used by a company to convert owned property and equipment into cash. The equipment is purchased by the lessor and then leased back to the seller.

Under a *facility lease*, an entire facility—a plant and its equipment—can be leased. Under this arrangement, a lessor may provide or arrange construction financing for a facility. Interest costs during construction can often be capitalized into the lease. The lease commences when the completed facility has been accepted by the lessee.

FINANCIAL REPORTING OF LEASE TRANSACTIONS BY LESSEES

Financial reporting considerations are important for most lessees and potential lessees. At one time, lessees needed only to disclose information regarding lease commitments in footnotes to their financial statements. Hence, leasing was often referred to as "off-balance-sheet financing." With the issuance of FASB Statement No. 13 (FAS 13), the accounting treatment of lease commitments changed. FAS 13 required that certain leases be recorded on the lessee's balance sheet as a liability and the leased property reported as an asset. This procedure is called "capitalizing a lease" or "lease capitalization." For leases that do not meet the test specified by FAS 13, the lessee need only disclose certain information regarding lease commitments in a footnote.

Classification of Leases

According to FAS 13 (paragraph 60), a lease is classified as either an operating lease or a capital lease. The principle for classifying a lease as either operating or capital for reporting purposes is as follows:

> [A] lease that transfers substantially all of the benefits and risks incident to the ownership of property should be accounted for as the acquisition of an asset and the incurrence of an obligation by the lessee. . . . All other leases should be accounted for as operating leases.

But how should the accountant interpret when substantially all of the benefits and risks of ownership are transferred? FAS 13 specifies that if one or more of the following four criteria are met for a noncancelable lease at the date of the lease agreement, the lease is to be accounted for as a capital lease:

1. The lease transfers ownership of the property to the lessee by the end of the lease term.
2. The lease contains a bargain purchase option.
3. The lease term is equal to 75% or more of the estimated economic life of the leased property.
4. The present value of the minimum lease payments (excluding executory costs)[3] equals or exceeds 90% of the fair value of the leased property.

A lease that does not satisfy at least one of the above four criteria is classified as an operating lease.

For reasons to be discussed below, lessees prefer a lease to be classified as an operating lease. While it may appear that FAS 13 limits management's ability to structure how a lease will be treated for financial reporting purposes, this is not true in practice. There are several ways in which a lessee can structure a lease to meet its objectives, as will be discussed later.

Accounting for Operating Leases

Because an operating lease does not represent the transfer of substantially all of the benefits and risks of ownership, the leased property is not capitalized, nor is the lease obligation shown as a liability on the

---

[3] Executory costs include insurance, maintenance, and property taxes.

balance sheet. Instead, the lease payments are charged to expenses over the lease term as they become payable.

Although neither the leased asset nor the obligation appears in the balance sheet, the lessee must disclose the following information in footnotes to its financial statements: (1) a general description of the leasing arrangement, which would include restrictions imposed by the lease arrangement, the existence of renewal or purchase options, and escalation clauses; (2) the lease expense for each year in which an income statement is presented; and (3) future minimum lease payments required in the aggregate and separately for each of the next five years.

Exhibit 11.1 is an illustration of a footnote disclosure of lease commitments taken from the fiscal 1999 annual report of Circuit City Stores, Inc. The disclosure of commitments for both operating and capital leases is shown. The latter disclosure requirements are explained in the next section.

Accounting for Capital Leases

A capital lease is treated for accounting purposes as if the leased asset were purchased and financed over time. The question then arises as to how the value of the leased asset and the corresponding liability should be recorded on the lessee's balance sheet at the inception of the lease. FAS 13 requires that these amounts be recorded at the inception of the lease as the lower of (1) the present value of the minimum lease payments during the lease term or (2) the fair market value of the leased asset.[4]

Once the asset and liability at the inception of the lease have been determined, the depreciation charge and the interest expense associated with the liability must be determined. Although the amounts of the asset and liability are the same at the inception of the lease, the subsequent depreciation and interest expense are computed independently.

In addition, the following footnote disclosures for capital leases are required in the lessee's financial statement:

1. The gross amount of assets recorded under capital leases presented by major classes according to nature or function. The lessee can combine

---

[4] The minimum lease payments are defined as the sum of (i) the minimum lease payments required during the lease term and (ii) the amount of any bargain purchase option. In the absence of a bargain purchase option, the amount of any guarantee of the residual value and the amount specified for failure to extend or renew the lease are used in lieu of (ii). Excluded from the minimum lease payments are executory costs where these are required to be paid by the lessee to the lessor.

EXHIBIT 11.1   Lease Commitments Footnote Disclosure in Fiscal 1999 Annual
Report of Circuit City Stores, Inc.

```
10. LEASE COMMITMENTS
The Company conducts a substantial portion of its business in leased premises.
The Company's lease obligations are based upon contractual minimum rates. For

certain locations, amounts in excess of these minimum rates are payable based
upon specified percentages of sales. Rental expense and sublease income for all
operating leases are summarized as follows:
```

(Amounts in thousands)	Years Ended February 28		
	1999	1998	1997
Minimum rentals.................	$302,724	$248,383	$184,618
Rentals based on sales volume.	1,247	730	2,322
Sublease income...............	(20,875)	(12,879)	(11,121)
Net..........................	$283,096	$236,234	$175,819

```
        The Company computes rent based on a percentage of sales volumes in excess
of defined amounts in certain store locations. Most of the Company's other
leases are fixed-dollar rental commitments, with many containing rent
escalations based on the Consumer Price Index. Most provide that the Company pay
taxes, maintenance, insurance and certain other operating expenses applicable to
the premises.
        The initial term of most real property leases will expire within the next
25 years; however, most of the leases have options providing for additional
lease terms of five years to 25 years at terms similar to the initial terms.
        Future minimum fixed lease obligations, excluding taxes, insurance and
other costs payable directly by the Company, as of February 28, 1999, were:
```

(Amounts in thousands) Fiscal	Capital Leases	Operating Lease Commitments	Operating Sublease Income
2000........................	$1,662	$296,674	$(14,684)
2001........................	1,681	293,961	(12,817)
2002........................	1,725	289,553	(11,605)
2003........................	1,726	285,710	(10,624)
2004........................	1,768	283,422	(9,123)
After 2004..................	16,464	3,289,107	(55,144)
Total minimum lease payments.................	25,026	$4,738,427	$(113,997)
Less amounts representing interest.................	12,298		

Present value of net
    minimum capital lease
    payments {NOTE 5}........
	$12,728		

this information for owned assets, which the company must also disclose.

2. Future minimum lease payments in the aggregate and for each of the
   five succeeding years (deducting executory costs) and the amount of
   imputed interest in reducing the minimum lease payments to present
   value.

3. Total contingent lease payments actually incurred for each period for which an income statement is presented.
4. A general description of the leasing arrangement, which would include restrictions imposed by the lease arrangement, the existence of renewal or purchase options, and escalation clauses.

Exhibit 11.1 provides an example of the footnote disclosure for capital lease commitments.

The impact of the accounting treatment of leases on reported income is usually minimal. The primary concern of management is therefore not with the impact on reported income, but with the effect on the firm's debt-to-equity ratio. This ratio is commonly employed by creditors and investors to determine whether a company is overburdened with debt. With a capital lease, the debt-to-equity ratio will be greater than if the lease is treated as an operating lease because of the lease obligation reported in the balance sheet. However, it is naive to assume that market participants are untutored about the impact of noncapitalized leases on the debt-equity ratio. Certainly rating agencies take into account leasing arrangements in assigning a credit rating.

FEDERAL INCOME TAX REQUIREMENTS FOR TRUE LEASE TRANSACTIONS

Remember that the Internal Revenue Service is concerned with the classification of a lease because tax benefits are affected. The Internal Revenue Code (IRC) has requirements for a lease to be treated as a true lease. These rules are independent of the rules for classifying a lease as set forth in FAS 13. The IRC distinguishes between nontax-oriented leases (i.e., conditional sale leases) and tax-oriented true leases. The major characteristic differentiating nontax-oriented and tax-oriented true leases is the type of purchase options available to the lessee. True leases have fair-market-value types of purchase options. Conditional sale leases have nominal fixed-price purchase options or automatically pass the title to the lessee at the end of the lease.

Revenue Ruling 55-540 (1955-2 Cum. Bull. 39) states:

Whether an agreement, which in form is a lease, is in substance a conditional sales contract depends upon the intent of the parties as evidenced by the provisions of the agreement, read in light of the facts and circumstances existing at the time the agreement was executed. In ascertaining such intent no single test, nor special combination of tests, is absolutely determinative. No general rule, applicable in all cases, can be laid down. Each case must be decided in the light of its particular facts.

A purchase option based on fair market value rather than a nominal purchase option is a strong indication of intent to create a lease rather than a conditional sale. The test is whether the interest of the lessor in the leased property is a proprietary interest with attributes of ownership rather than a mere creditor's security interest in the leased property.

A lease *generally* qualifies as a true lease for tax purposes if all of the following criteria are met:

1. At the start of the lease, the fair market value of the leased property projected for the end of the lease term equals or exceeds 20% of the original cost of the leased property (excluding frontend fees and any cost to the lessor for removal).
2. At the start of the lease, the leased property is projected to retain at the end of the initial term a useful life that (1) exceeds 20% of the original estimated useful life of the equipment and (2) is at least one year.
3. The lessee does not have a right to purchase or release the leased property at a price that is less than its then fair market value.
4. The lessor does not have a right to cause the lessee to purchase the leased property at a fixed price.
5. At all times during the lease term, the lessor has a minimum unconditional "at-risk" investment equal to at least 20% of the cost of the leased property.
6. The lessor can show that the transaction was entered into for profit, apart from tax benefits resulting from the transaction.
7. The lessee does not furnish any part of the purchase price of the leased property and has not loaned or guaranteed any indebtedness created in connection with the acquisition of the leased property by the lessor.

Additional criteria and guidelines for true leases are described in various IRS Revenue Rulings and Revenue Procedures.

In the United States, a taxable owner under a true lease cannot begin to receive tax benefits until its assets are completed and in service. Therefore, true leases are generally used to finance the acquisition of existing assets rather than greenfield projects—projects at the preconstruction stage. Some lenders, principally bank lenders, are willing to take construction risk on greenfield projects whereas other long-term lenders such as insurance companies generally make long-term loans on projects only after construction is complete. Some lease investors as well are reluctant to take construction completion risk. Sometimes financial institutions provide bridge leasing or other forms of bridge financing that is taken out by a longer-term true lease at the end of construction.[5]

In structuring a tax-oriented lease transaction, a corporation requiring the use of equipment will seek to have the lease treated as an operating lease for financial reporting purposes to avoid showing a debt obligation on the balance sheet but as a true lease for tax purposes so that the tax benefits of ownership can be transferred to the lender.

While the requirements and guidelines set forth for a lease transaction to be treated as a true lease for tax purposes are reasonably straightforward, there is sometimes room for interpretation; there are transactions intended to be true leases that the IRS might view as conditional sales leases. If this were to occur for a tax-oriented transaction, the economics of such a transaction would be changed by an adverse IRS ruling. Consequently, for complex transactions in which the parties fear they might be viewed by the IRS as not meeting the requirements and guidelines, the parties would seek an advanced ruling from the IRS as to how it would treat the transaction.

Lease agreements generally provide for an indemnity against the possible loss by the lessor of the income tax benefits the lessor expects to receive.

SYNTHETIC LEASES

One of the attractions of a true lease of equipment for lessees is the off-balance-sheet treatment of the lease obligation. One of the drawbacks of a true lease of equipment for many lessees (and particularly those able to utilize tax benefits associated with equipment ownership) is the possible loss to be experienced when the true lease terminates and the equipment may have to be acquired from the lessor.

The *synthetic lease* was developed to meet this need by providing the lessee with off-balance-sheet treatment of the lease obligation while at the same time protecting the lessee's cost of acquiring the residual value of the leased equipment at the termination of the lease. Tax benefits of equipment ownership are claimed by the lessee in a synthetic lease. The rental in a synthetic lease is approximately equivalent to the lessee's debt rate for comparable maturities.

Synthetic leases are operating leases for accounting purposes but they are structured as financings for tax purposes. They are off-balance-sheet leases in which the lessee remains the owner of the assets that are

---

[5] David Fowkes, Nasir Kahn, and Don Armstrong, "Leasing in Project Financing," *Journal of Project Finance* 6 (Spring 2000), pp. 21–32.

financed and retains the tax benefits associated with ownership while simultaneously enjoying the benefits of an operating lease. Such synthetic leases are structured using a lease agreement between the user or owner of equipment as the "lessee" and an investor as the "lessor" in a manner that satisfies the requirements for an operating lease defined in FAS 13 and related accounting rules.

VALUING A LEASE: THE LEASE OR BORROW-TO-BUY DECISION

Now that we know what a lease is and the key role of the treatment of tax benefits and residual value in a lease transaction, we will show how to value a lease. Several economic models for valuing a lease have been proposed in the literature. The model used here requires the determination of the net present value of the direct cash flow resulting from leasing rather than borrowing to purchase an asset, where the direct cash flow from leasing is discounted using an "adjusted discount rate."[6] The model is derived from "the objective of maximizing the equilibrium market value of the firm, with careful consideration of interactions between the decision to lease and the use of other financing instruments by the lessee."[7]

Direct Cash Flow from Leasing

When a firm elects to lease an asset rather than borrow money to purchase the same asset, this decision will have an impact on the firm's cash

---

[6] The adjusted discount rate technique presented in this chapter is fundamentally equivalent to, and results in the same answer as, that obtained by comparing financing provided by a loan that gives the same cash flow as the lease in every future period. This will be illustrated below.

Although the adjusted discount rate technique is fundamentally equivalent to calculating the adjusted present value of a lease, it is less accurate. The adjusted present value technique takes into consideration the present value of the side effects of accepting a project financed with a lease. (The adjusted-present-value technique was first developed by Stewart C. Myers, "Interactions of Corporate Financing and Investment Decisions: Implications for Capital Budgeting," *Journal of Finance* 29 (March 1974), pp. 1–26.) The reason for a possible discrepancy between the solutions to the lease versus borrow-to-buy decision using the adjusted-discount-rate technique and adjusted-present-value technique is that different discount rates are applied where necessary in discounting the cash flow when the latter technique is used.

[7] Stewart C. Myers, David A. Dill, and Alberto J. Bautista, "Valuation of Financial Lease Contracts," *Journal of Finance* 31 (June 1976), p. 799.

flow. The cash flow consequences, which are stated relative to the purchase of the asset, can be summarized as follows:

1. There will be a cash inflow equivalent to the cost of the asset.
2. The lessee may or may not forgo some tax credit. For example, prior to the elimination of the investment tax credit, the lessor could pass this credit through to the lessee.
3. The lessee must make periodic lease payments over the life of the lease. These payments need not be the same in each period. The lease payments are fully deductible for tax purposes if the lease is a true lease. The tax shield is equal to the lease payment times the lessee's marginal tax rate.
4. The lessee forgoes the tax shield provided by the depreciation allowance since it does not own the asset. The tax shield resulting from depreciation is the product of the lessee's marginal tax rate times the depreciation allowance.
5. There will be a cash outlay representing the lost after-tax proceeds from the residual value of the asset.

For example, consider the capital budgeting problem faced by the Hieber Machine Shop Company. The company is considering the acquisition of a machine that requires an initial net cash outlay of $59,400 and will generate a future cash flow for the next five years of $16,962, $19,774, $20,663, $21,895, and $26,825. Assuming a discount rate of 14% representing the company's weighted average cost of capital, the net present value (NPV) for this machine was found to be $11,540.[8]

Let's assume that the following information was used to determine the initial net cash outlay and the cash flow for the machine:

Cost of the machine = $66,000
Tax credit[9] = $6,600

---

[8] A company's weighted-average cost of capital (WACC) is commonly, though not always, used as the discount rate for capital budgeting analysis. As the term implies, WACC is a weighted-average cost of the company's equity and debt. Some, though not all, companies adjust their capital budgeting discount rates for riskier-than-normal projects. Practice is split about evenly between raising the discount rate and probability-adjusting the projected cash flows according to a survey of corporate financial officers. See Henry A. Davis, *Cash Flow and Performance Measurement: Managing for Value* (Morristown, NJ: Financial Executives Research Foundation, 1996).

[9] We use a tax credit in this illustration to show how the model can be applied should Congress decide to introduce some form of tax credit for capital investments in future tax legislation.

Estimated pretax residual = $6,000 value after disposal costs
Estimated after-tax proceeds from residual value = $3,600
Economic life of the machine = 5 years

Depreciation is assumed to be as follows:[10]

Year	Depreciation Deductions
1	$9,405
2	13,794
3	13,167
4	13,167
5	13,167

The same machine may be leased by the Hieber Machine Shop Company. The lease would require five annual payments of $13,500, with the first payment due immediately. The lessor would retain the assumed tax credit. The tax shield resulting from the lease payments would be realized at the time that Hieber Machine Shop Company made those payments. No additional annual expenses will be incurred by Hieber Machine Shop Company by owning rather than leasing (that is, the lease is a net lease). The lessor will not require Hieber Machine Shop Company to guarantee a minimum residual value.

Exhibit 11.2 presents the worksheet for the computation of the direct cash flow from leasing rather than borrowing to purchase. The marginal tax rate of Hieber Machine Shop Company is assumed to be 40%. The direct cash flow is summarized below:

			Year		
0	1	2	3	4	5
$51,300	($11,862)	($13,618)	($13,367)	($13,367)	($8,867)

The direct cash flow from leasing was constructed assuming that (1) the lease is a net lease and (2) the tax benefit associated with an expense is realized in the tax year the expense is incurred. These two assumptions require further discussion.

---

[10] The depreciation schedule to use at any given time is based on current tax law, which is subject to change. The depreciation in this example is based on a depreciable basis comprised of the cost of the asset, less one-half of the tax credit, or $66,000 − 3,300 = $62,700. The rates of depreciation for the five years, in order, are 15%, 22%, 21%, 21%, and 21%.

EXHIBIT 11.2 Worksheet for Direct Cash Flow from Leasing: Hieber Machine Shop Company[a]

	End of Year					
	0	1	2	3	4	5
Cost of machine	$66,000					
Lost tax credit	(6,600)					
Lease payment[b]	(13,500)	($13,500)	($13,500)	($13,500)	($13,500)	
Tax shield from lease payment[b]	5,400	5,400	5,400	5,400	5,400	
Lost depreciation tax shields[c]		(3,762)	(5,518)	(5,267)	(5,267)	($5,267)
Lost residual value						(3,600)
Total	$51,300	($11,862)	($13,618)	($13,367)	($13,367)	($8,867)

[a] Parentheses denote cash outflow.
[b] Lease payment multiplied by the marginal tax rate (40%).
[c] Depreciation for year multiplied by the marginal tax rate (40%).

228

First, if the lease is a gross lease instead of a net lease, the lease payments must be reduced by the cost of maintenance, insurance, and property taxes. These costs are assumed to be the same regardless of whether the asset is leased or purchased with borrowed funds. Where have these costs been incorporated into the analysis? The cash flow from owning an asset is constructed by subtracting the additional operating expenses from the additional revenue. Maintenance, insurance, and property taxes are included in the additional operating expenses. There may be instances when the cost of maintenance differs depending on the financing alternative selected. In such cases, an adjustment to the value of the lease must be made.

Second, many firms considering leasing may be currently in a nontaxpaying position but anticipate being in a taxpaying position in the future. The derivation of the lease valuation model presented in the next section does not consider this situation. It assumes that the tax shield associated with an expense can be fully absorbed by the firm in the tax year in which the expense arises. There is a lease valuation model that, under certain conditions, will handle the situation of a firm currently in a nontaxpaying position.[11]

Valuing the Direct Cash Flow from Leasing

Because the lease displaces debt, the direct cash flow from leasing should be further modified by devising a loan that in each period except the initial period engenders a net cash flow that is identical to the net cash flow for the lease obligation; that is, financial risk is neutralized. Such a loan, called an *equivalent loan*, is illustrated later. Fortunately, it has been mathematically demonstrated that rather than going through the time-consuming effort to construct an equivalent loan, all the decision-maker need do is discount the direct cash flow from leasing by an adjusted discount rate. The adjusted discount rate can be approximated using the following formula:[12]

Adjusted discount rate
= (1 − Marginal tax rate) × (Cost of borrowing money)

[11] The generalized model is explained and illustrated in Julian R. Franks and Stewart D. Hodges, "Valuation of Finance Contracts: A Note," *Journal of Finance* 33 (May 1978), pp. 657–669.

[12] As noted by Brealey and Myers, "The direct cash flows are typically assumed to be *safe* flows that investors would discount at approximately the same rate as the interest and principal on a secured loan issued by the lessee" (Richard Brealey and Stewart Meyers, *Principles of Corporate Finance* [New York: McGraw Hill, 1981], p. 629). There is justification for applying a different discount rate to the various components of the direct cash flow from leasing.

The formula assumes that leasing will displace debt on a dollar-for-dollar basis.[13]

Given the direct cash flow from leasing and the adjusted discount rate, the NPV of the lease can be computed. We shall refer to the NPV of the lease as simply the *value of the lease*. A negative value for a lease indicates that leasing will not be more economically beneficial than borrowing to purchase. A positive value means that leasing will be more economically beneficial. However, leasing will be attractive only if the NPV of the asset assuming normal financing is positive *and* the value of the lease is positive, or if the sum of the NPV of the asset assuming normal financing and the value of the lease is positive.

In order to evaluate the direct cash flow from leasing for the machine considered by the Hieber Machine Shop Company in our illustration, we must know the firm's cost of borrowing money. Suppose that the cost of borrowing money has been determined to be 10%. The adjusted discount rate is then found by applying the formula:

$$\text{Adjusted discount rate} = (1 - 0.40) \times (0.10) = 0.06, \text{ or } 6\% \text{ [14]}$$

The adjusted discount rate of 6% is then used to determine the value of the lease. The worksheet is shown as Exhibit 11.3. The value of the lease is −$448. Hence, from a purely economic point of view, the machine should be purchased by the Hieber Machine Shop Company rather than leased. Recall that the NPV of the machine assuming normal financing is $11,540.

---

[13] Brealey and Myers, *Principles of Corporate Finance*, p. 634. The formula must be modified, as explained later, if the lessee believes that leasing does not displace debt on a dollar-for-dollar basis.

[14] In this case, we consider the cost of borrowing to be most applicable opportunity cost to use for the adjusted discount rate. It is common practice for a company to use its WACC as a discount rate for capital budgeting (investment) decisions and its after-tax borrowing cost as a discount rate for financing decisions. WACC, being higher, takes the business risk of proposed projects into account. The cost of borrowing, being lower, is a more appropriate discount rate for financing decisions because the cash flows involved are more certain. It is best not to combine the cash flows used to make a capital budgeting decision, discounted at the WACC, and the cash flows underlying the related financing decision, discounted at the borrowing rate, in one consolidated analysis. If the investment and financing cash flows are combined and summed up on one spreadsheet, the financing cash flows can assume disproportionate importance in later years because they are discounted at a lower rate.

EXHIBIT 11.3   Worksheet for Determining the Value of a Lease

End of Year	Direct Cash Flow from Leasing	Present Value of $1 at 6%	Present Value
0	$51,300	1.0000	$51,300
1	(11,862)	0.9434	(11,191)
2	(13,618)	0.8900	(12,120)
3	(13,367)	0.8396	(11,223)
4	(13,367)	0.7921	(10,588)
5	(8,867)	0.7473	(6,626)
Value (or NPV) of lease			$(448)

Concept of an Equivalent Loan

The value of the lease considered by the Hieber Machine Shop Company was shown to be –$448. Suppose the firm had the opportunity to obtain a $51,748, 5-year loan at 10% interest with the following principal repayment schedule:[15]

End of year	0	1	2	3	4	5
Repayment	0	$8,757	$11,039	$11,450	$12,137	$8,365

(Recall that the firm's marginal borrowing rate was assumed to be 10%.)

Exhibit 11.4 shows the net cash flow for each year if the loan is used to purchase the machine. In addition to the loan, the firm must make an initial outlay of $7,652.

The net cash flow for each year if the machine is leased is also presented in Exhibit 11.4. Notice that the net cash flows of the two financing alternatives are equivalent, with the exception of year 0. Therefore, the loan presented above is called the *equivalent loan for the lease.*

We can now understand why borrowing to purchase is more economically attractive for Hieber Machine Shop Company. The equivalent loan produces the same net cash flow as the lease in all years after year 0. Hence, the equivalent loan has equalized the financial risk of the two financing alternatives. However, the net cash outlay in year 0 is $7,652 in the case of the equivalent loan compared to $8,100 if the machine is

---

[15] The loan payments are determined by solving for the set of repayments and interest each period that would result in the value of purchase (accompanied by a loan) being equivalent to leasing.

Period	0	1	2	3	4	5
Leasing: Cash flows:						
− Lease payments	−$13,500	−$13,500	−$13,500	−$13,500	−$13,500	$0
+ Tax shield	5,400	5,400	5,400	5,400	5,400	0
Net cash flow	−$8,100	−$8,100	−$8,100	−$8,100	−$8,100	$0
Purchasing: Cash flows:						
− Purchase cost	−$66,000					
+ Tax credit	6,600					
+ Residual value						$3,600
+ Depreciation tax shield	0	$3,762	$5,518	$5,267	$5,267	5,267
+ Loan	51,748					
− Principal repayment	0	−8,757	−11,039	−11,450	−12,137	−8,365
− Interest on loan	0	−5,175	−4,299	−3,195	−2,050	−836
+ Interest tax shield	0	2,070	1,720	1,278	820	334
Net cash flow	−$7,652	−$8,100	−$8,100	−$8,100	−$8,100	$0
Loan account:						
Previous balance	$0	$51,748	$42,991	$31,953	$20,503	$8,365
Principal repayment (+ loan)	+51,748	8,757	−11,039	−11,450	−12,137	−8,365
New balance	$51,748	$42,991	$31,953	$20,503	$8,365	$0
Value (NPV) of lease[a]	−$448					

[a] Difference between the net cash flows in year 0 [−8,100 − (−7,652)].

leased. The difference, –$448, is the value of the lease. Notice that the lease valuation model produced the same value for the lease without constructing an equivalent loan.

Comparison of Alternative Leases

The potential lessee may have the opportunity to select from several leasing arrangements offered by the same lessor or different lessors. From a purely economic perspective, the potential lessee should select the leasing arrangement with the greatest positive value. This requires an analysis of the direct cash flow from leasing for each of the leasing arrangements available.

For example, suppose that a firm has two leasing arrangements available to lease a given asset. The direct cash flow from leasing is shown below for each alternative:

End of Year	Direct Cash Flow from Leasing	
	Lease 1	Lease 2
0	$42,000	$45,800
1	(15,000)	(13,000)
2	(15,000)	(16,000)
3	(15,000)	(18,000)
4	(1,000)	(4,000)

The value of the lease using an adjusted discount rate of 6% and 8% is summarized below:

Adjusted Discount Rate	Value of	
	Lease 1	Lease 2
6%	$1,109	$1,015
8	2,663	2,818

When the adjusted discount rate is 6%, both leases are economically beneficial. However, Lease 1 is marginally superior to Lease 2. The value of both leases increases when the adjusted discount rate is 8%. In this case, Lease 1 is slightly less attractive than Lease 2. The NPVs of both leases for discount rates ranging from 4% to 10% are shown in Exhibit 11.5.

EXHIBIT 11.5 The NPV of Lease 1 and Lease 2 for Different Adjusted Discount Rates

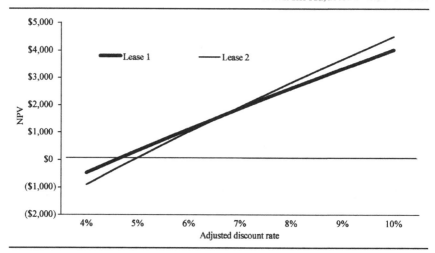

Another Approach to Lease Valuation

Rather than determining the NPV of a lease, many lessors use a different approach when attempting to demonstrate to potential lessees the economic attractiveness of a particular leasing arrangement. The approach is a comparison of the after-tax interest rate on the lease with the after-tax cost of borrowing money. The reason this approach appears to be popular is that management finds it easy to comprehend a rate concept but difficult to appreciate the NPV-of-a-lease concept.

The after-tax interest rate on the lease is found by determining the discount rate that equates the direct cash flow from leasing to zero; that is, it is the discount rate that makes the value of the lease equal to zero. This discount rate is also referred to as the *internal rate of return*. The after-tax interest rate on the lease is then compared to the after-tax cost of borrowing money. When the after-tax interest rate on the lease exceeds the after-tax cost of borrowing money, borrowing to purchase is more economical than leasing. Leasing is more economical when the after-tax cost of borrowing money is greater than the after-tax interest rate on the lease.

Exhibit 11.2 shows the direct cash flow from leasing for the lease arrangement available to the Hieber Machine Shop Company. The discount rate that produces a present value close to zero for the direct cash flow from leasing is 6.3%. Hence, the after-tax interest rate on the lease is about 6.3%.[16]

---

[16] The precise answer may be obtained using a financial calculator that has the IRR program or by using a spreadsheet program function, such as the IRR function in Microsoft's Excel.

When the after-tax cost of borrowing is 6%, the lease arrangement is not attractive. However, when the after-tax cost of borrowing money is 8%, the lease arrangement is attractive.

In the previous illustration, the determination that was made as to whether the lease was economically attractive was precisely the same determination that was made when the NPV lease valuation model was used. The identity of the result is not peculiar to this illustration. The two approaches will always produce the same result.

The advantage of the NPV lease valuation model presented is that it permits interaction of the investment and financing decisions. As a result, it is simple to determine whether an investment proposal that has a negative NPV assuming normal financing can be made economically attractive by a favorable lease arrangement. With the after-tax interest on the lease approach, this is not done as easily. That approach requires management to revise its estimate of the cost of capital when the after-tax interest rate on the lease is less than the after-tax cost of borrowing money and then to reevaluate the investment proposal with the revised cost of capital. This is an extremely complicated and awkward approach since it requires a continuous revision of the cost of capital as attractive lease arrangements become available. No simple solution to this problem has been proffered in the literature.

The rate approach will not always provide the same solution as the NPV approach when lease arrangements are compared. Differences in the selection of the best lease arrangement may result when the number of advance payments is different, when the lease payments are not uniform, or when the tax credit is handled any differently.[17] The best lease arrangement is the one with the greatest NPV. Therefore, if conflicts arise when comparing lease arrangements by the two methods, the decision should be based on the NPV of the lease.

---

[17] The situation is analogous to conditions in which the yield technique in capital budgeting may produce rankings conflicting with those produced by the net present value technique.

CHAPTER 12

Leveraged Lease Fundamentals

The leveraged form of a true lease of equipment is the ultimate form of lease financing. It allows a company, as lessee, to harness the lessor's capital, leveraged by institutional debt, as a source of funding somewhat like subordinated debt. The most attractive feature of a leveraged lease, from the standpoint of a lessee unable to use tax benefits of MACRS (Modified Accelerated Cost Recovery System), is its low cost as compared to that of alternative methods of financing. Leveraged leasing also satisfies a need for lease financing of especially large capital equipment projects with economic lives of up to 25 or more years, although leveraged leases are also used where the life of the equipment is considerably shorter. The leveraged lease can be a most advantageous financing device when used for the right kinds of projects and structured correctly.

Single-investor nonleveraged leases of equipment are simple two-party transactions involving a lessee and a lessor. In single-investor leases (sometimes called *nonleveraged leases* or *direct leases*), the lessor provides all of the funds necessary to purchase the leased asset from its own resources. While the lessor may borrow some or all of these funds, it does so on a full-recourse basis to its lenders, and it is at risk for all of the capital employed.[1]

A leveraged lease of equipment is conceptually similar to a single-investor lease. The lessee selects the equipment and negotiates the lease in much the same manner. Also, the terms for rentals, options, and responsibility for taxes, insurance, and maintenance are similar. However, a leveraged lease is appreciably more complex in size, documentation, legal involvement, and, most importantly, the number of parties involved and the unique advantages that each party gains.

---

[1] The single-investor lessor may securitize all or part of the lease receivables at a later date.

Leveraged leases of equipment are generally offered only by corporations and financial institutions acting as lessors. This is because in a leveraged lease the tax benefits available to individual lessors are much more limited than those available to a corporation. This chapter is devoted to leveraged leases offered by corporations and financial institutions.

The lessor in a leveraged lease of equipment becomes the owner of the leased equipment by providing only a percentage (20% to 30%) of the capital necessary to purchase the equipment.[2] The remainder of the capital (70% to 80%) is borrowed from institutional investors on a nonrecourse basis to the lessor. This loan is secured by a first lien on the equipment, an assignment of the lease, and an assignment of the lease rental payments. The cost of the nonrecourse borrowing is a function of the credit standing of the lessee.[3] The lease rate varies with the debt rate and with the risk of the transaction.

A "leveraged lease" is always a true lease. The lessor in a leveraged lease can claim all of the tax benefits incidental to ownership of the leased asset even though the lessor provides only 20% to 30% of the capital needed to purchase the equipment. This ability to claim the MACRS tax benefits attributable to the entire cost of the leased equipment and the right to 100% of the residual value provided by the lease, while providing and being at risk for only a portion of the cost of the leased equipment, is the "leverage" in a leveraged lease. Such leverage enables the lessor in a leveraged lease to offer the lessee much lower lease rates than the lessor could provide under a direct lease.

The legal expenses and closing costs associated with leveraged leases are larger than those for single-investor nonleveraged leases and usually confine the use of leveraged leases to financing relatively large capital equipment acquisitions. However, leveraged leases are also used for smaller lease transactions that are repetitive in nature and use standardized documentation so as to hold down legal and closing costs.

Several parties may be involved in a leveraged lease. Whereas direct or single-investor nonleveraged leases are basically two-party transactions with a lessee and a lessor, leveraged leases by their nature involve a minimum of three parties with diverse interests: a lessee, a lessor, and a nonrecourse lender. Indeed, leveraged leases are sometimes called three-party transactions.

---

[2] The exact amount is a function of the economic result the lessor seeks to achieve.

[3] If the credit of the lessee is insufficient to support the transaction, a guarantor of the lessee obligations under the lease including payment of rents may be necessary. This guarantor may, for example, be the parent or sister company of the lessee, an interested third party, or a government agency. As discussed elsewhere, leveraged debt cannot usually be directly guaranteed under the tax requirements of the IRS.

Several owners and lenders may be involved in a large leveraged lease. In such a case, an owner trustee is generally named to hold title to the equipment and represent the owners or equity participants, and an indenture trustee is usually named to hold the security interest or mortgage on the property for the benefit of the lenders or loan participants. Sometimes a single trustee may be appointed to perform both of these functions.

In this chapter we will review the rights, obligations, functions, and characteristics of the various parties that may be involved with a leveraged lease; the structure; the cash flows; and the debt arrangements possible.[4]

PARTIES TO A LEVERAGED LEASE

The parties to a leveraged lease include:

1. the lessee;
2. equity participants;
3. loan participants or lenders;
4. owner trustee;
5. indenture trustee;
6. manufacturer or contractor;
7. packager; and
8. guarantor.

We discuss each in the following subsections.

The Lessee

The lessee selects the equipment to be leased, negotiates the price and warranties, and hires the use of the equipment by entering into a lease agreement. The lessee accepts, uses, operates, and receives all revenue from the equipment. The lessee makes rental payments. The credit standing of the lessee supports the rent obligation, the credit exposure of the lenders of leveraged debt, and the credit exposure of the equity participants.

Equity Participants

The equity participants provide the equity contributions (20% to 30% of the purchase price) needed to purchase the leased equipment. They receive the rental payments remaining after the payment of debt service

---

[4] Tax requirements for leveraged leases are discussed in Chapter 5 in Peter K. Nevitt and Frank J. Fabozzi, *Equipment Leasing*, 4th ed. (Hoboken, NJ: John Wiley & Sons, 2000).

and any trustee fees. They claim the tax benefits incidental to the owner-ship of the leased equipment, consisting of MACRS tax depreciation deductions and deductions for interest used to fund their investment. They are entitled to receive the residual value of the equipment at the end of the lease subject to limitations provided by the lease agreement. The equity participants are sometimes referred to as the lessors. Actu-ally, in most cases they are the beneficial owners by way of an owner trust that is the lessor. Equity participants are also sometimes referred to as equity investors, owner participants, or trustors.

Loan Participants or Lenders

The loan participants or lenders are typically banks, finance companies, insurance companies, trusts, pension funds, and foundations. The funds provided by the loan participants, together with the equity contribu-tions, make up the full purchase price of the asset to be leased. The loan participants provide 70% to 80% of the purchase price on a nonre-course basis to the equity participants. As noted earlier, these loans are secured by a first lien on the leased equipment, an assignment of the lease, an assignment of rents under the lease, and an assignment of any ancillary agreements such as easements and supply contracts. Principal and interest payments that are due the loan participants (or lenders) from the indenture trustee are paid by the lessee to the indenture trustee, which then pays the loan participants.

Owner Trustee

The owner trustee represents the equity participants, acts as the lessor, and executes the lease and all of the basic documents that the lessor would normally sign in a lease. The owner trustee records and holds title to the leased asset for the benefit of the equity participants, subject to the mortgage or security agreement to the indenture trustee. The owner trustee issues trust certificates to the equity holders evidencing their beneficial interest as owners of the assets of the trust, issues bonds or notes to loan participants evidencing the leveraged debt, grants to the indenture trustee the security interests that secure repayment of the bonds (that is, the lease, the lease rentals, and a first mortgage on the leased asset), receives distributions from the indenture trustee, distrib-utes earnings to the equity participants, and receives and distributes any information or notices regarding the transaction that are required to be provided to the parties. The owner trustee has little discretionary power beyond that specifically granted in the trust agreement and has no affir-mative duties.

The owner participants indemnify the owner trustee against costs and liabilities arising out of the transaction, except for willful misconduct or negligence. It can be argued that an owner trustee is unnecessary. Where a leveraged lease has a single equity investor, the parties may conclude that an owner trustee is not needed and that the equity investor may act as the lessor. However, the cost of an owner-trustee for a leveraged lease is usually modest compared with the benefits unless the transaction is extremely simple and straightforward.

Indenture Trustee

The indenture trustee (sometimes called the security trustee) is appointed by and represents the lenders or loan participants. The owner trustee and the indenture trustee enter into a trust indenture whereby the owner trustee assigns to the indenture trustee, for the benefit of the loan participants and as security for the leveraged debt and any other obligations, all of the owner trustee's interest as lessor in:

1. the equipment to be leased and the lessor's rights under manufacturer's or contractor's warranties related to the equipment;
2. the lease agreement;
3. the lessor's right to receive rents (including all payments) owed by the lessee (subject to such exceptions as agreed between the lessor and lessee);
4. the lessor's rights to receive any payments under any guarantee agreements (subject to the same exceptions as the payments due the lessor); and
5. the lessor's rights under any ancillary facility support agreements such as easements, service contracts, supply contracts, and sales contracts.

The indenture agreement sets forth the form of the notes or loan agreements, the events of default, and the instructions and priorities for distributions of funds to the loan participants and other parties.

The indenture trustee receives funds from the loan participants (lenders) and the equity participants when the transaction is about to close, pays the manufacturer or contractor the purchase price of the equipment to be leased, and records and holds the senior security interest in the leased equipment, the lease, any ancillary facility support contracts, and the rents for the benefit of the loan participants. The indenture trustee collects rents and other sums due under the lease from the lessee. Upon the receipt of rental payments, the indenture trustee pays debt payments of principal and interest due on the leveraged debt to the loan participants and distributes revenues not needed for debt service to the owner trustee. In the event of default, the indenture trustee can foreclose on the leased equipment and take other appropriate actions to protect the security interests of the loan participants.[5]

Manufacturer or Contractor

The manufacturer or contractor manufactures or constructs the equipment to be leased. The manufacturer or contractor (or supplier) receives the purchase price upon acceptance of the equipment by the lessee and delivers the equipment to the lessee at the beginning of the lease. The warranties of the manufacturer, contractor, or supplier as to the quality, capabilities, and efficiencies of the leased equipment are important to the lessee, the equity participants, and the loan participants.

Packager or Broker

The packager or broker is the leasing company arranging the transaction. In many instances, the packager is purely a broker and not an investor. From the standpoint of the lessee, it may be desirable that the packager also be an equity participant. The packager may, in fact, be the sole equity participant.

Guarantor

A guarantor of the lessee's credit may be present in some leveraged lease transactions. Although a member of the lessee group may not guarantee the leveraged debt under Internal Revenue rules, a member of the lessee group may guarantee the lessee's obligation to pay rent. A party unrelated to the lessee may guarantee either rents or debt. Such a guarantor might be a third party such as a bank under a letter of credit agreement, an insurer of residual value, or a government guarantor.[6]

---

[5] A single trustee may assume the duties of both an owner trustee and an indenture trustee in a leveraged lease. Where a single trustee is used, the trustee is referred to as the owner trustee. Those who favor using a single trustee in a leveraged lease transaction argue that such an arrangement is simpler and reduces the costs of the transaction. Although the use of a single trustee in a leveraged lease has become an increasingly common arrangement, serious conflicts of interest may arise between the equity participants and the loan participants in the event of a default by the lessee. Such potential conflicts make the use of a single trustee unattractive if there is any question regarding the lessee's credit.

[6] Where rents are guaranteed by a third party, a controversy may arise under Revenue Procedure 75-21 that relates to whether the lessor is at risk for an amount equal to 20% of the cost of the equipment. It can be strongly argued that such a guarantee is merely the equivalent of a second credit exposure and does not alter the fact that the lessor is "at risk."

STRUCTURE OF A LEVERAGED LEASE

A leveraged lease transaction is usually structured as follows where a broker or a third-party leasing company arranges the transaction.

The leasing company arranging the lease, "the packager," enters into a commitment letter with the prospective lessee (obtains a mandate) that outlines the terms for the lease of the equipment, including the timing and amount of rental payments. Since the exact rental payment cannot be determined until the debt has been sold and the equipment delivered, rents are agreed tentatively based on certain variables, including assumed debt rates and the delivery dates of the equipment to be leased.

After the commitment letter has been signed, the packager prepares a summary of terms for the proposed lease and contacts potential equity participants to arrange for firm commitments to invest equity in the proposed lease to the extent that the packager does not intend to provide the total amount of the required equity funds from its own resources. Contacts with potential equity sources may be fairly informal or may be accomplished through a bidding process. Typical equity participants include banks, independent finance companies, captive finance companies, and corporate investors that have tax liability to shelter, have funds to invest, and understand the economics of tax-oriented leasing. The packager may also arrange the debt either directly or in conjunction with the capital markets group of a bank or an investment banker selected by the lessee or the lessor. If the equipment is not to be delivered and the lease is not to commence for a considerable period of time, the debt arrangements may be deferred until close to the date of delivery.

The packager may agree at the outset to "bid firm" or underwrite the transaction on the mandated terms and may then "syndicate" its bid to potential equity participants. However, the lessee may prefer to use a bidding procedure without an underwritten price on the theory that more favorable terms can be arranged using this approach.

In some instances, the lessee may prefer to prepare its own bid request and solicit bids directly from potential lessors without using a packager or broker to underwrite or arrange the transaction. This might be the case, for example, where the lessee has considerable experience in leveraged leasing and has already arranged leases of similar equipment, such as computers or computer systems.

If an owner trustee is to be used, a bank or trust company mutually agreeable to the equity participants and the lessee is selected to act as owner trustee. If an indenture trustee is to be used, another bank or trust company acceptable to the loan participants is selected to act as indenture trustee. As discussed previously, a single trustee may act as both owner trustee and indenture trustee.

Exhibit 12.1 illustrates the parties, cash flows, and agreements among the parties in a simple leveraged lease.

If the leveraged lease is arranged by sponsors of a project who want to be the equity participants, the structure and procedures are essentially the same as those for a leveraged lease by a third-party equity partici-

EXHIBIT 12.1   Leveraged Lease

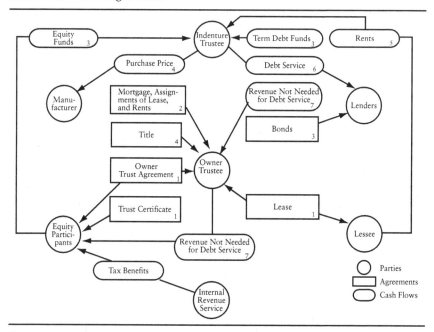

Summary:

1. An owner trust is established by the equity participants, trust certificates are issued, and a lease agreement is signed by the owner trustee as lessor and the lessee.

2. A security agreement is signed by the owner trustee and the indenture trustee, a mortgage is granted on the leased asset, and the lease and rentals are assigned as security to the indenture trustee.

3. Notes or bonds are issued by the owner trustee to the lenders, term debt funds are paid by the lenders (loan participants) to the indenture trustee, and equity funds are paid by the equity participants to the indenture trustee.

4. The purchase price is paid, and title is assigned to the owner trustee, subject to the mortgage.

5. The lease commences; rents are paid by the lessee to the indenture trustee.

6. Debt service is paid by the indenture trustee to the lenders (loan participants).

7. Revenue not required for debt service or trustees' fees is paid to the owner trustee and, in turn, to the equity participants.

Source: Exhibit 1 in Chapter 16 in Peter K. Nevitt and Frank J. Fabozzi, *Equipment Leasing*, 4th ed. (Hoboken, NJ: John Wiley & Sons, 2000), p. 328.

pant. In such circumstances, the sponsors are the equity investors. If some of the sponsors can use tax benefits and some cannot, the equity participants may include a combination of sponsors and one or more third-party leasing companies. This arrangement is more complex, but the structure and procedures are essentially the same as those for a leveraged lease by a third-party equity participant.

CLOSING THE TRANSACTION

Participation Agreement

The key document in a leveraged lease transaction is the participation agreement (sometimes called the *financing agreement*). This document is, in effect, a script for closing the transaction.

When the parties to a leveraged lease transaction are identified, all of them except the indenture trustee enter into a participation agreement that spells out in detail the various undertakings, obligations, mechanics, timing, conditions precedent, and responsibilities of the parties with respect to providing funds and purchasing, leasing, and securing or mortgaging the equipment to be leased. More specifically, the equity participants agree to provide their investment or equity contribution; the loan participants agree to make their loans; the owner trustee agrees to purchase and lease the equipment; and the lessee agrees to lease the equipment. The substance of the required opinions of counsel is described in the participation agreement. The representations of the parties are detailed. Tax indemnities and other general indemnities are often set forth in the participation agreement rather than the lease agreement. The exact form of agreements to be signed, the opinions to be given, and the representations to be made by the parties are usually attached as exhibits to the participation agreement.

Other Key Documents

The key documents in a leveraged lease transaction in addition to the participation agreement are: the lease agreement, the owner trust agreement, and the indenture trust agreement.

The lease agreement is between the lessee and owner trustee. The lease is for a term of years and may contain renewal options and fair-market-value purchase options. Rents and all payments due under the lease are net to the lessor, and the lessee waives defenses and offsets to rents under a "hell or high water clause."

The owner trust agreement creates the owner trust and sets forth the relationships between the owner trustee and the equity participants that it represents. The owner trust agreement spells out the duties of the trustee, the documents the trustee is to execute, and the distribution to be made of funds it receives from equity participants, lenders, and the lessee. The owner trustee has little or no authority to take discretionary or independent action.

The owner trust grants a lien or security interest on the leased equipment and assigns the lease agreement, any ancillary facility support agreements and right to receive rents under the lease to the indenture trustee (which may also be the owner trustee). It spells out the obligations of the indenture trustee to the lenders.

Indemnities by the Lessee

Lessee indemnities fall into three general categories:

1. A general indemnity that protects all of the other parties to the transaction from any claims of third parties arising from the lease or the use of the leased equipment.
2. A general tax indemnity that protects all of the other parties to the transaction from all federal, state, or local taxes arising out of or in connection with the transaction except for certain income tax or income-related taxes.
3. Special tax indemnities by the lessee that protect the owner participants from the loss of expected income tax benefits as a result of the acts and omissions of the lessee and certain other events.

The coverage of the special tax indemnities beyond the acts and omissions of the lessee is a matter of significant negotiation between the lessee and lessor.

CASH FLOWS DURING THE LEASE

The equity participants receive cash flow from three sources: rents after the payment of debt service and trustee fees, tax benefits, and proceeds from the sale of the equipment at the conclusion of the lease.

The lessee pays periodic rents to the indenture trustee, which uses such funds to pay currently due principal and interest payments to the loan participants and to pay trustee fees for its services. The balance of the rental payments is paid to the owner trustee. After the payment of any trustee fees due the owner trustee and any administrative or other expenses, the owner trustee pays the remainder of the rental payments to the equity participants.

The equity participants also realize cash flow from tax benefits as quickly as they can claim such benefits on their quarterly tax estimates and tax returns.

The leveraged debt is usually amortized over a period of time identical to the lease term, with payments of principal and interest due on or shortly after the due date of the rental payments. These payments may be monthly, quarterly, semiannual, or annual. Where "optimized debt" structures are used for competitive reasons, the rental payments approximately equal the debt service payments plus deferred income tax. This has the effect of reducing the leveraged debt payments in the later years of the lease. Rental payments are usually level but may vary upward or downward (sawtooth rents) to achieve a maximum yield for the lessor.[7] Also, debt payments may be concluded entirely before the lease term ends in order to generate additional cash for the lessor.

When the lease terminates, the equipment is returned to the owner trustee, who sells or releases the property at the direction of the owner participants.

The lease agreement usually requires the lessee to furnish the owner trustee and the indenture trustee with financial statements, evidence of insurance, and other similar information. The trustees distribute this information to all parties to the transaction.

DEBT FOR LEVERAGED LEASES

Debt for leveraged leases is usually at a fixed rate of interest although it also may be at a floating rate of interest. Such debt is available from a variety of sources. The lead equity source or packager may arrange the debt. Sometimes the lessee may prefer to have the debt arranged by its commercial bank, the capital markets group of its commercial bank, or its investment bank. Most leveraged lease debt is raised in the private placement market at little or no premium over what the lessee would expect to pay directly for such debt. The sources include:

- Insurance companies;
- Pension plans;
- Profit-sharing plans;
- Commercial banks;
- Finance companies;
- Savings banks;

---

[7] Subject to Internal Revenue Service limitations imposed by Section 467 of the Code and Proposed Regulations under Section 467.

- Domestic leasing companies;
- Foreign banks;
- Foreign leasing companies;
- Foreign investors; and
- Institutional investors.

Other less frequently used instruments and sources of debt that may be useful in special circumstances include the following:

Commercial Paper Investors. Commercial paper has sometimes been used for leveraged debt for short (five to seven years) leveraged leases. The major risks in using commercial paper are the floating interest rates and the possible inability to roll over the commercial paper. Such debt may require a backup line of credit. Interest rate risk can be hedged to some extent by using caps, interest rate futures, or interest rate swaps.

Public Debt Markets. It is possible, but not very practical, to use the public debt markets for leveraged debt. Public debt is expensive since it must be underwritten by an investment banking firm and registered under the Securities Act. For these reasons, issuance of public debt is not economical in amounts less than $50 million. Also, amending the lease difficult is when public debt is used.

Government Financing. If government financing is available, it can sometimes be used as leveraged debt.

Supplier Financing. Supplier financing can be an excellent source of leveraged debt (shipyard financing for a ship, for example). U.S. Export-Import Bank financing offers such opportunities. One difficulty in using this source is matching the debt maturities to the lease maturities. Where the lease is for a longer term than that of the supplier financing, wrap-around debt is difficult to arrange, particularly since the security interest of such debt usually must be subordinate to the supplier financing.

Multicurrency Financing. Where the lessee generates more than one currency from the sale of its product or service, it may prefer the leveraged debt to be in one or more matching currencies. Debt and rents can be arranged to satisfy this need. Currency swaps can be used to hedge the foreign exchange risk of foreign currency debt.

Bridge Financing. If interest rates on fixed long-term debt are, in the opinion of the lessee, unusually high, the lessee may arrange bridge financing on a floating-interest-rate basis with a view to refinancing term debt at a more favorable fixed-interest rate at a later time.

FACILITY LEASES

Leveraged leases have been used increasingly in recent years to finance the use of equipment that is impractical to move, such as electric generating plants, mining equipment, refineries, and chemical facilities.[8] A series of facility support agreements are needed in order to provide the lessor with rights to the leased equipment upon the conclusion of the original lease.

The lessor will want either to own the land on which the facility is located or to have a leasehold interest in the land that is at least 20% longer than the base lease term and any fixed-rate renewal lease terms available to the lessee. The lessor will also want easement and access rights to the property on which the facility is located. If supply contracts for raw material, fuel, or energy are necessary for successful operation of the facility, these must be assigned by the lessee to the lessor at the conclusion of the initial lease. Rights-of-way for power lines, rail lines, pipelines, and roads may be necessary, as may access rights to adjoining port, rail, or pipeline facilities. The leased equipment facility may be part of a large complex of similar facilities in some cases, and in such a case where the lessor should have rights to service, fuel, energy, and so forth, shared in common with the other facilities owned by the lessee or other parties.

Exhibit 12.2 is a diagram of a leveraged lease of an electric coal-fired generating facility that illustrates the parties, the cash flows, and the agreements involved in a facility lease transaction in which the owner trustee takes title during construction. This transaction contemplates the assignment of the facility support agreements.

In this example, the purpose of the facility support agreements between the lessee and the owner trustee is to provide the owner trustee with access to all properties and things necessary or desirable to allow the owner trustee (acting on behalf of the equity participants) to operate the electric generating facility as an independent commercial electric

---

[8] The equipment's lack of portability does not make it limited-use property for tax purposes so long as the facility is reasonably expected to have a fair market value equal to 20% of its original cost at the conclusion of the lease. The 20% useful life tests of Revenue Procedure 75-21 are met if, at the conclusion of the lease, the facility can continue to be used at its original location for a period of time equal to 20% or more of the base lease term plus any fixed-rate renewal terms.

EXHIBIT 12.2 Leveraged Lease of an Electric Generating Facility

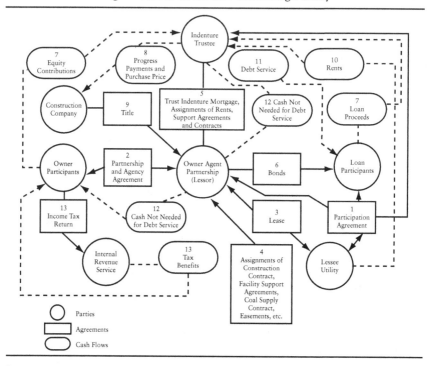

Summary:

1. A participation agreement is executed between the owner agent, the lessee, the loan participants, and the indenture trustee. This agreement constitutes the master agreement for the leveraged lease and spells out the general rights and obligations of the parties.

2. A partnership and agency agreement is entered into between the owner participants and a bank or trust company acting as the owner agent and lessor.

3. A lease agreement is signed between the partnership and the lessee for a term of 20 years. Rents are net to the lessor. The lessee assumes all obligations and risk that relate to the leased equipment. The lessee agrees to pay all rent and monetary obligations "come hell or high water" and waives defenses and offsets to such payments.

4. The lessee assigns to the partnership its interest in the construction contract, facility support agreements, coal supply contracts, easements, and so forth.

5. The owner agent, on behalf of the partnership, enters into a trust indenture and mortgage with the indenture trustee and assigns to the indenture trustee all rents and other payments to be received under the lease, the construction contract for the facility to be leased, the facility support agreements, coal supply contracts, easements, and so forth, all as security for bonds (leveraged debt) that are to be sold by the owner agent.

6. Bonds are issued to the bondholders.

7. Loan proceeds and equity contributions are paid to the indenture trustee.

EXHIBIT 12.2 (Continued)

8. The purchase price is paid to the construction company.

9. Title to the leased facility is conveyed by the construction company to the partnership.

10. The lease commences, and rental payments commence to be paid by the lessee to the indenture trustee.

11. The indenture trustee services the debt to the loan participants; cash not needed for debt service is distributed to the owner participants.

12. In the meantime the owner participants file income tax returns and receive tax benefits associated with equipment ownership such as MACRS tax depreciation.

Source: Exhibit 2 in Chapter 16 in Peter K. Nevitt and Frank J. Fabozzi, *Equipment Leasing*, 4th ed. (Hoboken, NJ: John Wiley & Sons, 2000), p. 336.

---

generating unit and to sell electricity generated by the facility into a grid. The agreements stipulate that maintenance services, fuel supply, power transmission and/or distribution, and other things are to be provided by the lessee (for which the lessee will be reimbursed), while a third party is operating the facility on behalf of the lessor or on lease from the lessor. Without facility support agreements the assets of the project have little value as collateral. The facility support agreements are assigned to the indenture trustee as support for the leveraged debt. They remain in effect throughout the interim lease term, the base lease term, and any renewal lease terms, and for at least long enough thereafter to meet the useful-life tests of the Internal Revenue Service. Another purpose of the facility support agreements is to ensure that the facility will have value to someone other than the lessee at the end of the lease so as to satisfy the true-lease requirements of the Internal Revenue Service.

For example, the mere ownership of the facility by the owner trustee, without the underlying supply contracts for coal to be used as fuel for the facility, might seriously undermine the value of the facility for collateral security purposes and residual value purposes. To protect the interests of the equity participants and the loan participants, it is necessary for the lessee to assign to the owner trustee any coal supply contracts that might be advantageous or valuable to it. The owner trustee, in turn, assigns its interest in such contracts to the indenture trustee for the benefit of the loan participants. The supplier to the facility must consent to the assignment, and the form of consent is usually included as part of the coal supply agreement.

The participation agreement and the lease agreement (as in Exhibit 12.2) may contemplate that the title to the property to be leased will be transferred to the owner trustee (lessor) while the facility is still in early stages of construction. In this situation, the construction contract is assigned by the lessee to the owner trustee, and construction financing is arranged as described next.

Although the facility will usually be constructed by a third-party contractor, the utility may wish to supervise the performance of the construction contract by that contractor. In this situation, the lessee and the owner trustee enter into a construction supervision agreement. The purpose of this agreement is to arrange for and require the owner trustee to use the services of the utility in the capacity of construction supervisor to oversee the construction testing, delivery, and acceptance of the facility.

CONSTRUCTION FINANCING

In the usual leveraged lease transaction, the equity participants pay in their equity funds simultaneously with the receipt of leveraged debt funds from the loan participants at the closing, when the leased equipment is accepted by the lessee and the lease begins.

However, where the construction period extends over a considerable time the contractor may require progress payments during construction. In such a situation the parties may agree that the owner trust will take title to the facility during construction, so that the lease involves an interim lease term during construction that precedes the base lease term. Where this type of arrangement is made, the lessee, the owner trustee, and the construction lenders, who usually are not also to be loan participants during the base term lease, enter into a separate interim loan (construction loan) agreement. The lessor's equity investment and short-term construction loan financing is used until the completion of construction, acceptance by the lessee, draw-down of the long-term financing (leveraged debt), and commencement of the base lease term. The lessee pays interim rents to the owner trustee in an amount sufficient to cover interest on the construction loan and an adequate yield to the equity participants. In the alternative, construction loan interest may be capitalized into the cost of the facility and included in the total cost of the facility which is to be financed by the lease.

Construction financing is usually provided by commercial banks. Such financing is secured by an assignment of interim rents and by the lessee's obligation to pay off the principal of the loan if the long-term lenders fail to provide the financing or if the facility is not constructed or completed by a certain date. In such a situation, the equity participants will also look to the lessee's guarantee to recover their investments plus an adequate yield. All of the lessee's guarantees of construction loans are eliminated on or before completion and acceptance of the leased equipment and commencement of the base term of the lease.

Eliminating lessee guarantees of the owner trust debt obligations is necessary in order to comply with the Internal Revenue guidelines.

CREDIT EXPOSURE OF EQUITY PARTICIPANTS

As noted earlier, equity participants realize their yields from the following sources:

1. the interest rate spread between their yield on investment and their cost of funds;
2. tax benefits from MACRS tax depreciation deductions; and
3. the residual value of the equipment at the conclusion of the lease.

Although equity participants sometimes like to view their credit exposure as being limited to their original equity investment, most of which may be recovered in the first few years of the lease term of a leveraged lease, this is not the case if a "forgiveness" of the leveraged debt occurs in the later years of the lease. In such a situation, the lessor may be deemed to realize taxable income from the forgiveness. A forgiveness might occur, for example, where the lessee defaults and the indenture trustee (on behalf of the loan participants) repossesses and sells the equipment for less than the outstanding principal of the leveraged debt.

For these reasons, leveraged leases are available only to lessees that present no apparent credit risk. Lenders and equity sources must be confident in the lessee's ability to meet all of its obligations under the lease, both for rental payments and for maintenance of the leased equipment.

TAX INDEMNIFICATION FOR FUTURE CHANGES IN TAX LAW

Where a company intends to use a true lease to finance the acquisition of equipment it needs, the lessee and lessor must agree as to which of them will bear the burden of future tax changes. The major tax benefits available to a lessor consist of MACRS-accelerated depreciation deductions. During the early years of a lease, tax deductions attributable to accelerated depreciation equal all or part of taxable rental income. This results in deferral of taxable income attributable to the lease rentals until the later years of the lease when depreciation deductions decline or are exhausted. If in the early years of a lease, the tax rate rises above that assumed by the lessor for pricing, the lessor's cash flows and yield will rise accordingly during those early years in which the lessor claims depreciation deductions. On the other hand, if the tax rate is higher than assumed by the lessor for pricing during the later years in which the rental income exceeds the depreciation deductions, the lessor's cash flow and yield will decline or even disappear.

Lessors generally take the position that they should be held harmless by the lessee in the event of any tax law changes or tax rate changes adversely affecting their contemplated yield or cash flow. Lessors argue that the lessee is no worse off under such an indemnification than the lessee would have been had the lessee purchased the leased equipment and directly claimed tax benefits associated with equipment ownership. Lessees, on the other hand, generally take the position that after delivery of the leased equipment, lessors should assume the risk of loss of tax benefits for any reason except as a result of acts or omissions of the lessee.

The problem facing both lessees and lessors is how to engage in equipment leasing and protect themselves in view of the future tax rate and tax law and uncertainties. A significant tax rate change can have disastrous consequences for a lessor, and the possibility of such a change is very real.

Initial questions facing lessors and lessees include the following:[9]

1. What is the definition of the tax-law risk and tax-rate risk covered by the indemnity?
2. What risk of tax-rate change that needs to be covered?
3. What event or events will trigger a tax indemnity?
4. For what period of time will tax indemnities apply? For the entire lease? Or for a limited number of months or years?
5. How will the loss (or gain) resulting from indemnified tax rate risks be computed?
6. How will the indemnified party be compensated?
7. Under what circumstances can the lessee or lessor terminate the lease?

NEED FOR A FINANCIAL ADVISER

An initial question for a company considering a leveraged lease is to determine its need for a financial adviser or broker.[10] Basically, this question boils down to whether the services performed by a financial

---

[9] For a further discussion of each, see Chapter 16 in Nevitt and Fabozzi, *Equipment Leasing*.

[10] Generally the lessee's financial adviser will locate the equity and/or debt investors and thus perform the brokerage function. From the standpoint of the investor and in the parlance of the trade, the lessee's financial adviser is a broker.

adviser will be cost effective as compared to the expenditure for the financial adviser's fee.

The services to be performed by a financial adviser for a company securing a leveraged lease include some or all of the following:

1. Advise the company in structuring financing of the planned equipment acquisition:
   a. Understand the company's objectives, priorities, and constraints.
   b. Analyze the tax, legal, accounting, and economic consequences for the company as well as the potential market acceptance of alternative approaches.
   c. Meet and work with the company's legal and tax counsel with regard to the proposed financing.
   d. Consider alternative methods of financing and compare their advantages and disadvantages with lease financing.
   e. If leasing is the best alternative, recommend the optimal lease financing strategy.
2. Assist the company in establishing a realistic transaction timetable, ensuring that all aspects of the financing progress in a timely and systematic fashion.
3. Assist the company in preparing an equity offering memorandum describing the transaction for distribution to prospective equity sources.
4. Identify the most appropriate equity investors for the transaction.
5. Solicit commitments on a consistent basis from prospective equity participants so as to ensure a complete underwriting of the equity investment in the transaction. Arrange meetings and make face-to-face presentations with priority prospects to explain the transaction.
6. Arrange meetings between the company's key executives and priority prospects where that is advisable.
7. Review, rank, and clarify the equity responses for the company. Evaluate the economics of the equity commitments, including all relevant terms and conditions. Assist the company in selecting the best equity investor(s).
8. Assist the company in negotiating and completing the commitment letter and any pricing adjustments with the equity participants.
9. Arrange for the private placement of the leveraged debt or assist in doing so. Advise the company with regard to structuring the leveraged debt to achieve optimal pricing, amortization, and flexibility, as well as favorable terms and conditions.
10. In conjunction with the company and its counsel, negotiate and document the terms and conditions of the various leveraged lease documents.
11. Assist in the closing of the transaction.

In order to proceed without a financial adviser, a prospective lessee must be satisfied that:

1. It has the technical and professional expertise to perform the above services with its own staff.
2. Those persons on its staff with the technical ability and expertise to arrange a lease can devote the time necessary to arrange, negotiate, and complete the transaction as successfully as a financial adviser would do.
3. It can gain access to the lease equity and/or debt placement markets as effectively and competitively as the financial adviser can.

Some companies that have regularly used leveraged leases to finance equipment feel comfortable with arranging additional leveraged leases themselves, particularly when the additional leases are repetitious and very similar to what they have done in the past. While such companies undoubtedly have the expertise to structure and negotiate leveraged leases, the questions they must address are whether they are familiar enough with changing lease equity markets to be up-to-date with regard to the latest innovative developments in those markets and whether they will be able to identify the full range of potential investors and lenders. Oftentimes the newest entrants are the most aggressive bidders as they seek to quickly build their portfolios.

THE STEPS IN STRUCTURING, NEGOTIATING, AND CLOSING A LEVERAGED LEASE

We conclude this chapter with a description of the various steps and milestones in structuring, negotiating and closing a leveraged lease are as follows:

1. Review of the transaction by the lessee and its counsel.
2. Preparation of drafts of the equity and debt-placement memos.
3. Preparation of the equity and debt-placement offering memorandums with the lessee and its counsel.
4. Preparation of equity and debt solicitation lists.
5. Completion of the equity solicitation and receipt of firm commitments from selected equity sources.
6. Completion and execution of the equity commitment letter.
7. Completion of a draft of all documents to be required.

8. Completion of debt solicitation and receipt of firm commitments from debt participants.
9. Review of debt documents by the lessee and equity participants.
10. Completion and execution of the debt commitment letter.
11. Completion of negotiations and agreement as to documents by the lessee and equity participants.
12. Review of documents by the debt participants.
13. Completion of negotiations and agreement as to debt documents by the equity participants, the lessee, and the debt participants.
14. Completion of final documents and signatures on all documents by all parties.
15. Delivery of the leased equipment, acceptance by the lessee, and payment of the purchase price.

The timetable for accomplishing those steps varies with each transaction depending upon the complexity of the structure, the strength of the lessee's credit, and the time remaining before the property to be leased is expected to be placed in service. While the placed-in-service date cannot in and of itself result in a rapid time schedule, it can motivate the parties to move with a greater sense of urgency than might otherwise be the case. As noted earlier, the lessee and the lessor can speed the process and hold down the costs by closely supervising their attorneys, segregating business decisions from legal decisions, and making business decisions promptly so that the documentation can move forward.

While it is possible to arrange a facility lease in a fairly short time, the financial planning for a large facility is complex and may involve a lead time extending over several months. Exhibit 12.3 is a flowchart for a facility leveraged lease transaction showing the decisions that will be made and the events that will take place from the inception to the completion of such a transaction.

EXHIBIT 12.3 Critical Path Chart of Leveraged Lease Financing for a Large Manufacturing Facility

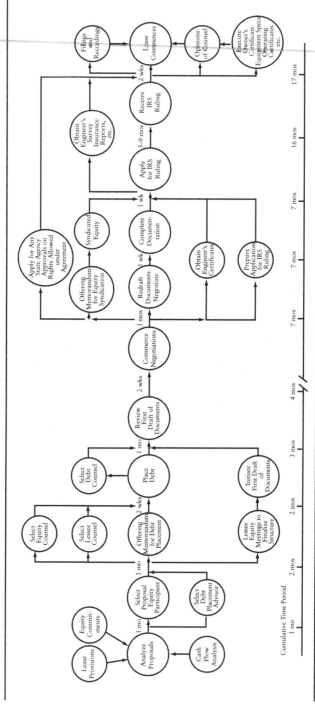

Source: Exhibit 1 in Chapter 17 in Peter K. Nevitt and Frank J. Fabozzi, *Equipment Leasing*, 4th ed. (Hoboken, NJ: John Wiley & Sons, 2000), p. 351.

258

CHAPTER 13

Project Financing

Among its many applications, structured finance may be used by corporations to fund major projects so that the lenders look to the cash flow from the project being financed rather than corporation or corporations seeking funding. This financing technique is called *project financing* (or *project finance*) and uses the special purpose vehicle (SPV) to accomplish its financing objectives. Both project financing and asset securitization use SPVs, yet project financing involves cash flows from operating assets, whereas asset securitization involves cash flows from financial assets, such as loans or as receivables.

Project finance is often used for capital-intensive facilities such as power plants, refineries, toll roads, pipelines, telecommunications facilities, and industrial plants. Before the 1970s, the majority of project lending was for natural resource ventures such as mines and oil fields. Since then the applications of project finance have broadened considerably, but power has been the largest sector.

Industries engaged in the production, processing, transportation, or use of energy have been particularly attracted to project financing techniques because of the needs of such companies for new capital sources. Enterprises located in countries privatizing state-owned companies have made extensive use of project financing.

In this chapter we look at the basic features of project financing. Discussions associated with project financing tend to focus on large complex projects. This might lead one to the conclusion that the project financing principles discussed in this chapter have little application to smaller, more ordinary financings. This is not the case. The same principles used to finance a major pipeline, copper mine, or a power plant can be used to finance a cannery, a hotel, a ship, or a processing plant.

WHAT IS PROJECT FINANCING?

Although the term "project financing" has been used to describe all types of financing of projects, both with and without recourse, the term has evolved in recent years to have a more precise definition:

> A financing of a particular economic unit in which a lender is satisfied to look initially to the cash flows and earnings of that economic unit as the source of funds from which a loan will be repaid and to the assets of the economic unit as collateral for the loan.[1]

A key word in the definition is "initially." While a lender may be willing to look initially to the cash flows of a project as the source of funds for repayment of the loan, the lender must also feel comfortable that the loan will in fact be paid on a worst-case basis. This may involve undertakings or direct or indirect guarantees by third parties who are motivated in some way to provide such guarantees.

Project financing has great appeal when it does not have a substantial impact on the balance sheet or the creditworthiness of the sponsoring entity or entities. Boards of directors are receptive to proceeding with projects that can be very highly leveraged or financed entirely or substantially on their own merits.

The moving party in a project is its *promoter* or *sponsor*. A project may have one or several sponsors. The motivation of construction companies acting as sponsors is to profit in some way from the construction or operation of the project. The motivation of operating companies for sponsoring a project may be simply to make a profit from selling the product produced by the project. In many instances the motivation for the project is to provide processing or distribution of a basic product of the sponsor or to ensure a source of supply vital to the sponsor's business.

The ultimate goal in project financing is to arrange a borrowing for a project that will benefit the sponsor but at the same time have absolutely no recourse to the sponsor, and therefore no effect on its credit standing or balance sheet. One way this can be accomplished is by using the credit of a third party to support the transaction. Such a third party then becomes a sponsor. However, a project is rarely financed independently on its own merits without credit support from sponsors who are interested as third parties and who will benefit in some way from the project.

---

[1] Peter K. Nevitt and Frank J. Fabozzi, *Project Financing*, 7th ed. (London: Euromoney, 2001), p. 1.

There is considerable room for disagreement between lenders and borrowers as to what constitutes a feasible project financing. Borrowers prefer their projects to be financed independently, off their balance sheets, with appropriate disclosures in financial reports indicating the exposure of the borrower to a project financing. Lenders, on the other hand, are not in the venture capital business and they are not equity risk takers. Lenders want to feel secure that they are going to be repaid either by the project, the sponsor, or an interested third party. Therein lies the challenge of most project financings.

The key to a successful project financing is structuring the financing of a project with as little recourse as possible to the sponsor while at the same time providing sufficient credit support through guarantees or undertakings of a sponsor or third party so that lenders will be satisfied with the credit risk.

There is a popular misconception that project financing means off-balance sheet financing to the point that the project is completely self-supporting without guarantees or undertakings by financially responsible parties. This leads to misunderstandings by prospective borrowers who are under the impression that certain kinds of projects may be financed as standalone, self-supporting project financings and therefore proceed on the assumption that similar projects that have no recourse to the sponsor are off the sponsor's balance sheet and need no additional credit support from a financially responsible third party.

It would be a happy circumstance if it were possible simply to arrange a 100% loan for a project (nonrecourse to sponsors) that looked as though it would surely be successful on the basis of optimistic financial projections. Unfortunately, this is never the case. There is no magic about project financing. Such a financing can be accomplished by financial engineering that combines the undertakings and various kinds of guarantees by parties interested in a project being built in such a way that none of the parties alone has to assume the full credit responsibility for the project, yet when all the undertakings are combined and reviewed together, the equivalent of a satisfactory credit risk for lenders has been achieved.

For lenders and investors, the essence of project finance is the analysis of project risks, including construction risk, operating risk, market risk (applying to both inputs and outputs of a project), regulatory risk, insurance risk, and currency risk. These risks often are allocated contractually to parties best able to manage them through construction guarantees, power purchase agreements and other types of output contracts, fuel and raw material supply agreements, transportation contracts, indemnifications, insurance policies, and other contractual agreements. But with many projects today in virtually all sectors, sponsors, lenders, and bank investors are exposed to significant market risk. Though recourse to the sponsors is usually limited, sponsors often provide credit support to the project through guarantees or other contractual undertakings. For example, an industrial sponsor of a cogeneration project may contract to buy steam from a project and another sponsor may contract to sell power to it. Also, the sponsors' economic interests in the success of a project are strong elements in the project's creditworthiness.

REASONS FOR JOINTLY OWNED OR SPONSORED PROJECTS

There has been an increasing trend towards jointly owned or controlled projects. Although most corporations prefer sole ownership and control of a major project, particularly projects involving vital supplies and distribution channels, there are factors that encourage the formation of jointly owned or controlled projects that consist of partners with mutual goals, talents, and resources. These factors include:[2]

- The undertaking is beyond a single corporation's financial and/or managerial resources.
- The partners have complementary skills or economic goals.
- Economics of a large project lower the cost of the product or service substantially over the possible cost of a smaller project if the partners proceeded individually.
- The risks of the projects are shared.
- One or more of the partners can use the tax benefits (i.e., depreciation and any tax credit).
- Greater debt leverage can be obtained.

The joint sponsors will select the legal form of the SPV (corporation, partner, limited partnership, limited liability company, contractual joint venture, or trust) that will be satisfy their tax and legal objectives.

CREDIT EXPOSURES IN A PROJECT FINANCING

To place a project financing into perspective, it is helpful to review the different credit exposures that occur at different times in the course of a typical project financing.

---

[2] Nevitt and Fabozzi, *Project Financing*, 7th ed., p. 265.

Risk Phases

Project financing risks can be divided into three timeframes in which the elements of credit exposure assume different characteristics:

- engineering and construction phase;
- start-up phase; and
- operations according to planned specifications.

Different guarantees and undertakings of different partners may be used in each timeframe to provide the credit support necessary for structuring a project financing.

Engineering and Construction Phase

Projects generally begin with a long period of planning and engineering. Equipment is ordered, construction contracts are negotiated, and actual construction begins. After commencement of construction, the amount at risk begins to increase sharply as funds are advanced to purchase material, labor, and equipment. Interest charges on loans to finance construction also begin to accumulate.

Startup Phase

Project lenders do not regard a project as completed on conclusion of the construction of the facility. They are concerned that the plant or facility will work at the costs and to the specifications that were planned when arranging the financing. Failure to produce the product or service in the amounts and at the costs originally planned means that the projections and the feasibility study are incorrect and that there may be insufficient cash to service debt and pay expenses.

Project lenders regard a project as acceptable only after the plant or facility has been in operation for a sufficient period of time to ensure that it will in fact produce the product or service at the price, in the amounts, and to the standards assumed in the financial plan that formed the basis for the financing. This startup risk period may run from a few months to several years.

Operations According to Specification

Once the parties are satisfied that the plant is running to specification, the final operating phase begins. During this phase, the project begins to function as a regular operating company. If correct financial planning was done, revenues from the sale of the product produced or service performed should be sufficient to service debt—interest and principal—pay operating costs, and provide a return to sponsors and investors.

Different Lenders for Different Risk Periods

Some projects are financed from beginning to end with a single lender or single group of lenders. However, most large projects employ different lenders or groups of lenders during different risk phases. This is because of the different risks involved as the project facility progresses through construction to operation, and the different ability of lenders to cope with and accept such risks.

Some lenders like to lend for longer terms and some prefer short-term lending. Some lenders specialize in construction lending and are equipped to monitor engineering and construction of a project, some are not. Some lenders will accept and rely on guarantees of different sponsors during the construction, startup, or operation phases, and some will not. Some lenders will accept the credit risk of a turnkey operating project, but are not interested in the high-risk lending during construction and startup.

Interest rates will also vary during the different risk phases of project financing and with different credit support from sponsors during those time periods.

Short-term construction lenders are very concerned about the availability of long-term "take-out" financing by other lenders upon completion of the construction or startup phase. Construction lenders live in fear of providing their own unplanned take out financing. Consequently, from the standpoint of the construction lender, take out financing should be in place at the outset of construction financing.

KEY ELEMENTS OF A SUCCESSFUL PROJECT FINANCING

There are several elements that both sponsors and lenders to a project financing should review in order to increase the likelihood that a project financing will be successful. The key ones follow:[3]

- A satisfactory feasibility study and financial plan has been prepared with realistic assumptions regarding future inflation rates and interest rates.
- The cost of product or raw materials to be used by the project is assured.
- A supply of energy at reasonable cost has been assured.
- A market exists for the product, commodity, or service to be produced.
- Transportation is available at a reasonable cost to move the product to the market.

---

[3] Nevitt and Fabozzi, *Project Financing*, 7th ed., p. 7.

- Adequate communications are available.
- Building materials are available at the costs contemplated.
- The contractor is experienced and reliable.
- The operator is experienced and reliable.
- Management personnel are experienced and reliable.
- Untested technology is not involved.
- The contractual agreement among joint venture partners, if any, is satisfactory.
- The key sponsors have made an adequate equity contribution.
- Satisfactory appraisals of resources and assets have been obtained.
- Adequate insurance coverage has been arranged.
- The risk of cost overruns have been addressed.
- The risk of delay has been considered.
- The project will have an adequate return for the equity investor.
- Environmental risks are manageable.

When the project involves a sovereign entity, the following critical elements are important to consider to ensure the success of a project:

- A stable and friendly political environment exists; licences and permits are available; contracts can be enforced; legal remedies exist.
- There is no risk of expropriation.
- Country risk is satisfactory.
- Sovereign risk is satisfactory.
- Currency is available and foreign exchange risks have been addressed.
- Protection has been arranged from criminal activities such as kidnaping and extortion.
- A satisfactory commercial legal system protects property and contractual rights.

CAUSES FOR PROJECT FAILURES

The best way to appreciate the concerns of lenders to a project is to review and consider some of the common causes for project failures, which include the following:[4]

- delay in completion, with consequential increase in the interest expense on construction financing and delay in the contemplated revenue flow;
- capital cost overrun;
- technical failure;

---

[4] Nevitt and Fabozzi, *Project Financing*, 7th ed., p. 2.

- financial failure of the contractor or other party essential to project operation;
- less-than-forecasted price or demand for project output;
- failure of offtaker to honor terms of contract for either financial or political reasons;
- uninsured casualty losses;
- increased price or shortages of raw material;
- technical obsolescence of the plant or equipment;
- loss of competitive position in the marketplace;
- poor management; and
- overly optimistic appraisals of the value of pledged security, such as oil and gas reserves.

In addition, for projects in a foreign country, the following are causes for project failures:

- government interference;
- expropriation;
- financial insolvency of the host government; and
- political changes resulting in failure of the host government to honor the terms of the contract.

For a project financing to be successfully achieved, these risks must be properly considered, monitored, and avoided throughout the life of the project.

The following 10 examples from the 1990s show how financial difficulty has resulted from various combinations of market, counterparty, currency, political, construction, and operating risk as well as high leverage and purchase prices or total investment amounts.

Market Risk

PYCSA, Panama

PYCSA Panama, SA, a project company, financed the $185.5 million construction cost of a Panamanian toll road in 1997 with $131 million Rule 144A, 15-year, senior secured project bonds and $54.5 equity. PYCSA Panama is an indirect subsidiary of Grupo PYCSA, a major Mexican contractor with experience in toll roads, bridges, tunnels, and other infrastructure and transport projects. The project bonds represented the first capital-market project financing in Latin America.

The toll road was designed to relieve traffic congestion around Panama City. It was part of a more comprehensive plan for toll roads to connect Panama City, the Tucumen International Airport, and Colon,

Panama's other major city on the Atlantic end of the canal. Under an agreement with the Republic of Panama, PYCSA Panama had a concession to construct, operate, and maintain the road for up to 30 years. Outside the scope of this project financing, the concession also provided for a second phase of toll road construction that would connect the first phase of the project with Colon. Vehicle traffic for the first phase, near Panama City, did not meet projections done at the time of the project financing in 1997 and revenues were lower than forecast because construction was delayed and fewer motorists than expected were willing to pay the toll despite heavy congestion on regular roads. In 2002, the project came close to defaulting on the bonds and PYCSA Panama considered withdrawing from the second phase of the project.

Before deciding to invest additional equity in the first phase of the project and to proceed to the second phase, PYCSA Panama asked the Panamanian government for some form of relief, either allowing the project company to raise its tolls, providing direct government financing, or handing over some government lands as the government did with another toll road concessionaire. PYSCA Panama reportedly justified investing additional equity in the first phase and preventing a default on the bonds by its projected earnings on the second phase of the project.

SCL Terminal Aéreo Santiago

SCL Terminal Aéreo Santiago is a bond-financed project to expand and operate the Arturo Merino Benitez International Airport in Santiago, Chile. The total project cost of $316 million was financed in late 1998 with $213 million in secured, 14-year bonds, $36 million in owners' equity, $42.5 million cash flow from commercial operations, and $24.9 million in interest earned on bond proceeds. The most important project risks were related to passenger growth and to a partial mismatch between the airports' revenues, paid in Chilean pesos, and debt service obligations, paid in U.S. dollars.

The project bonds received BBB-underlying ratings from three credit rating agencies, but credit insurance, resulting in AAA ratings, was required to sell the bonds in the difficult environment for emerging-market credit that followed the Asian currency crisis. Air traffic through the airport in the first several years after the project financing did not meet the projections made by the concessionaire. The underlying credit rating was downgraded several times between 2001 and 2003 because of a decline in civil aviation that followed the September 11, 2001 terrorist incident in the United States, a recession in Chile, and disputes between the concessionaire and Chilean regulators. The credit rating was upgraded again in 2004 after passenger traffic rose, the project company's financial results improved, and the project company signed an "income distribution mechanism" contract with the Chilean public works ministry. Under that contract, the government agreed to insure the concessionaire's revenue against a sudden drop in passenger flows in return for a premium paid by the concessionaire in kind via public works construction.

Market Risk, High Leverage, High Purchase Price

Drax, UK

Ofgem, the U.K. power industry regulator, and other power industry experts warned that electricity prices would decline when the New Electricity Trading Arrangements (NETA) were implemented in 2001. Despite those warnings, international power companies such as AES continued to pay high prices for assets such as Drax, a coal-fired power station located in North Yorkshire. Drax is one of the largest coal-fired plants in Western Europe and generates about 8% of the United Kingdom's electricity. National Power was required to divest some of its generation capacity when it purchased the distribution/supply business of Midlands Electricity, one of the Regional Electricity Companies (RECs). US-based AES Corporation purchased the plant for $3 billion, more than expected, and financed it with substantial leverage. One of the factors that justified the leverage was electricity price protection from a hedging contract with the U.K. subsidiary of TXU (a Dallas, Texas-based diversified energy company) that covered 60% of the plant's output. The remainder of the plant's output was subject to merchant risk. The senior bonds received investment-grade ratings in 1999.

Since the project financing in 1999, AES and its Drax power plant investment have been affected primarily by two important developments with far-reaching ripple effects: First, the combination of the U.K.'s New Electricity Trading Arrangements (NETA) and an oversupply of generating capacity reduced wholesale electricity prices in the United Kingdom even more than expected and consequently reduced the earnings and value of power plants such as Drax. Second, the Enron bankruptcy caused investors and lenders to take a more conservative stance toward the entire power industry, requiring companies such as AES and TXU to deleverage and sell off assets. When TXU, facing its own financial problems, terminated the hedging contract, it was clear that Drax would not be able to service its debt on an ongoing basis. In November 2002, Drax reached a six-month standstill agreement with its lending banks and bondholders to give it time to restructure.

In June 2003, AES made an offer to buy back part of its debt and to continue to operate and manage the plant in return for continued ownership of 20% of the equity and an annual management fee. AES walked away from the plant in August when the creditors did not accept its offer. The banks and bondholders took over the plant and replaced management with an independent board of directors. Over the next two years, electricity prices rose substantially, improving the plant's financial performance. The banks and bondholders negotiated with several bidders for the plant, but ultimately decided in favor of an IPO.

Drax was listed and started trading on the London Stock Exchange in December 2005. By then, Standard & Poor's had awarded Drax a BBB-corporate credit rating based on well maintained assets, efficient operations, production flexibility, and a solid financial profile compared to other merchant power suppliers. Some, noting Drax's dependence on a few large wholesale contracts and lack of a retail customer base to help hedge market price fluctuations, thought the IPO was a gamble on continued high electricity prices and that a publicly traded independent power station was unusual in a market then dominated by six vertically integrated utilities. Drax would continue seeking opportunities to take part in future mergers and acquisitions in the power sector, according to its CEO.

Market Risk, Political Risk

Dabhol, India

The Dabhol power project, as originally conceived, consisted of the development, construction, and operation of a power station to run on LNG, port facilities for the importation of LNG, and an LNG regasification facility. The principal project sponsors at the beginning were Enron (65%); General Electric, the turbine manufacturer and design contractor (10%); Bechtel, the construction contractor (10%); and the Maharashtra State Electricity Board (15%). The project represented the largest foreign investment and the largest energy infrastructure project financing in India.

Financing for the first phase of the project in 1995 was the first to close after foreign companies were allowed in the Indian power sector. It was facilitated by the first Indian government guarantee of a foreign corporation's liabilities. The power purchase agreement (PPA), signed in November 1993 after close to two years of negotiation, was politically controversial in India. Opponents criticized the agreement because the PPA was negotiated rather than open to tender, the deal was obsessively secret, and it allowed Enron excessive profits. Some also thought that LNG was the wrong fuel because it was too expensive. The project has been plagued by willful default by the Maharastra State Electricity Board (MSEB), the main offtaker; defaults by both federal and state governments on their guarantees; and the bankruptcy of Enron, the principal project developer. Among the underlying problems at the beginning were that the price of power supplied by Dabhol under the power purchase agreement (PPA) was more than the MSEB could afford, that the State of Maharastra had more power than it needed, and that the project was not allowed to sell power to other parties without state and federal government permission. Enron shut the plant down in 2001 after MSEB fell $240 million behind in payments.

A lengthy period of negotiations to restart or sell the plant ensued among the sponsors, Indian and foreign lenders, and the MSEB. GE and Bechtel filed arbitration claims of approximately $600 million each in September 2003 against the Indian government to recover their investments in the project and outstanding payments for work they had finished. At the same time, GE and Bechtel took claims under their political risk insurance policies with OPIC to an arbitration panel, which found that their interests in DPC were taken illegally and ordered OPIC to pay their political risk coverage claims. Emboldened by that arbitration panel decision, the foreign lenders initiated claims in November 2003 against the Indian government under bilateral investment treaties to put pressure on the government to restart the project. Bechtel and GE obtained U.S. bankruptcy court permission in 2004 to buy out Enron's 65% stake in the plant for a combined $20 million.

In July 2005, Bechtel agreed with the Government of India to settle all its claims against Dabhol Power Company for $160 million and GE reached a similar agreement for $145 million. GE reinvested the $145 million in India, where it already had significant and growing business interests. In July 2005, the Indian lenders developed a plan to pay $600 million to buy out the foreign lenders and allow the transfer of the project to a new SPV called Ratnagiri Gas and Power Ltd. The SPV would be owned by the lenders and two state-owned companies, Gail India, a gas company that would source the natural gas, and National Thermal Power Corporation, a generating company that would operate the plant and negotiate a new PPA with MSEB. The rising cost of natural gas made sourcing particularly difficult.

In August, MSEB was willing to buy electricity at 2.30 rupees per unit based on an estimated price of $3.65 per million British thermal units (MMBtu). By November 2005, price quotes were $7 to $8 per MMBtu. GE, by then no longer an equity holder, was commissioned in October 2005 on a contract basis to do an assessment study of what was needed to recommission the plant. By 2005, instead of a power surplus there was an acute shortage. As a result, the Government of India was working with all the parties even harder than before in an effort to reach a compromise and restart the plant.

Market Risk, Counterparty Risk, Currency Risk, Political Risk

Paiton Energy, Indonesia

Perusahaan Listrik Negara (PLN), the Indonesian state-owned utility, signed long-term, dollar-based PPAs with 27 independent power projects (IPPs) while the Suharto administration was in power. Paiton Energy was the first and therefore took the longest time to negotiate; it was intended to be a model for a large private power program. According to the project sponsors, being the first also explained why the $2.5 billion total cost of the plant was the highest of any of the Indonesian IPPs and the tariff charged to PLN was the highest.

Problems for PLN and the IPPs began with the decline of the Indonesian rupiah during the Asian financial crisis, starting in 1997. As the rupiah continued to decline, the IPPs' dollar-denominated electricity tariffs became increasingly unaffordable to PLN. For a 6-month period, PLN made no payments to Paiton Energy. After Suharto fell from power in 1999, PLN argued that it was forced to sign many of the contracts under pressure from his administration. Many of the IPPs involved relatives or associates of Suharto as local partners and none of the 27 IPP contracts was awarded in an open bidding process.

In the face of these pressures, both PLN and the Indonesian government refused to make payments under the PPAs and the support letters. PLN filed a lawsuit seeking to nullify its PPA with Paiton Energy, saying that the total cost of power was twice that of other comparable plants. President Wahid ordered PLN to drop the lawsuit and seek an out-of-court settlement. PLN and Paiton reached an interim agreement in 2000 that enabled the utility to purchase power at a reduced rate pending a full restructuring of the PPA.

After prolonged negotiations, the original 1994 PPA was amended in 2002, reducing the electricity price and extending the term from 30 to 40 years. Indonesia needed to settle its PPA disputes so it could attract investors in additional power projects to satisfy the country's growing electricity needs. After the amended PPA was signed, U.S. project sponsor Edison Mission Energy announced its plans to double the size of the plant, helping to mitigate earlier losses sustained on the project. In February 2003, the Export Import Bank of the United States converted a $507 million to a direct loan, as originally planned upon project completion but delayed by the Asian financial crisis.

In September 2003, Standard & Poor's raised its credit rating on the project from CCC to B–, citing a relatively strong PPA structure that provided stable cash flow generation, evidence of strong support provided by committed shareholders, strong electricity demand in Indonesia, and adequate operational performance of the plant over the preceding two years.

The agency also noted PLN's improved financial profile as a result of government approval to raise its electricity tariff and a stronger rupiah. Offsetting these strengths, the agency said that PLN's overall credit profile was weak because of poor operating performance, low profitability, and weak cash-flow-protection measures. In December 2004, Edison Mission Energy sold its interests in 10 international power projects, including Paiton Energy, to IPM Eagle, a 70–30 partnership between U.K.-based International Power and Mitsui & Co. International Power was expanding its international IPP investments while Edison International, Edison Mission's parent, was refocusing on domestic operations.

Counterparty Risk, Political Risk

Meizou Wan, China

The $725 million project cost of the Meizou Wan coal-fired power plant in the Fujian Province of the People's Republic of China was financed in 1998 with $158 million equity from its sponsors and $567 million in debt financing from the Asian Development Bank, Compagnie Française d'Assurance pour le Commerce Extérieur (Coface), Compania Espanola de Seguros de Credito (Cesce), and commercial banks. It was the second wholly foreign owned power project in China and the first entirely foreign-owned power project to be financed outside China's state-sponsored build-own-transfer (BOT) program.

Because the project does not rely on the BOT program, the sponsors could not take advantage of a comprehensive concession agreement with the provincial government or a preassembled regulatory approval and government support package. However, by not being bound by the BOT program, the sponsors had more freedom to design project arrangements and a financing package tailored to the project. The sponsors' objective was a true limited-recourse financing from international lenders with world-standard documentation that had never been used in China.

When the project was initially approved in 1993, China needed power plants and was willing to pay relatively high prices to get them. By 2002, however, there was an oversupply of power in Fujian province and the central Chinese government was restructuring the power sector to increase competition and cut electricity prices nationwide. In May 2002, the Fujian provincial government reneged on its obligations under the PPA with the Meizou Wan power project and proposed that the tariff be lowered. A temporary agreement in September 2002 helped Meizou Wan avoid default on its international loans and the sponsors refinanced a portion of the project debt with domestic Chinese banks to reduce the interest cost. Whatever the final agreement on the project tariff, the project sponsors' rate of return would be substantially less than originally anticipated. As a result of problems with Meizou Wan and concurrent problems with other overseas investments, major international power industry players became less enthusiastic about new Chinese projects.

Market Risk, Currency Risk, Political Risk, High Purchase Price

BCP, Brazil

BCP, a consortium led by Bell South, paid an unexpectedly high $2.5 billion for its cellular telephone license in São Paulo, Brazil and financed it with a high level of debt. Although operating performance and earnings before interest, taxes, depreciation, and amortization (EBITDA) exceeded its business plan, BCP had difficulty rolling over its local currency paper every two years and servicing its dollar-denominated debt as the value of the Brazilian real declined. Debt restructuring was impeded by disagreement between two deadlocked 47% shareholders, who eventually relinquished control of the project to bank lenders. At that time, two major players were beginning to dominate the Latin American telecommunications market. Over the following year, one of those players, America Movil of Mexico, bought BCP and the other, Telefonica of Spain, bought Bell South's other Latin American assets for considerably less than Bell South originally paid for them.

Market Risk, High Leverage

FLAG

Fiberoptic Link Around the Globe (FLAG) is a multinational submarine fiber-optic cable network that provides transmission services for telecommunications carriers, application service providers (ASPs) and Internet service providers (ISPs). Spanning 25 jurisdictions in North America, Europe, and Asia, the project is the first submarine cable system ever project-financed and the first major submarine cable system financed by private investors rather then international carriers. Insurance cover came from export credit agencies (ECAs) in 17 jurisdictions.

FLAG was able to repay its original $950 million project debt, arranged in 1995, but then continually borrowed and reinvested to expand its undersea cable network and could not service its debt after a worldwide drop-off in spending by major telecom carriers. The company declared bankruptcy in early 2002 and then reemerged six months later. As a result, creditors owned FLAG's equity, but the company's international undersea cable network and its relationships with 180 operators remained intact.

The principal lesson learned was that aggressive network expansion financed with high leverage may have been a viable strategy while Internet use, telecommunication traffic, and related capital spending were growing rapidly, but FLAG did not generate sufficient cash flow to service its debt when the market collapsed. Reliance Group, India's largest business group, acquired FLAG in early 2004, paying $211 million for a network that cost $4 billion to build. Reliance wanted to merge its domestic network with FLAG's international network to take advantage of the increased international traffic that resulted from Indian service companies' business with U.S. and other multinational customers.

Shortly after acquiring FLAG, Reliance announced a new $300 million undersea cable project to link Egypt and Persian Gulf countries with Hong Kong, crossing India to connect with Reliance's network. By this time the cost of building cable networks had dropped 60% since the telecom bubble, but because of continuing technological innovations, the growth of cable capacity was once again outpacing the growth of demand, leading to fears of another over-investment cycle. Now, however, FLAG was backed by a corporation with deep pockets.

Market Risk, Operating Risk

Andacollo Gold Mine, Chile

The Andacollo Gold Mine project financing in 1994 was the first in Chile without political risk insurance. Andocollo was the first major project and the principal asset of the Dayton Mining Company of Vancouver, British Columbia. The facility was built by Bechtel Corporation, one of the world's largest international engineering firms. The equity and loan financing for the project was on Dayton Mining's balance sheet, but because the project accounted for a large part of the company's balance sheet, the financing was considered in effect to be a project financing. By working with Bechtel, one of the most experienced contractors in the world, and structuring the loan as a project financing, Dayton was able to finance a project that its balance sheet alone could not have supported. The major themes in the story of Andacollo Gold since the project financing include lower-than-expected ore grades, resulting in higher-than-expected production costs; declining gold prices; continual losses reflected on Dayton Mining Corporation's income statements; defaults under the bank loan agreement and subsequent waivers; renegotiation of interest-rate and repayment terms with the banks; eventual repayment of the bank loan with the help of a convertible debenture offering; and continued efforts to evolve from a one-project company, which led to investment in new projects and to a recent merger.

Counterparty Risk, Political Risk

TermoEmcali, Colombia

TermoEmcali is a BOT power project that serves the city of Cali in Colombia. It was owned at the time of the original project financing in 1997 by Emcali, the local utility and sole offtaker, and InterGen, then an affiliate of Bechtel. (InterGen was later owned by Bechtel and Shell and then sold in 2005 to AIG Highstar Capital and the Ontario Teachers Pension Plan.) While this natural-gas-fired plant's marginal cost usually is higher than wholesale market energy prices, and the plant therefore serves primarily in a standby capacity, the rationale for the plant is to reduce the region's dependence on hydroelectric power and blackouts during droughts.

Whereas power projects in the past had been financed by banks during construction and then in some cases refinanced in the capital markets, but only after construction was completed, TermoEmcali was financed "out of the box" in the Rule 144A private placement market with a backup commercial loan commitment. The project's bonds had the longest term to date for a Colombian borrower and originally received an investment-grade credit rating.

A bank debt-service letter-of-credit facility replaced the government guarantee or power purchase agreement common in previous project financings. In addition to a conventional security package, Emcali's payment obligations to TermoEmcali under the PPA were secured by a *fiducia*, a trust that granted the project company a priority interest in a portion of Emcali's operating cash collections in case the latter defaulted in its payment obligations.

After a short delay in the beginning of commercial operations caused by problems with the combustion chamber, the performance of the power project was satisfactory. However, TermoEmcali was downgraded by the credit-rating agencies and eventually defaulted because Emcali, an equity holder and the principal offtaker, ran into financial difficulty as a result of a weak local economy and mismanagement. The utility went bankrupt, was taken over by the federal government, and then was handed back to Cali. Emcali's inability to pay for its power offtakes caused TermoEmcali to default on its bonds in 2003. Under a debt restructuring completed in 2005, the bondholders received $969 of new principal for each $1,000 of outstanding amount of the original notes.

Counterparty Risk, Construction Risk, Political Risk

Casecnan Water and Energy, Philippines

The Casecnan multipurpose power and irrigation project is a 20-year BOT project between the Philippine National Irrigation Administration (NIA) and CE Casecnan Water and Energy Corporation. After a 20-year cooperation period under the BOT contract, the project is to be turned over to the Philippine government at no cost and is expected to continue in commercial operation for another 30 years. The project consists of structures in the Casecnan and Denip Rivers that divert water into a 23-kilometer tunnel into the Pantabangan Reservoir for irrigation and hydroelectric use in the central Luzon area of the Philippines. An underground powerhouse located at the end of the water tunnel houses a 150 megawatt power plant.

The high-yield bond offering in 1995 illustrated the market's capacity to finance a large and complex project in an emerging-market country. It was structured in several tranches with 5-, 10-, and 15-year maturities to meet different investors' needs, and closed after a very tight time schedule to sell the bonds to institutional investors. During the course of construction, the original EPC contractor failed and was replaced, payment under a standby letter of credit backing the original EPC contactor's performance was made by a Korean bank only after a prolonged legal battle, and the replacement EPC contractor's completion was delayed by tunnel-drilling difficulties. Parent financial support was required because the construction-delay-strained project liquidity. The project was completed in December 2001.

After operations began, the NIA was consistently delayed in its monthly payments to the project company and failed to reimburse the project company for $52 million in taxes paid during construction as provided in the project agreement. The project company initiated international arbitration in August 2002 to force the NIA to reimburse the taxes paid. In 2003, the Philippine Supreme Court handed down a decision to nullify a contract between a Philippine government agency and the Philippine International Air Terminals Company to build Terminal Three at the Ninoy Aquino International Airport on the grounds that the contract was overpriced and the project company received a direct government guarantee contrary to Philippine BOT law. The Freedom from Debt Coalition, a think tank based at the University of the Philippines, called for the government to cancel its contract for the Casecnan project and several independent power producers because they had similar government guarantees and also had terms that were alleged to be too favorable to the contractors.

CREDIT IMPACT OBJECTIVE

While the sponsor or sponsors of a project financing ideally would prefer that the project financing be a nonrecourse borrowing that does not in any way affect its credit standing or balance sheet, many project financings are aimed at achieving some other particular credit impact objective, such as any one or several of the following:[5]

- to avoid being shown as debt on the face of the balance sheet so as not to impact financial ratios;
- to avoid being shown in a particular footnote to the balance sheet;
- to avoid being within the scope of restrictive covenants in an indenture or loan agreement that precludes direct debt financing or leases for the project;
- to avoid being considered as a cash obligation that would dilute interest coverage ratios and affect the sponsor's credit standing with the rating services;
- to limit direct liability to a certain period of time such as during construction and/or the startup period, so as to avoid a liability for the remaining life of the project; and
- to keep the project off the balance sheet during construction and/or until the project generates revenues.

Any one or a combination of these objectives may be sufficient reason for a borrower to seek the structure of a project financing.

Liability for project debt for a limited time period may be acceptable in situations in which liability for such debt is unacceptable for the life of the project. Where a sponsor cannot initially arrange long-term nonrecourse debt for a project that will not impact its balance sheet, the project may still be feasible if the sponsor is willing to assume the credit risk during the construction and startup phase, provided lenders are willing to shift the credit risk to the project after the project facility is completed and operating. Under such an arrangement, most of the objectives of an off-balance-sheet project financing and limited credit impact can be achieved after the initial risk period of construction and startup. In some instances, the lenders may be willing to rely on revenue produced by unconditional take-or-pay contracts from users of the product or services to be provided by the project to repay debt.[6] In other instances, the condition of the market for the product or service may be such that sufficient revenues are assured after completion of construction and startup so as to convince lenders to rely on such revenues for repayment of their debts.

---

[5] Nevitt and Fabozzi, *Project Financing*, 7th ed., p. 4.

Sources of Capital

Historically, commercial banks have provided construction financing for projects and insurance companies have provided take-out financing with terms of 20 years or more. Banks have been relatively more comfortable with construction risks and shorter-term loans, and insurance companies have been more comfortable bearing the longer-term operating risks after construction has been completed and the project has demonstrated the capability to run smoothly.

In the early 1990s, the investor base for project finance began to broaden. It now includes institutional investors such as pension and mutual funds, and investors in the public bond markets in a growing number of countries around the world. Two important developments made institutional investors more receptive to project finance investments than they had been in the past: a ruling by the U.S. Securities and Exchange Commission (SEC) and the issuance of project credit ratings by the major credit rating agencies.

SEC Rule 144a allows the resale of eligible unregistered securities to qualified institutional buyers and eliminates the requirement that investors hold on to securities for two years before selling them. Recently, some large power projects have aimed their financing solely at the institutional 144a market; others have been able to reduce their financing costs by committing to full registration for sale in the pubic markets within six months after the 144a securities are issued, thereby providing a more liquid market for the institutional investors that hold the securities.

Project Finance Credit Ratings

As the capital markets became an important source of funding, the amount of rated project debt grew rapidly. For example, in 1993, Standard & Poor's portfolio of rated project debt was $5.8 billion. The agency established its project rating team in 1994. By mid-1996, it had rated $16.3 billion and, by the end of 2002, $106 billion of project debt. Debt rated by the two other leading credit rating agencies, Moody's and Fitch, has grown in similar fashion.

---

[6] A *take-or-pay contract* is a long-term contract to make periodic payments over the life of the contract in certain minimum amounts as payments for a service or a product. The payments are in an amount sufficient to service the debt needed to finance the project and to pay the project's operating expenses. The obligation to make minimum payments is unconditional and must be paid whether or not the service or product is actually furnished or delivered. In contrast, a *take-and-pay contract* is a contact in which payment is contingent upon delivery and the obligation to pay is not unconditional.

Institutional Investors' Needs

For institutional investors, project finance offers a way to diversify and earn very good returns for the amount of risk. As more power and other infrastructure projects are financed and demonstrate a track record, more investors are becoming comfortable with the risk. William H. Chew, Managing Director, Corporate & Government Ratings at Standard & Poor's (S&P) sees project finance as not just another Wall Street invention, but a growing investment vehicle with strong demand on both the buy side and the sell side. It provides uncorrelated returns that portfolio managers have been looking for, and risks that are different from the credit of the sponsor or the offtaker of the project's product.

ACCOUNTING CONSIDERATIONS

Project financing is sometimes called "off-balance-sheet financing." However, while the project debt may not be on the sponsor's balance sheet, that debt still appears on the project balance sheet. The purpose of a project financing is to segregate the credit risk of the project from that of its sponsors so that lenders, investors, and other parties will appraise the project strictly on its own merits. The purpose is *not* to hide or conceal a liability of the sponsor from creditors, rating agencies, or stockholders. Of course, the obligations of a sponsor with respect to the project may have to be shown in the sponsor's financial statements or in footnotes thereto.

Under traditional guidance from generally accepted accounting principles (GAAP), the owner of a controlling financial interest (usually achieved through ownership of a majority of the voting equity) in a special-purpose entity (SPE) such as a project company should consolidate that entity. In so doing, the owner records its share of the entity's equity on its balance sheet and its share of the entity's income on its income statement. This is known as the *equity method of accounting*. If the project company has several owners, as many do, an owner with an interest of 50% or less includes its share of the project company's earnings below the line in "equity investment in unconsolidated subsidiaries" and its share of the equity on its balance sheet in "equity investment in unconsolidated subsidiaries." If the sponsor has less than a 20% interest in the project, it is presumed to lack significant influence over the project's management, and neither consolidation nor the equity method of accounting is required. Presumably, the sponsor's investment in a project and the related income or losses would be combined with other items on the balance sheet and income statement. It would be considered good practice to include some mention of the project investment in the footnotes, particularly given the sensitivity to disclosure and transparency in today's post-Enron environment. An important point to remember is that whether a project is financed on or off the balance sheet, analysts know where to look.

About 15 years ago, accountants realized that traditional GAAP guidance didn't work very well for SPEs whose activities and business decisions are limited, particularly in the case of leasing. In EITF Issue 90-15, Emerging Issues Task Force (EITF) of the Financial Accounting Standards Board (FASB) concluded that a lessee need not consolidate a lessor SPE if:

1. Its legal owner is an entity (or entities) other than the lessee and has a substantive equity investment at risk—and sometimes an interest as little as 3% was considered substantive, although the EITF considered this an absolute minimum and not the norm;
2. The SPE has significant transactions with other parties; and
3. Most of the residual risks and rewards related to the SPE's assets rest with other parties.

The EITF guidance was criticized for making it too easy for companies to avoid consolidating SPEs, and residual equity equal to 3% of assets was criticized as too little third-party investment at risk. Enron's use of such SPEs to hide corporate debt brought the potential abuses to public attention put pressure on FASB to issue new guidance on consolidation. FASB Interpretation (FIN) 46, *Consolidation of Variable Interest Entities,* an interpretation of Accounting Research Bulletin (ARB) 51, *Consolidated Financial Statements, Including Accounting and Reporting of Noncontrolling Interests in Subsidiaries*, was issued in January 2003 in response to that pressure. After much debate over FASB's complex solution to the SPE problem, the revised FIN 46R was released in December 2003.[7]

In FIN 46R, FASB concluded that consolidation guidance should be based on residual risks and rewards rather than on voting control and introduced a new concept of the *variable interest entity* (VIE). An entity is a VIE if:

1. It is so thinly capitalized that (a) it cannot finance its activities without additional subordinated financial support, or (b) its earnings volatility (expected residual returns plus expected losses) exceeds its equity investment at risk; or

---

[7] J. Paul Forrester and Benjamin J. Neuhausen, "Is My SPE a VIE under FIN 46R, and, If So, So What?" Chapter 30 in Christopher L. Culp, *Structured Finance & Insurance: The Art of Managing Capital and Risk* (Hoboken, NJ: John Wiley & Sons, Inc., 2006), p. 662.

2. its equity holders as a group do not have the ability, either directly or indirectly, to make decisions about its activities.

FIN 46R requires that the *primary beneficiary* (PB) of a VIE consolidate that entity. The PB is the holder of variable interests that will receive the majority of expected residual returns and bear the majority of expected losses. Variable interests may include equity investments, subordinated debt, guarantees, derivative instrument contracts, leases, service contracts, and commonly used project contracts such as power purchase agreements and operation and maintenance agreements.

If a project company is capitalized with a normal ratio of equity and debt to total capitalization considering the riskiness of the project, for example 15% to 30% equity to total capitalization for a power project, and its equity owners have the usual risks and rights, then it is generally not considered to be a VIE and the usual equity method guides whether or not an owner must consolidate its interest in the project company. However, if third-party contractors bear most of a project company's risk of loss and they rather than the equity holders make most of the decisions, then the project company may be defined as a VIE. If the PB is required to consolidate but does not have a majority voting interest in the VIE, the PB must disclose the following in addition to normal GAAP disclosures: the nature, purpose, size, and activities of the VIE; the carrying amount and classifications of assets posted as collateral for the VIE's obligations; and whether or not any creditors or other interest holders in the VIE have any recourse to the PB's general credit. If the PB has a majority voting interest in the VIE, it is not required to make these extra disclosures. A holder of a significant variable interest in a VIE that is not required to consolidate must disclose the nature, purpose, size and activities of the VIE, the nature of the holder's involvement with the VIE and when that involvement began, and the holder's maximum exposure to loss resulting from its involvement with the VIE.

These rules are still new as of this writing. Questions over what is a variable interest and whether a party is a PB are complex and will require professional advice. EITF 04-7, *Determining Whether an Interest Is a Variable Interest in a Variable Interest Entity*, has explored but not resolved issues such as:

- which of four approaches to use to determine to determine whether an interest in an entity is a variable interest ([1] fair value approach: whether the interest absorbs variability in the fair value of net assets; [2] cash flow approach: whether the interest absorbs variability in the entity's cash flows; [3] combination of fair value and cash flow approach, [4] design approach; whether the interest was originally intended to absorb the entity's variability); and

■ when determining whether an interest is a variable interest, whether long positions of a VIE that are created synthetically by derivative transactions or contract such as power purchase agreements should be considered in the same manner as long positions in the entity created by cash transactions.

Recently, J. Paul Forrester, Partner, Mayer, Brown, Rowe, & Maw LLP and Benjamin S. Neuhausen, National Director of Accounting, BDO Seidman LLP,[8] advised that given the wide variety of project-related agreements in practice and the significant variation of transaction-specific requirements contained in those agreements, the analysis of whether a party has a variable interest in a VIE is likely to be complex and time-consuming and different accounting firms may come to different conclusions in similar situations.

MEETING INTERNAL RETURN OBJECTIVES

Corporations set target rates of return for new capital investments. If a proposed capital expenditure will not generate a return greater than a company's target rate, it is not regarded as a satisfactory use of capital resources. This is particularly true when a company can make alternative capital expenditures that will produce a return on capital in excess of the target rate.

Project financing can sometimes be used to improve the return on the capital invested with a project by leveraging the investment to a greater extent than would be possible in a straight commercial financing of the project. This can be accomplished by locating other parties that have an economic interest in seeing the project completed, and shifting some of the debt coverage to such parties through direct or indirect guarantees. An example would be an oil company with a promising coal property that it does not wish to develop because of better alternative uses of its capital. It might bring in a company that requires the coal, such as a public utility. An indirect guarantee might be available in the form of a long-term take-or-pay contract, which would support long-term debt to finance the construction of the coal mine. This, in turn, would permit the oil company's investment to be leveraged more highly and consequently to produce a higher rate of return.

---

[8] Forrester and Neuhausen, "Is My SPE a VIE under FIN 46R, and, If So, So What?" p. 671.

OTHER BENEFITS OF A PROJECT FINANCING

There are often other side benefits resulting from segregating a financing as a project financing that may have a bearing on the motives of the company seeking such a structure. These benefits include:[9]

- Credit sources may be available to the project that would not be available to the sponsor.
- Guarantees may be available to the project that would not be available to the sponsor.
- A project financing may enjoy better credit terms and interest costs in situations in which a sponsor's credit is weak.
- Higher leverage of debt to equity may be achieved.
- Legal requirements applicable to certain investing institutions may be met by the project but not by the sponsor.
- Regulatory problems affecting the sponsor may be avoided.
- For regulatory purposes, costs may be clearly segregated as a result of a project financing.
- Construction financing costs may not be reflected in the sponsor's financial statements until such time as the project begins producing revenue.

In some instances, any one of the reasons stated above may be the primary motivation for structuring a new operation as a project financing.

TAX CONSIDERATIONS

Benefits available from any applicable tax credits, depreciation deductions, interest deductions, depletion deductions, research and development tax deductions, dividends-received credits, foreign tax credits, capital gains, and noncapital startup expenses are very significant considerations in the investment, debt service, and cash flow of most project financings. Care must be used in structuring a project financing to make sure that these tax benefits are used. In a new entity that does not have taxes to shelter, it is important to structure the project financing so that any tax benefits can be transferred to parties in a position currently able to use such tax benefits.

For U.S. federal income tax purposes, 80% control requires tax consolidation, except in the case of certain foreign subsidiaries, in which 50% control may require consolidation.

---

[9] Nevitt and Fabozzi, *Project Financing*, 7th ed., p. 5.

DISINCENTIVES TO PROJECT FINANCING

Project financings are complex. The documentation tends to be complicated, and the cost of borrowing funds may be higher than with conventional financing. If the undertakings of a number of parties are necessary to structure the project financing, or if a joint venture is involved, the negotiation of the original financing agreements and operating agreements will require patience, forbearing, and understanding. Decision-making in partnerships and joint ventures is never easy, since the friendliest of partners may have diverse interests, problems, and objectives. However, the rewards and advantages of a project financing will often justify the special problems that may arise in structuring and operating the project.

RECENT TRENDS

Among the recent trends in project finance have been the following:

- *Infrastructure requirements:* There continue to be massive infrastructure requirements, particularly in developing countries. For example, in 2001 the World Bank estimated that Latin America alone would need more than $70 billion per year in infrastructure investment through 2005 to meet the needs of a growing and largely impoverished population.
- *Privatization:* This is a worldwide trend that reflects political currents and one of the ways to provide needed infrastructure in light of government budgetary limitations. Variations on this trend include public/private partnerships and, in particular, the Private Finance Initiative in the United Kingdom.
- *Deregulation:* Along with privatization, deregulation in the power industry was intended to attract capital and ultimately to result in lower consumer prices. The crisis in 2000–2001 that resulted from a flawed deregulatory structure in California has caused skepticism and slowed the pace of worldwide power industry deregulation.
- *Securitization:* A trend over the past decade has been the growing use of bonds, both investment grade and high yield, for project financing sold to a broadening base of institutional investors and the consequent growth in credit-rated project debt. Related to this trend are investment funds comprised of projects from different industries are providing investors a way to spread risks and project sponsors an additional source of financing. Also related is the growing flexibility between bond and bank financing, helped by the increasing number of financial

institutions with both commercial and investment banking capabilities that can offer both loan and bond alternatives in a single project financing package.

■ *Increasing and then decreasing risk tolerance*: Until 1997, there was a trend of lengthening maturities, thinning prices (reflected in spreads over the cost of funds), looser covenants, and the extension of project finance to new industries and geographic regions and willingness of lenders and investors to assume new risks. This was partly a result of more institutional investors becoming interested in and developing expertise in project finance. This trend reversed as a result of the worldwide ripples caused by the Asian financial crisis starting in 1997, the Russian default in 1998, and the Brazilian maxidevaluation in 1999. Banks became less willing to commit to emerging-market credits and spreads on emerging-market bonds widened. To be financed, projects required increasing support from sponsors, multilateral agencies, export credit agencies (ECAs), and insurance companies. Since the Enron debacle, investors and lenders have reduced their tolerance for risk related to power companies with trading activities, overseas operations, and difficult-to-understand financial statements.

■ *Blending of project and corporate finance*: Lack of risk tolerance and market liquidity sometimes prevents projects from being financed off the corporate balance sheet on a pure nonrecourse basis. Projects today are financed along a spectrum ranging from pure project finance to pure corporate finance.

■ *Commodity price volatility*: Prices below long-term forecasted levels sometimes place commodity-based projects such as copper mines, gold mines, and oil fields "under water" in terms of profitability. With deregulation and merchant power, the "spark spread," the difference between a power plant's input (fuel) costs and output (electricity) prices, may at times not be sufficient for profitability.

■ *Insurance*: An emerging trend in project and concession financing is the use of targeted risk coverage, a structured financial mechanism that shifts specifically identified project risks to a third party that is willing to assume them such as a multi-line insurance or reinsurance company, a preferred creditor, or conceptually any party that is willing to assume those risks, including project sponsors. Among recent applications of targeted risk coverage have been revenue risk mitigation, including coverage against commodity pricing risk, revenue guarantees for toll road projects, and coverage against default of offtakers; substitutes for liquidity mechanisms such as fully funded debt-service reserves and standby letters of credit; and political risk coverage. Whereas just a few years ago, political risk insurance was provided mainly by government and multilateral agencies, it is now widely available from private insurance providers.

- *Financial innovation*: As innovations are made in other financial disciplines such as leasing, insurance, and derivatives-based financial risk management, they are applied quickly to project finance.
- *Interest rate volatility*: At the margin, rising and falling interest rates can affect whether or not projects are viable. In the early 1990s, and in the past several years, the interest-rate environment has been relatively benign.
- *Local currency financing*: As the role of pension funds and other institutional investors broadens in many emerging markets, local-currency funding is becoming increasingly available for project financing.
- *Bank capabilities*: The number of financial institutions with broad project finance syndication capabilities is shrinking as is the number with specialized project finance groups. Institutions with broad geographic scope and with both commercial and investment banking capabilities have a competitive edge in today's market.
- *Capital requirements*: In 1988, the Basel Committee on Banking Supervision, comprised of central bankers from the 13 biggest industrialized economies, published a framework for minimum bank capital requirements. Banks were required to set aside capital equal 8% of the amount of a loan if there was 100% risk associated with that loan and proportionately less for assets with a lower-percentage risk weighting. Corporate loans required 100% risk weighting while mortgages required 50% risk weighting and credit exposure to other banks required only 20% risk weighting. In 2004, the Basel Committee published *The International Convergence of Capital Measurement and Capital Standards: A Revised Framework,* known as Basel II. Under the new framework, project finance loans potentially have a higher risk weighting than corporate loans do, but there is a provision for banks to use their own risk estimation systems. As a result, the largest, most sophisticated banks may be able to use their precise risk calculations to avoid more onerous capital requirements on project finance loans. Basel II also distinguishes between typical project financing transactions, such as traditional oil and gas projects, and concession-based projects, where repayment depends on a creditworthy, contractually obligated end user such as a government entity. The latter are considered a secured exposure to the end user and therefore carry lower capital requirements. Basel II is discussed further in Appendix A of this book.

The Basel II Framework and Securitization

Banks and financial institutions are subject to a range of regulations and controls. Among the primary ones are concerned with capital adequacy, the level of capital a bank must hold to cover the risk of its many activities on and off the balance sheet. A capital requirements scheme proposed by a committee of central banks acting under the auspices of the Bank for International Settlements (BIS) in 1988 has been adopted universally by banks around the world. These are known as the BIS regulatory requirements or the Basel capital ratios, from the town in Switzerland where the BIS is based.[1] Under the Basel requirements all cash and off-balance-sheet instruments in a bank's portfolio are assigned a risk weighting, based on their perceived credit risk, that determines the minimum level of capital that must be set against them.

A bank's capital is, in its simplest form, the difference between assets and liabilities on its balance sheet, and is the property of the bank's owners. It may be used to meet any operating losses incurred by the bank, and if such losses exceeded the amount of available capital then the bank would have difficulty in repaying liabilities, which may lead to bankruptcy. However, for regulatory purposes, capital is defined differently. In its simplest form, regulatory capital is comprised of those elements on a bank's balance sheet that are eligible for inclusion in the calculation of capital ratios. "Regulatory capital" includes equity, preference shares, and long-term subordinated debt, as well as the general

---

[1] Bank for International Settlements, Basel Committee on Banking Regulations and Supervisory Practice, *International Convergence of Capital Measurement and Capital Standards*, July 1988.

reserves. The ratio required by a regulator will be that level deemed sufficient to protect the bank's depositors. The common element of these items is that they are all *loss-absorbing*, whether this is on an ongoing basis or in the event of liquidation. This is crucial to regulators, who are concerned that depositors and senior creditors will be repaid in full in the event of bankruptcy.

The Basel rules that came into effect in 1992 are popularly referred to as *Basel I*. Additional guidelines were published in final form in June 2004 with implementation set for 2006 to 2007 in Europe and 2008 to 2112 in the United States. These new guidelines are popularly referred to as Basel II. In this appendix, we present some highlights of the Basel II framework and offer some suggestions concerning its impact on securitization as well as credit derivatives.

BASEL RULES

A bank's total qualifying capital has two components: core capital, known as *Tier 1*, and supplementary capital, known as *Tier 2*. Tier 1 consists of the sum of three core capital elements minus goodwill. Those three elements are: (1) common stockholders' equity; (2) qualifying non-cumulative perpetual preferred stock; and (3) minority interests in the equity accounts of consolidated subsidiaries. The Tier 1 component must represent at least 50% of total qualifying capital. Tier 2 consists of four supplementary capital elements: (1) allowances for loan and lease losses; (2) perpetual preferred stock; (3) hybrid capital instruments and mandatory convertible debt securities; and (4) term subordinated debt and intermediate-term preferred stock, including related surplus.

The Basel I rules set a minimum capital-to-assets ratio of 8% of the value of *risk-weighted* assets. Assets are categorized and value-adjusted based on their risk and the resulting risk-weighted assets are multiplied by 8%. For the purpose of this calculation, each asset on a bank's balance sheet is assigned a risk weighting and the risk-weighting percentages are grouped into four categories: Category 1, with a 0% risk weighting, includes a bank's own cash and claims on U.S government agencies and the central governments of OECD countries. Category 2, with a 20% risk weighting, includes cash items in the process of collection, short-term claims (including demand deposits) on U.S. and foreign banks, and long-term claims on U.S. and OECD banks. Category 3, with a 50% risk weighting, includes residential mortgages and mortgage-backed securities. Category 4, with a 100% risk weighting, includes commercial loans and other assets not included in the first three categories. So, for example, a loan in the interbank market would be assigned a 20% risk weighting, a loan of exactly the same size to a corporation would receive the highest weighting of 100%.

There are also risk weights for off-balance-sheet items. The face amounts of certain specified off-balance-sheet items are assigned conversion factors and the resulting credit-equivalent amounts are assigned to the appropriate risk category according to the obligor, such as a commercial bank or corporation. Guarantees and other direct credit substitutes have a 100% conversion factor. Transaction-related contingencies such as bid bonds, performance bonds, and standby letters of credit related to particular transactions have a 50% conversion factor. Short-term, trade-related contingencies such as commercial letters of credit have a 20% conversion factor. Finally, unused portions of commitments, such as lines of credit that are cancelable and have original maturities of one year or less, have a 0% conversion factor.

For interest rate and foreign exchange contracts such as swaps, credit-equivalent amounts are calculated and multiplied by credit conversion factors. The credit-equivalent amount for an off-balance-sheet interest-rate or exchange-rate instrument is the sum of its mark-to-market value and the potential future credit exposure over its remaining life. The potential future credit exposure is estimated by multiplying the instrument's notional principal amount by the appropriate credit conversion factor, as defined in the table below:

Remaining Maturity	Interest-Rate Contracts	Exchange-Rate Contracts
One year or less	0	1.0%
Over one year	0.5%	5.0%

The resulting total credit-equivalent amount for the interest-rate or exchange-rate contract—the mark-to-market value plus potential future credit exposure—is assigned a risk weight according to the counterparty, such as a commercial bank or a corporation.

The perceived shortcomings Basel I attracted much comment from academics and practitioners alike, almost as soon as they were adopted. The main criticism was that the requirements made no allowance for the credit risk ratings of different corporate borrowers, and was too rigid in its application of the risk weightings. Recognizing how valid these concerns were, the BIS published proposals to update the capital requirements rules in 1999. The new guidelines are designed "to promote safety and soundness in the financial system, to provide a more comprehensive approach for addressing risks, and to enhance competitive equality."

Basel I was based on very broad counterparty credit requirements, and despite an amendment introduced in 1996 (covering trading book requirements), remained open to the criticism of inflexibility. The proposed new Basel II rules have three pillars, and are designed to be more closely related to the risk levels of particular credit exposures. These are:

Pillar 1: New capital requirements for credit risk and operational risk.
Pillar 2: The requirement for supervisors to take action if a bank's risk profile is high compared to the level of capital held.
Pillar 3: The requirement for greater disclosure from banks than before to enhance market discipline.

With respect to Pillar 1, the capital requirements are calculated using one of two approaches—the *standardized approach* and the *internal ratings based* (IRB) *approach*. In the standardized approach, also known as the basic indicator approach, banks will risk-weight assets in accordance with a set matrix, which splits assets according to their formal credit ratings. Within the IRB approach there is a *foundation approach* and an *advanced measurement approach*, the latter of which gives banks more scope to set elements of the capital charges themselves. In the IRB approach banks categorize assets in accordance with their own internal risk assessment. For a bank to undertake this approach, its internal systems must be recognized by its relevant supervisory body, and its systems and procedures must have been in place for at least three years. The bank must have a system that enables it to assess the default probability of borrowers.

In the United States, only the top dozen or so large international banks are required to adopt Basel II and a few more are expected to adopt the standards voluntarily. They will use the advanced measurement approach to calculate their minimum capital requirements. Other U.S. banks will continue to follow Basel I. In Europe, all financial institutions, regardless of size and complexity, must adopt Basel II, but they are free to choose which approach they take. European banks taking the standardized, basic-indicator approach or the foundation approach must comply by the end of 2006 and those taking the advanced measurement approach must comply by the end of 2007. The U.S Federal Reserve Board of Governors, the Federal Deposit Insurance Corporation, the Office of the Comptroller of the Currency, and the Office of Thrift Supervision approved new capital and risk management standards for U.S. banks under the Basel II framework in March 2006, setting a 4-year transition period starting in 2008 and also setting specific limits on any reduction in banks' risk-adjusted capital that may result from following the new guidelines. Even when Basel II is fully implemented, U.S. banks will be subject to regulators' minimum leverage ratio requirements and prompt corrective action rules. The bank regulatory agencies will prevent capital at large banks adopting Basel II from dropping more than 5% per year for three consecutive years. Also, if the aggregate level capital for all Basel II banks in the United States drops more than 10%, the regulators have said that they will reexamine the entire process.

It is generally believed that banks adopting Basel II will have a competitive advantage over banks continuing to follow Basel I because the advanced measurement approach will allow them to justify thinner capital charges than those allowed by formulas prescribed in the standardized approach. U.S. regulators plan to limit the competitive disadvantages for banks that do not follow Basel II in a new set of guidelines known as Basel IA.

Compared to the Basel I rules, general market opinion holds that the Basel II rules are an improved benchmark for assessing capital adequacy relative to bank risk. For the IRB framework, a significant change was the decision to base the capital charges for all asset classes on *unexpected loss* (UL) only, and not on both UL and *expected loss* (EL). In other words, banks must hold sufficient reserves to cover EL, or otherwise face a capital penalty. This move to an UL-only, risk-weight arrangement should result in the alignment of regulatory capital more closely with banks' actual economic capital requirement levels. A UL-only framework should result in banks regarding their capital base in a different light but should leave overall capital levels the same. The EL portion of risk-weighted assets is part of total eligible capital provision; and any shortage in eligible provisions will be deducted in a proportion of 50% from Tier 1 capital and 50% from Tier 2 capital. So the definition of Tier 1 and Tier 2 capital has changed under Basel II; the final framework withdraws the inclusion of general loan loss reserves in Tier 2 capital and excludes expected credit losses from required capital.

Note that the desire of the BIS to leave the general level of capital in the system at current levels means that a "scaling factor" can be applied to adjust the level of capital. This scaling factor has not been determined but will be assessed based on data collected by the BIS during the parallel running period. It will then be applied to risk-weighted assets to adjust for appropriate levels of credit risk.

The building blocks of the IRB approach are the following four measures of individual asset credit risk levels:

- *Probability of default* (PD): Measure of probability that the obligor defaults over a specified time horizon.

■ *Loss-given-default* (LGD): The amount that a bank expects to incur in the event of default (a cash amount measure per asset, showing value-at-risk (VaR) in the event of default).

■ *Exposure-at-default* (EAD). Bank guarantees, credit lines, and liquidity lines and is the forecast amount of how much a borrower will draw upon in the event of default.

■ *Remaining maturity of an asset* (M): Assuming that an asset with a longer remaining term to maturity will have a higher probability of experiencing default or other such credit event compared to an asset of shorter maturity.

Under the advanced IRB approach, a bank is allowed to calculate its own capital requirement using its own internal measures of PD, LGD, EAD, and M. These are calculated by the bank's internal model using historical data on each asset, plus asset-specific data.[2]

Basel II allows adjustments to capital requirements for credit risk mitigation mechanisms such as netting, guarantees, credit derivatives, and collateral. However, in order to recognize these credit risk mitigants for risk-based capital requirements, the institution must have operational procedures and risk management processes to ensure that all documentation used in collateralizing or guaranteeing a transaction is legal and enforceable under applicable law in relevant jurisdictions, and the institution must have conducted sufficient legal review to reach a well founded conclusion that the documentation meets this standard.

A separate regime will require banks following Basel II to set aside capital to cover operational risk, the risk of loss from inadequate or failed internal processes, people, and systems or from external events—including legal risk but excluding strategic or reputational risk. A bank operating under the advanced measurement approach for operational risk can use a standardized approach or an IRB approach. A bank using the IRB approach must have an operational risk data and assessment system that incorporates internal operational loss event data, external operational loss event data, results of scenario analyses, and assessments of the bank's business environment and internal controls.

---

[2] The calculation method itself is described in Basel II. However, a bank will supply its own internal data on the assets. This includes the confidence level: The IRB formula is calculated based on a 99.9% confidence level and a 1-year time horizon. This means there is a 99.9% probability that the minimum amount of regulatory capital held by a bank will cover its economic losses over the next 12 months. Put simply, that means that statistically there is only a 1 in 1,000 chance that a bank's losses would completely erode its capital base, assuming that this was kept at the regulatory minimum level.

A financial institution's total qualifying capital under Basel II will be essentially the sum of Tier 1 and Tier 2 capital elements as in Basel I with a few exceptions. The allowance for loan and lease losses will be removed as a Tier 2 capital element and replaced with a methodology for adjusting risk-based capital requirements based on a comparison of the institution's eligible credit reserves with its expected credit losses. An institution's total risk-weighted assets will be the sum of its assets risk weighted for credit risk and operational risk minus the sum of its excess eligible credit reserves (eligible credit reserves in excess of its total expected credit losses) not included in Tier 2 capital.

IMPACT ON SECURITIZATION AND CREDIT DERIVATIVES

We now offer some suggestions on the possible impact of Basel II on securitization and credit derivatives.

Exhibit A.1 shows the new risk categories for capital allocation under the new accord's IRB approach. Basel II recognizes that different types of assets behave differently, and is much more flexible than Basel I in this respect. Basel II provides specific capital calculation formulae for the following three asset types in a banking book: corporations, commercial real estate and retail. Different asset classes will be subject to different capital requirements under Basel II: Exhibit A.2 shows the BIS's own estimate of the change in requirements for Basel II compared to Basel I.

EXHIBIT A.1   Basel II Counterparty Risk Weights

Asset Type	AAA to AA–	A+ to A–	BBB+ to BBB–	BB+ to BB–	B+ to B-	Below B– (including defaulted)	Unrated
Sovereigns	0	20	50	100	100	150	100
Banks, option 1[a]	20	50	100	100	100	150	100
Banks, option 2[b] > three months	20	50	50	100	100	150	50
Banks, option 2 < three months	20	20	20	50	50	150	20
Corporations	20	50	100	100	150	150	100

[a] Risk weighting based on the sovereign in which the bank is incorporated.
[b] Risk weighting based on the rating of the individual bank.

EXHIBIT A.2   Basel II Capital Requirements for Different Asset Classes: Percent Change versus Basel I

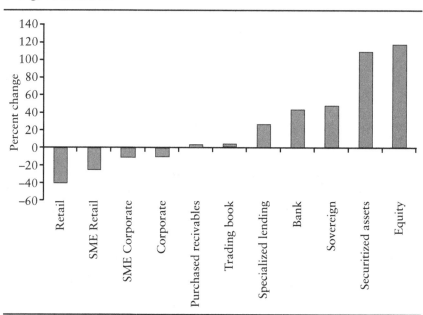

Source: Bank for International Settlements.

Under Basel I, banks had a great incentive to enter into credit derivative contracts because of the impact on their balance sheets and the reduced cost of capital that resulted. Under Basel II, some of this incentive may be reduced; for instance, banks would not necessarily need to buy credit protection on high-credit-quality corporate loans. For example, in Exhibit A.1, the risk weight of a loan to a corporation rated at AA would be 20%. Buying credit protection on this loan from an AA-rated bank would not reduce this charge, while buying protection from an A-rated bank would actually increase the charge, to 50%.

The same impact may be observed in the structured product market, as the incentive to securitize certain assets is also reduced. When first aired, the Basel II proposals were expected to have a significant impact on the securitization market but this is not so evident on final publication. There is now a common hierarchical approach to the calculation methodology that is applied under the IRB approach to determine risk-weighting for a securitization transaction. This applies irrespective of whether a bank is the originator or an investor in the transaction. Essentially, however, there is a uniform treatment of securitization transactions. For use with the ratings-based approach, there is a set of appropriate risk-weights to use to calculate the weightings in a securitization deal.

Unlike the proposed framework for wholesale and retail exposures, the securitization framework proposed in Basel II does not permit a bank to rely on its internal assessments of risk related to securitization exposures. The proposed securitization framework in the U.S. Federal Reserve Board's April 2006 *Notice of Proposed Rulemaking* (NPR) relies on two sources of information, to the extent available, to determine risk-based capital requirements: (1) a credit rating from a Nationally Recognized Statistical Rating Organization, i.e., a major credit rating agency such as Fitch, Moody's, or Standard & Poor's; or (2) risk-based capital requirements for the underlying exposures as if the exposures had not been securitized. The NPR suggests three general approaches for determining the risk-based capital requirements for securitization exposures: a *ratings-based approach*, an *internal assessment approach*, and a *supervisory-formula approach*. An institution is expected to apply a specified hierarchy of these approaches to determine the risk-based capital requirements for its securitization exposures.

An important objective of Basel II, with its closer alignment of regulatory capital to risk, is to address some of the capital arbitrage strategies that developed under Basel I. Because Basel I applies a flat 8% capital charge on all corporate assets, irrespective of the underlying credit quality of the borrower, the regulatory capital requirements on high-quality corporate assets were generally believed to be higher than the level of capital required to cover the economic risk of those assets. Therefore, Basel I gave banks an incentive to remove high-quality assets from their books by securitizing them. But originating banks often held on to the riskiest first-loss positions to help support their deals. So, even though they reduced their Basel I capital requirements, they did not necessarily reduce their economic risk exposure. By aligning regulatory capital on unsecuritized assets more closely to underlying economic risk than Basel I, Basel II reduces the incentives for banks to securitize loans to high-quality borrowers. Basel II also stems regulatory arbitrage by applying relatively stringent regulatory capital charges on junior securitization tranches, so banks will face higher costs if they retain those positions as credit enhancement for structured transactions. For example, for a bank using the standardized approach, unrated securitization positions must be deducted from capital—in other words the bank must set aside capital equal to that unrated securitization position.

For IRB banks that originate securitizations, a key element of the framework is the calculation of the amount of capital that the bank would have been required to hold on the underlying pool had it not securitized the exposures. This amount of capital is known as K_{IRB}. If an IRB bank retains a position in a securitization that obliges it to absorb losses up to or less than K_{IRB} before any other holders bear losses (i.e., a first-loss position), then the bank must deduct this position from capital. The Basel Committee on Banking Supervision believes this requirement is warranted in order to provide strong incentives for originating banks to shed the risk associated with highly subordinated securitization positions that inherently contain the greatest risks. For IRB banks that invest in highly rated securitization exposures, a treatment based on the presence of an external rating, the granularity of the underlying pool (the number and diversity of the underlying exposures), and the thickness of the exposure (the dollar amount of the tranche) has been developed.

We surmise that there may be regulatory capital advantages to securitizing lower-rated assets to a greater extent than has been seen hitherto. This is because under the new ratings-based approach (see Exhibit A.1), under certain circumstances very low-rated assets, for instance below BB, attract a very high risk weighting. It remains to be seen what structured products arise to meet this potential requirement.

Synthetic Securitization: Case of Mortgage-Backed Securities

The securitization technique described in Chapters 4 and 5 has been applied widely in capital markets worldwide since its introduction in the U.S. residential mortgage market in the 1970s. In those two chapters, we discussed cash flow securitizations. In Chapter 7, we discussed synthetic collateralized debt obligations (CDOs). Here we look at synthetic mortgage-backed securitization, both commercial and residential. We will see that the transaction is based on exactly the same principles as CDOs and that deals are originated for roughly similar reasons as balance sheet static synthetic CDOs.[1]

TRANSACTION DESCRIPTION

As has been observed in the synthetic CDO market, the European and U.S. commercial mortgage-backed securities (CMBS) and residential mortgage-backed securities (RMBS) markets have witnessed a range of different synthetic deal structures. The first deal was issued in 1998. As with synthetic CDOs, synthetic mortgage-backed securities (MBS) deal structures involve the removal of the credit risk associated a pool of mortgages by means of credit derivatives, rather than by recourse to a true sale

---

[1] A quantitative model for issuers in evaluating cash and synthetic securitizations is provide in Ian Barbour and Katie Hostalier, "A Framework for Evaluating a Cash ('True Sale') versus Synthetic Securitisation," Chapter 6 in Frank J. Fabozzi and Moorad Choudhry (eds.), *The Handbook of European Structured Financial Products* (Hoboken, NJ: John Wiley & Sons, 2004).

to a special purpose vehicle (SPV). The originator, typically a mortgage bank, is the credit protection buyer and retains ownership, as well as the economic benefit, of the assets. The credit risk is transferred to the investors, who are the protection sellers.

The main market for synthetic MBS to date has been Germany, although deals have also been seen from U.K., Swedish, Italian, and Dutch originators.

DEAL STRUCTURES

As with synthetic CDOs, there exist funded and unfunded synthetic MBS deals, as well as partially funded deals. The type of structure adopted by the originator will depend on the legal jurisdiction, the regulatory environment, capital requirements, and also the preferences of investors.

Unfunded Synthetic MBS

An unfunded synthetic MBS deal uses CDS to transfer the credit risk of a pool of mortgages from the originator to a swap counterparty. There is no note issuance and frequently no SPV involved. The investor receives the CDS premium during the life of the transaction. In return for which, he agrees to pay out on any losses incurred by the originator on the pool of assets. The CDS references the pool of mortgages, which remain on the originator's balance sheet.

The CDS protection seller will pay out on occurrence of a credit event. The precise definition and range of credit events differs by transaction and jurisdiction, but generally there are fewer credit events associated with a synthetic MBS compared to a synthetic CDO deal. This reflects the nature of the reference assets. Credit events are defined in the deal documentation and their occurrence will trigger a payment from the protection seller. The common credit events described in a synthetic MBS are "Failure to Pay" and "Bankruptcy."

As with vanilla CDS, in an unfunded synthetic MBS the investor is exposed to a counterparty risk if the originator is unable to continue paying its premium. To overcome this, some shorter-maturity deals are arranged with a one-off premium aid at the start of the deal, which covers the credit protection for the life of the deal. Conversely, the risk for the protection buyer is if the protection seller becomes bankrupt, in which case the former will no longer receive any credit protection.

As there is no SPV involved, unfunded deals can be brought to market relatively quickly, and this is a key advantage over funded deals. Because the credit default swap (CDS) counterparty needs to be equivalent rated to an OECD bank, the investor base is narrower than for funded deals.

Funded Synthetic MBS

In a funded synthetic MBS structure, an SPV is set up that issues a tranched series of credit-linked notes (CLNs), which are discussed in Chapter 9. These CLNs are referenced to the credit performance and risk exposure of a portfolio of reference assets, which may be residential mortgages, real-estate loans, or commercial mortgages. The proceeds of the CLNs are either:

- invested in eligible collateral, such as a guaranteed investment contract (GIC) account[2] or AAA rated government securities; or
- passed to the originator or a third party.

If the note issue proceeds are invested in collateral, this is known as a *collateralized funded synthetic MBS*, otherwise the deal is uncollateralized.

Although fully funded synthetic MBS deals have been observed in the market, it is more common to see partially funded transactions, in which a portion of the reference pool credit risk is transferred via a CDS. This achieves credit risk transfer from the SPV to investors without any funding issues.

Exhibit B.1 shows a typical funded synthetic MBS structure. Exhibit B.2 shows a simplified structure for a synthetic CMBS where the originator is transferring credit risk on assets spread across more than one legal jurisdiction.

The structure is usually brought to market first by the originator entering into a credit protection agreement with the SPV, which requires it to pay the protection premium (or interest on par value) to the SPV, and second by the SPV ("issuer") transferring this risk exposure to investors by means of the note issue. These investors ultimately pay out upon occurrence of a triggering event. The credit risk of the CLNs is in effect linked to the aggregated credit performance for the relevant tranche of risk of the reference pool. It is also linked to the risk profile of the collateral assets, but this should not be significant because only very high-quality investments are eligible for the collateral pool.

If the CLN(s) is (are) to be collateralized, the cash raised from the issue is used to purchase eligible securities or placed in a reserve cash account. The note collateral is used to back the coupon payments on the CLNs. It is also a reserve fund that can be used to cover losses in the reference asset

---

[2] We refer here to the European market definition of a GIC, which is a bank account with a fixed spread to LIBOR.

EXHIBIT B.1   Synthetic MBS Generic Structure

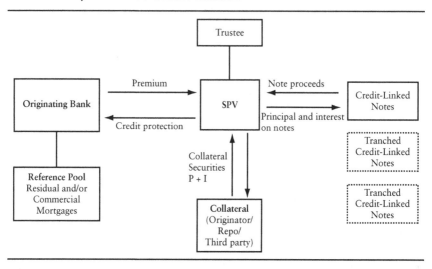

EXHIBIT B.2   Pan-European Synthetic CMBS Generic Structure

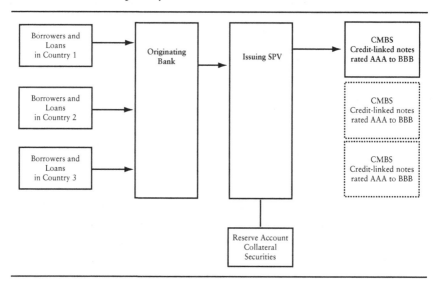

pool and to pay expenses associated with the vehicle. If the losses suffered by the reference assets are greater than any reserve account, or the nominal value of the junior note, the note collateral is available to cover the originator for the loss. This is the loss borne by the investors who purchased the CLNs. This arrangement, because it is funded, eliminates the counterparty risk (for the protection buyer) associated with unfunded structures. This reason is that investors have covered the credit risk exposure with an up-front payment. If the CLNs are not to be collateralized, the note proceeds are passed to the originator directly or to a third-party agent. The originator or third party is of course obliged to repay principal on the CLNs upon maturity, but only if no triggering events have occurred.

Upon occurrence of losses in the reference pool, the allocation of those losses follows established synthetic deal procedures. Each loss is applied only to the most junior CLN (or CDS in an unfunded or partially funded deal) outstanding. More senior noteholders should not see their cashflows affected until the note below them is fully absorbed by continuing losses.

Partially Funded Synthetic MBS
In a partially funded deal, the issue of CLNs is combined with a CDS that transfers part of the credit risk but on an unfunded basis. Frequently this will be a basket or portfolio CDS that is ranked above the CLNs, so it becomes a super-senior CDS.

INVESTOR CONSIDERATIONS[3]

Traditional cash MBS and synthetic MBS deals have several features in common, and both aim to achieve several common objectives. The main objective is the transfer of the credit risk associated with a pool of mortgage assets away from the originating bank, usually via an SPV. Key to the attraction of a synthetic deal is the fact that it can be customized to investors' requirements more closely. In a synthetic deal, the credit risk exposure that is transferred is (in theory) defined precisely, compared to a cash deal where any and all risks associated with the assets are transferred. Thus a synthetic deal can be structured and documented to transfer precisely the risk exposures that the investors are looking for.

Below we highlight three areas of difference between the two products:

---

[3] For a comprehensive discussion of synthetic MBS transactions, see Ian Barbour, Katie Hostalier, and Jennifer Thym, "True Sale versus Synthetics for MBS Transactions: The Investor Perspective," Chapter 5 in *The Handbook of European Structured Financial Products*.

■ originator issues,
■ cash flow liquidity risk; and
■ loss severity.

Originator Issues

As a synthetic MBS does not involve a true sale of assets, investors' fortunes are still connected with those of the originator. Therefore, if the originator becomes insolvent, the deal can be expected to terminate. Should this happen, an estimated loss is calculated, which is then applied starting with the most junior note in the structure.[4] The collateral assets are then realized and the proceeds used to pay off the outstanding CLNs.

In a traditional cash MBS, there may be occasion when a shortfall in cash in the vehicle may lead to disruption of cash receipts by investors. Typically, cash MBS deals are structured with a *liquidity provider* or *liquidity facility* to cover such temporary shortfalls, which may be the arranging bank for the deal. With such an arrangement, the credit rating of the deal will be linked to some extent to that of the liquidity provider. With a synthetic MBS, this does not apply. Losses in the reference pool are applied to the note structure in priority order not when a credit event has been verified, but when the loss has been realized. In these circumstances, investors should continue to receive cash flows during the time interval up to the loss realization. Consequently, a liquidity provider is not required.

Cash Flow Liquidity Risk

In a customized structure aimed at transferring credit risk, the probability of default is an important factor but not the sole factor. The severity of loss is also significant, and the impact of this will differ according to whether it is a cash or synthetic deal. Under a cash structure, if an event occurs that results in potential loss to investors, any outstanding principal, together with accrued interest and recovery costs, will need to be recovered from the securities. So the performance of a cash deal is dependent on the recovery time and costs incurred during the process (such as legal costs of administration).

Loss Severity

With a synthetic deal, the originator may customize the type and level of risk protection for which it pays. So it may, if it wishes, purchase protection for one or a combination of the following: (1) principal outstanding, (2) interest costs (capped or uncapped), and/or (recovery costs).

---

[4] Under this approach, an expected loss is calculated on nonperforming loans, although the actual credit event may or may not have occurred.

Home Run! A Case Study of Financing the New Stadium for the St. Louis Cardinals

CYNTHIA A. BAKER AND J. PAUL FORRESTER

CYNTHIA A. BAKER
is a partner at Chapman and
Cutler LLP in Chicago, IL.
cbaker@chapman.com

J. PAUL FORRESTER
is a partner at Mayer, Brown,
Rowe & Maw LLP in
Chicago, IL.
jforrester@mayerbrownrowe.com

On the morning of December 23, 2003, the City of St. Louis, Missouri awoke to a banner on the highway ramp closest to Busch Stadium in downtown St. Louis trumpeting "This Ramp is Coming Down," a line of bulldozers on the lot next to Busch Stadium, and a *St. Louis Post-Dispatch* front-page headline reading "Cards Are Set To Announce Stadium Financing Deal Today." When the St. Louis Cardinals (Cardinals) closed on the financing and broke ground for their new stadium adjacent to the current Busch Stadium, it was the culmination of many years of considerable effort by the Cardinals. Earlier plans for a publicly funded stadium encountered the same public opposition found in other cities. With a stagnant economy, and state and city budgets stretched thin, new sports facilities are not a budget priority. Only two other Major League Baseball teams have privately financed ballparks. Against this background, the Cardinals retained Banc of America Securities' Sports Finance Advisory Team in the Spring of 2003 to act as advisor and placement agent. Banc of America Securities and the Cardinals developed an innovative hybrid securitization/project finance/leveraged lease structure to turn the Cardinals' strong fan base into an investment-grade credit that would support the 20-year financing for the new $330 million stadium. Notably, the structured financing that closed on December 23—including $200.5 million of private placement bond debt, a $45 million subordinated

loan from St. Louis County, $30 million generated from the sale of various tax credits, a tax abatement by the City of St. Louis, and an equity investment by the Cardinals' ownership—was not the leveraged lease financing described in the *Post-Dispatch* on the morning of the closing. Unbeknownst to the *Post-Dispatch*, and notwithstanding months of intense efforts in pursuit thereof, the leveraged lease financing had been abandoned a week earlier because it could not be closed within the time available.

The structured transaction that did close, illustrated in Exhibit 1, was the largest private placement of debt for a Major League Baseball (MLB) stadium, the first MLB stadium transaction using a bankruptcy-remote structure, the first set of cash flows from a baseball stadium to be rated investment grade by both Moody's and Standard and Poor's and insured to "AAA" by Ambac Assurance, and only the third privately financed MLB home stadium. How is it that the Cardinals, who are not located in a major media market, were able to bring home such a major-league financing? What is the structure of the financing that closed and how is it different from the leveraged lease structure? Why was the hybrid leveraged lease structure abandoned, and what were the obstacles to closing such a transaction? This article examines these issues. The article will not examine why public financing ultimately was not available for the stadium or that the stadium is only a part of an impressive redevel-

303

E X H I B I T   1
Final Structure—Cardinals Transaction

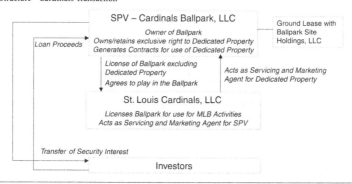

opment plan (known as "Ballpark Village") for a portion of downtown St. Louis in the shadow of St. Louis' symbolic Gateway Arch. While interesting for their own reasons, these subjects are beyond the scope of this article.

In the current market, major league sports arenas and stadiums often are funded by monetizing "contractually obligated income" or "COI." Stadium naming rights, luxury suites, sponsorships (i.e., signage within the stadium), pouring rights, concessions, and other multi-year contracts that result in future revenue streams are examples of COI. Premium seats, sometimes known as "club seats," also may be COI if sold pursuant to multi-year subscriptions. These revenues may be substantial. For example, naming rights for Minute Maid Park, home of the Houston Astros, is at the high end, generating an average of $6.07 million per year for 28 years. Naming rights for Safeco Field, home of the Seattle Mariners, still generates on average $2 million per year for 20 years, even though it falls at the low end of the range for ballparks that have sold naming rights.[1] Luxury suite prices for MLB teams vary widely, with the Toronto Blue Jays charging prices ranging from $37,000 to $120,000 per season and the New York Yankees charging $300,000 per season. Suite prices in the Cardinals current home, Busch Stadium, are reported to range from $79,000 to $205,000.[2] Teams typically offer luxury-suite contracts with 3-, 5-, 7-, or 10-year terms and often include incentives for renewal. In the National Football League, the trend in recent years to build new stadiums with luxury suites is

driven in part by league revenue-sharing rules that require teams to share "ticket" revenues but not luxury-suite revenues. Major League Baseball's revenue-sharing rules do not provide such incentives. Instead, managers of baseball stadiums are driven solely by the premiums that can be charged for luxury suites (and club seats) with additional amenities. Generating contractually obligated income that will be eligible for monetization requires a strong fan base and strong corporate and community support for a sports team or franchise.

The St. Louis Cardinals have such a strong fan base and strong corporate and community support in spades. The Cardinals, the first team west of the Mississippi, began play in 1875, first as the St. Louis Brown Stockings, then as the Browns, then as the Perfectos, and finally, in 1900, as the Cardinals. Their overall record, second only to the New York Yankees, includes 8,514 wins with 20 first-place division finishes, 15 National League Championships, and 9 World Series Championships. The team has produced 48 hall-of-fame players and coaches including Enos Slaughter, Rogers Hornsby, Red Schoendienst, "Dizzy" Dean, Stan "The Man" Musial, Bob Gibson, Lou Brock, and Ozzie Smith. Twice in the past five years, most recently in 2003, the Cardinals were designated as MLB's fan-friendliest teams by the United Sports Fans of America. The Cardinals rank second among all MLB teams in tickets sold over the past 20 seasons with average annual ticket sales in excess of 2.8 million. The Cardinals have projected sales of 19,300 season tickets for

Exhibit 2
Traditional Securitization

Sponsor/Originator

Generates and Sells Receivables

| Sale and Contribution of Receivables | Purchase Proceeds |

SPV

Purchases Receivables and Funds through Secured Loan or Sale of Undivided Interest in Receivables

| Transfer of Undivided Interest / Security Interest in Receivables | Loan/Purchase Proceeds |

Investors / Commercial Paper Conduit

the 2004 season. This compares to 28,000 projected by the San Francisco Giants, 18,000 by the Baltimore Orioles, 17,000 by the Boston Red Sox, 14,000 by the Chicago Cubs, 11,000 by the Chicago White Sox, and 8,000 by the San Diego Padres. Cardinals games have been broadcast by KMOX, a megawatt AM station that can be heard nearly coast to coast, since the 1950s. It was Harry Caray's broadcasts of Cardinals' games on KMOX to which Luke Chandler—the young protagonist in John Grisham's bestseller *A Painted House*—would tune in every Saturday evening when growing up in rural Arkansas in the 1950s. Although St. Louis ranks only18th among metropolitan areas in United States, it ranks 7th in the nation for corporate headquarters. The Cardinals' seat deposit program for season tickets in the new ballpark has been over-subscribed and letters of intent for 10-year, luxury-suite contracts were signed in the summer of 2003 for all 52 suites then offered. The Cardinals' well-established, sustained relationship with the local community has resulted in strong corporate sponsorship for the team.

The Cardinals' strong fan base turned into an investment-grade credit through creative application of structured finance techniques—this despite the fact that the organization itself is unrated. In a typical securitization, illustrated in Exhibit 2, an operating company originates receivables by signing and performing contracts. That originator then sells fully performed receivables to a special purpose vehicle (SPV) formed solely for the purpose of purchasing the receivables. An SPV generally has no

employees and its constitutive documents prohibit it from incurring any debt or conducting any activities other than those necessary for the related securitization. In addition, its constitutive documents and the transaction documents require it to maintain at least one independent director, unrelated to the originator or any of its affiliates, whose affirmative vote is required for the SPV to seek or consent to relief as a debtor under the United States Bankruptcy Code. The SPV finances its purchase either by issuing securities (typically, debt securities), by selling an undivided interest in the receivables to a commercial paper conduit, or in some instances through a borrowing arrangement with a commercial paper conduit. Such a sale of receivables, combined with certain corporate separateness and organizational limitations placed on the SPV, works to isolate the receivables from the bankruptcy and credit risks of the originator and can allow the receivables to be self-financing at a higher credit rating than that of the originator. In the case of a ballpark, however, a classic sale-securitization structure may not isolate the COI from the bankruptcy risk of the originator because of the executory nature of most, if not all, of the related COI. Failure of the originator to perform on those contracts most likely will excuse the related obligors from having to pay, such that the contracts are subject to rejection in the bankruptcy of an originator. Accordingly, different techniques must be used to isolate the COI receivables from the credit risk of the team.

In the structure developed with Banc of America Securities, the Cardinals formed a special purpose vehicle, Cardinals Ballpark, LLC ("Ballpark LLC"), with the typical organizational limitations and independent directors. However, Ballpark LLC itself will originate the contracts giving rise to the COI pledged to support the ballpark financing. In the final transaction, Ballpark LLC, as lessee, entered into a long-term ground lease with Ballpark Site Holdings, LLC ("Site Holdings") for the site and will own all improvements when complete. As the owner of all improvements and rights to use of the site, Ballpark LLC also holds all rights that give rise to contractually obligated income associated with the site, including naming rights, luxury suites, and rights to post signs and advertisements, conduct concession activities, and all other activities on the site and its improvements. Under a license agreement with Ballpark LLC, the Cardinals have the right (and are required to) conduct Major League Baseball games and related activities in the stadium and on the site. The license agreement gives the Cardinals only a subset of the rights giving rise to COI. Ballpark LLC retains for itself

E X H I B I T 3
Lease Structure—Cardinals Transaction

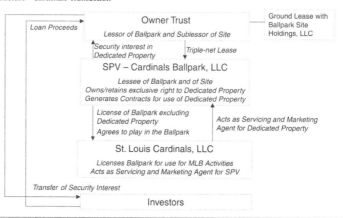

naming rights, rights to conduct concession activities, rights to license luxury suites and certain club seats, and certain sponsorship (signage) rights (collectively, the "dedicated property"). The dedicated property is marketed and serviced by the Cardinals under a contractual arrangement, much like a publicly owned stadium might contract with a service company. The dedicated property effectively is isolated from the credit risk of the Cardinals, because it never was owned by the Cardinals.

Contractually obligated income from the dedicated property is pledged to the bondholders and was sufficient to earn the bonds an underlying investment-grade rating by both Standard and Poor's (BBB–) and Moody's (Baa3). The bonds also are supported by a leasehold mortgage on the site, and a security interest (and backup mortgage) on the stadium and other site improvements. Revenues from the dedicated property are directed to a lockbox and applied through a priority-of-payments waterfall, much like a typical securitization. Ballpark LLC is further capitalized by a $45 million subordinated loan from St. Louis County and a substantial equity investment by the Cardinals' owners. The bonds were wrapped to an "AAA" rating by Ambac Assurance Corporation. The proposed leveraged lease transaction, shown in Exhibit 3, would have adopted most of this basic structure, with the debt

issued by the owner trust and the debt portion of rent achieving the same ratings, except that the dedicated property would have been pledged by Ballpark LLC to support its rent obligations under the lease.

Participants in the structured finance markets may find the abandoned leveraged lease structure of some interest. The introduction of securitization techniques to big-ticket leasing is the point where securitization, project finance, and lease finance converge.

A leveraged lease financing structure may offer a number of benefits to the sponsor/lessee. A lease introduces another source of capital to a structure—equity capital provided by the owner participant ("OP"). The tranche of capital provided by the OP is subordinate to debt and, since the OP is the owner of the leased property, it is entitled to the tax depreciation and other related tax benefits. These tax benefits subsidize the lease rate offered to the lessee to the point where the cash-on-cash return required by the OP is commonly less than the senior debt rate. The tax benefit subsidization reduces the all-in, pre-tax lease-financing rate to less than comparable debt financing rates. The lease structure can provide a higher percentage of the aggregate capital needs of the project than can debt alone—in some cases 100% or more of the cost of the leased asset. Another important consideration for sports facilities is that the required rate of return for the institutional OP may be less than the entrepreneurially driven return requirements of a sports franchise owner. A lease can allow a franchise owner to deploy its equity capital into more lucrative or shorter-term investment opportunities.

The hybrid leveraged lease structure appeared to offer many advantages to the Cardinals over the structured debt transaction described above. Ownership of a sports stadium offers certain tax benefits. A major league sports team typically is held by a limited liability company, limited partnership, or other tax-pass-through entity, with the owners being some combination of individuals, family trusts, and corporations. Because of the usually diverse tax status, including rules limiting the efficacy of "passive tax losses," team owners are often inefficient (or at least uncertain) users of tax benefits. The question of whether a hybrid leveraged lease provides the best after-tax financing rate only can be answered if it is known whether the franchise owner can make efficient use of the tax benefits associated with ownership of the related facilities. Given the favorable attributes of the leveraged lease structure and its ability to accommodate the structured finance techniques described above, a hybrid structure seemed to be the logical choice.

Generally, debt and equity investors in a traditional leveraged lease are looking to the corporate credit quality of the lessee/sponsor for repayment. An owner trust buys or builds the asset to be leased and funds that price through an investment by the OP (approximately 20% of the value of the asset under tax rules) and by borrowing money through bank loans or the issuance of bonds or other debt securities. The asset is leased to the sponsor with rent payments due under the lease being exactly the amount necessary to pay debt service and a fixed rate of return to the OP. The rent due is determined through a "black box" calculation that, after taking into account the depreciation deductions, optimizes the amount and timing of rent, debt service, equity cash flows, and all of the related tax attributes for the OP on one hand, while minimizing the present value of payments due by the lessee on the other.

The Cardinals' lease transaction would have largely followed this traditional structure, with a few important variations. An owner trust, as lessee, would have entered into a long-term ground lease with Site Holdings for the site and contracted for the construction of improvements. At closing, the owner trust would have entered into a triple net lease with Ballpark LLC covering both the site and the improvements. As the lessee with the right to use all improvements and the site, Ballpark LLC also would

have held all rights that give rise to contractually obligated income associated with the facility, including the dedicated property. As in the debt structure described above, Ballpark LLC would have licensed the stadium and site to the Cardinals for the purpose of conducting Major League Baseball games and related activities and retained for itself the sole ownership of the dedicated property and related revenue streams. Lockbox arrangements and a pledge of the COI and dedicated property would have supported Ballpark LLC's obligation to pay rent to the owner trust. The senior debt and subordinated county debt issued by the owner trust would have been secured by a leasehold mortgage and security interest on the site and improvements and a further assignment of the secured rents. This structure would have required debt and equity to look to the credit of Ballpark LLC and the dedicated property, and not the Cardinals, for repayment.

Why abandon a transaction that offered 100% financing, a subsidy of cash payments by the equity investor's use of tax benefits, and a lower-cost source of equity capital? The answer: time—or lack thereof. The construction schedule (driven by a completion date tied to the opening of the baseball season in 2006), necessary work on an interstate interchange (the ramp serving the new stadium), the subordinated loan from St. Louis County, the sale of tax credits to fund site remediation, and state funding of infrastructure improvements in surrounding areas all required that the private financing close before the end of 2003. The timing explanation, however, is incomplete. A question remains as to why a hybrid transaction would take more time and be more difficult to complete than the structured debt transaction.

With the clarity of 20/20 hindsight, several explanations appear. Within financial institutions and within law firms, those involved in structured finance transactions tend to specialize, whether in securitization, project finance, or lease finance. Each specialty has its own paradigm, and specialists approach a new structure in light of that often unspoken paradigm leading to frequent misunderstandings and miscommunication. For example, in securitization the investor's credit decision is based on an analysis of the credit quality of the asset and the effectiveness of the structure to isolate the asset. In project finance, investors look to the strength of the contracts that support the asset being financed and the credit quality of the contracting parties. If there are gaps in the contracts that support the project financing, the investor has to evaluate "gap risk," including in some cases an evaluation of the operational risks of the related asset. In contrast, generally speaking, OPs look primarily to the corporate credit of the lessee/sponsor. In a hybrid structure, which by its very nature requires a change in this fundamental paradigm, a difficulty lies in harmonizing the approach across these different disciplines.

Differences in the paradigms may heighten traditional points of controversy. Particularly in transactions where buyout rights give the lessee the ability to capture upside appreciation in the asset, OP equity looks more like subordinated debt than traditional equity. Accordingly, standard senior-subordinated points of controversy—control, consents, and foreclosure rights—play out as debt-equity issues in leveraged leases. But, differences in paradigm can make *all* the difference. Tranches of debt and equity in securitizations are very common, with senior classes taking all of the cash flow from, and controlling decisions with respect to, the assets following a default or early amortization event. Because all parties are looking to asset performance, and discretion to manage the assets is circumscribed by contract, they may be relatively less concerned about which party holds control over the assets. In contrast, an investor relying on a corporate credit alone typically will require greater and greater control over a borrower/lessee's actions the further down that credit falls on the ratings ladder, particularly after default. "Standard" foreclosure rights differ substantially between the securitization and leveraged lease markets. These differences, and others, may exaggerate the ordinary senior/subordinated tensions. A securitized-debt investor may reject as "off-market" an OP's insistence on restricted or delayed foreclosure rights. So too, a leveraged-lease investor may reject as off-market the debtholders' insistence on all control and consent rights following default. Both are right within their respective paradigms, but a hybrid requires a shift in the "market." To add to the confusion, the jargon of each field uses similar terms that mean different things, and these differences can be material. Without a means of bridging the differences in perspective and communication, a lease equity investor's credit committee may never get comfortable with a below-investment-grade sponsor regardless of the credit quality of the assets supporting the transaction. Similarly, without a bridge, a securitization investor looking solely to asset value, along with its usual expansive rights to take control of the liquid assets supporting the financing, may never be comfortable with sharing operational control with subordinated lease equity investors.

The different approaches each financing discipline brings to a hybrid structure can be addressed in a number of ways. An institution considering such a transaction might staff its deal team from across specialty areas. For example, a securitization/project finance/lease hybrid that cannot be sold to a "pure lease" investor might be more attractive to project finance-type investors. Alternatively, financial guaranty companies already bridge knowledge and risk assessment gaps in the market. In a hybrid securitization/project finance/lease structure, a financial guaranty provider might be asked to wrap the entire rent due under the lease, and not just the related debt. Obtaining a rating of the equity cash rent might be another solution.

The Cardinals achieved a rare result: competitive, attractive financing for a cutting-edge, but retro-look, ballpark with modest financial support from state and local governments and manageable equity support by the franchise owners. The transaction advanced the state of the art for privately financed sports and entertainment venues. Fans of the St. Louis Cardinals and of Major League Baseball will be the ultimate winners. Finally, the lessons learned from the Cardinals stadium transaction will benefit the financing and construction of other stadiums with ever-more-efficient blends of capital sources to better balance and serve the goals of team owners, players, municipalities, and the fans, while meeting the requirements of financial investors.

Editor's Note

Ms. Baker was formerly a partner with Mayer, Brown, Rowe & Maw LLP. The authors represented Banc of America Securities' Sports Finance Advisory Team, as structuring agent, and the private placement debt investors in the financing described. All information with respect to the specifics of the transaction or the Cardinals has been publicly reported in various sources. The analysis of the issues and the conclusions drawn herein are those of the authors, and not the views of Mayer, Brown, Rowe & Maw LLP or any of its clients. Our special thanks to Jim Nash and Tucker Sampson of Banc of America Securities, David McIlhenny and Gareld Gray of Banc of America Leasing, and O. Kirby Colson III of Armstrong Teasdale LLP, counsel to the St. Louis Cardinals, for their helpful insights and comments. Any errors are those of the authors alone.

ENDNOTES

[1]Street & Smith's Sports Business Journal, By the Numbers 2004, p. 10.

[2]Street & Smith's Sports Business Journal, By the Numbers 2004, pp. 106 and 107.

To order reprints of this article, please contact Dewey Palmier at dpalmieri@iijournals.com or 212-224-3675.

Municipal Future-Flow Bonds in Mexico: *Lessons for Emerging Economies*

JAMES LEIGLAND

JAMES LEIGLAND
is a senior municipal
finance advisor at the
Municipal Infrastructure
Investment Unit in
Midrand, South Africa.
jamesl@miiu.org.za

I n late August 2003, a small group of South African municipal officials and their advisors visited Mexico for a week to learn about recent developments in the Mexican municipal bond market. The trip, financed by the South African government, reflects a growing interest among developed as well as developing countries in a surprisingly sudden blossoming of the municipal bond market in Mexico. Beginning with no previous experience in municipal bond issuance, the Mexican market registered 10 municipal or state bond issues in less than two years, beginning in December 2001, with many more issues in preparation by the end of that period. The country now boasts a higher percentage of state and local governments with credit ratings from agencies like Fitch, Standard & Poor's, and Moody's than any other country except the United States. International donors and development finance institutions now regularly cite Mexico as an emerging economy that clearly is leading the way in terms of innovative municipal finance.

The Mexico case has generated considerable interest in a country like South Africa, which had a municipal bond market of sorts for decades before it became dormant in the early 1990s. Since the end of the apartheid government in 1994, the country has begun to focus on the massive numbers of formerly disenfranchised South Africans who still do not have access to basic municipal services. Borrowing directly from the capital markets

appears to be an essential element of any successful nationwide effort to close the municipal infrastructure investment gap. However, neither issuers nor investors in South Africa have demonstrated much enthusiasm for municipal bonds.

This article reviews developments in the Mexican municipal bond market, and explains how legal and regulatory reforms in the country adapted innovative private-sector financing techniques, like future-flow securitization, to pave the way for a small, but active municipal bond market. The question of whether or not such an approach can or should be used in other developing countries is explored, with special reference to South Africa. This article concludes by suggesting that in many countries, the specific techniques used in Mexico may not be cost-effective, but the basic principles underlying the financial mechanics clearly have application.

MEXICO IN THE LATE 1990s

The 1994–95 financial crisis in Mexico led the federal government to take stock of its public financial health. Among many other things, government officials began to look for better ways of financing investments by state and local governments. The existing method involved loans by development and commercial banks backed by intercepts of intergovernmental tax-sharing grants, known as "tax participations." Loan agreements typically

309

allowed creditors, in case of default, to request the federal government to deduct debt-service payments from the borrower's monthly tax participation payments. The deduction amounted to an intercept of payments, executed by federal authorities, before the funds were transferred to the state or local borrower.

The intercept arrangement created an implicit federal guarantee of state and local borrowing, and a massive contingent liability for the federal government, at least in the eyes of lenders. This in turn meant that lenders paid little attention to the purpose of the borrowing or the credit standing of the borrower—all such loans were considered to be backed by the federal government's creditworthiness. The moral hazard associated with this kind of lending was significant.

The federal government began a series of reforms in the late 1990s designed to increase the financial autonomy and accountability of state and local entities by making clear that new debt no longer could be viewed as a risk of the federal government. Beginning in March 2000, no state or municipal debt would be backed with the tax-sharing intercept mechanism. Tax-sharing grants would continue to be made to states and municipalities, but borrowers and lenders would have to create new arrangements to secure repayment with no further direct federal involvement in the intercepts or any implication of federal guarantees. Requirements for bank capitalization also were changed, motivating banks to pay attention to the credit standing of their local government borrowers by seeking two ratings from nationally recognized credit rating agencies before making loans.

The reforms caused concern among lenders and borrowers alike because of other government reforms underway that were increasing the need for state and municipal borrowing. By the late 1990s, the government's fiscal decentralization program was in full stride. Between 1994 and 2001, the state and municipal government share of all public expenditure grew from 47% to 64%, reflecting the decision by federal officials to require those government entities to do more of the work in financing and managing government programs (Protego [2003]).

At the same time, a substantially new class of lender was emerging in the market—one with a rapidly growing need for long-term, high-quality, fixed-income debt denominated in local currency. In the late 1990s, the federal government privatized the management of its mandatory pension funds for private-sector employees. The new fund managers, known as *afores*, quickly transformed the funds into fast-growing pools of cash in need of good-

quality investments. From 1998 to 2001 the assets managed by the *afores* increased by almost 600%, with the total expected to reach 20% of GDP by 2015 (Protego [2003]). In allowing these funds to invest in municipal bonds of at least single-A quality (as determined by two rating agencies), the government created instant demand for state and municipal securities of strong credit quality.

However, after the end of active federal involvement in the interception of tax-participation grants to states and municipalities, the challenge was to find some other way of enhancing the credit quality of debt issued by those entities. U.S.-style general obligation borrowing, backed by the full faith and credit of local governments, was not attractive to investors because the short terms of local elected officials (three years with no possibility of re-election) gave rise to worries that promises to pay debt service might be amended or retracted for political reasons. Revenue bonds, backed by the revenues from projects to be built with bond proceeds, were even less attractive because the years of reliance on tax-participation grants to back borrowing had allowed state and local officials to ignore the need for improvements in local revenue generation and collection. State and municipal services often were not managed efficiently and the revenues from those services usually were not dependable sources of debt repayment.

The tax-participation grants remained a large and predictable source of revenue, accounting for over 90% of state revenues and over 70% of municipal revenues (Fitch [2002]). The challenge was to find a way of convincing investors that state and local officials would be willing to use those revenues to repay debt in future situations where money was tight and new decision makers were tempted to withhold payments for projects approved by their predecessors.

FUTURE-FLOW SECURITIZATION

An idea for a solution came from the future-flow securitizations that allowed public and private companies in below-investment-grade countries to access affordable international finance. In traditional asset-backed securitizations, lenders repackage existing pools of home mortgages or car loans for resale as tradable securities. Credit card securitization is one of several variations of the asset-backed technique, in which both existing and future receivables are sold to a trust that in turn issues securities to investors. The receivables are associated with particular identified accounts, but also include future receivables that are generated through those accounts. In a sense, these are future flows, although generated by accounts specified at the initial closing, and typically the securities held by investors are backed by an equal amount of receivables. For these reasons, credit card securitizations are usually considered to be asset backed.

True future-flow transactions are usually transactions in which a borrower (referred to as the "originator") raises funding on the basis of expected future sales. Because these are expected rather than existing sales (or existing, identified accounts), the outstanding principal amount of the securities is not always exactly equivalent to the outstanding principal amount of the underlying receivables. This quality makes them "future-flow" rather than "asset-backed" securitizations (Rough [2000]).

The first major future-flow securitization in a developing country was structured in Mexico by Citibank in 1987. It involved the securitization of telephone service receivables owed to Mexico's monopoly phone company, Telmex. The receivables arose when Telmex completed more calls for AT&T customers calling into Mexico than AT&T completed for Telmex customers calling into the U.S. The net international settlement receivables paid by AT&T to Telmex were relatively easy to estimate based on market history.

Telmex isolated debt-service payments to bond holders from any possibility of misdirection by company or government officials by selling the receivables to a U.S.-based trust, and instructing AT&T to pay its Telmex invoices to the trust, thus generating secure revenues for the holders of the securities (trust certificates) sold by the trust to investors. As the securities amortized, the residual liquidated receivables flowed back to Telmex. The future-flow mechanism represented a way for Telmex to issue investment-grade bonds at a time when Mexico was restructuring its sovereign debt, and Mexican companies, particularly state-owned enterprises, were unable to access international capital markets.

The Telmex deal was copied many times by many different kinds of companies. The number of such deals increased sharply after Mexico's 1994-95 crisis, with Latin American countries dominating the market. A key reason the future-flow mechanism became so popular so quickly in countries at or below investment grade was that the deals proved to be exceptionally resilient, even in situations of severe national economic distress. For example, in 1999 Pakistan defaulted on its sovereign debt, but an offshore trust continued to pay debt service on US$250 million in Pakistan Telecommunications Company bonds backed by future telephone-settlement receivables. According to Ketkar and Ratha [2001], by the end of 2001, the principal rating agencies reported having rated more than 230 future-flow deals worth more than $44 billion.

APPLICABILITY TO MEXICO

Although such deals vary greatly depending on types of collateral, legal and regulatory frameworks, and operational characteristics of the originators (borrowers), they share many common features, most of which were attractive to Mexican officials interested in finding a mechanism to help states and municipalities access the domestic capital market:

- Future-flow securitizations typically are driven by the need for capital market access by a company located in a developing country where a low sovereign rating (at the bottom of or below investment grade) capped the maximum rating that the company could earn. Mexican municipalities had a similar problem in the sense that their own low ratings tended to cap the ratings of their individual investment projects.

- In future-flow deals, the borrowing company normally has significant, dependable foreign-currency export receivables owed to it by creditworthy customers in other countries, who are able to pay in hard currency, usually U.S. dollars. Mexican municipalities had a significant, dependable source of domestic currency in the form of grant-participation grants. Federal reforms had made grant flows highly predictable via transparent formulas formalized in national legislation.

- In future-flow deals, the company establishes some form of special purpose vehicle (SPV), often a trust, in a tax-neutral jurisdiction outside the company's home country, where the court system is trusted by investors. The shift in jurisdiction helps ensure that the trust arrangements cannot be restructured easily. SPVs were not a new concept in Mexico. Federal officials were willing to authorize states and localities to create trusts that could handle debt service outside of the normal local government budget process. States and municipalities also were allowed to enter into debt covenants that would make any premature unwinding of trust arrangements particularly difficult.

- In future-flow deals, the company sells its existing and future export receivables to the trust in return for an upfront purchase price. In Mexico, federal officials did not want state and local authorities to actually securitize their debt in this sense because they wanted local entities to remain fully responsible for their obligations, but they were willing to allow local officials to pledge their tax-participation revenues to "administrative" trusts in exchange for loans.

- In future-flow deals, customers are given irrevocable instructions to pay their invoices to a collection account in which the trustee has a security interest for the benefit of the owners of the trust certificates. In Mexico, federal officials were willing to accept irrevocable instructions from local officials and legislatures to make tax-participation payments to administrative trusts rather than directly to the relevant state or municipality.

- In future-flow deals, the trust finances the purchase of future receivables by issuing securities subject to a series of stringent covenants with bondholders. In June 2001, Mexican federal government officials allowed states and municipalities to begin issuing securities similar to the bonds or commercial paper involved in most future-flow deals. Exchange certificates (*certificados bursatiles*) were introduced as direct, negotiable municipal debt instruments that, unlike the simple promissory notes traditionally used in Mexico for state and local borrowing, could include covenants, specify events of default, identify different maturity dates and amortization schemes, etc.

- Future-flow deals are particularly subject to "collateral performance risk," the risk that in almost any portfolio of future receivables some customers will become delinquent or even default on payments (Roever and Fabozzi [2003]). Accordingly, the trust is often over-collateralized with several times more receivables pledged than are actually required to back the securities, in order to provide investors with a layer of protection against non-payment by customers, variations in the value of the exports, or other unexpected changes in anticipated revenues. In Mexico, because secure federal grants constitute such a high percentage of state and municipal revenues, over-collateralization was a feasible way to reassure investors against unanticipated reductions in intergovernmental grant flows.

ARGENTINA: AN EARLY TEST OF THE METHODOLOGY

A handful of municipal future-flow deals in Argentina during the late 1990s provided some key lessons for Mexican officials. Several Argentine provinces issued bonds backed by future streams of federal tax-sharing revenues. For example, in August 1997 Tucumán Province issued $200 million in seven-year bonds over-collateralized by a pledge of 35% of its total tax-sharing revenues. The revenues were transferred on a daily basis by the Argentine federal government to a local bank acting as a collection agent. The funds then were exchanged into U.S. dollars and transferred to a New York-based trust that made debt service payments.

Technically, this was not a future-flow securitization, because the flows were not securitized and sold to a trust. The province continued to "own" the revenue streams and remained fully responsible for the debt obligation. But Argentine officials successfully simulated key aspects of the securitization technique. For example, the fact that the debt was over-collateralized by tax-sharing revenues was recognized as a credit strength by the rating agencies.

Other features of the deal made rating agencies somewhat cautious, however. They were particularly concerned that government officials had not done enough to isolate the revenues from potential government interference. The province explicitly maintained the right to dissolve the trust arrangement if the province itself first declared an economic emergency. The deal also included a cross-default provision that required acceleration of bond repayments in the event that other, unsecured provincial debt defaulted. In the view of the rating agencies, all of this tied the revenue flows too closely to national and provincial government performance and processes. As a result, the rating of the deal failed to pierce the sovereign rating ceiling. Fitch-IBCA assigned the issue a grade of "BB−," a notch below the sovereign rating at that time.

The rating agency concerns were confirmed later during the Argentine financial crisis. After the national government defaulted on its sovereign debt, the tax-sharing bonds were downgraded to default status as well, because of the national government's intention to divert revenues from the provinces, devalue the currency, and restructure existing government debt. By declaring a financial emergency, the province was able to unwind the deal and regain control over whatever revenues still were flowing from the national government.

EXHIBIT 1
Municipal Future Flow Bonds: Flow of Funds

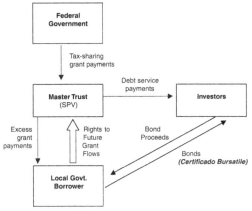

IMPLEMENTATION IN MEXICO

The Argentine experience with the tax-sharing future flows was instructive for Mexico. Mexican officials realized two things about the future-flow mechanism as a way to facilitate municipal bonds issuance: 1) the mechanism as used in Argentina could be perfected by using covenants to strengthen the isolation of revenue flows from potential government interference; and 2) when perfected, the mechanism offered a way of simulating the federal intercept arrangements that had made borrowing possible for Mexican states and municipalities prior to 2000. Instead of the federal government actively intercepting grant flows on behalf of lenders or investors, administrative trusts run by professional financial managers could receive grant revenues and make debt-service payments before local officials ever received the money. Accordingly, federal officials proposed that states and municipalities create administrative trusts into which tax-sharing revenues could be deposited directly by federal authorities, and out of which debt-service payments could be made directly to bond holders (*see Exhibit 1*).

The government entity could issue exchange certificates (*certificados bursatiles*), and use the trust to make debt-service payments, or the trust itself could sell "ordinary participation certificates" (*certificados de participación*

ordinarios) and pay them off with tax-sharing revenues assigned to it by the state or local government. In this way, trusts could isolate debt-service payments from any general government expenditure accounts. As legal, tax-neutral entities under Mexican law, trusts could be created relatively easily by local officials, and professional financial managers hired to manage debt-service payments. So-called "master" trusts could allow management of several debt obligations at the same time, with funds going into designated sub-accounts.

Like the Argentine arrangements, Mexican deals stopped short of true securitization, although that term is sometimes used to characterize the deals (Standard & Poor's [2001]). The trust mechanism involved is a debt repayment vehicle only—an administrative trust rather than a guarantee trust. The debts managed by the trust remain direct obligations of the state or municipal borrower, whose revenues are used by the trust to make debt service payments. Those revenues are not packaged and sold to investors, as they would be in a future-flow securitization.

The use of such trusts quickly caught on, beginning in late 2000, with a number of Mexican states and municipalities using master trusts as payment mechanisms for infrastructure domestic currency bonds sold with relatively high ratings, low coupons, and terms ranging from five to seven years. Exhibit 2 shows bond issues involving trusts over the past two years.

CREDIT ENHANCEMENT FEATURES

Perhaps the most important feature of the Mexican version of the municipal future-flow mechanism is its ability to assure rating agencies that they can give a higher rating to a municipal project than they would to the parent state or municipal government. Exhibit 3 compares Fitch's credit ratings on the five future-flow financings they had rated as of April 2003, with Fitch's general obligation ratings for the parent state or municipal entity benefiting from the trust financings. The rating differentials are dramatic, averaging an improvement of nearly five rating grades per deal.

The future-flow mechanism achieves these kinds of rating improvements because various features of the mech-

Eₓ H I B I T 2
Mexican State and Municipal Bond Issues

Issue Date	Government Entity	Millions of Pesos
December 1, 2001	Aguascalientes	90
December 1, 2001	State of Morelos	216
July 1, 2002	San Pedro Garza Garcia	110
August 1, 2002	Monterrey	168
September 1, 2002	Zapopan	147
November 1, 2002	Guadalajara	800
December 1, 2002	State of Mexico	2,000
May 1, 2003	State of Guerrero	1,500
June 1, 2003	Tlalnepantla	96
August 1, 2003	State of Nuevo Leon	978

Source: Protego [2003]

Eₓ H I B I T 3
Ratings on Future-Flow Financings vs. Government-Obligation Ratings

Government Entity	GO Rating	Rating on FF Financing
State of Morelos	A	AA+
San Pedro Garza Garcia, NL	AA	AAA
State of Mexico	BB+	AA
Guadalajara, Jal	AA-	AAA
State of Guerrero	A-	AA+

Source: Fitch IBCA, Duff & Phelps [2003]

anism function as a web of sometimes overlapping internal credit enhancements to mitigate precisely the kinds of key borrowing risks that concern Fitch and the other credit rating agencies. It is no surprise that rating agencies respond favorably to this kind of structuring. Because issuers often target a particular rating as a desired outcome of the structuring process, they often attempt to engage rating agencies before the deal is structured. As a result, instead of reacting with a rating to a deal as it has been structured, rating agencies often advise issuers on enhancements for future-flow deals *before* the bonds come to market. With some early Mexican municipal issues,

for example, rating agencies recommended less severe covenants in order to make events of default less likely.

The web of internal credit enhancements on municipal future-flow deals includes many of the key elements that make future-flow securitizations successful:

*   The *administrative trust structure* provides enhancement by isolating the debt-service payment process from normal municipal budgets and expenditure processes. The money used to pay debt service is from a strong, reliable source, but it is especially attractive to investors because it does not pass through the hands of municipal officials—it cannot be diverted or withheld for political reasons.
*   Additional credit enhancement results from *irrevocable instructions* to the federal government regarding deposit of tax-sharing grant revenues in the trust rather than with the municipality. In Mexico, these instructions often have been strengthened by being issued directly by state or local legislatures.
*   Trusts are further strengthened with *over-collateralization* of debt, in the sense that the tax-sharing grant revenues pledged to support the outstanding debt, and secured in the trust's reserve accounts, typically are worth several times more than the par value of the debt itself. This surplus provides comfort to investors that in cases of underperforming tax revenues, or changes in federal allocation policies, a trust will still be able to repay bondholders.

Mexican officials have added several additional mechanisms to the future-flow technology to help avoid the kinds of problems evident in Argentina. The new types of securities authorized for use by Mexican municipalities make possible for the first time a variety of covenants with bondholders, and in Mexico covenants also provide a form of internal enhancement by requiring certain remedial actions by the trust to be triggered by different kinds of "credit events." Remedial actions can include larger contributions to reserve accounts, the creation of additional reserve accounts to serve as a first line of defense against revenue problems, acceleration of debt repayment, or immediate repayment of all debt using all pledged revenues as they become available. Credit events can include rating downgrades, reductions in debt-service reserve accounts, or any other proxy for reduced revenue performance and increased bondholder risk.

Some covenants provide an extra measure of credit support with extreme penalties for breach. For example, any attempt by a municipality to re-take control of grant streams (e.g., via a court case to dissolve a trust) typically triggers full and immediate default. This kind of enhancement has been used in Mexico to assure investors that parent local governments will not attempt to unwind trust structures, as was done in Argentina during the national financial crisis.

VARIATIONS ON THE BASIC MODEL

One claim made for future-flow deals is that they help establish a credit history for borrowers, as well as market familiarity with municipal bonds (Chalk [2002]). All of this is expected to facilitate a gradual move to more traditional, less expensive borrowing techniques. In Mexico, there have been recent deals that make use of own-source municipal revenues rather than intergovernmental grants to back the borrowing. In this sense they are arguably more traditional, but the structuring involved is as aggressive—and expensive—as any deals seen in the market to date.

In Tlalnepantla de Baz, the most industrialized municipality in Mexico, a unique bond issue was sold in early 2003 backed by municipal revenues rather than federal tax-participation grants. To enhance the deal, a letter of credit for up to $5.3 million was issued in support of just over 50% of the borrowing by Dexia Credit Local, a development bank subsidiary of the Dexia Group, one of the largest financial groups in Europe. An additional 30% of the Tlalnepantla deal was backed by a municipal bond guarantee, worth up to $3 million, sold by the International Finance Corporation (IFC), the first such guarantee ever offered by the IFC.

In Mexico, credit providers to municipalities must be Mexican-based companies. Because Dexia is not a Mexican-based company it could not guarantee bonds directly sold by the municipality. Instead, the bonds were sold by the trust established by Tlalnepantla, and the proceeds on-lent to the municipality. The external enhance-

ments helped raise the local currency credit rating on the bonds from "AA" to "AAA," without a sovereign guarantee or the backing of intergovernmental grant flows.

The Tlalnepantla de Baz bond issue represents perhaps the most innovative variation to date on the future-flow model. The inability to use tax-participation revenues to back the bonds stimulated the search for external credit enhancement—often used in future-flow securitization. The deal also made use of a so-called double-barreled pledge of revenues, often used in municipal bond issues sold in the U.S. market. The Tlalnepantla issue was backed primarily by revenues from the municipally-owned water utility. Should those revenues prove to be insufficient, municipal tax revenues of the parent municipality will provide a "second barrel" of support. The two underlying projects are also very much like what one would find financed by a U.S.-style revenue bond issue. Some bond proceeds will be used for the construction and operation of a wastewater treatment plant that will recycle wastewater for industrial re-use. The rest of the proceeds will be used to reduce physical and commercial water losses. In other words, the bond proceeds will be used directly for activities that eventually should pay for themselves.

A second variation on the Mexican municipal future-flow model, used in most of the early bond issues, involves the use of payroll tax revenues to back the borrowing. The State of Mexico sold such an issue in 2002, worth more than all previous municipal issues at the time. Other than the source of revenue for repayment, most of the rest of the deal is similar to earlier future-flow transactions, including a master trust, over-collateralization, etc. A debt-service reserve established at the time of issuance holds an amount equal to 10% of the principal. Covenants require that a second 10% reserve account be established in response to a variety of "credit events," for example in the event that payroll tax revenues fall below minimum expected levels.

Like Tlalnepantla's water tariffs, payroll taxes are a local government revenue rather than intergovernmental grant income. However, as with intergovernmental grants, payroll taxes can be handled largely outside the local government expenditure process. Nationwide, approximately 85% of payroll tax revenues are collected by commercial banks, which can be given irrevocable instructions to turn those revenues over to administrative trusts established to handle debt-service payments for outstanding bond issues.

The state's congress issued a decree creating the trust and authorizing the issuance of irrevocable instructions to banks acting as tax collection agents. The decree formalized the trust mechanism in administrative law as well as in covenants with bondholders, thus adding to the legal strength of the arrangement. The various enhancements earned the deal a local currency rating of "AA," at a time when the state's government obligation rating was just "BB+." Mexico City (a federal district with the right to collect payroll taxes) has been working on a similar issue for several years.

COSTS AND RISKS

Mexican municipal future-flow bonds clearly constitute a powerful financing tool that has helped states and municipalities access badly needed capital at affordable interest rates. However, a variety of other kinds of significant costs and risks are associated with these mechanisms.

Transaction Costs

Although higher ratings reduce interest costs, the high fixed costs of these transactions can contribute to high overall borrowing costs. The deals are by definition highly structured and involve relatively long lead times and high transaction costs in the form of legal, banking, and management fees. The trust administration fees in Mexico also can be high. The International Monetary Fund (2003) estimates that the transaction costs on these kinds of deals are three to four times higher than on "plain vanilla" external bond issues. The complicated structure of these deals, and the practice of paying transaction costs from the proceeds of the bond issues, make the overall impacts of transaction costs much harder to evaluate than interest costs on the issue. In Mexico, the very heavy reliance of issuers on expensive advisors for due diligence, structuring, and underwriting has suggested to some local officials that whenever possible and practical, tasks be assigned separately so as to establish at least minimal checks and balances among advisors.

Enhancement Costs

Although attractive to investors, enhancements like over-collateralization are expensive ways to mitigate portfolio performance risks. The revenues pledged are much higher than normally are needed for debt service. This leaves less than usual to back future borrowing, potentially increasing the cost. The irrevocable nature of the pledge also makes any future debt restructuring difficult. Because of these high costs, it is clearly in the interests of

the issuer that over-collateralization and other internal and external enhancements be used cost-effectively in optimizing the marketability of a bond issue. One method of encouraging this, employed on some Mexican deals, is to hire a specialized advisory firm to structure the issue, but not to do the underwriting. In that way, the deal structure can be optimized to suit the needs of the issuer, rather than the needs of investors who make up an underwriter's primary distribution network. The specialized advisor can help select an underwriter with experience and underwriting networks suited to the particular issue structure chosen.

Moral Hazard

Perhaps of most concern are the potential moral hazards associated with both the borrowing and lending activities involved in future-flow deals. Moral hazard was of course one of the reasons for the Mexican government's determination to end the implied federal government guarantee of local government borrowing. However, the future-flow mechanism clearly allows for several kinds of moral hazard to persist in the Mexican municipal debt market:

Over-borrowing. The mechanism can enable borrowing in situations where high interest rates might otherwise not allow it. A result of this is the temptation to over-borrow, by avoiding financing limits normally imposed by government policy or market discipline, and delaying needed improvements in financial management and other aspects of corporate governance.

Over-lending. Investors and lenders have little incentive to enforce normal market limits, because they bear very little risk in these deals. The various enhancements ensure that risk-sharing with lenders or investors is virtually non-existent. Lenders and investors are motivated to make capital available because the enhancements make the underlying credit strength of the issuer almost irrelevant.

Lack of Stakeholder Scrutiny. A third kind of moral hazard associated with these deals relates to the two above, but also derives from the unique and almost total separation in these deals between 1) the use of debt proceeds and 2) sources of revenue for debt repayment. In practice, this separation means that the purpose of the borrowing does not come under as much scrutiny as in other forms of borrowing.

- Revenue bonds of course closely link these two elements. Because the debt will be paid back from revenues generated by the investments to be made with bond proceeds, bondholders have an interest in the purpose of the borrowing. Government officials and the general public have a relatively clear indicator of the need for the borrowing and the rationale of the underlying project: if debt service is payable from project revenues, the deal has at least demonstrated financial self-sufficiency.

- In typical general obligation borrowing the link still exists, particularly in the minds of taxpayers. Such bonds are normally backed by local tax revenues, and have a direct impact on local tax rates. Consequently, taxpayers have an immediate interest in ensuring that the borrowing is necessary and cost-effective. This kind of municipal borrowing is the most closely monitored by citizens in a country like the United States.

- Locally issued debt backed by taxes set and collected at the national level weakens this link, and results in borrowing that few stakeholders have a strong interest in scrutinizing. Taxpayers have little incentive to monitor how the loan proceeds are spent locally, because their local projects—whether or not needed, well designed, or efficiently managed—have little impact on national tax rates. Taxpayer complaints about bond proceeds misspent on local projects typically do not lead to changes in national tax rates; the money is just spent on something else. Bondholders also have little incentive to monitor implementation if the bonds are secured with an over-collateralization of reliable tax revenues. In other words, responsible future-flow borrowing depends heavily on the integrity of local government officials, because there are few stakeholders looking over their shoulders.

Market participants in Mexico cannot point to specific examples of these sorts of moral hazards actually giving rise to serious problems, but there clearly is some concern in the marketplace that the potential for such problems exists.

APPLICABILITY TO OTHER EMERGING ECONOMIES: THE CASE OF SOUTH AFRICA

How applicable is the municipal future-flow mechanism to local government borrowing in other countries? This was the question asked by the South African local government officials and advisors who visited Mexico in late August 2003.

Similarities Between the Two Countries

The key municipal finance problem in South Africa is similar to the one affecting municipalities in Mexico and in many other emerging economies—not enough capital investment in municipal infrastructure. As in Mexico after the 1994-95 financial crisis, South African officials realized by the end of the 1980s that a perceived sovereign guarantee of local government borrowing was creating large contingent liabilities for the national government and retarding the development of a normal market in local government debt. A municipal bond market of sorts had existed for decades, but most of the debt was sold under the apartheid government's "prescribed investment regime," which required institutional investors to hold 54% of their investment portfolios in a range of government securities, including municipal bonds.

The high, fixed percentage and an implied sovereign guarantee meant that virtually all municipal securities could be sold quickly via private placement to a relatively small number of institutional investors. The system fed capital to municipalities and helped to build and maintain Western-style urban infrastructure services for the white minority under apartheid, but encouraged little development of the market practices and investor skills associated with a viable municipal bond market. Investors were required to buy bonds, and bond proceeds were used to build infrastructure for white citizens who were mostly willing and able to pay for it (or other sources of revenue were found to repay bondholders). In other words, there was little incentive for lenders to do credit analysis, and agency credit ratings were unnecessary. There was virtually no trading of bonds; investors simply bought and held them to fulfill their portfolio requirements.

The prescribed regime ended in the early 1990s. Municipal bond sales stopped entirely (the last municipal bond issue listed on the Bond Exchange was sold by the City of Durban in 1993). Private bank lending to municipalities also began to decline after 1994, largely because municipalities were expanded to include disadvantaged areas and, as a result, became much less attractive to private sector lenders. Amalgamations dramatically increased the need for municipal infrastructure finance by formally bringing disadvantaged citizen inside municipal boundaries, but made municipal debt even less attractive to private banks because the added areas reduced average payment levels as well. In the eyes of many traditional commercial bankers, the creditworthiness of these municipalities declined sharply after 1994.

Like Mexico's parastatal development bank, Banobras, South Africa's Development Bank of Southern Africa (DBSA) was used by government to fill some of the infrastructure investment gap in the late 1990s. But like Banobras, DBSA could not supply all municipal investment needs, and its strong presence in the market was somewhat counterproductive because it tended to discourage private lenders from returning to the market and discouraged stronger municipalities from actively pursuing bond issues.

Key Differences

Unlike Mexico, South Africa could not identify innovative municipal financing techniques in the 1990s to replace the prescribed investment regime, and is unlikely to make use of the future-flow bond technology. The reasons for this reflect important differences between South Africa and Mexico, but also suggest that Mexico may not be as typical an emerging economy as its South African visitors hoped in August 2003.

Revenue. Without large, reliable revenue flows that can be intercepted before they enter the municipal bank accounts, there is little rationale for going through the expensive process of establishing privately managed trusts to isolate debt repayment from normal government decision-making. In Mexico, state and local governments have such flows because 88% of total state and municipal revenue comes from federal transfers. South African municipalities, on the other hand, receive just 17% of their revenue from intergovernmental grants (Republic of South Africa [2003]). The numbers mean that South African municipalities are more self-sufficient and have much stronger incentives to manage their affairs efficiently, but by the same token will not gain much by creating administrative trusts to enhance borrowing.

Legal Framework. Without a legal and regulatory framework that strongly and clearly sanctions the use of trusts and other internal credit enhancements in municipal borrowing, investors are likely to question the reliability of the future-flow mechanism. Partly because of the municipal future-flow bond experience in Argentina, Mexican authorities recognized early on that such arrangements must be firmly rooted in law to assure investors that trusts cannot be unwound or revenues diverted at some point in the future. In establishing such a legal and regulatory framework, national policy makers in Mexico also displayed a substantial measure of confidence in the integrity of local officials, because of the moral hazard potential described above. National government officials in South Africa, on

the other hand, are concerned about the misuse of trusts and similar mechanisms by municipalities, particularly in terms of reduced financial accountability and transparency. Consequently, the government's new Municipal Finance Management Act, passed by the National Assembly in September 2003, prohibits the use of trusts by municipalities for purposes related to borrowing, and requires that all intergovernmental grant revenues be transferred directly into a "primary" municipal bank account.

Credit Ratings. Without market respect for agency credit ratings, and without the presence of the international rating agencies to provide authoritative ratings, it is difficult to gauge the value of the structuring that goes into a future-flow deal, and to know how much structuring is enough. A country in which many municipalities have ratings also tends to have more competition among lenders, some of which may not be willing or able to invest in their own in-depth credit analysis. Mexican officials took advice from World Bank experts in the late 1990s and encouraged banks to solicit two ratings every time they made a municipal loan. That helped attract the major international rating agencies to Mexico and helped poise them to play an active role in future-flow structuring. In South Africa, national officials have taken an approach that is much more common in the developing world. Detailed government data on municipal performance has not been released to the public, and ratings have not been encouraged, apparently out of a concern about embarrassing under-performing municipalities. In any case, the reliance on ratings in investment decision-making has been slow to take off in the South African capital market; credit ratings still represent only a minor factor in such decisions. Several local rating agencies exist in South Africa (including one affiliate of an international agency), but only one international firm has opened an office in the country.

Role of the Development Bank. For any kind of competitive, private-sector financing of municipalities to thrive, subsidized government "development banks" must be prevented from crowding out private-sector lenders or investors from deals involving the upper tier of creditworthy municipal borrowers. As the impressive recent history of bond issuance activity in Mexico confirms, the country's powerful development bank, Banobras, generally has been either unwilling or unable to crowd out private-sector lenders and investors. Indeed, Banobras recently has entered into a preliminary agreement with the IFC to develop mechanisms for insuring municipal bonds, presumably in recognition of the value of an active municipal bond market. In South Africa, the government's Development Bank of Southern Africa (DBSA) is the most active lender to municipalities, but an overwhelming percentage of its funding (65%) goes to the six largest "metropolitan" municipalities such as Johannesburg, Durban, and Cape Town, effectively keeping those municipalities largely away from private commercial lenders, and completely out of the bond market (Republic of South Africa [2003]). Many market participants in South Africa, including many commercial banks, argue that DBSA strongly crowds the private sector out of municipal lending.

Market Size. Finally, of course, larger and more liquid markets attract more competition among purveyors of financial innovation and expertise. South Africa, with a population of 44 million, is not even half the size of Mexico (102 million). More important, Mexico has 31 states and 2,431 municipalities. Market participants expect that 150 of these local governments soon will have credit ratings and begin weighing various forms of borrowing, including future-flow bonds. The country's proximity to the United States ensures a steady and productive interaction among legal and financial experts on both sides of the border. In South Africa, the capital market is small, volatile, and isolated. The potential for municipal bond market activity is vastly smaller than in Mexico, with just 284 municipalities, including only one or two with the size or credit strength to access the capital market directly without extensive internal and/or external credit enhancement.

CONCLUSION: BACK TO BASICS

South African municipalities are unlikely to find significant value in Mexico-style municipal future-flow bonds. Indeed, such instruments do not appear to offer much help for the financing problems of municipalities in the many developing countries where the various special conditions that gave rise to the future-flow approach do not exist. However the Mexican model is useful in underscoring some basic principles of municipal bond market development.

The Role of National Government

The use of municipal future-flow bonds in Mexico is probably more a result of political will than the structuring innovations of legal and financial experts. The federal government made intergovernmental transfers a reliable and predictable source of local government revenue; introduced modern, flexible investment instruments; ensured that the legal/regulatory framework supported the use of trusts and the various other credit enhancements required by investors; strongly promoted the use of credit ratings; and condoned

a more progressive stance toward municipal bond issuance by its own development bank. It is possible to argue that the federal government took this action only after the financial crisis of 1994-95 highlighted the weaknesses of the existing system of municipal finance, including the implicit federal government guarantee of municipal borrowing, and the government's resulting contingent liability. However, similar circumstances have not prompted many other developing country governments to such creative action. As is the case so often in the developing world, political will to act can have a profound impact on development, but is extremely rare. This is certainly the case with development of municipal bond markets.

The Role of Local Government

In addition to political will, Mexico displays another quality that is often a key missing ingredient in efforts to kick-start municipal bond markets—a willingness to give local government officials the benefit of the doubt when it comes to municipal borrowing. Decentralization is an often-expressed goal in the developing world, but when it comes to finance, national government officials often are unwilling to let their local government counterparts operate without close supervision. Municipal bond borrowing is an area of finance notorious for wasteful spending and corruption, even in so-called developed economies. Municipal future-flow bonds appear to increase the temptation to misbehave. Nevertheless, Mexican officials are to some extent giving the benefit of the doubt to local officials in an effort to promote innovative financing of municipal infrastructure. Critics in countries such as South Africa accuse national government officials of micro-managing local government affairs in an effort to eliminate every opportunity for corrupt behavior, but at the same time forestalling meaningful decentralized public finance. Mexico has far to go in improving the management and self-sufficiency of its municipalities, but that process has begun in notable fashion with a decentralized approach to borrowing.

Municipal Bond Market Basics

The structuring techniques involved in Mexico's municipal future-flow deals are mostly mechanisms for achieving in a nascent municipal bond market the kinds of minimally acceptable deal characteristics that often are taken for granted in more developed markets. Finding short cuts or proxies to achieve these kinds of characteristics, sometimes at significant risk and cost, is a common strategy in efforts to develop municipal bond markets in emerging economies (Leigland [1997]). Municipal future-flow bonds may not be cost-effective in South Africa's capital market, but whether or not the specific structuring techniques are appropriate, the basics that underlie the future-flow approach are essential to successful municipal bond sales in any market:

Ability to Pay. Municipalities must have revenue streams that are large and reliable enough to repay investors, and must be able to demonstrate convincingly to prospective investors that those revenue streams are thoroughly predictable. If intergovernmental grant flows are formalized and predictable, as they are in Mexico, they are often particularly attractive to investors because they do not depend on the ability of the municipality in question to carry out effective revenue management. Obviously, the more of such revenue that can be pledged for exclusive use in repayment of debt, the more comfortable investors are. This is the benefit of over-collateralization techniques used in Mexico.

Willingness to Pay. Municipalities also are expected to demonstrate that they will be willing to repay debts, regardless of changes in politicians or administrative personnel. However, the most convincing way to deal with this issue is not through elaborate promises to pay, but by showing that revenues needed to repay bondholders will be used for that purpose regardless of the intentions of officials. Various kinds of intercept mechanisms have been used, particularly in developing countries, to ensure that kind of repayment. The administrative trusts used in Mexico maximize the impact of the intercept concept by allowing all debt-service payments to be made before the revenues even reach municipal bank accounts. To ensure that municipal officials cannot redirect the revenues to the municipality, irrevocable instructions are given to depositors.

Binding Promises. Investors must be convinced that the various commitments to repay them are legally binding on the municipal issuer. This is accomplished through a variety of contractual promises, with painful sanctions for breach. Some Mexican local governments also have backed these commitments with formal resolutions of the local legislatures, thus recognizing the promises in administrative law as well. And of course legal opinions by reputable law firms are required on all of these arrangements.

Extra Enhancement. From the perspective of investors, there is no such thing as too much credit enhancement. As long as the costs of enhancements, including municipal bond insurance, are outweighed by savings achieved for the municipal issuer (e.g., in the form of lowered interest rates), such enhancements make financial sense.

REFERENCES

Chalk, Nigel. "The Potential Role for Securitizing Public Sector Revenue Flows: An Application to the Philippines." IMF Working Paper No. 02/106. Washington, DC: International Monetary Fund, 2002.

Fitch IBCA, Duff & Phelps. "Financing of Mexican States, Municipalities, and Agencies: Alternatives and Strategies." *Fitch Ratings: Public Finance,* January 31, 2002.

———. "Special Report: Boom Times at the Rio Grande: U.S.-Mexico Border Region Expands." *Fitch Ratings: International Public Finance,* May 1, 2003.

International Monetary Fund. "Assessing Public Sector Borrowing Collateralized on Future-flow Receivables." Washington, DC: International Monetary Fund, June 11, 2003.

Ketkar, Suhas, and Dilip Ratha. "Development Financing During a Crisis: Securitization of Future Receivables." Policy Research Working Paper No. 2582. Washington, DC: World Bank, 2001.

Leigland, James. "Accelerating Municipal Bond Market Development in Emerging Economies: An Assessment of Strategies and Progress." *Public Budgeting and Finance,* Vol. 17, No. 2 (Summer 1997).

Protego. "Development of the Mexican Bond Market for Sub National Governments." Unpublished; Mexico City: Protego, August 2003.

Republic of South Africa. *Intergovernmental Fiscal Review.* Pretoria: RSA National Treasury, 2003.

Roever, W. Alexander, and Frank J. Fabozzi. "A Primer on Securitization." *The Journal of Structured and Project Finance,* Vol. 9, No. 2 (2003), pp. 5-19.

Rough, Clive. "Future-flow Securitisation in Asia." *The Asian Securitisation and Structured Finance Guide 2000.* London: White Page, January 2000.

Standard & Poor's. "Securitization of Federal Tax Participations by Mexican States and Municipalities." *Standard & Poor's RatingsDirect Research,* May 17, 2001.

To order reprints of this article, please contact Dewey Palmieri dpalmieri@iijournals.com or 212-224-3675.

STRUCTURED FINANCE	Pre-Sale Report

Crown Castle Towers LLC
Senior Secured Tower Revenue Notes, Series 2005-1

EXPECTED CLOSING DATE:
June 2005

AUTHOR:

Taimur Jamil
Analyst
(212) 553-4181
Taimur.Jamil@moodys.com

CONTACTS:

Jay Eisbruck
Managing Director
(212) 553-4377
Jay.Eisbruck@moodys.com

Kumar Kanthan
Managing Director
(212) 553-1428
Kumar.Kanthan@moodys.com

Linda Stesney
Managing Director
(212) 553-3691
Linda.Stesney@moodys.com

Brett Hemmerling
Investor Liaison
(212) 553-4796
Brett.Hemmerling
@moodys.com

WEBSITE:
www.moodys.com

This pre-sale report addresses the structure and characteristics of the proposed transaction based on information provided to Moody's as of May 17, 2005.

Investors should be aware that certain issues concerning this transaction have yet to be finalized. Upon conclusive review of all documents and legal information as well as any subsequent changes in information, Moody's will endeavor to assign definitive ratings to this transaction. The definitive ratings may differ from the preliminary ratings set forth in this report. Moody's will disseminate the assignment of definitive ratings through its client service desk.

PROVISIONAL (P) RATING		
Class	Rating	Amount ($)
A	(P)**Aaa**	$1,198,460,000
B	(P)**Aa2**	$233,845,000
C	(P)**A2**	$233,845,000
D	(P)**Baa2**	$233,850,000

OPINION

Crown Castle International Corp. (NYSE ticker CCI), intends to use the proceeds from the sale of the notes by Crown Castle Towers LLC (the Issuer Entity), Crown Castle PT Inc., Crown Communication Inc., Crown Communication New York, Inc., Crown Castle GT Company LLC, Crown Castle South LLC, Crown Castle International Corp. de Puerto Rico and Crown Atlantic Company LLC (the Asset Entities) to re-balance its capital structure. The Issuer Entity as well as the Asset Entities are all Delaware limited liability companies or Delaware Corporations, with the exception of Crown Castle International Corp. de Puerto Rico, and fully wholly owned subsidiaries of Crown Castle International Corporation.

Crown Castle International Corp. is a large wireless communications tower owner with a presence throughout the United States and Australia. The firm derives approximately 90% of its revenues by leasing site space on its 10,618 towers to wireless service providers and constitutes the cash flow stream for this securitization. The remaining revenue is derived from its services business, which provides network services relating to sites or wireless infrastructure for customers, including project management of antenna installation.

Crown Castle PT Inc., Crown Communication Inc., Crown Communication New York, Inc., Crown Castle GT Company LLC, Crown Castle South LLC, Crown Castle International Corp. de Puerto Rico and Crown Atlantic Company LLC own the 10,618 towers.

The Asset Entities were converted into special purpose entities and prohibited from having any employees, owning any other asset other than their own tower sites and from incurring any indebtedness other than the notes. The ownership of the towers was transferred via a True Contribution ("Sale") of equity in the Asset Entities holding them to the Issuer Entity. The bond holders will have a priority security interest in 100% of the equity interests of the Issuer Entity. The assets owned by the Issuer Entity through its 100% ownership of the Asset Entities include communication towers, real property and associated rights, managed and leased third-party sites, tenant leases, owned equipment on towers or at sites, FCC licenses and systems.

Moody's ratings on this transaction are derived from our projected net cash that the pool will generate from leasing the tower sites over the life of the transaction, the structural enhancement including the subordinate tranches, and the legal structure.

Strengths
- The cross-collateralization of the large pool with diverse sites and locations reduces the volatility of the cash flows.
- Miscellaneous reserves accounts will be established including a Cash Trap Reserve Sub-Account that will become active should the DCSR fall below 1.75x over a trailing 12 month period at the end of any calendar quarter. In addition, if the DSCR falls below 1.45x over a trailing 12 month period at the end of any calendar quarter the bonds will start to amortize.
- 96% of the revenue is being generated by telephony tenants. From a technology perspective this is a positive as other components such as paging will experience a decline in revenues over time.
- The subordination provided by the rated tranches supports the ratings on the transaction.

Concerns
- No principal amortization occurs during the term of the loan. After May 2010, the loan needs to be refi-nanced. Should that fail to occur all cash is trapped and used to pay interest due and outstanding principal sequentially. In the event of a default the Servicer can either sell the assets to retire the bonds or continue operating the portfolio and use all the excess cash to retire outstanding principal. Given the large size of the portfolio, it is conceivable that asset disposal on such a large scale may significantly depress the value of the towers, far below their value as of this transaction date.
- The Borrower has the right, subject to the payment of release premiums, to release collateral. The release premium required to release a tower from this transaction is stipulated at 125% of the allocated loan amount and provided the DSCR post-release is greater than or equal to the DSCR immediately prior to such release. Similarly, property can be substituted but limited to 5% of the allocated loan amount per year. There are cer-tain controls affecting how the pool composition may change in the event of a release, but some risk of adverse selection remains.
- Crown Castle has an arrangement with Verizon pertaining to two Asset Entities; Crown Atlantic and Crown GT. In the event of a default if the servicer opts to dispose of all the Asset Entities, the arrangement with Ver-izon may potentially reduce the equity value of Crown GT and Crown Atlantic.
- Verizon (**A3**) and AT&T-Cingular (**Baa2**) account for more than 50% of the portfolio's revenue. On a combined basis they could not only seek to influence Crown Castle to lower the tenant rent structure to their advantage but could also seek to cause significant disruption to the revenue stream if either one were to default on its rental obligations.

TRANSACTION OVERVIEW

The Asset Entities

All of the tower sites are currently owned, leased or managed by the Asset Entities, which are in turn wholly owned by Crown Castle Towers LLC. The ownership of the towers is disbursed among the Asset Entities as follows:

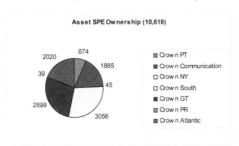

Securities Issued

The Notes have a balance of $1,900,000,000. The Issuer Entity will issue Class A, Class B, Class C, and Class D fixed rate Notes.

Release Provisions Protected via Premiums and Portfolio Tests

Wireless Towers can be released from the portfolio upon payment of a cash release price, which is an amount equal to 125% of the allocated loan amount for the property to be released. The amount will be applied towards the outstanding principal on the mortgage loan.

Moody's believes that the release premium imposed in connection with a release of property from the pool is adequate to protect pool diversity and property quality to a degree consistent with the ratings.

Property Substitution

Sites within the securitized portfolio may at any time prior to the maturity date be replaced with other sites given certain covenants are met. In any given year the number of sites that can be substituted is limited to 5% of the allocated loan amount, however, any unused portion can be carried over into subsequent years.

The substitution criteria that must be followed are:
- The combined % of telephony and investment grade tenants for the replacement tower sites must be 90% or greater,
- the new sites' ground leases, for real estate that is not owned, must have an unexpired term at least as long as the towers being replaced,
- the weighted average remaining term of tenant leases on the replacement sites must be the same or better, and
- the maintenance capital expenditures for the replacement sites is not materially greater than for the replaced sites.

These covenants are adequate to protect pool diversity and property quality to a degree consistent with the ratings.

Issuance of Additional Notes

The transaction structure allows for the issuance of additional notes based on newly acquired tower sites by a newly formed or existing Issuer Entity wholly owned by the Issuer. Additional notes may also be issued without additional collateral provided that the DSCR, after giving effect to such issuance is not less than the original DSCR. In either case, Moody's must affirm that such an action will not cause it to downgrade, withdraw or qualify its outstanding ratings for the existing notes solely as a result of the issuance of the additional notes.

In the instance additional notes are issued, the criteria Moody's may use to evaluate the portfolio may be different from the criteria utilized to rate this transaction. The evolving nature of this asset class as well as technological developments may warrant a different approach; consequently, the advance rates at that time may be different than what was attained for this transaction. Moody's may not necessarily rate the issuance of the additional notes.

In the instance Moody's is unable to affirm the ratings and conclude that the issuance of additional notes would warrant a negative ratings action on the existing notes, additional notes will not be issued. Instead, Crown Castle may seek other financing alternatives, such as a completely new structured transaction or issuance by Crown Castle International.

Pay Structure

The loan requires payment of interest only until the scheduled balloon payment date, which will be in June 2010. The loan must be repaid in full or refinanced in June 2010. Should that fail to occur all cash will be trapped and used to pay interest due and outstanding principal sequentially. In the event of a default, the Servicer can either sell the assets to retire the bonds or continue operating the portfolio and use all the excess cash to retire outstanding principal.

Prior to this date, pre-payment is generally limited to any funds that are generated if assets in the portfolio are disposed of.

Portfolio Overview

The cash flow to service the debt for this transaction will be backed by revenues from 10,618 tower sites located throughout the United States.

Technology

There are approximately five different types of technology services that are provided by tenants of the portfolio and can be categorized as such:

Telephony accounts for 96% of existing revenues. Telephony functions are those normally found in cellular phones such as call transmission and reception, voicemail, messaging, etc. This is considered a high growth market since U.S. cellular phone penetration lags behind those of other developed and developing countries.

Land Mobile Radio & Specialized Mobile Radio (LMR/SMR) constitutes a very small percentage of revenue. This service is by government agencies such as the police and dispatch services for conveying and transmitting brief messages.

Over time as telephony functions become more specialized and inclusive, it is predicted that revenue from this segment will disappear and be served by the telephony component.

Paging only constitutes 1% of the portfolio's current revenue. This function has become somewhat obsolete since cellular phones have become more prevalent. Over time as the process of value migration continues it is expected that revenues from this segment will disappear as well without a correlated increase in the telephony sector. It must be noted that paging has far greater reach than cellular phones; however, this advantage has eroded considerably over the past few years.

The *Data* component also does not constitute a significant portion of the portfolio's revenue; however, the same logic applies to this segment as that mentioned for paging and LMR/SMR. Over time, it is expected that this function will become an inclusive part of the telephony component and the portfolio will realize an eventual decline in revenue from this segment.

Revenue from the *Broadcasting* segment is expected to remain at par with current projections. Even though satellite dishes have become more prevalent, it is still expected that for local channels local broadcasting capability will continue to be required at current levels.

4 • *Moody's Investors Service*   Crown Castle Towers LLC

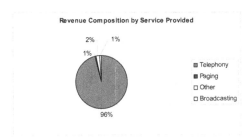

Revenue Composition by Service Provided

Tower Stratifications

The stratification depicted below reflects the 10,618 sites that are owned by the Asset Entities and constitute the portfolio.

Geographic Distribution

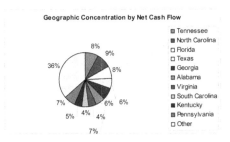

Geographic Concentration by Net Cash Flow

Revenue Composition by Tenants

Top 10 Tenants	Ratings	% of Revenue
Cingular/AT&T	Baa2	28.3
Verizon	A3	23.8
T-Mobile	Baa1	10.5
Nextel	Ba3	8.2
Sprint PCS	Baa3	6.3
Alltel	A2	4
Nextel Partners	Ba3	2.6
Triton PCS	Caa1	1.9
Leap Wireless	B3	1.9
Airgate	Caa1	1.1
Other	NA	11.4

Investment Grade vs. Non-Investment Grade Tenants

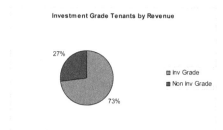

Land Designation

Type of Tower

Towers are vertical metal structures of three types and are selected by tenants based on the range coverage they seek. The higher the tower the greater the range.

Guyed Towers range in height between 200 and 2,000 feet. They are supported by cables attached at different levels on the tower that run anchor to anchor foundations. They have the capacity to accommodate equipment for up to 30 tenants.

Lattice Towers range in height between 150 and 400 feet. They are self supporting with three or four legs that act as anchors. They have the capacity to accommodate equipment for up to 12 tenants.

Monopole Towers range in height between 50 and 200 feet and are self supporting vertical tubular structures. They have the capacity to accommodate equipment for up to 5 tenants.

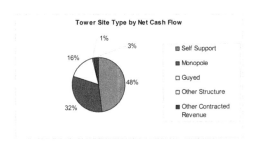

The average number of tenants per tower for the current portfolio of 10,618 towers is 2.3, whereas the industry average is 2.5. Barring the growth affiliated with annual rent escalators, the portfolio should also experience organic growth until the number of tenants per tower in the portfolio is equals the industry average.

Legal Structure

The Issuers will be the Issuer Entity, Crown South, Crown Communication, Crown PT, Crown NY and Crown PR. These entities were initially not organized in contemplation of a securitized financing. Their charter and organizational documents will be changed and certain provisions will be added to limit their business purpose, and to comply with special purpose entity requirements.

The Guarantor will be CC Towers Guarantor LLC, a newly-formed special purpose entity whose sole purpose will be to hold the equity interests of Issuer Entity and to guarantee repayment of the Notes. It will pledge the equity interests of Issuer Entity to the Indenture Trustee as security for the guarantee.

The bond holders will have a priority security interest in 100% of the equity interests of the Issuer Entity with the following exception:

- Crown Atlantic and Crown GT were formed as joint ventures between Crown Castle International and entities that are now owned by Verizon. While Crown Castle International now owns all of the ownership interests in both Crown Atlantic and Crown GT, Verizon remains a Tenant of Crown Atlantic and Crown GT and has various protective rights regarding the business and activities of Crown Atlantic and Crown GT. In particular, Crown Atlantic and Crown GT are prohibited from incurring certain indebtedness, guaranteeing debt and granting liens on their assets without Verizon's approval. Accordingly, the Notes will not be obligations of Crown Atlantic or Crown GT, and the Notes will not be secured by, and Noteholders will not have the benefit of any direct liens on, the assets of Crown Atlantic and Crown GT.

The diagram[1] below depicts organizational structure of the Issuer Entity.

---

1   From the Offering Memorandum

ORGANIZATIONAL STRUCTURE OF CROWN CASTLE INTERNATIONAL CORP.

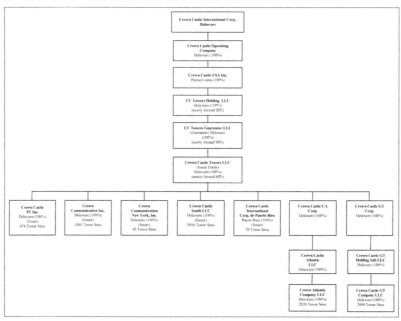

REPAYMENT SUMMARY	
Variable	**Terms**
Loan Amount	$1,900,000,000
Loan Term	60 months
Payment Type	Interest only. No principal amortization occurs during the term of the loan. On or after May 2010, the loan must either be refinanced or paid in full. Should that fail to occur all cash will be trapped and used to pay interest due and outstanding principal sequentially. In the event of a default, the Servicer can either sell the assets to retire the bonds or continue operating the portfolio and use all excess cash flow to retire outstanding principal.
Payment Frequency	Monthly
First Payment Date	07/15/2005
Expected Maturity Date	06/15/2010
Legal Final Maturity Date	06/15/2035
Balloon	Yes
Prepayment Clause	The Asset Entities may dispose of tower sites having an allocated note amount of up to $20 million per year prior to the second anniversary of the closing date. After the second year the Asset Entities may dispose of tower sites at any time without limit.
Lockbox Required	Yes
Release Provision Terms	Sites can be released from the portfolio upon payment of the release price of 125% of the allocated loan amount.
Property Substitution	Property substitution is limited to 5% of allocated loan amount in any given year provided certain covenants are met. Any amount that is not used can be carried over into subsequent years until June 2010.
Events of Default	Failure to pay any scheduled amounts due Failure to comply with financial reporting and compliance requirements Any breach or default under covenants of the indenture Any breach of representation or warranties Involuntary or voluntary bankruptcy Default under the management agreement or any injunctions
Reserve Accounts	*Impositions and Insurance Reserve Sub-Account:* Funded at the onset in the amount of $24.5 million. The account will be funded on each due date in an amount equal to 1/12 of the real estate taxes and other impositions that will be payable during the ensuing 12 months. *Cash Trap Reserve Sub-Account:* To reserve 100% of any excess cash flow should the DSCR fall below 1.75x over a trailing 12 month period at the end of any calendar quarter. *Advance Rents Reserve Sub-Account:.* To (a) reserve eleven twelfths of the amount of rent paid by lessees under tenant leases require annual rent be paid in advance (b) five-sixths of the amount of rent paid by tenants under space licenses that require semi-annual rent be paid in advance, and (c) two-thirds of the amount of rent paid by lessees under tenant leases that require that quarterly rent be paid in advance. Funded at the onset in the amount of $21.9 million. *Environmental Remediation Reserve Sub-Account:* To reserve for payment of potential environmental remediation costs with respect to the tower sites. This account will be funded at the outset with $2.5 million, increasing to $5.0 million 12 months post closing.

Payment Priority

The order of priority for payments from the cash management account is depicted below:

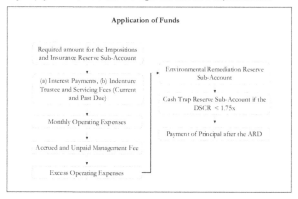

MOODY'S REVIEW AND CASH FLOW ANALYSIS

In deriving the value of the assets, Moody's considered Crown Castle's historical operating performance, evaluated and analyzed comparable public company data and market information from various third party sources. Emphasis was placed on analyzing expense components as well as future revenue growth potential for the sector. This was of particular concern since companies aggressively moved to acquire wireless tower portfolios at significant premiums, which led to unsustainable leverage and several bankruptcies in the latter part of the 1990s.

One inherent feature built into all tenant leases is a mandatory annual rent escalator that ranges from 3% to 5% depending on the location, type and height of the tower. Even if organic growth in the sector comes to a standstill, revenue from the portfolio will continue to increase every year by a minimum of 3% until the termination of the underlying tenant leases. Local zoning and building regulations make it quite difficult for competitors to erect new towers and offer tenants other options; should such an option exist it is unlikely that the value that can be derived from such a shift would outweigh the associated moving costs. Furthermore wireless carriers optimize and fine tune their services for optimal coverage in geographic locations, and disturbing that equilibrium by locating to another tower in a different vicinity can affect that coverage.

Given the above, it is very likely that tenants will opt to renew their lease contracts upon expiration. However it is to be noted that Verizon and AT&T/Cingular on a combined basis account for more than 50% of this portfolio's revenue, and in turn can influence Crown Castle to lower its tenant rental structure to their advantage. Such an outcome will not only have negative margin consequences for the industry, but also an immediate impact to this securitization in terms of reduced cash flows servicing the bonds.

The exhibit below outlines lease expirations over the coming years in terms of contribution to total revenue.

Tenant License Expiration (Months)	% of Revenue
0 - 12	14.2
13 - 24	10.4
25 - 36	7.7
37 - 48	10.4
49 - 60	29.9
> 61	27.0
Carrier Swap Agreements	0.4

The average industry Broadband Equivalent Tenants (BBE), a measure used by the tower industry to normalize tenant additions, is 2.5. The BBE is 2.6 for this portfolio, in line with the indsutry average, and an indicator that the portfolio is performing slightly better than its peers, and should experience growth if management continues to implement is current strategy to acquire tenants.

Moody's was provided with projected cash flows along with the underlying assumptions such as SG&A expenses, capital expenditures and other general operating line items for the 10,618 sites that constitute the portfolio. Revenues were based on leases in place, operating expenses were based on historical operating statements, and capital expenditures were based on recent experience at the properties.

Environmental reviews were performed for all of the Tower Sites. Environmental consultants performed reviews of government environmental databases for information concerning the Tower Sites in accordance with the standards for such review as part of an American Society for Testing and Materials environmental assessment. Based on their database reviews, of the 10,618 Tower Sites, 9640 Tower Sites were identified by the environmental consultants as not having any environmental issues. The remaining 978 Tower Sites were subjected to drive-by observations and additional data reviews, 967 Tower Sites were cross-referenced to environmental reports that the Asset Entities had maintained, and a Phase I environmental assessment was performed at one Tower Site. No environmental issues were raised as a result of this due diligence.

Crown Castle also demonstrated established procedures and policies to ensure that its tower portfolio is in compliance with zoning and permitting requirements, something that is fundamental for a tower operator; the firm has never been fined by the FAA or FCC for non-compliant activities.

8,821 out of the 10,618 tower sites consist of a leasehold interest under a ground lease, which represents approximately 77.2% of the of the cash flows. The cash flows from owned sites and leasehold sites where an estoppel has been obtained, represent approximately 68.9% of annualized run rate net tower cash flow.

Value of Assets

To calculate the value of the entire portfolio, a scenario based analysis was conducted. Revenue growth rates were varied on the multiple technology services that the tenants of this portfolio provide. Telephony, which constitutes 96% of the services provided, was given credit for growth. Higher growth rates for the sector were used at the onset of the transaction and perpetual growth rates with a triangular distribution of 3%, 4% and 5% for the duration. The service sectors such as Paging, Broadcasting and LMR/SMR were given no growth credit.

Expenses were varied such that EBITDA margins ranged from 40% to 75% based on a triangular distribution. This factored in not only Crown Castle's current EBITDA margins that were a little below the industry average (excluding its services business), but also that of other competitors which ranged within the specified band above.

Maintenance capital expenditures were correlated to revenue growth. Crown Castle had provided baseline maintenance capital expenditure projections that ranged in the $700 - $1000 per tower per annum, and capital expenditures incurred in excess of the specified ranged was considered "revenue enhancing", such as new tower construction. Factoring in Crown Castle's past financials and that of its competitors, this range was considered low. The range for the required maintenance capital expenditure per tower was modified to $1,200 - $1,600 with minimum annual increments of 3%; a triangular distribution of 3%, 4% and 5% was used to simulate variability.

On the Anticipated Repayment Date (ARD), Crown Castle will seek to re-finance the portfolio. However our analysis assumes that such an event does not occur; instead the assets continue to operate on an "as-is" basis with an additional 5% interest penalty applied to all classes of notes post ARD. The rationale for this assumption is to ensure that the bonds are re-paid in full by the legal final maturity should market conditions prove unfavorable for such a re-financing. Analysis was also done on the potential impact on revenues, should the larger tenants default or were to exercise influence to affect rental pricing to their advantage; the objective was to ensure that the bonds were re-paid in full by the legal final maturity.

The servicer also has the option to sell the assets upon an event of default. Given the large size of the portfolio it is conceivable that asset disposal on such a large scale may significantly depress the value of the towers, far below their value as of this transaction date. The servicer is therefore expected to exercise its discretion and pursue the best course of action in the interest of the bond holders.

In conjunction to the revenue and expense stresses, we applied a series of different discount rates based on the riskiness of the future cashflow stream. Discount rates used varied between 10.00% and 12.00%.

The analysis resulted in a loan amount of $1,900,000,000 and tranched as depicted below:

Class	Rating	Amount ($)
A	(P)**Aaa**	$1,198,460,000
B	(P)**Aa2**	$233,845,000
C	(P)**A2**	$233,845,000
D	(P)**Baa2**	$233,850,000

STRUCTURE AND CREDIT ENHANCEMENT

The Crown Castle Towers LLC, Senior Secured Tower Revenue Notes Series 2005-1 transaction is structured as multi-class, fixed, senior-subordinate notes. The notes are issued in four sequential classes (Class A, Class B, Class C, and Class D). The certificates have not been and will not be registered under the Securities Act of 1933, as amended. The issuance has been designed to permit resale under SEC Rule 144A.

Payment Priority

Class A are senior securities, supported by subordinate securities. Class B, Class C and Class D are subordinate securities and provide credit support for notes with an earlier alphabetical class designation. Any shortfalls in payments resulting from losses and delinquencies will be borne first by the junior participation, then by the holders of the Class D notes, then by the holders of the Class C notes, then by the holders of the Class B notes, and finally by the holders of the Class A notes.

REPRESENTATIONS AND WARRANTIES

In the indenture, the Issuer Entity and the Asset Entities made certain representations and warranties concerning the properties. The representations and warranties cover such items as title to the properties, the environmental condition of the properties.

MANAGER

Crown Castle USA Inc. (a wholly owned subsidiary of Crown Castle International Corp.), will act as manager for the Issuer Entity. The responsibilities will include services necessary to the ownership and operation of the sites, including acting as leasing agent for the sites. In addition, the manager will also perform administrative services relating to accounting, litigation management and finance. The management agreement will have successive terms of 30 days, and will terminate automatically at the end of any 30-day period unless renewed by the Issuer Entity or an event of default has occurred or the DSCR falls below 1.1. The manager can be replaced in an event of default, or by the Issuer Entity if it chooses to as long as an event of default has not occurred.

SERVICER

Midland Loan Services, Inc will act as the Servicer under the trust agreement. The responsibilities of the Servicer will include advancing delinquent interest payments (other than balloon payments) on the senior participation and such other sums necessary for the protection of the property (e.g., real estate taxes, insurance, etc.) all to the extent deemed recoverable. Midland Loan Services, Inc. has been reviewed by Moody's and found acceptable in the role of Servicer.

RATINGS

Moody's ratings are based on the quality of the collateral, the leverage on the portfolio, and the structural and legal integrity of the transaction. The ratings on the notes address the likelihood of receipt by note holders of timely payment of interest and of all distributions of principal by the final rated distribution date of June 2035 with respect to the notes.

Moody's ratings address only the credit risks associated with the transaction. Other non-credit risks, such as those associated with the timing of principal prepayments and the payment of prepayment penalties, have not been addressed and may have a significant effect on yield to investors.

TRANSACTION SUMMARY

Structure Summary

Structure:	Senior/subordinate
Whole Loan Balance:	$1,900,000,000
Collateral:	The bond holders will have a priority security interest in 100% of the equity interests of the Issuer Entity. Each Issuer will grant a security interest in substantially all of its personal property as collateral for the Notes. The assets owned directly by the Issuer Entities include communication towers, real property and associated rights, managed and leased third-party sites, tenant leases, owned equipment on towers or at sites, FCC licenses and systems
Guarantor:	CC Towers Guarantor LLC
Manager:	Crown Castle USA Inc.
Servicer:	Midland Loan Services, Inc.
Indenture Trustee:	JPMorgan Chase Bank, N.A.
Anticipated Repayment Date:	June 2010
Rated Final Repayment Date:	June 2035

STRUCTURED FINANCE

New Issue Report

MVL Film Finance LLC

CLOSING DATE:
September 1, 2005

AUTHOR:

Olga Filipenko
Assistant Vice President
(212) 553-4624
Olga.Filipenko@moodys.com

CONTACTS:

Jay Eisbruck
Managing Director
(212) 553-4377
Jay.Eisbruck@moodys.com

Linda A. Stesney
Managing Director
(212) 553-3691
Linda.Stesney@moodys.com

Nicolas Weill
Managing Director
(212) 553-3877
Nicolas.Weill@moodys.com

Brett Hemmerling
Investor Liaison
(212) 553-4796
Brett.Hemmerling@moodys.com

WEBSITE:
www.moodys.com

ASSIGNED RATINGS

	Amount($)	Maturity	Rating
Class A	465,000,000	September 2016	Aaa

OPINION

Moody's **Aaa** rating of the Class A Notes is based on the following:

- The support of a financial guarantee insurance policy from Ambac Assurance Corporation (Ambac), whose insurance financial strength rating is **Aaa**. Ambac will guarantee timely interest and ultimate principal payment.

Moody's underlying investment grade rating of the facility is based on:

- The historical performance of live-action films based on Marvel characters and the anticipated slate of films.
- Structure of the deal.

Moody's Investors Service

October 5, 2005

RATING SUMMARY

MVL Film Finance LLC (MVL) was created to partially finance Marvel Studios' production of a slate of 10 live-action or animated films based on up to 10 of Marvel's comic book characters, including Captain America and Nick Fury. The securitization will own the film rights to the characters as well as the film library created featuring the characters.

The facility will fund a portion of aggregate costs associated with producing each film. It will function as a revolving credit facility whereby the issuer can borrow, pay down and re-borrow amounts on a revolving basis for seven years. Revenues from the exploitation of the film slate, net of participations, residuals, print and advertising expenses and distribution costs will provide a source of debt repayment. An additional source of repayment is the monetization of the intellectual property value of the character film rights and the library of completed films, as well as the sequel and spin-off rights to the completed films.

The film slate will be marketed and distributed by Paramount Pictures Corporation (Paramount), with the exception of certain foreign territories that MVL Productions LLC, an affiliate of Marvel Studios, expects to pre-sell to leading distributors in such territories and domestic free TV, which will be self-distributed by MVL Productions LLC. Paramount is a wholly-owned subsidiary of Viacom.

The rating on the transaction was based on the analysis of the projected slate of films and the projection of revenues and expenses for these films in conjunction with the transaction's structural features and enhancements.

Company Background

Marvel Studios, Inc. (Marvel Studios) is a subsidiary of Marvel Entertainment, Inc (Marvel). Marvel is a publicly traded character-based entertainment company with a market capitalization of approximately $1.7 billion as of September 30, 2005. Marvel owns and commercializes rights to an intellectual property library consisting of over 5,000 characters, including some of the most recognizable characters in the entertainment industry, including Spider-Man, X-Men, Hulk, Captain America, Fantastic Four and Nick Fury.

Historically, Marvel has licensed characters to major film studios (Fox, Sony, Universal) that finance the production of and distribute films based on those characters while paying Marvel a licensing fee in the form of an advance against a revenue or profit participation. Films based on Marvel characters such as Spider-Man, X-Men and Fantastic Four have experienced dramatic success in the marketplace. While Marvel has historically licensed out its characters, it has remained an integral part of the film production process and has the knowledge and experience to run its own film studio. This facility will allow Marvel to act as a stand-alone film studio producing films based on its characters, as well as to maintain control of the film properties through all windows of the film cycle.

Film Slate

The film slate will be produced by Marvel Studios and will be based on the original Marvel characters and comic book stories of "Captain America", "Nick Fury", "Ant-Man", "The Avengers", "Black Panther", "Cloak and Dagger", "Doctor Strange", "Hawkeye", "Power Pack", and "Shang-Chi".

The films are intended to be major event films with production budgets of between $60 million and $165 million. The historical box-office performance of films Marvel has produced in partnership with the major studios has been outstanding. The inherent uncertainty of film performance is further mitigated by the ability to use existing storylines in developing films, as well as audience awareness of the Marvel characters.

Transaction Structure

The facility will fund a portion of the aggregate film production costs during the production of each film. To mitigate film completion risk, prior to the initial advance on each film, the special purpose production company formed to produce each applicable film will be required to obtain an acceptable completion guarantee. The advances under the facility will not exceed the amounts covered by the completion guarantee.

Credit enhancement for the Class A Notes is provided by $60 million in unwrapped Class B Notes. The Class B Notes will be fully funded prior to any draws on the rated portion of the facility and will be subordinated to the Class A Notes.

Cash generated in the transaction will be trapped in a Borrower Blocked Account, and no distributions to Marvel are permitted until a certain number of films have been released and specific coverage and minimum balance tests have been satisfied.

In addition, as a condition precedent to funding for any individual film, the issuer is required to pre-sell certain international distribution rights in Japan, Germany, France, Spain and Australia and may engage in other acceptable alternative financings to reduce the advances required to be funded through the facility. The target for the foreign territory pre-sales is 33% of each film's production budget. Moody's believes that this target is achievable based on analysis of current and historical data for the pre-sale of foreign territories for high-budget event films. Pre-selling territory rights has the effect of reducing the potential upside from exploitation in the applicable territories in exchange for reducing performance risk by covering a portion of production budgets with upfront cash.

Credit enhancement is also provided by a true sale of the film rights to the characters; triggers based on the performance of the films and foreign territory pre-sales; the value of the intellectual property pledged as collateral; and a cap on overhead expenses payable to Marvel. In addition, MVL Productions LLC will self-distribute domestic TV rights at no cost to the film credit facility.

The facility also benefits from a three-month interest reserve as well as a $25,000,000 Class A liquidity reserve. The liquidity reserve is available to cover insurer expenses, administrative costs up to $600,000 per annum, insurance premium and interest payments on the Class A Notes, and will provide protection against timing delays of cash flow collections from Paramount.

Quantitative Analysis

Moody's reviewed historical data for the films released by some of the major studios between 2000 and 2004 that met the eligibility criteria for this transaction, including a subsample of films produced by Marvel in partnership with major studios. The data included production costs as well as different line items for revenues and expenses and overall profit for the movies. The line items for revenue included amounts received from theatrical, home video, pay TV, and network/syndication/non-theatrical channels. Line items for expenses included domestic and foreign theatrical distribution costs, home video manufacturing and shipping, participations, and residuals.

Using this historical data, a relationship was developed between production and revenues as well as production, revenues and distibution expenses. Using these relationships as well as anticipated production expenses for the upcoming slate of films which were provided to Moody's, a Monte Carlo simulation was performed. The resulting amounts were then used to derive net cash flows, which were then used to pay down the notes.

After several thousand potential slates were simulated, the expected loss experienced on the Class A Notes was found to be consistent with an investment grade rating.

STRUCTURE SUMMARY

Structure

Issuer:	MVL Film Finance LLC
Studio:	Marvel Studios, Inc.
Distributor:	Paramount Pictures Corporation[1]
Administrative Agent:	General Electric Capital Corporation
Collateral Agent:	HSBC Bank USA, National Association
Amount Rated:	$465,000,000
Rating:	**Aaa**
Financial Guarantee Providor:	Ambac
Credit Support:	$60 million in subordination
Placement Agent:	Merrill Lynch
Transfer Period:	7 years
Legal Final Maturity:	11 years from closing

1   The film slate will be marketed and distributed by Paramount Pictures Corporation, with the exception of (i) certain foreign territories, and (ii) domestic free TV, both of which will be self-distributed by Marvel.

Doc ID# SF63119

STANDARD &POOR'S

Structured Finance

ABS

Presale: Honda Auto Receivables 2006-1 Owner Trust

$1.261 Billion Asset-Backed Notes Series 2006-1

Primary Credit Analyst:
Amanda M Soriano
New York
(1) 212-438-2609
amanda_soriano@
standardandpoors.com

Secondary Credit Analyst:
Nadine E Gunter
New York
(1) 212-438-2475
nadine_gunter@
standardandpoors.com

This presale report is based on information as of March 21, 2006. The ratings shown are preliminary. This report does not constitute a recommendation to buy, hold, or sell securities. Subsequent information may result in the assignment of final ratings that differ from the preliminary ratings.

Preliminary Ratings As Of March 21, 2006			
Class	Preliminary rating*	Preliminary amount (mil. $)	Recommended credit support (%) ¶
A-1	A-1+	298.00	3.75
A-2	AAA	316.00	3.75
A-3	AAA	400.00	3.75
A-4	AAA	247.13	3.75

*The rating of each class of securities is preliminary and subject to change at any time. ¶Hard credit support at closing will be 3.75% plus excess spread.

Profile

Expected closing date: March 28, 2006.

Collateral: The $1.303 billion collateral pool consists of 74,512 fully amortizing, level, monthly pay auto loan contracts.

Underwriters: Barclays Capital and Citigroup.

Seller: American Honda Receivables Corp.

Servicer: American Honda Finance Corp.

Indenture trustee: JPMorgan Chase Bank N.A.

Owner trustee: Citibank N.A.

Rationale

RatingsDirect
Publication Date
March 21, 2006

The preliminary ratings assigned to Honda Auto Receivables 2006-1 Owner Trust's auto receivables asset-backed notes series 2006-1 reflect:

- The credit enhancement provided by the 3.25% subordinated certificate s, a 0.50% reserve fund building to 0.75% of the initial pool balance, and excess spread;
- The pool composition, which continues to represent high-quality prime loans, of which approximately 66% are loans under credit tier A with a weighted average FICO score of 753 and 89% are new vehicles; and
- The sound legal structure.

Transaction Overview

This is American Honda Finance Corp.'s (Honda) 29th retail auto loan securitization and its first in 2006. The hard credit support of 3.75% plus the available excess spread in this transaction will provide a sufficient multiple of expected cumulative losses for the designated ratings.

The transaction is structured as a true sale of the receivables from the originator, Honda, to American Honda Receivables Corp. (AHRC), a bankruptcy-remote, special-purpose entity. AHRC, in turn, transfers the receivables through a pledge to the owner trust, the issuer of the rated notes. The notes total $1.261 billion. The trust will also issue $42.36 million of certificates, representing 3.25% of the collateral pool, which will be retained by AHRC. Initially, the class A-1 money market and the class A-2 notes receive all principal payments until fully retired. Thereafter, the notes will share the principal distributable amount with the certificates pro rata, provided that the specified reserve fund balance is not less than 0.25% of the initial pool balance. Certificate principal will be paid as discussed below.

Credit Enhancement

Subordination

On each distribution date, payments to the certificateholders are subordinated to note interest and principal. Principal due on the certificates will not be paid until the required interest and principal pay ments on the notes and the interest on the certificates have been made (see Payment Structure). The reserve fund is topped up after payment of the principal distributable amount on the certificates. The certificates are not entitled to receive an y principal payments until after the class A-1 money market and the class A-2 notes are retired. Thereafter, the payment priority switches to pro rata between the noteholders and the certificateholders according to the applicable noteholders' percentages. This may result in the amortization of credit support provided by the certificates for the class A notes. However, if the specified reserve fund balance is less than 0.25% of the initial pool balance and as long as this occurs, principal payments will not be made on the certificates until all outstanding notes have been paid in full. This mitigates the risk of amortizing the subordination too quickly in the event of performance deterioration.

Reserve fund

The reserve fund is available to cover shortfalls of required interest and principal on the notes and the certificates and will increase to a target of 0.75% of the initial pool balance from 0.50% of the initial pool balance at closing. The reserve floor will be maintained at 0.75% of the initial receivables. In addition, if certain charge-off or delinquency triggers are breached, the reserve fund requirement will increase.

Excess spread

The annual excess spread for this securitization is greater than that of the previous transaction (series 2005-6), primarily due to a lower composition of loans with APRs of less than 4.00%. The $25.7 million yield supplement amount contributes approximately 90 basis points to annual excess spread.

Yield supplement account

A yield supplement account will be available to cover interest deficiencies on any discounted receivable.

On each payment date, the indenture trustee will withdraw from the yield supplement account the amount by which one month's interest on the principal balance of each discount receivable (excluding defaulted receivables) at a rate equal to 6.60%, exceeds one month's interest on the principal balance of each discount receivable (excluding defaulted receivables) at the annual percentage rate of that receivable.

For this transaction, approximately 68.52% of the collateral pool has APRs below 6.60%. The weighted average APR for the entire collateral pool, including the estimated yield supplement account, is approximately 7.24%.

Payment Structure

Distributions will be made from all available collections in the following order of priority:

- The 1% servicing fee and nonrecoverable servicer advances;
- Any accrued and unpaid trustee fees and expenses (capped at $100,000 per year);
- Interest to the class A noteholders, including class A-1 noteholders;
- Principal first to the class A-1 noteholders until the principal amount is reduced to zero, and then to the remaining class A noteholders, sequentially, based on the noteholders' percentage of the outstanding principal balance;
- Interest to the certificateholders, from remaining available amounts;
- Principal to the certificateholders, after the class A-1 and A-2 noteholders have been paid in full, based on the certificateholders' percentage of the outstanding principal balance;
- Amount needed to bring the reserve fund to its target level;
- Any accrued and unpaid trustee fees and expenses not previously paid; and
- Any remaining amounts to the seller.

Performance

Honda is the originator and servicer of the receivables. As of Dec. 31, 2005, Honda's serviced portfolio consisted of 1,828,660 contracts amounting to $23.6 billion. The year-to-year growth in serviced loans was 13.80% through Dec. 31, 2005.

Honda has consistently maintained the loss performance of its managed portfolio at low levels over the past five years. Net losses as a percentage of the average amount outstanding were 0.49% as of Dec. 31, 2005, compared with 0.87% as of Dec. 31, 2004. Delinquencies and repossessions decreased to 2.05% of the outstanding loan balance as of Dec. 31, 2005, compared with 2.13% as of Dec. 31, 2004.

Standard & Poor's Ratings Services' cumulative net loss projections for Honda's more recent securitized pools (series 2002-3 through 2004-2) range from 0.46%-1.00%. Paid-off securitizations in 2000 and 2001 have experienced lower cumulative net losses, ranging from 0.31%-0.42%.

Honda implemented a new servicing computer system in August 2004. Standard & Poor's continues to monitor the impact of this transition on Honda's managed portfolio and securitized transactions.

The Pool

The $1.303 billion collateral pool consists of 74,512 fully amortizing, level monthly pay contracts. Each receivable selected for the pool is less than 30 days past due. The weighted average original term to maturity and the remaining term to maturity are 57.92 months and 52.88 months, respectively, resulting in approximately five months of seasoning. No loans have an original maturity longer than 60 months. The weighted average APR of the pool is 6.34%. Approximately 66% of the initial pool balance consists of loans with a weighted average FICO score of 753. This should have a positive effect on pool performance, as loans with high FICO scores usually perform better than loans with low FICO scores. New vehicles represent 89% of the pool. This further enhances credit quality because loans for new vehicles exhibit lower losses than loans for used vehicles. The only significant geographic concentration is California, representing 14.65% of originations measured by principal. The next highest concentration is Texas, which accounts for 8.46% of the pool.

Honda

Honda is a wholly owned subsidiary of American Honda Motor Co. Inc., which, in turn, is a wholly owned subsidiary of Honda Motor Co. Ltd. (A+/Stable/A-1), a Japanese corporation that is a worldwide manufacturer and distributor of motor vehicles, motorcycles, and power equipment.

Honda was incorporated in 1980 and its principal offices are located in Torrance, Calif. The company provides wholesale and retail financing to authorized dealers in the U.S. and Canada.

STANDARD &POOR'S	RATINGSDIRECT

RESEARCH Return to Regular Format

Presale: ACG Trust III

Publication date:	19-Dec-2005
Primary Credit Analyst:	Anthony Nocera, New York (1) 212-438-1568; anthony_nocera@standardandpoors.com
Secondary Credit Analysts:	Ted Burbage, New York (1) 212-438-2684; ted_burbage@standardandpoors.com
	Philip Baggaley, CFA, New York (1) 212-438-7683; philip_baggaley@standardandpoors.com
	Michael K Vernier, Esq., New York (1) 212-438-6629; michael_vernier@standardandpoors.com

$1.86 Billion Floating-Rate And Deferrable Interest Notes Series 2005-1

This presale report is based on information as of Dec. 19, 2005. The ratings shown are preliminary. This report does not constitute a recommendation to buy, hold, or sell securities. Subsequent information may result in the assignment of final ratings that differ from the preliminary ratings.

Preliminary Ratings As Of Dec. 19, 2005		
Class	Preliminary rating*	Preliminary amount (mil. $)
G-1A	AAA/Stable¶	1,620.0
B-1§	A-/Stable	117.5
C-1§	BBB-/Stable	122.5

*The rating of each class of securities is preliminary and subject to change at any time. ¶The 'AAA' rating is based on a financial guaranty policy provided by Ambac Assurance Corp., Finance Guaranty Insurance Co., and MBIA Insurance Corp., all of which have an 'AAA' insurer financial enhancement rating. §The class B-1 and C-1 notes are subordinate and allow the deferral of interest payments.

Profile

Expected closing date: Dec. 29, 2005.

Collateral: Shares in entities that directly and indirectly receive lease and residual cash flows associated with a portfolio of aircraft.

Underwriters: UBS Investment Bank and Deutsche Bank.

Seller and remarketing and administrative agent: Aviation Capital Group Corp.

Statutory trustee: Wells Fargo Delaware Trust Co.

Monitoring agent: Aircraft Monitoring Services LLC.

Servicing agent and cash manager: Pacific Life Insurance Co. (AA/Stable/A-1+).

Capital markets structuring agent: UBS Securities LLC.

Financial guaranty providers: Ambac Assurance Corp, Finance Guaranty Insurance Corp., and MBIA Insurance Corp. (the policy providers). Each policy provider has an 'AAA' insurer financial enhancement rating. The rating on the class G notes will be linked to the lowest-rated policy provider and, consequently, a downgrade of any policy provider would result in a downgrade of the class G notes.

Liquidity facility provider: Calyon.

Rationale

The preliminary ratings assigned to ACG Trust III's $1.86 billion floating-rate and deferrable interest notes series 2005-1 reflect the estimated credit quality of the initial and future lessees; the value and quality of aircraft collateral; the legal and cash flow structure, which support full and timely payment of interest and ultimate repayment of principal on or before the final maturity date on the class G notes; and the ultimate repayment of interest and principal on the class B and C notes on or before the final maturity date.

The preliminary ratings do not address the payment of step-up or additional premium that may be due to noteholders due to the refinancing of existing notes or the issuance of additional notes. Both the refinancing of existing notes or the issuance of additional notes require rating agency confirmation that the ratings on the existing notes would not be lowered or withdrawn as a result of such action.

The cash flow modeling of stress tests appropriate to each rating incorporate assumptions regarding airline default rates, maintenance costs, time off-lease for repossessed aircraft, reduced rental rates on leases as a result of a downturn, and expenses associated with repossessions. The rating approach follows a similar methodology that Standard & Poor's Ratings Services used in its analysis of all previously rated aircraft operating lease pool securitizations.

The ratings approach considers cash flow primarily from the 74 aircraft in the portfolio; structural safeguards; and reserve facilities to cover amounts associated with maintenance expenses, repossession costs, and security deposits. Cash generation consists of payments made under the leases or replacement leases, proceeds from aircraft disposition, net payments under the swap agreements, security deposits, liquidity reserves, and interest earned on invested cash. The leases are operating leases, signed initially for fixed periods with a remaining weighted average term of 3.84 years at the expected closing date.

The stable outlook reflects the expectation of a continued moderate industry recovery.

Issuer Overview

ACG Trust III represents the third securitization issued by Aviation Capital Group Corp. (ACG). The company previously issued Aviation Capital Group Trust Series 2000-1 and ACG Trust II Series 2003-1. In June 2005, ACG acquired Boullioun Aviation Services from West LB AG. The Boullioun fleet was composed of 102 aircraft, which increased ACG's total owned and managed fleet to 214 aircraft. The ACG Trust III securitized portfolio contains 74 aircraft, many of which were purchased in the Boullioun acquisition.

Collateral Pool Characteristics

The initial appraised value of the portfolio, which is made up of young, widely used aircraft manufactured by Airbus and Boeing, is $2.27 billion. At closing, the aircraft will be on lease to 45 lessees in 28 countries. ACG will act as the remarketing agent for the aircraft.

The portfolio contains three aircraft representing 2.76% of the pool that will initially be on lease to Skynet Asia Airways Ltd. (Skynet), which is based in Japan. Japanese law requires that the title to the aircraft must be held by a Japanese entity; the title is held by Venus Aircraft Ltd., a Japanese limited liability company owned by Sojitz Corp. (BB-/Stable). Beneficial ownership in the aircraft is vested in Wells Fargo Bank Northwest, as the owner trustee for three separate trusts, which are in turn beneficially owned by ACG Trust

III. At the expiration of each Skynet lease, the title will be purchased by the owner trustee for $1. Should Sojitz become insolvent before the purchase option is exercised, Sojitz's interest in the aircraft would become part of the Sojitz bankruptcy proceedings, which would result in additional time for the servicer to access the aircraft. Standard & Poor's has addressed this issue by incorporating prolonged downtime of up to 24 months in the cash flow analysis performed to account for this delay. Two of the three leases expire in early 2007, while the third lease expires in 2010. If the leases are not extended, and are released to non-Japanese airlines, the ownership structure will unwind.

Strengths And Concerns

Strengths
The strengths of this transaction include:

- The majority of the aircraft in the portfolio are popular models that should enjoy good release and resale markets;
- The portfolio is well-diversified by model, lessee, and country;
- The portfolio consists of 98.5%, by value, narrow-body (which tend to have a more liquid resale and releasing market) and 1.5% wide-body aircraft;
- The servicer, Aviation Capital Group, is a highly experienced aircraft lessor; and
- The fleet is one of the youngest fleets securitized, with an average age of 4.8 years.

Concerns
The following concerns have been identified:

- The portfolio was recently acquired and has doubled the size of ACG's owned and managed fleet, which could stress ACG's operations in the near term; and
- The ownership structure of the aircraft under lease to Skynet adds an additional element of risk.

These concerns have been addressed by applying appropriate stress assumptions into the cash flow analysis performed for this transaction.

Transaction Structure
On the closing date, ACG Trust III will issue rated bonds of approximately $1.86 billion in aggregate principal amount in three classes of notes: the class G-1 notes, which will be insured by the policy providers, all of which have an 'AAA' insurer financial enhancement rating; the class B-1 notes; and the class C-1 notes. The notes issued subsequent to this transaction, if any, will rank pari passu with existing notes in the same class or, in the case of the class D notes, will be subordinated to the existing notes. There will be no class D notes issued at closing. All newly issued or refinanced notes require rating agency confirmation affirming the ratings of the existing outstanding notes before such issuance or refinancing.

Similar to previous transactions, the issuer does not directly own or possess a security interest in the aircraft. Noteholders do not have certain rights and remedies that would normally pass to them on an occurrence of an event of default. ACG Trust III and its subsidiaries pledged to the security trustee as security for ACG Trust III obligations, the leases and associated lease payments, the ownership or beneficial interest in the aircraft-owning entities, proceeds from the disposition of aircraft, cash on hand and invested cash, payments under the swap agreement, and all credit facilities. ACG Trust III is a newly formed Delaware statutory trust and will have 100% interests in each of the aircraft-owning entities.

The proceeds of the issuance of the class G-1, B-1, and C-1 notes will be used by ACG Trust III to purchase the equity interest in the aircraft-owning entities, fund the liquidity reserves, and pay expenses of the offering.

The structure benefits from rental payments received from the lessees from closing, including payments from aircraft that have not yet been transferred. Funds for undelivered aircraft will be maintained in separate trust accounts and will not be transferred to the seller until the assets are delivered. At closing, it is expected that not all of the aircraft will be delivered.

In addition to a $25 million primary cash reserve, the transaction contains a $35 million credit facility to support expenses, class G-1 interest, and senior swap payments. The initial liquidity provider will be Calyon. The facility may be fully drawn upon a provider downgrade or the provider's decision not to extend the facility. Should this occur, either an eligible provider may be used as a replacement or the funds will be drawn and deposited into a cash collateral account. There are also two $15 million cash reserves for each of the class B-1 and C-1 notes.

Legal opinions, subject to various assumptions and qualifications, address certain insolvency risks, including true sale of the assets to ACG Trust III and consolidation of ACG Trust III with certain ACG affiliates and security interests, and certain other matters, will be delivered by White & Case LLP and other New York, Delaware, and Irish counsel, along with special Nebraska insurance counsel for Pacific Life Insurance Co.

Payment Structure

The rated classes of notes bear a floating rate of interest at LIBOR plus a margin. The interest on the notes is payable on each payment date according to the following priority of payments:

- Required expense amount;
- Class G interest, senior swap payments, and reimbursements of prior policy and credit facility draws;
- Senior swap payment draws made by the policy provider;
- Replenishment of the primary liquidity reserve account up to the required amount, the payment of any credit facility advance obligations, the replenishment of any cash collateral account up to the required amount, and the reimbursement of any credit facility obligation paid by the policy provider;
- Policy premium to the policy provider;
- Class G minimum principal;
- Class B interest;
- Class B minimum principal;
- Class C interest;
- Class C minimum principal;
- Class G scheduled principal;
- Class B scheduled principal;
- Class C scheduled principal;
- Modification and refinancing expenses;
- Class D interest (if issued);
- Class D scheduled principal (if issued);
- Accrued interest to the policy providers;
- Class G supplemental principal;
- Replenishment of the secondary liquidity reserve;
- Replenishment of the tertiary liquidity reserve;
- ACG Trust III distribution amount;
- Class B supplemental principal;
- Class C supplemental principal;
- Special indemnity expenses;
- Class G outstanding principal;
- Class B outstanding principal;
- Class C outstanding principal;
- Class D outstanding principal (if issued);
- Subordinated swap payments;

- Subordinated indemnity payments; and
- All remaining amounts to the statutory trustee.

If the acceleration of the notes occurs due to an event of default, the transaction follows a sequential pay structure, thus the senior class of notes is paid out in full before the more junior classes receive any distributions.
The structure is designed to maintain credit enhancement levels and adjust payments to the notes in line with expected principal pay-down schedules. To the extent that cash collections are less than expected, principal payments are made to the notes in order of priority. Reserves for aircraft maintenance and potential interest shortfalls have been provided by a liquidity facility and cash reserves.

Events Of Default

Each of the following constitute a note event of default:

- Failure to pay interest, when due, for a period of five or more business days;
- Failure to pay principal on any subclass by the final maturity date;
- Failure to pay, when due, any amount if there are amounts available in the collection accounts that are not applied, and the failure continues for five or more days;
- Failure by ACG Trust III to comply with any covenants or obligations under the indenture;
- Insolvency (voluntary or involuntary) relating to ACG Trust III or its subsidiaries;
- Judgments in excess of 5% of the adjusted portfolio value; or
- The constitutional documents of ACG Trust III cease to be in full force and effect and are not replaced with documents that have the same terms.

Roles Of The Parties

Ambac, FGIC, and MBIA financial guaranty policies

The policy providers will each issue a financial guaranty policy covering only the class G notes. Each policy provider will have an equal share and will be obligated to pay a pro-rated share of all claims on a several basis. The rating of the class G notes will be based on the lowest rating of the three policy providers. The policy will cover the following:

- The timely payment of class G interest;
- The ultimate payment of class G note principal on its final maturity date;
- After an indenture event of default regarding the class G notes and upon the sale of an aircraft, any shortfall between the proceeds of such sale and the class G note target price;
- Twenty four months after an acceleration event, class G minimum principal; and
- Avoidance payments relating to a bankruptcy of the issuer.

Remarketing agent/administrative agent

ACG will act as the remarketing agent for the aircraft. In this role, ACG will collect rentals and maintenance payments due from lessees, enforce rights against lessees, and remarket aircraft for release or sale.

ACG, established in 1989, leases and manages commercial aircraft under leases for its own portfolio and for third-party financial institutions, and two prior securitization transactions. The company is 100% owned by Pacific Life Corp. With its recent acquisition of the Boullioun Aviation portfolio, the company is one of the top four aircraft lessors in the world.

Monitoring agent

Aircraft Monitoring Services Ltd., which was formed by an aviation industry expert, will act as the monitoring agent. In this role, the company will monitor the performance of the remarketing agent and will assist the controlling trustee in making lease, sale, and capital investment decisions.

Remarketing Agent Evaluation

ACG will act as the remarketing agent for the transaction. The company was founded in 1989 and is one of the world's larger managers of commercial aircraft, managing a fleet of 214 aircrafts. In 2005, the company purchased the 102-aircraft portfolio of Boullioun Aviation Services. ACG's management team is very experienced, with the CEO having approximately 25 years in the aviation industry.

ACG's ability to market and release aircraft in a timely manner is critical in maximizing the cash flows generated by rental revenues, and its ability to dispose of aircraft after their useful life is another key factor in cash optimization. It is Standard & Poor's view that ACG's ability to release and dispose of aircraft is very strong and consistent with the assigned ratings. Because of the company's strong market position, its commitment to the aircraft leasing business, and the financial strength of its parent company, Pacific Life Corp., no committed back-up servicer was deemed necessary in this transaction.

Portfolio Details

The portfolio's characteristics include:

- The portfolio consists of 74 aircraft with an initial appraised value of $2.27 billion;
- There are 73 narrow-body (98.5% by value) and one wide-body aircraft (1.5%);
- Both Boeing (62.7%) and Airbus (37.3%) aircraft are represented in the portfolio;
- The weighted average age from manufacture is 4.8 years;
- The total number of initial lessees is 45 in 28 countries;
- The largest lessee concentration is Air Europa Lineas Aereas (approximately 6.97% by value), followed by Air Berlin (approximately 6.09%), and TAM (approximately 4.08%);
- Of the initial leases, 54.3% by value is currently leased to developing countries; and
- Spain is the largest country concentration at 10.7%.

Table 1 shows a portfolio comparison between the ACG Trust III transaction and previous aircraft transactions.

Table 1 – ACG Trust III Versus Most Recent Previous Transactions					
	ACG Trust III	Aircraft Lease Securitization Ltd.	Castle 2003-2 Trust	Castle 2003-1 Trust	Aviation Capital Group Trust II
No. of aircraft	74	42	34	37	37
Weighted avg. age (yrs.)	4. 80	8.20	7.37	6.73	6.25
Developing market exposure (%)	54.38	44.70	54.91	24.91	44.86
Narrow-bodies/wide-bodies (%)	98.5/1.5	67/33	58/42	83/17	93.9/6.10
Max. country concentration (%)	Spain (10.74)	Japan (13.00)	China (14.33)	U.S. (25.38)	U.K. (15.76)
Largest initial lessees (%)	Air Europa Lineas (6.97%)	Tombo Capital (13.00)	Emirates (10.56)	Air France (7.93)	GB Airways (12.13)

Table 2 shows a typical range of cash flow stresses for an operating lease transaction of this kind.

Table 2 - Typical Range Of Cash Flow Stresses For An Operating Lease Transaction			
	AA*	A*	BBB*
Depression 1 start (mos.)	1	1	13
Depression 2 start (mos.	109	109	120
Depression 3 start (mos.)	217	217	217

Length of depression (yrs.)	3-4	3-4	3-4
Lessee defaults (depression 1) (%)	75-90	65-85	55-70
Lessee defaults (depression 2) (%)	85-98	75-90	60-75
Lease rate decline (depression 1) (%)	50-70	40-60	30-50
Lease rate decline (depression 2) (%)	65-85	55-75	40-60
Repossession/remarketing time (mos.)	6-12	6-11	4-10
Lease term (depression 1) (yrs.)	4	4	4
Lease term (depression 2) (yrs.)	3	3	3
Repossession costs ($000)	750-1,000	750-1,000	750-1,000

*Rating stress analysis; not indicative of the notes' ratings.

ACG Trust III's ability to honor its note obligations was analyzed using a model designed to test the robustness of the transaction's cash flow factoring in the above stresses. Lessee defaults and the timing of the defaults were simulated using a Monte Carlo approach. Remarketed leases during the assumed depressions are released at reduced market lease rates.

Asset Analysis

The aircraft portfolio is considered to be the strongest fleet securitized to date. The average age of the fleet is 4.8 years and the pool is primarily composed of popular, modern-technology narrow-body aircraft, most notably the Airbus A320, representing 26.66% of the fleet; and the Boeing 737-700 and 737-800, which together represent 41.85% of the fleet. The portfolio is made up of nine different aircraft types; Boeing manufactures 63%, with the remaining 37% manufactured by Airbus.

The largest concentrations are new technology desirable aircraft. The Airbus A320 and the slightly larger A321 represent 27% and 8% of the pool by value, respectively, with the A320 one of the most popular narrow-body planes. Lease rates for these models have held up fairly well through the global airline downturn (and have since rebounded), although high production rates of the A320 through the downturn caused some oversupply and thus impeded lease rate recovery compared with Boeing's B737-800. The portfolio contains 28% of the 737-800 and 14% of the 737-700, which are included in Boeing's "next generation" 737 family of aircraft. Lease rates for both aircraft held up well through the downturn and have strengthened recently due to high demand (especially for the B737-800). Boeing's B737 "classics" (B737-300 and B737-400) represent approximately 18.4% of the portfolio. These planes were introduced in the 1980s, but continue to be widely used. While their lease rates declined more significantly than newer models during the downturn, they have recovered fairly well since then. The three remaining aircraft types represent a relatively small percentage of the fleet: the A319 (2.5%), a smaller version of the A320 and another popular narrow-body; the B767-300ER (1.5%), a small wide-body (the portfolio's only wide-body aircraft) introduced in the 1980s and which has rebounded strongly from lease rate declines of several years ago; and the 757-200 (1%), a large narrow-body that, while widely used, has seen lease rate weakness due to the bankruptcy of several large U.S. airlines that use it.

Lessee Analysis

The lessees in the current portfolio represent a diverse mix of airline credits, with significant representation from Europe and Asia. The five-largest lessees represent 25% of the portfolio by value, with Air Europa Lineas Aereas, a major Spanish airline and part of the Globalia tourism group, being the largest concentration at 7%. Other airlines with high concentrations include Air Berlin (6.0%), a German low-cost carrier; TAM-Linhas (4%), a major Brazilian airline; and My Travel Group (4%), a U.K.-based charter airline.

Overall, the credit quality of the portfolio was determined to be average for portfolio securitizations.

Maintenance

The initial lessees for the aircraft contain provisions specifying maintenance standards and the required condition of the aircraft on redelivery. A certain portion of the initial leases stipulate that the lessee is required to provide monthly maintenance reserves, but in other leases there is no provision for payment of maintenance. In these instances, the lessor must rely on the credit of the lessee and the ability of the lessee to perform scheduled maintenance throughout the lease term, and must return the aircraft in the condition required by the lease on termination.

Separate cash flows that model the sources and uses of maintenance expenditures have been reviewed and stressed, and it was found that the costs associated with these risks are sufficiently addressed in the proposed $25 million cash reserves and the $35 million credit facility. The class B and C notes each have a $15 million cash reserve, which provides liquidity to those notes, but is not available to cover maintenance and other expenses.

Surveillance

Standard & Poor's will maintain active surveillance on the rated notes until they mature or are retired. The purpose of surveillance is to assess whether the rated notes are performing within the initial parameters and assumptions applied to each rating category. The issuer is required to supply periodic reports and notices to Standard & Poor's to maintain continuous surveillance on the rated notes.

STANDARD &POOR'S	RATINGSDIRECT

RESEARCH   Return to Regular Format

ACG Trust III Notes Series 2005-1 Assigned Preliminary Ratings; Outlook Stable

Publication date: 19-Dec-2005
Primary Credit Analyst: Anthony Nocera, New York (1) 212-438-1568;
                               anthony_nocera@standardandpoors.com
Secondary Credit Analysts: Ted Burbage, New York (1) 212-438-2684;
                               ted_burbage@standardandpoors.com
                               Philip Baggaley, CFA, New York (1) 212-438-7683;
                               philip_baggaley@standardandpoors.com
                               Michael K Vernier, Esq., New York (1) 212-438-6629;
                               michael_vernier@standardandpoors.com

NEW YORK (Standard & Poor's) Dec. 19, 2005--Standard & Poor's Ratings Services today assigned its preliminary ratings to ACG Trust III's $1.86 billion floating-rate and deferrable interest notes series 2005-1 (see list). The outlook is stable.

The preliminary ratings are based on information as of Dec. 19, 2005. Subsequent information may result in the assignment of final ratings that differ from the preliminary ratings.

The preliminary ratings reflect the estimated credit quality of the initial and future lessees; the value and quality of aircraft collateral; the legal and cash flow structure, which support full and timely payment of interest and ultimate repayment of principal on or before the final maturity date on the class G notes; and the ultimate repayment of interest and principal on the class B and C notes on or before the final maturity date.

The preliminary ratings do not address the payment of step-up or additional premium that may be due to noteholders due to the refinancing of existing notes or the issuance of additional notes. Both the refinancing of existing notes or the issuance of additional notes require rating agency confirmation that the ratings on the existing notes would not be lowered or withdrawn as a result of such action.

The stable outlook reflects the expectation of a continued moderate industry recovery.

A copy of Standard & Poor's complete presale report for this transaction can be found on RatingsDirect, Standard & Poor's Web-based credit analysis system, at www.ratingsdirect.com. The presale can also be found on Standard & Poor's Web site at www.standardandpoors.com. Select Credit Ratings, and then find the article under Presale Credit Reports.

PRELIMINARY RATINGS ASSIGNED
ACG Trust III

Class	Rating	Amount (mil. $)
G-1A	AAA/Stable*	1,620.0
B-1**	A-/Stable	117.5
C-1**	BBB-/Stable	122.5

*The 'AAA' rating is based on a financial guaranty policy provided by Ambac Assurance Corp., Finance Guaranty Insurance Co., and MBIA Insurance Corp., all

of which have an 'AAA' insurer financial enhancement rating. **The class B-1 and C-1 notes are subordinate and allow the deferral of interest payments.

FitchRatings
KNOW YOUR RISK

Structured Finance

Asset-Backed
Presale Report

CNH Equipment Trust 2006-A

Expected Ratings

Class	Amount ($ Mil.)	Expected Rating	CE (%)*
A-1	293.0	'F1+'	4.60
A-2	280.0	'AAA'	4.60
A-3	360.0	'AAA'	4.60
A-4	181.4	'AAA'	4.60
B	35.7	'A'	1.50

*Does not include excess spread. CE – Credit enhancement.

Analysts
Transaction
Du Trieu
+1 312 368-2091
du.trieu@fitchratings.com

Bradley Sohl
+1 312 368-3127
bradley.sohl@fitchratings.com

Joseph S. Tuczak
+1 312 368-2083
joseph.tuczak@fitchratings.com

Performance Analytics
Peter Manofsky
+1 312 368-2068
peter.manofsky@fitchratings.com

Expected Closing Date
March 16, 2006

The preliminary ratings do not reflect final ratings and are based on information provided by the issuer as of Feb. 28, 2006. These preliminary ratings are contingent on final documents conforming to information already received. Collateral may be added or dropped from the portfolio. Ratings are not a recommendation to buy, sell or hold any security. The prospectus and other offering material should be reviewed prior to any purchase.

■ Summary
Fitch expects to rate the class A and B notes to be issued by CNH Equipment Trust 2006-A as listed at left. The notes will be backed by retail installment sales contracts on new and used agricultural and construction equipment originated by CNH Capital America LLC (CNH Capital). The 2006-A transaction will be the 14th U.S. public securitization issued by CNH Capital LLC that includes receivables originated by CNH Capital.

The expected ratings are based on the following:

- Available credit enhancement: the class A notes will be supported by subordination (3.10% class B notes), a cash reserve account funded at 1.50% of the initial pool balance upon closing that will grow and be maintained at the greater of 1.50% of the initial pool balance and the balance of all subsequent receivables or 1.50% of the outstanding receivables balance, and excess spread.
- Role of New Holland Credit (New Holland) as master servicer.
- The integrity of the legal structure.
- Cash flow stress test results.

■ Strengths
- Obligor and geographic diversity, which helps mitigate the effects of any regional construction or agricultural downturns.
- Higher concentration of annual pay contracts, which historically have performed better than other payment types.
- New Holland Credit's experience as a servicer, as demonstrated by consistent loss performance.
- The CNH Capital dealership networks, which greatly aid the collection, repossession and remarketing processes.

■ Concerns
- A potentially weak economic environment may accelerate near-term repossessions and losses.
- Uncertainty as to ongoing support from FIAT S.p.A., which owns approximately 85% of the stock of CNH Global N.V. (CNH). Fitch's rating of FIAT S.p.A. was affirmed at 'BB–' and the Outlook was upgraded to Stable from Negative on Jan. 20, 2006.

March 6, 2006

www.fitchratings.com

FitchRatings
KNOW YOUR RISK

Structured Finance

■ **Noteworthy Changes**

• **Decline in Enhancement Levels:** Initial enhancement has been reduced by 65 basis points (bps) for the class A notes and 125 bps for the class B notes from the closing levels in the CNH 2005-B transaction. The 2006-A transaction will not include a class C tranche, which provided subordination for the class A and B notes in the prior transactions. These reductions in enhancement are the net result of changes in the size of the class B notes (decrease of 60 bps), removal of class C notes (decline of 100 bps) and a reduction in the reserve account of 25 bps.

When sizing enhancement levels, Fitch took into consideration, among other things, the continually improving static-loss performance of both new and used agricultural and construction equipment, the collateral characteristics and certain structural features of the 2006-A transaction. These features include a $387 million prefunding amount (approximately 33.6% of initial receivables). Fitch notes that, given the size of the prefunding amount, the addition of new loans should not significantly

affect closing date pool characteristics and concentrations.

• **Shifting Payment Priority:** The 2006-A transaction incorporates a shifting payment priority, where initially principal is distributed sequentially between the class A and B notes. However, if the class A notes are ever undercollateralized, interest allocable to the class B notes is made available to pay class A principal (see the Principal Allocation section on page 7). Once collateralization is restored, the class B notes will resume interest payments. The 2005-B transaction included a fully sequential payment priority.

• **Reserve Account Step-Down Trigger:** Similar to the 2005-B transaction, the 2006-A structure incorporates a reserve step-down feature whereby the reserve account will step down by 25 bps (floored) to 1.25% in month 24 or 30, as long as the collateral performs as expected and does not hit certain defined performance triggers. In the 2005-B transaction, the reserve account stepped down 25 bps (capped) on the 18th, 24th or 30th month. The step-down trigger is fully explained in the Reserve Account section on page 6.

• **The Discount Rate:** The discount rate utilized in the 2006-A transaction is 7.80%, 80 bps greater than the 2005-B transaction. However, excess spread remains virtually the same in the 2006-A transaction (1.65% per annum [p.a.]) when compared with the 2005-B transaction (1.62% p.a.).

Deal Structure

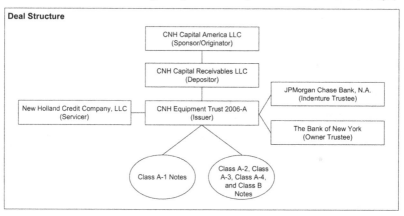

CNH Equipment Trust 2006-A

FitchRatings
KNOW YOUR RISK

Structured Finance

■ CNH Global N.V.
- **Role:** Parent of seller/servicer.
- **Risk to Transaction:** As parent company of servicer, bankruptcy may invoke a servicer transfer.
- **Mitigants:** Strong financial performance and condition.

CNH is a leading manufacturer of agricultural and construction equipment whose products (including brands such as Case, Case IH, New Holland and Kobelco) are sold in more than 160 countries through a network of more than 11,400 dealers and distributors worldwide. CNH was formed in 1999 in connection with New Holland N.V.'s acquisition of Case Corporation.

CNH's three primary business segments are as follows:

- **Agricultural Equipment:** CNH manufactures a broad range of equipment used in farm and livestock operations, as well as equipment for large-scale growers, utility producers, and orchard and livestock operations.
- **Construction Equipment:** CNH manufactures heavy construction and light industrial equipment for use in road building, mining, demolition, excavation and commercial building.
- **Financial Services:** CNH Capital and New Holland Credit provide financing for new and used agricultural, construction and other equipment to

dealers and customers. Various forms of insurance are also available to customers and dealers to help support the purchase and lease of equipment.

As of Dec., 31 2005, CNH reported revenues of $12.6 billion. FIAT S.p.A. owns approximately 85% of the stock of CNH. (For more information, see the press release, "Fitch Affirms Fiat's Ratings On Deal With GM," dated Feb. 14, 2004, and available on Fitch's Web site at www.fitchratings.com.).

■ CNH Capital America LLC
- **Role:** Seller (CNH Capital)/servicer (New Holland Credit)
- **Risk to Transaction:** New Holland Credit as servicer, transaction's performance is strongly tied to New Holland maintaining servicing rights.
- **Mitigants:** Stresses and credit enhancement, as well as New Holland's experience as a servicer on prior transactions.

On Dec. 31, 2004, Case Credit Corporation was converted into CNH Capital, which is an indirect wholly owned subsidiary of CNH and provides financing to customers and dealers for the purchase and lease of CNH equipment. New Holland Credit is an indirect, wholly owned subsidiary of CNH and provides equipment financing to customers and dealers. As servicer of the 2006-A transaction, New Holland Credit will receive a servicing fee each month equal to one-twelfth of 1.00% of the pool balance as of the first day of the preceding calendar month.

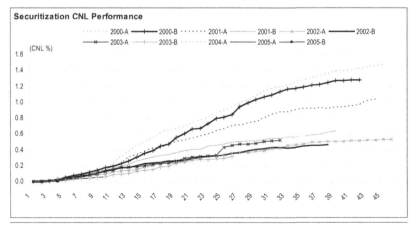

CNH Equipment Trust 2006-A

FitchRatings

Structured Finance

■ Legal Structure

Fitch believes the legal structure of the transaction ensures that the bankruptcy of CNH would not impair the timeliness of payments on the securities. Fitch expects to receive and review legal opinions to the effect that the transfer of loans to the trust will constitute a true sale and not a secured financing and that the assets of CNH 2006-A would not be consolidated with the assets of CNH in the event of the bankruptcy of CNH. Furthermore, Fitch expects to receive an opinion of counsel that the trustee will have a first perfected security interest in the assets transferred to CNH 2006-A.

■ Portfolio Performance

CNH Historical Portfolio Performance

Historical delinquency and loss performance on CNH's captive portfolio is presented in the table on page 9. Delinquency, repossession and loss rates on agricultural and construction equipment have experienced downward trends over the past four years. Total delinquencies were 2.22% of the portfolio at year-end 2005, down from 2.35% at year-end 2004, and 3.41% in 2003. Net losses as a percentage of the CNH's portfolio have remained almost unchanged at 0.46% in 2005,

versus year-end 2004 (0.47%). Net losses in 2003 and 2002 were 0.69% and 0.93%, respectively.

As delinquency, repossession and loss rates fluctuate with the economy, Fitch factored into its analysis the effect of a weak economic environment on pool performance when determining an expected base-case loss rate, stress multiples and stressed recovery rates used in the cash flow analysis to size credit-enhancement levels. (For more detail on specific assumptions used, see the Credit Enhancement section on page 5.)

■ Securitization History

CNH 2006-A will be the 14th U.S. public securitization issued by CNH. Fitch has rated eight prior transactions. As part of its funding strategy, CNH comes to the asset-backed securitization (ABS) market several times per year.

■ Collateral Analysis

The notes will be backed primarily by a pool of retail installment sales contracts on new and used agricultural and construction equipment originated by CNH Capital. Noteworthy differences in the underlying collateral of CNH 2006-A from prior transactions are listed below.

Collateral Comparison
(%)

	2006-A	2005-B	2005-A	2004-A	2003-B
Initial Statistical Contract Value ($)	810,394,179	634,064,454	929,984,960	1,218,743,947	687,386,393
Initial Receivables as % of Total	70.47	52.47	78.09	89.90	89.80
Number of Contracts	26,805	22,302	45,227	48,376	28,899
Average Contract Balance ($)	30,233	28,431	20,563	25,193	23,786
Retail Installment Sales Contracts	100	100	100	100	100
Weighted-Average Annual Percentage Rate	5.04	4.69	5.31	4.21	4.50
Weighted-Average Original Term (Months)	53.72	52.30	53.84	52.40	52.70
Weighted-Average Remaining Term (Months)	47.69	50.33	43.45	49.10	48.80
Weighted-Average Seasoning (Months)	6.03	1.97	10.39	3.30	3.90
Equipment					
Agricultural	68.66	69.49	70.16	73.59	73.26
New	38.79	48.86	38.44	45.38	40.47
Used	29.87	22.63	31.72	28.21	32.79
Construction	31.34	30.51	29.83	26.42	26.74
New	23.73	22.82	22.73	20.15	20.71
Used	7.61	7.69	7.10	6.27	6.03
Payment Frequency					
Monthly	42.82	50.59	44.45	49.16	46.51
Annual	48.03	40.03	46.17	42.41	42.78
Other (Semiannual, Quarterly and Irregular)	9.16	9.38	9.37	8.43	10.71
Geographic Concentrations					
Largest State	6.99 (IA)	7.44 (TX)	6.37 (IL)	7.10 (TX)	5.42 (TX)
Second-Largest State	6.53 (IL)	4.64 (IL)	6.20 (TX)	4.64 (IL)	5.18 (IL)
Third-Largest State	6.25 (TX)	4.61 (CA)	5.86 (IA)	4.38 (CA)	5.15 (CA)
Fourth-Largest State	5.16 (MN)	4.51 (MN)	4.93 (MN)	4.31 (AR)	4.97 (PA)
Fifth-Largest State	4.89 (CA)	3.59 (IA)	4.58 (CA)	4.27 (PA)	4.01 (AR)

CNH Equipment Trust 2006-A

FitchRatings

Structured Finance

Collateral Attributes

Equipment Type – Stable

The split between agricultural and construction equipment in the 2006-A transaction is comparable with the 2005-B transaction. However, there is a higher percentage of used agricultural equipment: 29.87% versus 22.63% in the 2005-B transaction. The concentration in the 2006-A, however, is consistent with prior transactions, which have been composed of approximately 30% used agricultural equipment. Used agricultural equipment loss experience is similar to new agricultural equipment; therefore, the 2006-A transaction's performance should be in-line with prior transactions.

Geographic Concentration – Stable

Consistent with prior transactions, the largest concentrations of loans are located in Iowa (7.0%), Illinois (6.5%), Texas (6.3%), Minnesota (5.2%) California (4.9%) and Indiana (4.0%). No other state accounts for more than 4.0% of the pool. Geographic diversification is important to shield the pool from rolling recessions and regional economic downturns.

Loan Attributes

Seasoning, Contract Balance and APR – Stable to Improving

Installment sales contracts in the 2006-A transaction are noticeably more seasoned (approximately 6.18 months versus 1.97 months in the 2005-B transaction). The 2006-A transaction has higher seasoning due to the addition of $64 million in seasoned and significantly amortized contracts from the CNH 2002-A transaction that was called in January 2006. The average contract balance ($30,233) is slightly higher when compared with the 2005-B transaction's average contract balance of $28,431. The weighted-average annual percentage rate in the 2006-A transaction is 5.04%, which is higher than in the 2005-B transaction (4.69%), but still results in the same amount of excess spread.

Payment Frequency – Decreasing

Payment frequency in the 2006-A transaction is slightly lumpier due to an increase in annual pay contracts, comprising 48.03% of the pool, versus 40.03% in the prior transaction. Although the 2006-A annual pay concentration is the highest, dating back to the 2002-A transaction, the increase is mitigated

by the fact these contracts historically have performed the best.

■ Credit Analysis

Annual Static Pool Review

Fitch took into consideration both quantitative and qualitative factors in evaluating CNH's credit-enhancement structure. Fitch reviewed historical annual repossession, delinquency and net loss data on CNH's managed portfolio, as well as static pool performance data from prior CHN securitizations to develop an expected loss rate.

Loss Estimate

Fitch expects performance to be consistent with historical managed portfolio net losses, which have ranged from 0.29%–1.54%. On a securitization basis, net losses have ranged from 0.01%–1.48% for transactions dating back to 2000. Based on the collateral characteristics and the economic environment, Fitch anticipates lifetime losses will be consistent with historical averages.

Credit Enhancement

To achieve high investment-grade ratings, credit enhancement is needed to protect securityholders against the realization of losses due to poor collateral performance. Credit-enhancement levels were based on several qualitative and quantitative factors. Risk factors influencing performance may include the following:

Equipment Descriptions

Agricultural Equipment: Agricultural equipment (68.66%) underlying the receivables generally includes tractors, combines, cotton pickers, soil management equipment, planting and seeding equipment, hay and forage equipment, crop care equipment (e.g., sprayers and irrigation) and small telescopic handlers.

Construction Equipment: Construction equipment (31.34%) underlying the receivables generally includes excavators, backhoes, wheel loaders, skid steer loaders, tractor loaders, trenchers, horizontal directional drilling equipment, telescopic handlers, forklifts, compaction equipment, crawlers and cranes.

FitchRatings
KNOW YOUR RISK

Structured Finance

- National or regional economic downturns;
- Weather, commodity prices and crop yields could affect agricultural equipment borrowers;
- Interest rates, housing starts, and government and private appropriations could affect construction equipment borrowers ; and
- Inattentive servicing or a servicing transfer.

The senior notes are supported by subordination (3.10% class B notes), a cash reserve initially set at 1.50% and maintained at the greater of 1.50% of the initial balance and the balance of all subsequent receivables or 1.50% of the outstanding balance, and initial excess spread of approximately 1.65% on an annual basis. Total excess spread over the life of the transaction is expected to be approximately 2.95% (1.65% times a 1.79-year weighted-average life).

Reserve Account
Amounts in the reserve account on each payment date will be available to cover shortfalls in distributions of principal and interest on the notes. On the closing date, the reserve account will be funded with an amount equal to 1.50% of the initial receivables balance. The reserve account will grow and be maintained at greater than 1.50% of the initial receivables balance and the balance of all subsequent receivables or 1.50% of the outstanding receivables balance through the trapping of excess spread. The nondeclining feature of the reserve account provides additional credit enhancement over time to protect noteholders.

Similar to the 2005-B transaction, the reserve account in the 2006-A transaction incorporates a reserve step-down feature whereby the reserve account will step down by 25 bps (floored) at a predefined period, as long as the collateral performs as expected and does not hit certain defined performance triggers. The required reserve account amount will decrease 25 bps from 1.50% to 1.25%, with a target of 1.50% of the outstanding pool balance at month 24. The step-down feature in the 2005-B transaction began in month 18 and also in months 24 and 30 if the step down feature was not utilized earlier. The specified spread account reduction triggers are shown in the table at right.

Excess Spread
Annual excess spread in the CNH 2006-A transaction is anticipated to be approximately 1.65%, which, as mentioned earlier, is slightly higher than the 1.62% annual excess spread in the CNH 2005-B transaction.

Expected Initial Annual Excess Spread (%)

7.80	WAC on collateral
(5.13)	WA note coupon (expected)
2.67	
(1.02)	Servicing and back-up servicing fee (annual)
1.65	Initial annual excess spread (expected)

WAC – Weighted-average coupon. WA – Weighted average.

■ **Cash Flow Modeling**
Fitch analyzed cash flows reflecting stressed default rates, recovery rates and recovery timing lags under several default timing scenarios. Fitch derived an expected loss rate based on an analysis of annual performance data (see the table on page 9) and static pool performance data from CNH's managed portfolio and prior securitizations (as shown in the chart on page 3). As the 2006-A pool will not include receivables originated by non-CNH dealers, Fitch also took into consideration the more favorable historical performance of receivables originated by CNH dealers.

In addition, Fitch's analysis took into consideration the current nature of the agricultural industry and the cyclicality of the construction industry to assess the effect of an economic downturn on the frequency of repossessions and on recovery rates (and timing lags) on repossessed equipment.

Modeling Comments
- Recovery rate of 40%.
- Six-month recovery lag.
- Even, back-end and front-end loaded loss-timing scenarios.
- Delinquency rate stress (50 bps) applied to servicing fee.
- Stresses on expected prepayment speeds (20%) to reduce the availability of excess spread.

Specified Spread Account Reduction Triggers

Month	Three-Month Average 61+ Delinquency Ratio (%)	Cumulative Net Loss Ratio (%)
24	2.50	0.55
30	3.00	0.65

Structured Finance

Expected Credit Enhancement
(%)

Class	% of Total	Subordination	Cash Reserve	Expected Credit Enhancement Excluding Excess Spread
Class A	96.9	3.1	1.5	4.6
Class B	3.1	N.A.	1.5	1.5

N.A. – Not applicable.

Stress Scenarios Results
The break-even losses sustained by the enhancement structure were then compared with Fitch's expected loss rate stressed by a multiplier consistent with the rating being sought. Under Fitch's 'AAA' scenario, the class A notes were able to withstand 5.0 times (x) the expected net loss rate. The class B notes sustained more than a 3.0x stress scenario. Fitch reviewed all cash flow runs to verify that each class of notes would be paid in full by its respective legal final maturity date.

■ **Structural Considerations**

Prefunding Account
Approximately $387 million of the proceeds from the sale of the notes was deposited into a segregated trust account that will be used from time to time to purchase additional receivables, subject to certain eligibility criteria, for addition to the trust pool. Funds remaining in the account after June 15, 2006, will be used to make principal payments on the notes. A capitalized interest account was also funded with proceeds from the sale of the notes. This account will be used to cover interest shortfalls attributable to any negative carry during the prefunding period. Funds remaining after the end of the prefunding period will be released to the seller.

Based on historical origination volume, subsequent receivables added to the trust during the prefunding period have characteristics comparable with the initial receivables as of the transaction's closing date

Named Back-Up Servicer
Systems & Services Technologies, Inc. (SST) is the named back-up servicer for the 2006-A transaction. Initially, the back-up servicer will obtain data and systems information from the servicer's servicing system, in addition to confirming that such data are readable by the back-up servicer, and will map the data to its systems. Additionally, the servicer will provide the back-up servicer with data from the servicer's servicing system on a monthly basis. Within 10 business days of the receipt of the data, the back-up servicer is expected

to use its best efforts to identify any discrepancies or confirm that the information concerning delinquency aging, defaults and month-end contract value contained in the monthly servicer report distributed by the servicer corresponds with the monthly data provided to the back-up servicer. SST will receive a fee of 2 bps for these activities. In the event SST was to take over servicing, it would receive the greater of the following: one-twelfth of 2 bps of the pool balance as of the first day of the preceding calendar month; $8.50 per contract in the trust as of the first day of the applicable calendar month; or $4,000. A servicer transfer will be triggered if CNH files for bankruptcy or an event of default occurs. A $150,000 reserve account will also be funded upon closing and available only to pay certain expenses and fees associated with the back-up servicer.

Interest Allocation
Interest will be allocated pro rata among the class A and B notes on the 15th of every month (or the next business day), starting in April 2006.

Principal Allocation
Principal will be allocated sequentially among the class A and B notes on the 15th of every month, starting in April 2006. In addition, if the class A notes are ever undercollateralized or if the maturity of the notes has been accelerated after an event of default, interest allocable to the class B notes is made available to pay class A principal. Once collateralization is restored, the class B notes will resume interest payments.

Payment Waterfall
The trustee will generally distribute funds in the following order of priority:

- Back-up servicing fee (2.0 bps).
- Servicing fee.
- Administration fee, payable to the administrator.
- Class A interest.
- To pay principal on the class A notes in an amount equal to the excess of (x) the outstanding principal balances of the class A notes over (y) the asset balance.

FitchRatings
KNOW YOUR RISK

Structured Finance

- Class B interest.
- To pay principal on the notes in an amount equal to the note monthly principal distributable amount.
- Reserve account deposit, up to the required amount.
- Certain indemnities of a successor servicer and any accrued expenses of the back-up servicer.
- The remaining balance, if any, to the certificateholders, initially CNH.

Events of Default

To protect the bondholders from issuer insolvency or deterioration in credit, the structure includes several events of default. Fitch believes the occurrence of these events is unlikely.

Any of the following constitutes an event of default under the indenture, which can result in all accrued interest and unpaid principal becoming due and payable immediately:

- A default in the payment of interest to the rated notes for five consecutive business days.
- A default in the payment of principal when due and payable.
- Failure to perform any covenant or agreement of the trust in the indenture within specified cure periods.
- Failure to cure any incorrect representation or warranty made by the trust in the indenture within specified cure periods.
- Certain events of bankruptcy, insolvency, receivership or liquidation of the trust.

Following an event of default related to either a default in payment of principal or a default for five days or more in the payment of interest on any class of notes that has resulted in an acceleration of the notes, class B noteholders will not receive interest until payment in full of principal and interest on the class A notes.

Loss Allocation

Losses stemming from defaulted receivables will be covered by the enhancement in the following order:
- Excess spread.
- Reserve account.
- Class B notes.
- Class A notes.

■ Operations Review

Originations

The collateral in the 2006-A transaction was initially originated through independently owned dealerships that have entered into a retail financing agreement allowing them to sell contracts and leases to CNH Capital. Approximately 1,400 Case Credit and New Holland Credit dealers are located in the United States. Dealerships are subject to periodic financial review and may be terminated due to either a lack of volume or a violation of the dealer responsibilities in the retail financing agreement.

Underwriting

Credit applications are sent to one central finance office for review and risk-rating assessment. Part of this review includes credit scoring by a credit model that incorporates variables predictive of future loan performance. Previously, CNH Capital utilized a Fair, Isaac & Co., Inc. (FICO)-based scoring system installed in 1994, and New Holland Credit used an Experian-based scoring system that was originally installed in 1997. However, in April 2002, an integrated Experian-based model, developed using CNH Capital's customer database, was implemented for both CNH Capital and New Holland Credit applications. Additionally, the underwriting criteria now focus solely on receivables originated through the captive dealer network.

In addition to the credit-scoring model, credit bureau reports, bank or trade references and, in some cases, financial statements are reviewed during the underwriting process. Credit managers have an average of more than 10 years of underwriting experience and are aligned by usage (agricultural and construction) rather than by brand. Collateral- and application-specific guidelines are also incorporated into the underwriting process. Guidelines for used equipment (which represents approximately 38.56% of the 2006-A pool) typically require shorter terms and higher down payments. Obligors are also required to obtain physical damage insurance on the equipment.

Collections and Servicing

Servicing, collection and customer service activities are based out of regional centers in Wisconsin and Pennsylvania. Delinquent customers are generally contacted by phone at 10 days past due; however, they may be contacted sooner if the obligors have had problems in the past. Letters are also sent if telephone

FitchRatings
KNOW YOUR RISK

Structured Finance

Credit Loss/Repossession/Delinquency Experience — Excluding Non-CNH*
(Years Ended Dec. 31)

	2005	2004	2003	2002	2001
Average Portfolio Outstanding ($)	4,772.50	4,494.80	4,434.50	4,616.40	4,824.40
Repossessions (%)	0.76	1.02	1.55	1.93	1.95
Net Loss as % of Liquidations	0.94	0.90	1.23	1.66	1.59
Net Loss (%)	0.46	0.47	0.69	0.93	0.87
Portfolio Outstanding ($)	4,914.10	4,630.80	4,358.70	4,510.30	4,772.50
Total Delinquent ($)	109.10	109.00	148.70	214.60	251.20
Total Delinquent (%)	2.22	2.35	3.41	4.76	5.32

*All performance data exclude the effect of financing receivables from non-CNH Global N.V. dealers.

contact is not successful. The local dealer is typically contacted at 45 days past due and may assist in the collection process by visiting the obligor and/or developing collection strategies specific to an obligor and that obligor's financial situation. At 60 days past due, general procedures to prepare for repossession are initiated. Outside companies may also be utilized to locate a customer and/or the equipment.

Repossession

At 90 days past due, repossession of the equipment will generally take place, often with the assistance of the local dealership. Once repossessed, the equipment is generally taken to a secure location and inspected to assess its value. Repairs may also be done at this point to enhance the resale value of the equipment. Dealerships are notified of used equipment that is currently or will soon be available. Most recoveries on repossessed equipment are realized through resale on the equipment at auctions.

Loss Recognition

At 120 days past due, a receivable is treated as nonperforming. For purposes of the securitization, losses will be recognized when a receivable is liquidated through sale or other disposition, which typically occurs within 30–60 days after the equipment is repossessed.

Extensions

An obligor experiencing a temporary cash flow problem may request an extension or deferral of one or more installment payments. Extensions are given on a case-by-case basis and will only be granted if it can be determined that the obligor can meet its obligation once rescheduled and that there is sufficient security in the equipment. Loans with seasonal payment schedules require a minimum curtailment of the original installment amount as a condition of extension. The allowed duration of the extension is a function of the outstanding balance and requires various levels of authorization. Extensions and modifications are rarely granted.

CNH Equipment Trust 2006-A

FitchRatings
KNOW YOUR RISK

Structured Finance

Asset-Backed
Presale Report

CIT Equipment Collateral 2006-VT1

Expected Ratings

Class	Amount ($ Mil.)	Expected Rating	CE (%)
A-1	330.00	'F1+'	14.25
A-2	179.00	'AAA'	14.25
A-3	330.00	'AAA'	14.25
A-4	93.53	'AAA'	14.25
B	22.68	'AA'	12.00
C	22.68	'A'	9.75
D	30.25	'BBB'	6.75

CE – Credit enhancement.

Analysts

Transaction

Brigid E. Fitzgerald
+1 312 606-2361
brigid.fitzgerald@fitchratings.com

John Bella, Jr.
+1 212 908-0243
john.bella@fitchratings.com

Performance Analytics
Peter Manofsky
+1 312 368-2068
peter.manofsky@fitchratings.com

Expected Closing Date
March 23, 2006

The preliminary ratings do not reflect final ratings and are based on information provided by issuers as of March 9, 2006. These preliminary ratings are contingent on final documents conforming to information already received. Collateral may be added or dropped from the portfolio. Ratings are not a recommendation to buy, sell or hold any security. The prospectus and other offering material should be reviewed prior to any purchase.

■ Summary
Fitch expects to rate the class A, B, C and D notes to be issued by CIT Equipment Collateral 2006-VT1 (CITEC 2006-VT1) as listed at left. The notes will be backed by equipment lease contracts on new and used technology and other small-ticket equipment originated or acquired by the commercial business units of the Specialty Finance (SF) segment of CIT Group Inc. (CIT). The expected ratings address the likelihood that noteholders will receive full payments of interest and principal in accordance with the terms of the transaction. The expected ratings are based on the following:

- Initial credit enhancement (CE) equal to 14.25% for the class A notes (7.5% subordination, 6.75% initial cash collateral account [CCA] deposit), initial CE of 12.00% for the class B notes (5.25% subordination, 6.75% initial CCA), 9.75% initial CE for the class C notes (3.0% subordination, 6.75% initial CCA) and initial CE for the class D notes provided by the 6.75% initial CCA.
- Target CE with the reserve account growing to 7.75% of the outstanding contract principal balance (CPB) and an initial floor of 3.00% of the original CPB, subject to step down.
- The integrity of the legal structure.
- Cash flow stress test results.

■ Strengths
- Financial strength of CIT ('A'/'F1') as seller/servicer.
- Improving performance of the originators' managed portfolio and previous securitizations.
- Dell Financial Services' (DFS, 57.41% of pool) and Snap-On Tools' (2.48%) collateral have never suffered a net loss within securitizations due to reserves.
- Diverse geographic concentrations.
- Structural features, including subordinate note floors and a cumulative net loss trigger.

■ Concerns
- Vendor concentrations (76.32% DFS and Avaya, Inc.).
- Equipment concentrations (75.56% computers and telecommunications).

March 13, 2006

FitchRatings
KNOW YOUR RISK

Structured Finance

Transaction Structure

CIT Financial USA, Inc.
(Originator and Servicer)

100%
Ownership

*Leases, Loans,
and Equipment*

Proceeds

CIT Funding Company

*Leases
And Loans*

Proceeds

CITEC 2006 VT1

Notes

Proceeds

CITEC 2006 VT1 Investors

CITEC 2006-VT1– CIT Equipment Collateral 2006 VT1.

■ Noteworthy Changes

Initial Credit Enhancement
Initial CE levels are lower by 62.5 basis points (bps) for the class A notes, 62.5 bps lower for the class B notes, 87.5 bps lower for the class C notes and 37.5 bps lower for the class D notes versus CITEC 2005-VT1. Lower CE levels are primarily due to performance improvements within the SF managed and securitized portfolios, as well as the higher concentration of DFS assets, the best performing origination source on a net basis.

CCA Step-Down Feature
At close, the CITEC 2006-VT1 CCA will be initially funded at 6.75% of the original CPB and, thereafter, targeted at 7.75% of the outstanding CPB. The initial CCA level is a 37.5 bps reduction versus the CITEC 2005-VT1 initial funding of 7.125%. Meanwhile, the targeted 7.75%, and 3.00% CCA floor (prior to step-down) remain consistent with the prior transaction.

New to the 2006-VT1 structure is the CCA stepdown. This feature enables the CCA to step down by 0.25%/0.25%/0.25%, respectively, on three specific payment dates if the transaction performs within predetermined performance metrics (see page 5).

CIT Equipment Collateral
2006-VT1

Parties to Transaction
Issuer: CIT Equipment Collateral 2006-VT1
Indenture Trustee: Bank of New York
Servicer: CIT Financial USA, Inc.

Tighter Sequential Trigger Levels
Similar to the CITEC 2005-VT1 transaction, CITEC 2006-VT1 will feature a cumulative net loss trigger that alters the payment priority to full sequential pay if certain loss levels are surpassed at designated intervals. The measurement intervals will remain the same for CITEC 2006-VT1; however, the net loss amounts have been reduced by as much as 1.00%, primarily at the tail end of the transaction. The sequential trigger protects the noteholders in the event that the CITEC 2006-VT1 portfolio performs outside of expectations, while the tighter levels are the result of lower cumulative net loss expectations relative to prior transactions.

■ CIT Group Inc.
- **Role:** Parent of seller/servicer.
- **Risk to Transaction:** As parent company of servicer, bankruptcy may invoke a servicer transfer.
- **Mitigants:** Strong financial performance and condition.

CIT is a diversified finance company engaging in vendor, equipment, commercial, consumer and structured financing and leasing activities. Rated 'A' by Fitch's Financial Institutions group, CIT was founded in 1908, and has more than $60 billion in assets under management. CIT possesses the financial resources, industry expertise and product knowledge to serve the needs of clients across approximately 30 industries and operates extensively in the United States and Canada, with strategic locations in Europe, Latin and South America, and the Pacific Rim. CIT is a Fortune 500 company and a component of the S&P 500 Index. At Dec. 31, 2005, stockholders' equity totaled $6.96 billion.

■ CIT Financial USA, Inc.
- **Role:** Seller/servicer.
- **Risk to Transaction:** As servicer, transaction's performance is strongly tied to CIT Financial maintaining servicing rights.
- **Mitigants:** Stresses and CE, as well as CIT Financial's experience as a servicer on prior transactions.

2

FitchRatings
KNOW YOUR RISK

Structured Finance

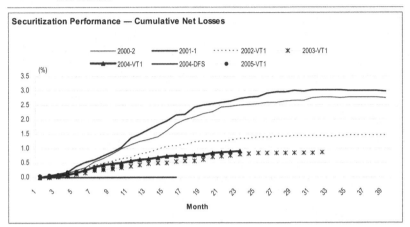

Securitization Performance — Cumulative Net Losses

CIT Financial USA, Inc., which is a wholly owned subsidiary of CIT, is the seller and servicer for this transaction. The equipment contracts serving as collateral for the CITEC 2006-VT1 transaction were originated under the SF/vendor technology (VT) portfolio of CIT Financial USA. Through various contract purchase agreements, profit-sharing arrangements and joint ventures, CIT Financial USA both originates and purchases equipment contracts from select vendors. As servicer of the CITEC 2006-VT1 transaction, CIT Financial USA will receive a servicing fee each month equal to one-twelfth of 0.75% of the CPB as of the first day of the related collection period.

■ Legal Structure

Fitch believes the legal structure of the transaction ensures that the bankruptcy of CIT would not impair the timeliness of payments on the securities. Fitch expects to receive and review legal opinions to the effect that the transfer of loans to the trust will constitute a true sale and not a secured financing and that the assets of CITEC 2006-VT1 would not be consolidated with the assets of CIT in the event of the bankruptcy of CIT. Furthermore, Fitch expects to receive an opinion of counsel that the trustee will have a first perfected security interest in the assets transferred to CITEC 2006-VT1.

■ Portfolio Performance

Historical Portfolio Performance

Historical delinquency and loss performance on similar contracts within CIT's managed portfolio is presented in the table on page 6. Since 2002, the SF/VT portfolio has demonstrated continued improvement from both a delinquency and loss perspective. In addition to a rebound in the economy, CIT notes that factors behind the performance improvements include continued stability of the portfolio's management and servicing environment and the overall vendor and industry mix.

The average year-end delinquency rate since 2002 has been 3.62%, with annual losses of 0.95%, 50%, 0.41% and 0.28% in 2002, 2003, 2004 and 2005, respectively. Such delinquency and loss rates are toward the low end of industry averages (see the Delinquency and Loss table on page 6).

■ Securitization History and Performance

CIT Equipment Collateral 2006-VT1 represents the sixth equipment lease securitization of assets generated by CIT's SF segment since the business unit's formation in 2001 and the ninth securitization backed by small-ticket equipment contracts since the acquisition of Newcourt Credit Group Inc. (Newcourt) by CIT in November 1999.

FitchRatings
KNOW YOUR RISK

Structured Finance

Collateral Comparison

	CITEC 06-VT1 ($ Bil.)	CITEC 05-VT1 ($ Mil.)	CITEC 04-VT1 ($ Mil.)	CITEC 03-VT1 ($ Mil)	CITEC 02-VT1 ($ Bil.)	CITEC 01-1 ($ Mil.)
CPB	1.01	804.68	936.72	869.08	1.07	844.05
Number of Contracts	74,262	61,944	62,780	62,416	73,864	47,846
Average Balance	13,576	12,990	14,921	13,924	14,435	17,641
WAOT	43.0	45.0	44.0	45.0	44.0	44.0
WART	37.0	38.0	36.9	39.0	38.0	41.0
WAS	6.0	7.0	7.1	6.0	6.0	4.0
Business Unit (%)						
Dell	57.41	46.82	48.63	47.60	49.55	41.83
Avaya	21.20	29.25	30.62	35.76	34.30	36.15
Small Ticket	18.91	20.45	18.30	12.85	12.64	13.99
Snap-On Tools	2.48	3.48	2.45	3.80	3.51	5.39
Equipment Types (%)						
Computers	60.70	49.70	51.41	50.34	54.00	47.25
Telecommunications	14.86	23.30	25.50	29.34	32.54	37.36
General Office	19.87	18.42	15.62	10.30	6.46	7.31
Customer Type (%)						
Service Organizations	48.04	45.27	42.30	41.29	38.66	38.09
Manufacturing/Construction	15.87	14.32	18.98	21.26	21.46	17.24
Retail and Wholesale	7.99	9.93	10.18	10.90	11.16	11.12

CPB – Contract principal balance. WAOT – Weighted-average original term. WART – Weighted-average remaining term. WAS – Weighted-average seasoning.

Similar to the managed portfolio, CIT's SF securitizations have shown marked reductions in the delinquency, default and loss columns. This positive trend and the resultant building of CE prompted Fitch to upgrade both the 2003-VT1 and 2004-VT1 transactions in December 2005. Both transactions are reporting losses and delinquencies at levels noticeably lower than prior deals. This improvement is representative of a broader macroeconomic upturn and is also a result of changes in underwriting criteria that took place over 2001 and 2002. In addition, as mentioned in the Historical Portfolio Performance section on page 3, consistency in management and servicing greatly contributed to the positive progression of the securitized figures.

■ Collateral Analysis
The underlying pool of contracts backing the CITEC 2006-VT1 notes consists primarily of equipment lease contracts. The initial CPB is approximately $1.01 billion. The pool contains 74,262 contracts with a weighted-average seasoning of approximately six months. For collateral characteristics of the 2006-VT1 transaction versus the prior five transactions, see the table above.

Borrower Concentrations – Weakening
The largest and top five largest obligors constitute approximately 1.74% and 6.35%, respectively, of the pool balance as of the cut-off date. Comparatively higher than the top one and five exposures of 1.50% and 5.21% for the CITEC 2005-VT1 transaction, the credit quality of the underlying obligors largely negates any concentration concerns.

Geographic Concentrations – Stable
Consistent with prior transactions, the largest concentrations of loans are located in California (11.57%), Texas (11.37%), New York (8.68%), Florida (8.58%) and New Jersey (5.61%). No other state accounts for more than 4.26% of the pool. Geographic diversification is important to shield the pool from rolling recessions and regional economic downturns.

Vendor Concentrations – Stable
Similar to CITEC 2005-VT1, approximately 76.3% of the CITEC 2006-VT1 transaction is related to two vendor relationships (DFS and Avaya). While CIT's historical performance demonstrates vendor efficiencies and recourse arrangements through certain joint-venture programs, future performance relies on the continued success of such programs.

CIT Equipment Collateral
2006-VT1

FitchRatings
KNOW YOUR RISK

Structured Finance

Credit Enhancement
(%)

Class	% of Total	Subordination	Initial Reserve Account	Total Expected CE*
Class A	92.50	7.50	6.75	14.25
Class B	2.25	5.25	6.75	12.00
Class C	2.25	3.00	6.75	9.75
Class D	3.00	—	6.75	6.75

*Total does not include expected increase in reserve account. CE – Credit enhancement.

Equipment Concentrations – Weakening
More than 75% of the CITEC 2006-VT1 collateral is related to computers and telecommunications equipment. This exposure is mitigated by diversification within other segments of the portfolio, such as by industry, geography and obligor. In addition, the majority of the top 10 obligors in the CITEC 2006-VT1 portfolio are investment-grade rated entities.

Industry Concentrations – Stable
Consistent with the prior transaction, the largest obligor industry exposure within the 2006-VT1 collateral pool is the services industry at 48.04%, followed by the manufacturing industry at 15.87%.

Seasoning – Weakening
The weighted-average remaining term is 37.1 months, resulting in 6.1 months of initial seasoning compared with the initial 7.3 months of aging in the 2005-VT1 transaction. Fitch took this into consideration when formulating the 2006-VT1 expected-loss figure, as pools with lower seasoning will likely experience higher cumulative net losses than a seasoned pool, since a portion of losses have occurred prior to securitization.

■ Credit Analysis

Annual and Static Pool Review
Fitch considered both quantitative and qualitative factors in evaluating the credit-enhancement structure of the CITEC 2006-VT1 transaction. Fitch reviewed the contributing business segments' delinquency and default histories on both a managed and a securitized basis, projecting cumulative defaults on pools that have not fully paid down using segment-specific loss-timing curves.

Ultimately, in determining the expected net loss proxy for the CITEC 2006-VT1 portfolio, Fitch first determined an expected gross default rate for each contributing segment. Subsequently, Fitch ascribed

segment-specific recovery rates and, finally, weighted the individual segment's expected losses by its 2006-VT1 portfolio proportion.

Loss Estimate
Fitch expects performance of the CITEC 2006-VT1 pool to remain within ranges established by historical securitization performance measures dating back to 1999. Based on the collateral characteristics, including vendor, equipment, obligor and industry concentrations, Fitch utilized a cumulative net loss assumption of 2.75% for the 2006-VT1 portfolio in its analysis in determining CE.

Credit Enhancement
To achieve high investment-grade ratings, CE is needed to protect securityholders against the realization of losses due to poor collateral performance. Risk factors influencing performance may include the following:

• National or regional economic downturns;
• Industry weakness resulting in higher defaults and lower recovery rates;
• Vendor or manufacturer bankruptcy; and
• Inattentive servicing or a servicing transfer.

The initial CE for the class A, B, C and D notes is 14.25%, 12.00%, 9.75% and 6.75%, respectively. Additionally, the reserve account will grow to a target 7.75% of the outstanding CPB and have a floor of 2.25% of the original CPB (after stepdown).

Cash Collateral Account
The CCA is a segregated trust account established by the indenture trustee for the benefit of the noteholders

CCA Stepdown
(%)

Payment Period	Cumulative Net Loss Test	Floor Reduction	Floor Amount
20	2.50	0.25	2.75
23	2.75	0.25	2.50
29	3.00	0.25	2.25

CIT Equipment Collateral
2006-VT1

FitchRatings
KNOW YOUR RISK

Structured Finance

Delinquency and Loss Performance — Specialty Finance
(%, Years Ended Dec. 31)

	2001	2002	2003	2004	2005
Aggregate Net Investment of Contracts ($ 000)	6,349,420	5,785,894	5,697,658	5,727,548	5,358,963
Period of Delinquency					
31–60 days	3.15	2.28	1.65	2.09	2.04
61–90 days	1.06	0.74	0.67	0.81	0.85
91+ days	1.36	0.83	0.76	0.93	0.90
Total Delinquencies	5.57	3.85	3.08	3.83	3.79
Gross Losses as a Percent of Net Investment	3.00	2.71	1.73	1.57	1.35
Recovery Percent	1.84	1.76	1.22	1.16	1.07
Net Losses as a Percent of Net Investment	1.15	0.95	0.5	0.41	0.28

Note: Numbers may not add due to rounding.

and may be used to pay interest and principal on the notes to the extent that amounts on deposit in the collection account are insufficient.

At closing, the CCA will be funded in an amount equal to 6.75% of the initial CPB, with a target amount of 7.75% of the outstanding CPB and a floor of 3.00% of the initial CPB prior to stepdowns. According to projected cash flows, the CCA should reach its target of 7.75% of outstanding CPB by May 20, 2006, which is the second payment date.

The 2006-VT1 CCA incorporates a step-down feature, whereby the CCA can step down by 0.25%/0.25%/0.25%, respectively, on three specific payment dates if the transaction performs within predetermined performance metrics.

■ Cash Flow Modeling
The cash flow model was customized to capture the structural features of the 2006-VT1 transaction. Stresses were applied to base-case performance assumptions and incorporated into the model to project the effects of deteriorating asset performance on noteholder cash flows.

Modeling Comments
• A six-month lag from default to recovery was implemented for all scenarios.
• Recovery rates were limited to 30% across rating categories.
• Loss-timing curves were adjusted to test the ability of the structure to withstand different default distributions, including front-, middle- and back-loaded loss curves.
• To incorporate a supplementary stress on the amount of cash available to cover losses and pay interest and principal on the notes, Fitch also

implemented a higher servicing fee within cash flow models.

Stress Scenarios Results
The break-even losses sustained by the enhancement structure were then compared with Fitch's expected-loss rate stressed by a multiplier consistent with the rating being sought. Under Fitch's 'AAA' scenarios, the class A notes were able to withstand a minimum of 4.5 times (x) the expected net loss rate. Meanwhile, the class B, C and D notes sustained more than a 4.0x, 3.0x and 2.0x stress in each relevant cash flow scenario. Under stress scenarios consistent with the ratings sought, the credit-enhancement structure was sufficient to ensure payment of the class A, B, C and D notes in accordance with the legal documents.

■ Structural Considerations

Priority of Payments
The owner trust will pay note principal and interest on each payment date from the available pledged revenues for the payment date, as well as allowable amounts withdrawn from the CCA. Interest and principal will be paid monthly, and principal on the notes will be paid on a pro rata basis between classes but distributed sequentially within class A.

Available pledged revenues will be allocated in the following order of priority:

• Reimbursement of servicer advances.
• Servicing fee.
• Interest on class A-1, A-2, A-3 and A-4 notes, including any overdue interest.
• Interest on class B notes.
• Interest on class C notes.

CIT Equipment Collateral
2006-VT1

FitchRatings
KNOW YOUR RISK

Structured Finance

- Interest on class D notes.
- Principal on class A notes, sequentially, beginning with class A-1 notes.
- Principal on class B notes.
- Principal on class C notes.
- Principal on class D notes.
- Any amount necessary to increase the CCA balance to its required level.
- Amounts payable in connection with the CCA.
- Any remainder to the holder of the equity certificate.

If an event of default occurs, all principal will be allocated to the most senior class of notes then outstanding. Repayment continues in this sequential manner until the outstanding principal balance of each class is reduced to zero.

Net Loss Trigger

The cumulative net loss amount is the ratio of the cumulative reported net losses since the initial cut-off date over the initial CPB. If on any payment date the amount of cumulative losses exceeds the trigger level for the applicable period, principal payments will be allocated sequentially to the senior-most class of notes then outstanding (principal payments are allocated pro rata between the class A-2, class A-3 and class A-4 notes under these circumstances once the class A-1 notes have been paid in full). Payment periods and their respective trigger levels are as shown in the table at right.

As demonstrated in the table, the cumulative net loss trigger is tested primarily at three-month intervals. Violation of the trigger can be cured upon the cumulative amount of net losses falling below the specified amount at any tested payment date. Any such cure reverts the sequential pay structure back to the modified pro rata payment priority.

Floors

Within CITEC 2006-VT1, each subordinate class is subject to a floor and, as long as any more senior class is outstanding, will not receive payments that would reduce its principal balance below its specified floor. A principal payment that would reduce the principal balance of a subordinate class below its floor is reallocated to the most senior class then outstanding.

For CITEC 2006-VT1, the levels of the subordinate class floors are variable and will increase if cumulative contract pool losses cannot be funded

Cumulative Net Loss Trigger
(%)

Payment Period	Cumulative Loss Trigger
1	0.50
2	0.50
5	1.00
8	1.75
11	2.75
14	3.25
17	4.00
20	4.25
23	5.00
26	5.25
29	5.25
32	5.50
35	5.50

from current available pledged revenues and the CCA. If losses become severe and credit-enhancement levels are reduced, the principal paydown would result in a sequential-pay senior subordinated structure among the various note classes.

■ Operations Review

Segment Overview and Originations

CIT conducts its operations through strategic business units that market products and services to satisfy the financing needs of specific customers, industries, vendors/manufacturers and markets. CIT is focused on serving midsized to large businesses through the following four business segments:

- Specialty Finance.
- Equipment Finance.
- Commercial Finance.
- Capital Finance.

The CITEC 2006-VT1 transaction will contain assets originated or acquired by the commercial business units of the Specialty Finance segment of CIT.

As of Dec. 31, 2005, SF's managed assets totaled $29 billion, representing 46.26% of CIT's total managed assets. The SF segment has total managed commercial assets of $14.3 billion, total managed consumer assets of $14.8 billion, new business volume in 2005 of $6.3 billion and more than 3.5 million customers worldwide.

SF's commercial business builds alliances with industry-leading vendors to deliver customized financing solutions to support manufacturers, dealers

FitchRatings
KNOW YOUR RISK

Structured Finance

and distributors in the sale or distribution of their products. Its primary market focus is on computer hardware, software and peripherals; voice, data and video communications; and electronics. The majority of these operations were acquired in the Newcourt transaction, with some operations having originated from AT&T Capital Corp. (Newcourt acquired AT&T Capital in 1998).

SF also consists of joint ventures and profit-sharing arrangements with top-tier manufacturers that benefit from CIT's sales financing programs while providing CIT with considerable volume on an annual basis. Manufacturers use CIT to reduce balance sheet and capital needs and simultaneously share credit risk and profitability. Through joint ventures, CIT has established partnerships with Dell, Inc. (Dell), Avaya (spun off from Lucent Technologies, Inc.), Snap-On Tools and others.

Underwriting

CIT utilizes a proprietary facility risk-grading system, which serves as the cornerstone for both CIT's and DFS's underwriting and credit-risk management processes. The risk-grading system is a credit-scoring model designed to provide a comprehensive review of the factors that affect the risk of a transaction. The system provides a systematic methodology for uniformly analyzing risk across the institution and comparing risk in different portfolios.

CIT's policy requires that all facilities be graded under the facility risk-grading system. This includes all new business and annual renewals of existing credit facilities. In addition, when there is a change in the credit facility or the financial condition of a client, risk grades should be reviewed and adjusted accordingly.

Collections and Servicing

Each vendor program is serviced through a dedicated servicing operation generally located near the vendor headquarters to improve synergies. As a result, certain vendors within the 2006-VT1 transaction will act as subservicers for the relative contracts.

In general, delinquent customers are contacted by phone at 10 days past due; however, obligors may be contacted sooner if it is determined to be appropriate. Letters may also be sent if telephone contact is not successful. Collection notes and research are maintained in InfoLease. A delinquent contract may be escalated to management or placed with a third-party collection agency, if needed.

Outside collection agencies and attorneys are frequently used to supplement collection activity for SF accounts. Typically, an account is placed with an outside collection agency or attorney when it is 180 days or more past due. However, accounts past due less than 180 days may be placed with a collection agency or attorney depending upon the circumstances of its delinquency. Equipment may be repossessed at any time after the contractual default, but repossession typically is not made until the account is at least 90 days past due.

SF policies require that accounts that are 90 days past due, or less given appropriate evidence of impairment, be placed on nonaccrual and written down to their underlying collateral value no later than at 180 days past due.

Index

Printed in the United States
By Bookmasters